PRINCIPLES
OF
FEDERAL
JURISDICTION

Second Edition

By

James E. Pfander
Owen L. Coon Professor of Law
Northwestern University School of Law

CONCISE HORNBOOK SERIES®

WEST®
A Thomson Reuters business

Mat #41033246

Concise Hornbook Series and Westlaw are trademarks registered in the U.S. Patent and Trademark Office.

© West, a Thomson business, 2006
© 2011 Thomson Reuters
    610 Opperman Drive
    St. Paul, MN 55123
    1–800–313–9378
Printed in the United States of America

ISBN: 978–0–314–26523–4

For Laurie, Sarah, Samantha and Benjamin

Preface

This book provides an introduction to the principles of federal jurisdiction, aimed primarily at law students in advanced courses. It seeks to convey two related bodies of knowledge. First, the book offers students an overview of certain canonical features of jurisdictional law. Most courses in federal jurisdiction include discussions of *Marbury v. Madison* (1803), *Erie R. Co. v. Tompkins* (1938), the Madisonian Compromise, the abstention doctrines, and the jurisdictional rules of standing, ripeness, and mootness. Knowledge of these rules, which structure (and sometimes frustrate) an individual's attempt to invoke the power of federal courts, will serve students well on bar exams and in practice. Such knowledge will also enable the student to evaluate the impact of changes in the rules. If Congress or the Supreme Court curtails access to federal trial courts, for example, students should know that the decision may put more pressure on the Court's appellate docket as the only federal forum in which litigants can seek review of state court decisions.

Second, and more importantly, the book will encourage students to make sophisticated arguments about the evolution of jurisdictional law. Law school graduates tend to think that the rules of law in their casebooks will remain fixed for the foreseeable future. But dramatic changes in law can occur in a very short time, occasioned by the government's responses to world events and subtle changes in legal culture. If the Bush Administration's response to terrorist attacks illustrates the impact of world events, shifting attitudes toward diversity jurisdiction provide a serviceable example of cultural change. A generation ago, many saw diversity jurisdiction as a waste of federal judicial resources, and influential organizations such as the American Law Institute (ALI), the Judicial Conference of the United States, and the Federal Courts Study Committee called for its legislative repeal. See ALI (1969). Today, diversity jurisdiction has enjoyed something of a rebirth. Not only has Congress redrawn jurisdictional boundaries to expand federal diversity jurisdiction over class actions, the federal courts have relaxed some doctrines to give parties easier access to federal diversity dockets.

This book attempts to convey both the canonical doctrines and the argumentative possibilities that together make up the principles of federal jurisdiction. In addition to providing background information on the leading doctrines, the book will set out the principles articulated in the cases and the impact those principles have had on the shape of jurisdictional law. By necessity in a book of relatively compact size, the discussion will focus on the field's leading cases and will omit many issues of detail that one can readily find in more encyclopedic treatises. Decisions of the Supreme Court provide the foundation for much of the discussion, but the book also draws on the work of scholars to probe judicial pronouncements. For simplicity, I have cited judicial decisions by name, year of decision, and court, if not the Supreme Court. I have cited scholarly authorities by referring to the author's last name and the year of publication. More complete citations appear in tables at the back of the book.

A word about my sources, and debts of gratitude. Like Justice Ginsburg, I am a devoted fan of the Hart & Wechsler casebook, both as a teaching tool and as a scholarly reference. I have relied on it extensively in framing and thinking through the problems addressed in this book, and wish to acknowledge my debt to its current authors, Dick Fallon, John Manning, Dan Meltzer, and David Shapiro. My indebtedness also runs to the authors of the many other fine casebooks in the field; I have often turned to them to challenge my thinking and deepen my understanding. Finally, let me mention my hope that the field's senior scholars will continue to review and criticize the contributions of new scholars. The practice sets a praiseworthy standard of unselfish engagement and helps to sustain the tradition of excellence that characterizes scholarship on the law of federal jurisdiction.

Special thanks to Akhil Amar, Willy Fletcher, Vicki Jackson, John Jeffries, Henry Monaghan, Marty Redish, Judith Resnik, Suzanna Sherry and William Van Alstyne for words of encouragement, to Eddie Hartnett and Bob Pushaw for unstinting collegiality, and to Jane Brock for expert secretarial help. Thanks most of all to my family for maintaining an attitude of bemused toleration.

JIM PFANDER

Evanston, Illinois

Summary of Contents

Table of Contents

PRINCIPLES
OF
FEDERAL
JURISDICTION

Second Edition

Chapter One

THE ARCHITECTURE OF ARTICLE III

1.1 Introduction

To a degree some may find surprising, the text, history, and structure of Article III continue to play an important role in arguments about the scope of federal jurisdiction and the nature of judicial authority. Justice Felix Frankfurter explained the instinct behind this focus on text, history, and structure more than half a century ago: he characterized the words of Article III as technically framed to establish clear limits on the federal judicial power and contrasted such technical precision with the Constitution's more generalized references to liberty, property, and due process of law. See *National Mutual Ins. v. Tidewater Transfer Co.* (1949) (dissenting opinion). Although many observers share Frankfurter's view of the comparative specificity of Article III, the sheer number of competing accounts of the federal judicial power would seem to belie any claim of technical precision and clarity. See Brest (1980). Disputes over Congress's power to strip the federal courts of jurisdiction feature plausible but quite different accounts of the text of Article III. As with many interpretive tasks, then, the interpretation of Article III often begins, but rarely ends, with the text and history of the judicial article. This chapter introduces the text and the way it structures current thinking about federal jurisdiction.

1.2 The Vesting Clause

Article III of the Constitution provides the framework of the federal judicial system (and influences the organizational structure of this book). The first section of Article III declares that the "judicial Power" shall be vested in one Supreme Court, and in such inferior courts as the Congress may from time to time ordain and establish. Known as the vesting clause, this richly evocative provision performs a wide range of functions. Perhaps most importantly, the vesting clause establishes the federal judiciary as one of three independent departments of the federal government with a special set of powers all its own. The judicial power differs from the legislative and executive power that Articles I and II vest in the Congress and President, respectively. The parallel vesting of three different powers implicitly but unmistakably suggests that each of the branches should refrain from exercising the powers that have been assigned to another department and provides the textual predicate for the principle of separation of powers.

In laying the constitutional foundation for the separation of powers, the vesting clause assigns judicial power to the federal judiciary. As a general matter, one can describe the judicial power as the power to adjudicate disputes; that was the function of the court systems (in Britain and in the several states) with which the framers of Article III were most familiar. But what were proper contours of the adjudicative function, and what sources of law were the federal courts to draw upon in resolving disputes? Chief Justice John Marshall answered certain of these questions in *Marbury v. Madison* (1803), proclaiming that the judicial function entailed the enforcement of the rights of individuals, including rights they held in relation to the federal government, and encompassed the power to interpret and apply the Constitution itself. Other early judicial pronouncements shape our conception of the judicial power by disclaiming any power to issue advisory opinions, see *Correspondence of the Justices* (1793), and by refusing to hear matters in which the judgments of the courts were subject to review by the political branches of government. See *Hayburn's Case* (1792). Over time, and especially in the last century, a host of mostly judge-made restrictions on the judicial power have arisen, including the doctrines of standing, ripeness, mootness, and the political question doctrine. The justiciability doctrines, the subject of Chapter 2 of the book, derive from the fact that Article III limits the federal courts to the exercise of powers of a judicial character.

1.3   One Supreme Court, Multiple Inferior Courts

Apart from vesting the federal courts with judicial power, Article III specifies to some extent the courts that are to exercise such power. Article III vests the judicial power in "one supreme Court, and in such inferior Courts as the Congress may from time to time ordain and establish." This portion of Article III does at least three things. First, it requires Congress to provide for the operation of a single "supreme court," and implicitly prohibits Congress from creating additional supreme courts with competing or overlapping jurisdiction. Second, it authorizes Congress to ordain and establish as many "inferior courts" as the judicial needs of the country may require. Third, it incorporates the Madisonian Compromise, which authorizes Congress to establish lower federal courts or to rely instead upon the state courts as courts of first instance. This section will briefly consider the unity, supremacy, and inferiority requirements; the next section will explore the

Madisonian compromise and its provision for reliance on state courts.

The requirement that a single Supreme Court act as the head of the judicial department operates in tandem with the requirements of supremacy and inferiority to provide a firm basis for the creation of a hierarchical judicial department. Consider first the constitutional vesting of judicial power in a single Supreme Court. This requirement of unity grounds the Court's familiar role in expounding a nationally uniform body of law. Today, the Court sits atop a judicial pyramid, made up of a variety of state and federal judicial tribunals. In addition to its power to review decisions from the fifty state court systems, the Court may consider cases coming from any of the regional appellate courts, the Court of Appeals for the Federal Circuit, and a range of other federal tribunals. Article III provides for the creation of this multitude of lower federal courts and tribunals but empowers the Supreme Court to articulate uniform legal rules to harmonize otherwise discordant voices.

Supremacy and inferiority help cement the Court's role in unifying federal law by creating a hierarchical relationship between superior and inferior courts. In such a hierarchy, lower courts must obey the decisions of their judicial superiors, and give effect to the Court's pronouncements. If they fail to do so, they invite an appeal to a superior court and a reversal of their decision. See Caminker (1994). Such a hierarchical system also enables individual litigants to secure the enforcement of their rights at relatively lower levels of the Article III pyramid, and avoid the expense and inconvenience of litigating all the way to the Supreme Court to obtain access to controlling federal law. Hierarchy thus plays an important role in ensuring the application of the Supreme Court's controlling determinations of federal law by lower tribunals throughout the country.

Equally important, the supremacy and inferiority requirements help to protect the independence of the judicial department from politically motivated attacks at the hands of Congress and the President. Congress has broad power to establish lower federal courts, a power recognized in Article III and confirmed in Article I. Yet the courts that Congress establishes must remain inferior to the Supreme Court. See Pfander (2009). The requirement of inferiority prevents Congress (and by implication the President) from establishing a new set of tribunals, vesting the new tribunals with some portion of the judicial power, and directing them to adjudicate disputes free from the oversight and control of the Article III judiciary. See Pfander (2007). By requiring that all federal courts operate within the Article III hierarchy, subject to the ultimate oversight and control of the Supreme Court, the supremacy and inferiority requirements forestall the creation of new more politically pliable tribunals for the final determination of federal rights. See Pfander (2004). Chapter 10 discusses the implications of supremacy and inferiority for the power of Congress to regulate the jurisdiction of the state and federal courts.

1.4   The Madisonian Compromise

Article III vests the judicial power in the Supreme Court, and in "such inferior courts as the Congress may from time to time ordain and establish." The permissive phrasing of the provision reflects the decision of the framers to empower, but not require, Congress to establish inferior federal courts. Known as the Madisonian Compromise, the provision grew out of a debate between those (like James Madison and James Wilson) who regarded inferior federal courts as essential to an effective judicial department and those (like Roger Sherman and Luther Martin) who thought the state courts could act as courts of first instance, subject to an appeal to the Supreme Court. Although the advocates of reliance on the state courts won an initial vote to eliminate a provision mandating lower federal courts, Madison and Wilson engineered a compromise that restored Congress's power to provide for such federal bodies if, in its judgment, they were necessary. See Collins (1995).

The Madisonian Compromise informs debates about both Congress's authority to control the jurisdiction of the lower federal courts and the degree to which state courts provide an adequate alternative forum. As for the federal courts, most observers see the Madisonian Compromise as giving Congress broad control over the existence and powers of the inferior federal courts. (The evident recognition of congressional discretion as to lower courts also helps to cement the perception that Article III creates and mandates the preservation of the Supreme Court.) For these observers, the greater power to deny all jurisdiction to the lower federal courts also gives Congress the power to create such courts and confer part, but not all, of the jurisdiction specified later in Article III section 2. As for state courts, the Madisonian Compromise implies as a matter of constitutional law that the state courts may serve as appropriate substitutes for lower federal courts. While the Compromise assumes some degree of federal judicial oversight, it treats the state courts as proper tribunals for first instance determination of many federal claims.

The presumed competence of the state courts may shed light on what has come to be known in federal jurisdictional circles as the parity debate. Critics note that the judges of state courts (unlike their federal counterparts) often serve without the benefit of life tenure and may thus be more responsive to subtle, and not so subtle, forms of political influence. State judicial elections may exacerbate the problem, as candidates for state judicial office stake out politically popular positions that may influence their judgment after they take their seats on the bench and make them less willing to enforce unpopular federal constitutional rights. Defenders of the state courts often point to the Madisonian Compromise, and its assumption that state courts (despite their lack of life-tenured judges) were presumptively appropriate forums for the adjudication of federal matters. Here, then, lies a fundamental issue of institutional competence that often arises in debates over the allocation of federal jurisdiction between state and federal courts. Such doctrines as the well-pleaded complaint rule, the abstention doctrines, and the scope of federal habeas corpus review of state criminal proceedings all rest to some degree on assumptions about state judicial willingness to enforce federal rights.

The Compromise may also help to explain the framers' decision to divide judicial business between the Supreme Court's original and appellate dockets. As the nation's only mandatory federal court, the Supreme Court provides the only constitutionally assured federal forum for the determination of federal claims. The Compromise assumes that many claims within federal jurisdiction may receive their original determination in the state courts, subject only to appellate review in the Supreme Court. Yet for some kinds of claims, the framers may have viewed appellate review as inadequate to protect federal interests and may have sought to secure their original federal determination. The two categories of litigation that appear on the Court's original docket—cases affecting ambassadors and public ministers and cases involving the states themselves as parties—may appear there in part due to some distrust of state court original jurisdiction. Ambassador cases, if brought in state court, might violate the doctrine of ambassadorial immunity under the law of nations, and state-party cases might encounter the states' own reluctance to entertain suits against themselves.

Finally, the Madisonian Compromise may shape perceptions about the nature of the state courts' obligation to entertain federal proceedings. Congress and the Supreme Court frequently assume that state courts will voluntarily hear federal claims, and the state courts have generally acted on the same assumption. If the states refuse to provide a forum for the adjudication of federal claims, the Madisonian Compromise may raise questions about Congress's ability to force them to do so. After all, the Compromise empowers Congress to establish (or expand the jurisdiction of) lower federal courts if, for any reason, it finds itself dissatisfied with the quality of justice in the state courts. With the power to rely on federal courts as an alternative, Congress's ability to force state courts to hear federal claims in the teeth of state opposition might fairly be questioned.

On the other hand, Article I of the Constitution specifically empowers Congress to "constitute tribunals inferior to the Supreme Court." With its distinctive use of the word "tribunals" instead of courts, this provision may give Congress authority not only to fashion formal federal courts with life-tenured judges but also to incorporate state courts into the federal judicial hierarchy. Article III vests the judicial power in federal "courts," but not in "tribunals"; similarly, its requirement that the judges of the federal courts enjoy life tenure and salary protections does not apply to the judges of tribunals, at least as a textual matter. The distinctive use of the word tribunals in Article I suggests that Congress could assign power to determine federal causes to the state courts, thereby constituting them as tribunals inferior to the Supreme Court, a possibility that Alexander Hamilton highlighted in *Federalist No. 81.* See Pfander (101 Nw. 2007). Chapter 10 discusses the obligation of state courts to hear federal claims.

1.5   Tenure in Office and Salary Protections

The next provision of Article III, section 1 declares that federal judges of both the supreme and inferior courts shall serve "during good behavior," a phrase understood to mean tenure for life, subject to removal for misconduct. Section 1 further prohibits any reduction in judicial salary and requires the payment of salaries at "stated times." Designed to insulate federal judges from political pressure and reprisal, these tenure-in-office and salary protections were modeled after tenure protections that the British Parliament extended to the judges of the superior courts at Westminster in 1701. Throughout the eighteenth century, the colonists of North America had chafed under a series of royal judges who served during the king's pleasure, rather than during good behavior; the grievances listed in the Declaration of Independence included a complaint about the lack of judicial independence. Experience after the nation won its independence from Great Britain had seemed to confirm the need for some judicial insulation. In one early case from Rhode Island, the state legislature threatened to discharge state judges who questioned the constitutionality of debtor relief legislation. Many state judges were subject to removal from office upon the passage of a legislative resolution to that effect.

The tenure-in-office protections do permit the removal of federal judges who violate the requirement of good behavior. Article II deals with judicial misconduct, empowering the House of Representatives to impeach a sitting federal judge by making a formal accusation of misconduct (high crimes and misdemeanors). Following impeachment, the Senate conducts a trial of the charges and may convict the judge and remove him or her from office. Scholars disagree as to whether the provision for House impeachment and Senate trial provides the exclusive mode of removing federal judges. Compare Prakash & Smith (2006) (urging that Congress could invest a court with the power to remove federal judges for misbehavior) with Pfander (74 Chi. 2007) (arguing that the Constitution's provision for impeachment and trial of federal judges provides the exclusive mode of removing them from office).

What constitutes a breach of good behavior, thereby subjecting a judge to removal, remains a subject for debate. Serious criminal activity clearly qualifies but controversial judicial decisions probably do not. In the early years of the Republic, especially in the wake of *Hayburn's Case* (1792), there was talk about the impeachment of judges who questioned legislative policy. Following the election of Thomas Jefferson, the House impeached Samuel Chase, a Supreme Court justice and member of the opposition Federalist party, for his heavy-handed role in trials under the Sedition Act of 1798. The Senate refused to convict Justice Chase, however, and established the principle that legislative disagreement with judicial decisions does not warrant impeachment. Former Chief Justice William Rehnquist cited this example as a precedent in arguing that the political branches should channel their efforts to influence judicial selection into the appointment process and refrain from threatening judges with removal from office through the impeachment power. See Rehnquist (2005).

The judicial independence proclaimed in Article III stands in contrast, then and now, to the situation of state judges. Although a handful of state constitutions provide for life tenure, most call for the election or appointment of judges to specific terms in office. At the conclusion of such terms, state judges often run in retention elections to hold their positions and they may face direct competition. A reflection of the democratic impulse, the provisions for judicial elections may create a somewhat more politically responsive state judiciary than obtains at the federal level. Political campaigns to oust controversial judges have occurred from time to time, particularly under California's provision for judicial recall. Recent Supreme Court decisions expand the free-speech right of state judicial campaigners, and threaten to transform the normally staid judicial election into a more freewheeling affair. See *Republican Party v. White* (2002). As suggested above, some critics of reliance upon the state courts—especially for the enforcement of unpopular constitutional rights—emphasize state judicial politics in arguing for the transfer of cases to federal court.

State judicial elections of the future promise to feature more special interest involvement and single-issue electioneering. Business groups have devoted considerable resources to the campaigns of judicial candidates who support some restriction on tort liability. Trial lawyers have funneled contributions to their opponents. With candidates unable to invoke the judicial canons of ethics to avoid taking positions on these issues, interest groups may demand relatively clear statements of judicial position as a condition of support. Such statements of position may compromise the objectivity and independence of sitting judges. Campaign contributions may also raise questions of impartiality, particularly in the wake of *Caperton v. A.T. Massey Coal Co.* (2009), in which the Supreme Court recognized a due process right to the recusal of state judges whose receipt of contributions from a party to litigation create the appearance of an "extreme" conflict of interest.

Questions of judicial independence also arise in debates over the power of Congress to shift cases from federal courts, established under Article III, into other federal tribunals, such as legislative courts and administrative agencies. The practice of relying upon non-Article III tribunals took root before the Constitution was ratified; Congress authorized courts-martial to hear claims of misconduct in the military, established boards and commissions to pass upon various financial disputes, and created a general court for Northwest territory. Today the practice of relying upon non-Article III courts and tribunals to hear federal disputes has become quite widespread; the federal government employs far more administrative law judges than Article III judges to perform the business of adjudication. Although the judges of these agencies and territorial courts often enjoy civil service protections and lengthy terms of office, they are not Article III judges and lack life tenure. The proliferation of such tribunals may thus seem to depart from Article III's inflexible command that all federal courts employ life tenured judges. Many observers, however, believe that judicial review in Article III courts can help to lessen the problems associated with the creation of non-Article III courts, and that such review may be constitutionally required. Chapter Ten addresses the constitutional puzzles of legislative courts.

1.6   The Scope of the Judicial Power

Section 2 of Article III specifies a series of "cases" and "controversies" to which the judicial power "shall extend." This list of items on the jurisdictional menu defines the scope of federal judicial power, and gives rise to the conception of the federal courts as courts of limited jurisdiction. But in defining the outer limits of federal judicial power, Article III section 2 does not clearly specify the minimum amount of work, if any, that Congress must assign to the federal courts. Most observers agree that Article III actually confers original and appellate jurisdiction on the Supreme Court, subject to the possibility (discussed below) of some congressional reallocation. But Article III does not specify the jurisdiction of the lower federal courts, seemingly leaving Congress to define their jurisdiction under the Madisonian Compromise.

One consistent challenge to the argument of congressional discretion has been based upon the requirement that the judicial power "shall extend" to the specified cases and controversies. Beginning with Justice Joseph Story's opinion in *Martin v. Hunter's Lessee* (1816), many have read the seemingly mandatory declaration as imposing an obligation on Congress to "extend" the judicial power to the various matters that appear on the jurisdictional menu. Supporters of such theories of congressional obligation point out that the Constitution often uses the term "shall" as a term of obligation, as in the Article III section 1 requirement that the judicial power shall be vested in one or more federal courts. See Amar (1985). Others read the provision as defining the maximum extent of the judicial power, while leaving Congress with discretion over how much jurisdiction actually to confer on the federal courts. On this reading, Article III defines a ceiling on the extent of the judicial power but not a floor. See Harrison (1997).

Similar questions have surfaced about the reason for the framers' use of the terms "cases" and "controversies" to describe the various matters of federal cognizance that appear on the jurisdictional menu. A quick look at the text will confirm that Article III uses the term "cases" to describe matters brought within judicial power by reference to the subject matter of the dispute; cases arising under the Constitution, laws, and treaties of the United States, for example, call for an interpretation or application of one of those controlling provisions of federal law, just as a case affecting ambassadors may draw into question the nature and extent of ambassadorial authority, immunity, or wrongdoing. Controversies, by contrast, do not identify a particular subject or body of law; instead, these jurisdictional provisions define judicial power by reference to the parties to the dispute. Thus, Article III extends the judicial power to controversies to which the United States shall be party, and to those between two or more states; it does not require that the controversy itself depend on the meaning of federal law (although they often do). For example, controversies between citizens of different states—commonly known as diversity jurisdiction—often turn on state common or statutory law and may not present any issues of federal law.

While scholars broadly accept the distinction between cases as defined by the subject matter of the dispute, and controversies as defined by party alignment, they disagree about why Article III uses these different terms to describe the matters that appear on the jurisdictional menu. Some scholars believe the term "cases" to be the broader of the two, encompassing both criminal and civil matters. These scholars read the term controversies, by contrast, as extending only to civil disputes. See Pfander (1994). Others read the distinction as one between cases that invite the federal courts to pronounce and expound the law, and controversies that call upon the federal courts simply to resolve a particular dispute between opposing parties. See Pushaw (1994). This account has the virtue of linking the function of law exposition to the cases arising under the Constitution, laws and treaties that the Supreme Court now regards as lying at the center of its expositional role.

The terms might serve, somewhat more prosaically, as simple placeholders to help with the interpretation of other provisions of Article III. The next clause of section 2 declares that the Supreme Court—the only court created by the Constitution—shall have original jurisdiction in certain "cases" and appellate jurisdiction in all the "cases" before mentioned. The reference to cases "before mentioned" might seem to invite a reading that takes account of the distinction between cases and controversies, thereby vesting the Court only with original and appellate jurisdiction of matters previously identified as cases on the menu. Such an approach would make the Court's jurisdiction over controversies dependent on legislative assignment and would cast doubt upon the Court's traditional understanding of its original jurisdiction as primarily made up of the controversies involving state parties that the menu identifies as such. Chapter 3 explores these possibilities.

Whatever the function of the case-controversy distinction, the definition of specific items on the jurisdictional menu has proven quite durable. Although the Eleventh Amendment curtailed the jurisdiction somewhat to foreclose the assertion of certain claims against the states as states, the menu of federal proceedings has remained unchanged for over two centuries. This durability owes much to the decision to define federal jurisdiction in terms co-extensive with the powers of the federal government. Co-extensivity inheres in the grant of federal-question jurisdiction over cases arising under the Constitution, laws, and treaties of the United States. The federal question grant ensures that the federal courts' jurisdiction extends to any dispute that implicates supreme federal law. When the content and scope of that law changes over time, jurisdiction follows. The Fourteenth Amendment (and the other acts of the Reconstruction Congress) vastly expanded federal power but did not require any formal change in the scope of judicial power under Article III. New constitutional and statutory rights were proper subjects of federal adjudication as cases arising under the Constitution and laws of the United States.

1.7   Supreme Court Original and Appellate Jurisdiction

Article III section 2, clause 2 declares that the Supreme Court shall have original jurisdiction over certain specified proceedings and appellate jurisdiction over all the rest.   The Court itself has long taken the position that these provisions actually confer the jurisdiction in question and that its power to hear cases comes directly from the Constitution.   Congress, on the other hand, has never been content to leave the Court's jurisdiction to that specified in the Constitution; jurisdictional statutes confer both original and appellate jurisdiction on the Court in certain cases and decline to do so in others.   On the appellate side of its docket, the Court has tended to defer to such legislation, emphasizing Congress's power to fashion "exceptions" to and "regulations" of its appellate jurisdiction.   How far Congress may go in fashioning such exceptions remains unresolved, due in part to the Court's reluctance to interpret statutory restrictions on its authority as foreclosing appellate review in its entirety.   See Felker v. Turpin (1996).

Congressional power over the Court's original docket also remains a topic of some dispute.   In *Marbury v. Madison* (1803), of course, the Court found that Congress lacks power to expand its original jurisdiction.   While the holding survives, the rationale has faded over time.   Chief Justice Marshall based his decision in *Marbury* on a negative inference; he claimed that Article III makes a fixed distribution of the jurisdiction between the Court's original and appellate dockets and implicitly deprives Congress of power to re-draw the lines.   But the broadest implications of this ban on congressional reallocation have not taken hold.   Thus, the Court itself has recognized that some matters, arguably assigned to its original jurisdiction, may originate elsewhere and still provide a proper case for the exercise of its appellate jurisdiction.   See *Cohens v. Virginia* (1821).   It has also upheld legislation that gives the lower federal courts concurrent jurisdiction over matters within its original jurisdiction.   While such legislation does not deprive the Court of original jurisdiction, it does set the stage for the Court's refusal to hear the matters originally.   The Court often declines to exercise original jurisdiction if an alternative forum may hear the dispute, a development that stands in some tension with a conception of the Court's original jurisdiction as fixed by the Constitution.

1.8   Congress and Judicial Architecture

Congress has played an important role in developing the structure of the federal courts, exercising powers conferred by the Inferior Tribunals and Necessary and Proper Clauses of Article I and by the range of Article III provisions that explicitly contemplate legislative action. Chapter Ten will examine some of the limits on congressional power. Even in those areas where Congress enjoys broad regulatory authority, many of the institutional features of the interlocking state and federal judicial systems have become too deeply ingrained to uproot. In the Judiciary Act of 1789, Congress chose to create a system of lower federal courts, instead of relying as it might have on the state courts to hear federal claims. Congress also took steps to integrate the state judiciaries into the federal system, providing for Supreme Court review of state court decisions on any conclusive questions of federal law. Further, Congress provided for the removal of certain matters from state to federal court at the trial court level, thus giving defendants a chance to transfer certain state court proceedings into a federal forum. Many of these early decisions continue to shape judicial federalism today. Individual litigants throughout the United States thus have access to a dual system of state and federal courts and often have a choice about where to raise their federal claims.

In addition to the dual system of state and federal courts, Congress has created a series of adjudicative bodies outside of Article III. One such group of Article I tribunals has come to be known as legislative courts. These legislative courts include territorial courts, which handle judicial business in territories under federal control that have yet to achieve formal statehood; courts-martial, which hear criminal charges arising from military service; and the US Court of Federal Claims, which hears suits against the United States for breaches of contract and takings of property. Legislative courts differ from Article III courts in that they often employ judges who lack life tenure and often hear matters that have been regarded as lying outside the scope of the judicial power under Article III. Other non-Article III adjudicators include the judges who staff federal bankruptcy courts, the magistrate judges who serve as adjuncts to federal district courts, and the administrative agencies.

One can gain some appreciation for the scope of non-Article III adjudication by considering raw numbers. A study by Professor Resnik compares the number of Article III judges to the number of non-Article III adjudicators of all varieties. See Resnik (2002). The results are striking. In 1999, Congress had authorized a total of only 834 Article III judgeships, including justices of the Supreme Court, and judges of the appellate and trial courts. In comparison, there were nearly 2400 non-Article III adjudicators, including 845 bankruptcy and magistrates judges, well over 100 judges of Article I and territorial courts, and some 1400 administrative law judges. Indeed, the number of ALJs employed to hear disability and other benefit claims at a single federal agency (the Social Security Administration) exceeds the number of Article III judges at all levels of the Article III judicial establishment.   These ALJs handled over 500,000 cases a year in the late 1990s, whereas federal district court judges were completing roughly 270,000 cases a year in the same period.

If these numbers reveal the relative significance of non-Article III adjudicators in the federal judicial hierarchy, they remain incomplete.   To fill out the picture of the distribution of judicial resources requires some data on the number of judges who serve in state courts.   According to a Federal Bureau of Justice Statistics report, California alone employed more trial judges (1480) than the entire federal judiciary combined.   State courts as a whole employed some 26,500 judges at the trial and appellate levels.   See Federal Bureau Justice Statistics (1998).   Thus, Article III judges (834) represent a very small portion of the total number of state and federal judges in the United States; only 3% of the nation's judges serve in federal court, whereas 97% serve in state courts.

Chapter Two

THE NATURE OF THE JUDICIAL POWER

2.1 Introduction

The separation of the powers of government into three departments suggests that federal courts have a distinctively judicial role to play in deciding, with final and binding effect, concrete disputes between adverse parties. Such an understanding of the judicial power gives rise to a number of corollaries. Judicial independence necessitates some restrictions on the power of the political branches to review the work of the judiciary (the principle of finality) and on the power of courts to review political questions (the political question doctrine). It also implies limits on the willingness of the federal courts to offer advice or other non-binding declarations of the law in an abstract or hypothetical setting (the ban on advisory opinions). The focus on adjudication of genuine disputes has also been thought to preclude the federal courts from hearing claims in which one of the parties lacks a concrete interest in the litigation (the principle of standing). Finally, adjudication necessitates the interpretation and application of possibly overlapping and competing bodies of law and may call for the interpretation of the Constitution. The connection between adjudication and the accompanying power to interpret the Constitution finds its canonical expression in the Supreme Court's decision in *Marbury v. Madison* (1803).

2.2 The *Marbury* Decision

As the case mostly closely associated with the Supreme Court's power to review the constitutionality of acts of Congress, *Marbury v. Madison* invites analysis on a variety of levels. Apart from the decision's rationale, scholars have explored the political setting of the case, which arose from the sharp partisan conflict between the Federalist party of Washington, Hamilton, and Adams and the Republican party of Jefferson, Madison, and Monroe. The conflict began with the adoption of the Judiciary Act of 1801, which empowered the lame-duck Federalist President, John Adams, to appoint a number of new judges to the federal bench in the waning moments of his term. The Jeffersonians fought back against what

they viewed as a form of court packing by repealing the Act and
eliminating the new circuit courts.

William Marbury's claim arose from these political machinations. Jefferson and Madison refused to honor his last-second
appointment as a justice of the peace for the District of Columbia
on the ground that his commission had not been delivered to him
before the Federalists left office. (Marbury's lawyer, Charles Lee,
had served as the Attorney General of the United States under
Adams; the Chief Justice, John Marshall, had served as the secretary of state under Adams before his appointment to the Court in
1801.) The action began as a petition for a writ of mandamus that
would direct James Madison as secretary of state to deliver the
disputed commission and honor Marbury's claim to the office.
Marbury filed the action in the Supreme Court of the United States
in December 1801, invoking the Court's rather open-ended power
to issue writs of mandamus in appropriate cases. The Court
promptly granted an order to show cause, directing Madison to
answer Marbury's claim.

Perceiving the order as evidence that the federal courts had
become Federalist courts, the Republican Congress responded with
some vehemence. During 1802, Congress repealed the Judiciary
Act of 1801 and restored the provisions of the Act of 1789. The
repeal had three consequences. First, it turned a number of Article
III judges out of office, not by firing them directly, but by closing
the new circuit courts that they had been appointed to staff.
(Federalists in Congress argued eloquently, but unsuccessfully, that
the measure violated the tenure provisions of Article III.) Second,
Congress reimposed on the Justices of the Supreme Court the
onerous duty of riding the circuits, a chore from which the Act of
1801 had relieved them by creating new judgeships. Third, it
changed the terms of the mandamus power that Marbury had
invoked, switching back to the somewhat more limited terms of the
Act of 1789. Other legislation changed the dates for the Court's
next term or sitting. This clever strategy meant that the Justices
would not sit again as a full Court until February 1803, well after
they would face the obligation of riding their circuits in Fall 1802.
As the first practical test of the constitutionality of the repeal,
circuit riding put the Justices in an awkward position. If they
agreed to hear cases on circuit, they would effectively confirm the
legality of legislation that displaced the judges of the circuit courts;
if they refused, they would invite impeachment.

Scholars who describe the *Marbury* decision as the product of
political defeat properly emphasize the changed situation the Justices confronted in February 1803, when they re-convened as a full
Court after having meekly ridden the circuits the previous Fall.
But if the Court's political weakness necessitated an order dismiss-

ing Marbury's petition, it certainly did not determine the rationale for the dismissal. That task fell to John Marshall, and he performed it with great political flair. En route to a jurisdictional dismissal, the Chief Justice gave voice to lasting restrictions on the political branches of the federal government, branches then firmly within the control of the Jeffersonians. While the decision also disabled the judicial branch to some extent, Marshall worked hard to limit these consequences for his department.

2.2.1 The *Marbury* Decision: Marshall's Opinion

Marshall's opinion for the Court began with a discussion of the first principles of mandamus jurisdiction aimed at articulating limits on the executive branch. Here, he faced a potential problem. Marbury claimed a property right in his office and argued that the right had vested upon President Adams's execution of the commission (the document that evidences the appointment). Although they did not formally appear through counsel in response to the mandamus petition, Madison and Jefferson obviously believed that the commission did not take effect because it had not actually been delivered to Marbury. In any case, the government could argue that decisions about Marbury's continuation in office were left to the executive and not subject to judicial review. Notably, Marbury did not claim title to a life-tenured job in the federal judiciary but to a five-year post as a justice of the peace.

Marshall stiff-armed the potential clash between the branches. He defined the proper role of the courts in overseeing executive branch decisions by developing a distinction between matters of executive discretion and matters of legal right. While Marshall disclaimed any judicial authority to hear merely political questions, he explained that claims of legal right were matters for the courts to resolve. He borrowed this distinction from the great English cases on mandamus, which had recognized the availability of the writ to compel an inferior officer to perform a non-discretionary act but had refused to compel action when the matter had been left to the officer's judgment or discretion. Viewing Marbury as enjoying a legal right to his commission on the basis of its having been signed and sealed, Marshall treated delivery and investiture in office as merely ministerial acts that were subject to judicial compulsion through the writ of mandamus.

Having affirmed Marbury's title to his office, and having concluded that mandamus afforded him a proper remedy for the ministerial act of the commission's delivery, Marshall turned to consider the authority of the Supreme Court to award the relief in question. Marbury had filed the petition in the Supreme Court as an original matter, invoking the Court's authority under the mandamus provisions that Congress first enacted in section 13 of the

Judiciary Act of 1789. (The intervening expansion of the Court's mandamus authority in 1801 had been repealed a year later, before Marshall addressed the issue in February 1803.) Marshall had little doubt that section 13 conferred an original power to issue mandamus; he (somewhat selectively) quoted the statute's provision for the issuance of writs of mandamus in accordance with the principles and usages of law and found without much discussion that the statute allowed Marbury to initiate proceedings for the writ as an original matter.

Scholars have been quite critical of Marshall's interpretation of the statute, arguing that section 13 did not so obviously confer original jurisdiction on the Court to issue the writ of mandamus. Partly, these criticisms focus on the text of the statute and its grant of "power" instead of "jurisdiction"; critics have suggested that the Court should have read the provision as conferring power to issue the writ only when the Court has acquired jurisdiction of the case on some other basis. See Amar (1989); Van Alstyne (1969). These criticisms may appear to gain strength from the doctrine of constitutional avoidance, under which the Court construes statutes so as to avoid constitutional issues. Had the Court found an absence of statutory authority to entertain original mandamus proceedings, it would have had no occasion to consider the constitutional question to which it next turned.

Subsequent scholarship has offered support for Marshall's interpretation of the statute. See Pfander (2001); Weinberg (2003). The original text of the statute appears to confer a freestanding grant of mandamus authority, independent of other jurisdictional grants. Its grant of "power" was perfectly consistent with the exercise of the discretionary mandamus authority that had arisen in English practice; elsewhere, the statute uses the term jurisdiction to refer to judicial authority that individuals could invoke as a matter of right. Moreover, the consistent practice of supreme courts both in England and the United States was to exercise mandamus authority on an original petition to oversee the work of both inferior courts and inferior officers. Against this backdrop, Marshall's decision to regard the statute as a grant of original mandamus authority to proceed seems relatively well justified.

Marshall next considered the constitutionality of this grant of mandamus power in light of the specific terms of Article III. Marshall focused on Article III, section 2, which confers original jurisdiction on the Court in a few cases (those affecting ambassadors and involving state parties), and appellate jurisdiction in all the rest. Marshall first found that these grants of jurisdiction were mutually exclusive and prevented Congress from reallocating the Court's jurisdiction. As a consequence, Marshall found that the Court could exercise original jurisdiction in mandamus only where ambassadors or state parties were involved. Marbury's petition did not fit within one of the appropriate categories of original jurisdiction and thus required dismissal. (Apparently no one regarded Madison as an "ambassador, other public minister, or consul" within the meaning of the original jurisdiction clause; these terms referred to diplomatic officers rather than to the heads of the federal departments.)

None of these conclusions as to the meaning of Article III was self-evident. While Marshall treated the grants of original and appellate jurisdiction as a distribution of the Court's authority, the provisions do not expressly foreclose some reallocation by Congress. Many scholars have argued that Congress's power to fashion exceptions to and regulations of the Court's appellate jurisdiction may imply a power of reallocation; cases excepted from the appellate docket might be reassigned to the Court's original jurisdiction. See Calabresi & Lawson (2007). Moreover, it seems entirely conceivable that cases within the Court's original jurisdiction might originate elsewhere, perhaps in proceedings before state courts. A strict denial of appellate jurisdiction in such cases would disable the Court from correcting errors in potentially sensitive state-party and ambassador cases. Marshall came to recognize this problem with his *Marbury* rationale, and quietly abandoned this implication in a later case. See *Cohens v. Virginia* (1821).

Marshall may have been on firmer ground in asserting that Article III's specific grant of original jurisdiction to the Supreme Court was understood as foreclosing Congress from expanding the Court's original docket. Original jurisdiction operated to provide for trial of claims at the Supreme Court, and trials at the nation's capital could burden the parties and the Court.[1] All such burdens would have been magnified in 1788, when canals and railroads were still years away. While the Justices might travel through the country to conduct trials of matters on the Court's original docket, following the model of the superior courts in England, original litigation on the English model would have still required the filing of papers, issuance of writs, and entry of judgments at the Court's home base. Geographic convenience may help to explain the parties who appear on the Court's original docket; the states had representatives in Congress, and ambassadors were likely posted to the nation's capital. See Amar (1989). By limiting the original docket to these parties, Article III promises that the exercise of original jurisdiction in other federal cases will occur before a court (state or federal) in the vicinity of the parties. Members of the

---

1. During the 1790s, the Court actually impaneled a jury to hear a suit for damages against the State of New York; the Eleventh Amendment's ratification swept such claims from its docket.

First Congress who shared this understanding spoke of the need to carry federal justice to every person's door.

If Marshall's conclusion was correct that Congress lacked power to expand the Court's original jurisdiction (and *Marbury*'s holding on that point has survived), it set up a conflict between the terms of section 13 and Article III that forced Marshall to consider the Court's power to ignore an unconstitutional act of Congress. Or did it? Many scholars have argued that Marshall created the conflict that led to his discussion of judicial review, a conflict he might have sidestepped. We have seen two possible avoidance strategies: a narrow interpretation of section 13 as not conferring the power or jurisdiction in question and a narrow interpretation of Article III as not limiting the power of Congress to expand the Court's original jurisdiction. Another possibility may have been to have treated the mandamus power as part of the Court's supervisory authority, grouped alongside its appellate jurisdiction. But mandamus, as Marshall explained, would operate as an assertion of appellate jurisdiction only insofar as it sought to "revise and correct" the proceedings of a lower court. In seeking to compel action by an executive branch official, not to correct a lower court error, Marbury's petition fell on the original jurisdiction side of the line Marshall defined.

2.2.2 The *Marbury* Decision: Judicial Review

All of which led Marshall to take up the "deeply interesting" question whether "an act, repugnant to the constitution, can become the law of the land." Marshall did not invent judicial review in the *Marbury* decision: State court decisions during the 1780s had tentatively explored the idea of ignoring an unconstitutional statute. Alexander Hamilton had built on those developments in justifying judicial review in *Federalist No. 78* (from which Marshall borrowed liberally); and early Supreme Court decisions had presumed the inapplicability of unconstitutional legislation. See Treanor (2005). But Marshall did give the doctrine of judicial review its first extended treatment in the pages of the Supreme Court reports, and his analysis remains a starting point for understanding the origins of this distinctly American development.

As with many of his great opinions, Marshall derived his conclusions in *Marbury* from a set of principles or political axioms that he simply proclaimed. The government of the United States, and its various departments, were obliged to respect limits specified in a written Constitution. The Constitution, as the expression of popular sovereignty, established a "superior paramount law," unchangeable by ordinary legislative act. As a consequence, any legislative act repugnant to the Constitution was simply void. Courts were empowered to consider the conflict between the Constitution and a legislative act and to declare legislation void in appropriate cases. After all, the Constitution bound the judicial department, just as it did the legislative branch, and the courts were obliged in a case of conflict to give effect to the higher law. For Marshall, constitutional interpretation and judicial review followed from the duty of the judicial department to resolve the litigated case.

Marshall added a number of references to provisions of the Constitution that were said to confirm the propriety of judicial review. He noted that the jurisdiction of the federal courts extended to cases arising under the Constitution, a fact that tended to confirm that constitutional law was a matter for judicial interpretation. He pointed to the fact that several provisions of the Constitution, including those relating to bills of attainder and treason, appeared to have been specially designed for judicial application. He cited the judicial obligation, under oath, to support the Constitution. Finally, he noted that the Supremacy Clause places the Constitution first on the list of federal laws made binding on state court judges as the supreme law of the land.

Scholars have debated whether Marshall's opinion provides a convincing justification for the doctrine of judicial review. Many have concluded that, standing alone, it does not. See Hand (1959). Nowhere in the Constitution does the document itself proclaim that the federal courts may declare particular acts of Congress unconstitutional. The many provisions Marshall cites can all have their expected operation without positing such a judicial power. For example, the judicial oath to support the Constitution would make sense even if the Constitution to be supported did not contemplate the exercise of judicial review. Such a view would not deny higher law status to the Constitution, but would only assign Congress final responsibility for passing on constitutional challenges to proposed legislation. Even Marshall's argument for the judicial power to invalidate a law in direct contradiction to the Constitution has failed to persuade the critics. Congress rarely flouts the Constitution directly; more often, it takes a position in an area where the Constitution does not speak clearly and the precedents point in various directions. In such areas, constitutional interpretation may well intrude on the making of legislative policy. See Posner (2005); Bickel (1962).

If the Constitution, standing alone, fails to persuade, many scholars have concluded that the drafting and ratification history supports Marshall's conclusion. Those who participated in the debates at the Philadelphia convention in 1787 often spoke on the assumption that the federal courts would have the power to ignore unconstitutional laws. Such views fueled opposition to the proposed creation of a Council of Revision, comprised of officers of the

executive and judicial branches. According to those who successfully opposed that plan, judicial officers were expected to invalidate
unconstitutional laws in the course of adjudication and should not
play that role as part of any such Council. During the ratification
debates, moreover, supporters of the Constitution often invoked the
presumed power of judicial review, portraying it as a tool for the
enforcement of limits on the federal government. If not written in
the document, judicial review might well be seen as an implicit part
of the ratification bargain.

Scholars continue to debate the origins of American doctrine of
judicial review and its various historical precursors. Notable recent contributions include Bilder (2004), which emphasizes the
historical power of Privy Council to review final judicial decisions of
the colonial courts of British North America for repugnancy to
British law, and Hamburger (2008), which highlights the judicial
oath and the accompanying duty to apply law to the litigated case.

2.2.3   The *Marbury* Decision: Departmentalism

Marshall's decision in *Marbury* required dismissal of the mandamus proceeding for want of original jurisdiction and ended the
dispute with James Madison. (Marbury did not obtain his position
as justice of the peace, and the federal judges who lost their jobs
following the repeal of the Judiciary Act of 1801 did not win
reinstatement to their posts or monetary compensation. So much
for Marshall's optimistic assurance of remedies for violations of
legal rights.) If Marshall's disposition was brief, his opinion was
far reaching, laying the foundation for judicial review of acts of
Congress and for the modern development of judicial review of
administrative action. In both areas, the *Marbury* decision continues to empower and constrain the judicial department and to
structure its relationship with the political branches.

Much of the terrain remains contested, as the nation's great
debates over the acceptance of judicial decrees nicely reveal. Following *Marbury*, the Court did not invalidate an act of Congress
again until its decision in *Scott v. Sandford* (1856) helped to propel
the nation into civil war. Abraham Lincoln challenged the legitimacy of the *Scott* Court's conclusion that Congress could not
constitutionally ban slavery in the territories. In what has come to
be known as a "departmental" conception of judicial review, Lincoln viewed the Court's decision as settling the particular dispute
over Dred Scott's status but not as establishing a political rule that
would require immediate acceptance by the people of the United
States. While the federal courts were free to construe the Constitution to resolve concrete disputes within their department, other
departments of government were free to develop and act on an
alternative vision of the Constitution.

Many figures in American history have embraced a limited, departmental conception of the judicial power to expound the Constitution. Thomas Jefferson took the position that the Sedition Act of 1798 violated the first amendment; the federal courts disagreed and convicted certain publishers of violating the law. After becoming President, Jefferson acted on his own constitutional view in pardoning the targets of such prosecutions. President Jackson similarly invoked constitutional scruples to support his decision to veto legislation to re-establish the second national bank. His veto message acknowledged the contrary view of the federal courts, see *McCulloch v. Maryland* (1819), but refused to treat the judicial opinion as binding the president when acting within his own department. A more complex form of federal departmentalism (involving courts at the national level and political actors at the state and local level) may have encouraged the Southern architects of massive resistance to defy the Supreme Court's decision in *Brown v. Board of Education* (1954). Some respectable observers defended the right of Southern officials to oppose the decision, at least until they were brought before the federal courts in a litigated case. See Bickel (1964). The Court's contrary assertion in *Cooper v. Aaron* (1958) invoked *Marbury* in contending that state officials have an obligation to obey the Court's pronouncements. But *Cooper* remains a disputed landmark and failed to end Southern resistance to *Brown*.

2.2.4 The *Marbury* Decision: Interpretive Theory

Marbury asked little of the political branches and thus does little to resolve the debate over who must comply with the Court's decisions (beyond the parties to the particular dispute). Nor does it shed much light on the proper method by which the Justices of the Court should discern constitutional meaning. As noted, Marshall's opinion relied heavily on a statement of first principles and did not draw upon earlier decisions of the Supreme Court or on the (then as yet unpublished) drafting history of the Constitution. He treated the *Federalist Papers* as a source of inspiration but not as an authoritative account of the public understanding of the Constitution. The opinion was not self-consciously originalist; Marshall did not proclaim himself bound to give effect to the original understanding of the Constitution. But Marshall nonetheless took for granted that the words in the document had a meaning that the federal courts could grasp and apply to litigated disputes. That seems clear both from his analysis of the interplay between Article III's provisions for original and appellate jurisdiction and from his recitation of examples in which the Constitution directly constrained the exercise of legislative power.

Questions about interpretive method range more widely today. Just as the Constitution fails to set forth an explicit power of judicial review, so too does it fail to specify the rules by which it should be interpreted. Constitutional theory seeks to fill the gap. One can divide theorists into a variety of camps. Originalists (once called interpretivists) tend to focus on the text, structure, and history of the Constitution; they argue that the Constitution's status as law depends on its having been ratified by the people in conventions. Such formal acts were based upon a conception of the document's public meaning at the time of ratification, an understanding that continues to control until changed through the amendment process. Originalists consult a variety of sources in the search for public meaning, including public statements by those who participated in the ratification debates and dictionaries that were in current usage at the time.

Theorists reject originalism for a variety of reasons. Some doubt that modern interpreters can reliably reconstruct the public meaning of a document now well over 200 years old. Others note that the Supreme Court has repeatedly departed from the originalist theory of interpretation, producing precedents on which government institutions and the people themselves have come to rely (such as the decisions upholding the constitutionality of paper money). Originalism may cast doubt on a great many precedents, but it furnishes no tools for selecting from among the precedents that the Court should retain and those it should abandon.[2] Some critics have demonstrated the unconventional nature of the founding, casting doubt on the originalist construct of a stable and publicly understood meaning and an orderly process of ratification. Others have argued that the founders and amenders may have expected some evolution in the meanings of the many open-ended provisions of the Constitution, such as equal protection and due process of law.

Among non-originalist theories of interpretation, the principle of institutional settlement often helps to frame the debate over questions of federal jurisdiction. Associated with the Legal Process School of the 1950s, the principle of institutional settlement holds that courts should (as a normative matter) and do (as a descriptive matter) interpret jurisdictional principles so as to assign particular decisions to the branch or department of government best suited to their competent resolution. Crudely put, the principle of institutional settlement operates as a theory of the separation of powers,

2. In Brown v. Board of Education (1954) (ending segregation) and Roe v. Wade (1973) (recognizing a woman's right to terminate a pregnancy), for example, the Court pronounced rules of law said to have been derived from the Constitution, but not from the original understanding of the Fourteenth Amendment's equal protection and due process clauses.

under which the political branches of government (and administrative agencies) bear responsibility for developing many of the rules that govern life in a modern democratic society and the more insulated ·judicial branch applies the rules in concrete disputes between parties. Essentially court-centered, the principle of institutional settlement seeks to justify a narrow conception of the judicial role: settling disputes, enforcing rights, confining other institutions within their proper· boundaries, and giving voice to constitutional values of which the political branches may lose sight.

Legal process thinking may help to refocus the debate over *Marbury* to some extent. While the Court dismissed the action on jurisdictional grounds, the decision makes a number of claims about the proper role of the three branches of government. For starters, Chief Justice Marshall identified the judiciary with the task of articulating and enforcing individual rights against the political branches. Many legal process thinkers would agree that courts can better consider individual claims than their political branch counterparts, who often must ignore the particular in framing a general rule (and who may rely on the courts to prevent any resulting unfairness). Legal process thinking may help to illuminate a second feature of the *Marbury* decision: Marshall's decision to reject an assignment of expanded original jurisdiction. The Court's important role today lies in defining uniform rules of law for national application, work done primarily as an appellate body. An expanded grant of original jurisdiction may interfere with the Court's appellate function. Moreover, a congressional power to broaden original jurisdiction in the political context of *Marbury* (where an implicit threat of impeachment loomed had the Justices declined their circuit riding duties) may have seemed especially ominous.

A more subtle form of legal process argument might emphasize the importance of maintaining judicial distance as an argument against expanded original jurisdiction. Frequently today, the Court hears questions of constitutional law some months or years after the passage of the immediate crisis that gave rise to the issue. Exceptions do exist; the Pentagon Papers case proceeded swiftly to the Court's appellate docket, see *New York Times v. United States* (1971), as did the Steel Seizure case. See *Youngstown Sheet & Tube v. Sawyer* (1952). But often an issue will work its way through the lower state and federal courts for a time before it comes to the Court for ultimate resolution. At this later stage, the Court may have the benefit of the considered opinions of several lower court judges as well as those of legal scholars. Meanwhile, political passions may have cooled, enabling the Court to speak as an organ of sober second thought. See Bickel (1962). If Congress were free to expand the Court's original jurisdiction, it might hurry constitutional questions onto the Court's docket for possibly premature determination and deprive the Court of the benefit of lower court development of the issues.

2.3   The Requirement of Judicial Finality

In declaring limits on the power of the political branches to dictate terms to the federal courts, *Marbury* followed a pattern set early in the history of the federal judiciary. Two decisions—both dating from the early years of the Washington Administration—helped to establish enduring principles of judicial finality and freedom from political branch encroachment. In *Hayburn's Case* (1792), the justices of the Supreme Court (sitting as judges of the federal circuit courts) agreed that the federal courts should refuse to hear claims under a statute that subjected judicial decisions to the oversight and control of the political branches. In the *Correspondence of the Justices* (1793), the Court refused to provide advisory opinions in response to questions from the executive branch about the nation's obligations under its treaty with France. Citing the separation of powers and the need to preserve judicial independence, the decisions emphasize judicial finality as a defining feature of the judicial power.

Hayburn's Case was really a series of cases in which disabled veterans of the Revolutionary War sought the payment of pensions promised in an Act of Congress. Under the terms of the legislation, veterans were to apply to the federal trial courts with proof of their disability and their military service. Following a favorable judicial determination, the claims went to the secretary of war for review of the claimant's military service. Then, the claims went to Congress for a determination as to whether the pension should be paid. The structure had a certain geographic logic; the courts could take evidence and make the initial determination in the veterans' home states followed by review on the part of officials at the nation's capital. But as the (circuit-riding) Justices noted in refusing to hear the claims of the veterans, the system subjected the decisions of the circuit courts to review by both the executive and legislative branches of government. This was seen as a violation of the principle of judicial finality (and the lack of finality made the work non-judicial, or inappropriate for federal courts). While the decisions of the federal courts may be reviewed by superior courts in the Article III hierarchy, judicial finality forbids review by the political branches of government.

The requirement of judicial finality creates a potentially awkward relationship with the legislative branch, especially as it relates to the determination of money claims against the government of the United States. Before the Constitution's ratification, the practice of legislative assemblies throughout the colonial period had been one of requiring individuals with claims against the state (such as claims by government contractors) to submit legislative petitions in support of their claims. Individuals would submit their claims to a committee of the assembly, the committee would determine the claim, and if favorably disposed, recommend payment of the claim in the next appropriations bill. See Pfander (2010). Payment of the claims of disabled veterans thus implicated congressional power over the purse strings, a power reflected in the constitutional requirement that all payments from the treasury receive the approval of Congress.

Article III does not answer the question of how Congress can preserve its prerogative over appropriations, even as it enlists the federal courts in the determination of money claims. Article III does contemplate judicial involvement; it provides for the assertion of jurisdiction over claims in which the United States appears as a party. But the Court has not read this language as compelling the assertion of federal jurisdiction or as effecting a waiver of the government's immunity from suit. In other words, the Constitution seemingly leaves Congress free to decide whether to retain its control over public claims (through the process of legislative petitions), or to cede such control to the federal courts. See Figley & Tidmarsh (2009). Following *Hayburn's Case*, Congress cannot invite federal judicial involvement without surrendering some portion of its own control over the payment of claims. Federal judicial involvement requires federal judicial finality and a relatively firm agreement on the part of Congress to pay any claims that the federal courts approve.

Congress's agreement to pay was some time in coming, but it has now arrived. As a first measure, Congress in 1855 created the Court of Claims to hear the claims of government contractors who were supplying goods and services to the federal government. Like the veterans' benefit statute invalidated in *Hayburn's Case*, the provision for the judicial determination of claims reserved legislative control of payment decisions. The Supreme Court found that the lack of judicial finality foreclosed it from exercising appellate jurisdiction over the decisions of the Court of Claims. *See Gordon v. United States* (1864). The Court of Claims was thus said to function as a legislative or Article I court, established outside the strictures of Article III and not subject to the same finality requirements. (For a more detailed analysis of legislative courts, see Chapter 10.) In keeping with its status as a legislative court, the Court of Claims long exercised an advisory jurisdiction, proposing the disposition of issues referred to it by Congress. The current US Court of Federal Claims remains an Article I court, staffed by judges who serve for a renewable term of 14 years.

Although the Court of Federal Claims continues to operate outside of Article III, Congress has now provided sufficient finality to clear the way for appellate review in the Article III courts. Under the terms of a standing appropriation law, known as the Judgment Fund, Congress will pay any judgment rendered by the US Court of Federal Claims (and by any Article III court). The Supreme Court has ruled that this standing authorization provides the practical finality that was missing in *Hayburn's Case* and thus permits Article III courts to hear money claims against the government. See *Glidden Co. v. Zdanok* (1962). The US Court of Appeals for the Federal Circuit, an Article III court, now reviews decisions of the Court of Federal Claims without concern that such review exceeds the scope of the judicial power.

Finality issues also arise when Congress takes steps through legislation to re-open a particular judicial decision or set of decisions. In *Plaut v. Spendthrift Farm* (1995), for example, the Court invalidated legislation that proposed to re-open a set of federal decisions that dismissed securities fraud claims. The dismissals came after an earlier decision by the Court defined a surprisingly short limitation period for the claims in question. Congress responded by extending the limitation period for future claims and by providing past claimants with a new window in which to re-file actions previously dismissed on limitations grounds. The *Plaut* Court ruled that this re-opening of prior cases violated the principle of judicial finality and the doctrine of separation of powers. While Congress remains free to change the law prospectively and to apply the new law to pending cases, it may not re-open final decisions or subject them to review other than by a superior court within the Article III hierarchy.

The principle of judicial finality applies with somewhat reduced force when the judicial decisions at issue grant injunctive relief. As a general matter, injunctions remain subject to the ongoing supervision of the federal courts and may be modified in light of changed circumstances, including a change in the relevant legal or factual framework. In one famous old case, the Court had ruled that a bridge over the Delaware river should be torn down as an impediment to navigation. Congress responded by passing legislation confirming the legality of the bridge. The Court vacated its prior decision, deferring to congressional power over navigation and concluding that the new statute required the termination of the prior injunction. See *Pennsylvania v. Wheeling & Belmont Bridge* (1855). The ongoing nature of the judicial role in supervising injunctive relief also played a crucial role in the Court's decision to uphold aspects of the Prison Litigation Reform Act (PLRA). See *Miller v. French* (2000). Congress adopted the PLRA in 1996 to provide for the re-consideration of structural injunctions in prison litigation and the termination of relief in many situations. But the legislation left the courts in control of the extent to which changed circumstances (including the new standard of narrowly tailored relief) necessitated termination of existing decrees.

As *Miller v. French* illustrates, the Court has been less concerned by threats to finality in which the courts themselves retain control over the extent to which an earlier decision remains binding. Under the doctrines of claim and issue preclusion, for example, the courts have traditionally exercised control over the degree to which earlier judicial decisions foreclose later litigation. Similarly, modern systems of procedural law, including the Federal Rules of Civil Procedure, typically permit the parties to file motions for relief from a judgment based on fraud or factual error. See Fed. R. Civ. P. 60(b). The possible threat to finality that such procedures pose has not been interpreted as a barrier to the exercise of judicial power. Similarly, in the context of naturalization proceedings, the Court has ruled that the federal courts appropriately exercise the judicial power in playing their largely ceremonial role in overseeing the formal approval of applications for citizenship. See *Tutun v. United States* (1926). Today, a federal agency reviews these applications. To be sure, naturalization judgments that have been procured on the basis of fraud or factual error may (like erroneous patents or land grants) be canceled upon the suit of the federal government. But federal courts would hear the suit to cancel and would determine the legality of the prior naturalization proceeding.

2.4   The Ban on Advisory Opinions

Early in the nation's history, the Supreme Court concluded that it could not issue advisory opinions: opinions offered in response to abstract legal questions propounded by another branch. As with judicial finality, the need to preserve judicial independence and the desire to avoid extra-judicial chores shaped the Court's rejection of an advisory opinion practice. The ban on advisory opinions remains intact today as a limit on the power of federal courts. It grows out of the same family of justiciability concerns that animate the doctrines of finality and standing and that informed the *Marbury* decision. In other words, the Court's rejection of an advisory role reflects the notion that the power of the federal courts to expound the law derives from the power to resolve concrete disputes and does not exist outside of that dispute-resolution context.

The issue first arose during the Washington administration, which had established a policy of neutrality as between the warring powers of Europe. France insisted on help from the United States, citing the provisions of the treaty of 1778. Out of this foreign policy stew arose a host of legal questions concerning the scope of French rights and US obligations under the treaty. The executive branch sought advice from the Court, noting that the first question would be whether the Justices could, with propriety, proffer their advice on abstract questions. The Court's answer arrived a few weeks later in the *Correspondence of the Justices* (1793). In a letter to President Washington, the Court concluded that such extra-judicial decision making was inconsistent with the "lines of separation" drawn in the Constitution. The Court also pointed out that the power of the executive to request advice from the cabinet was expressly limited to the executive departments and seemingly excluded the judicial department from an advice-giving role.[3]

As a fundamental limit on the power of the federal courts, the ban on advisory opinions draws support from a number of considerations. Had the Court recognized a right in the executive branch to seek advice, requests for advice may have crowded out the Court's adjudicative function (in somewhat the way that expansions in original jurisdiction may impede the Court's appellate function). Requests for advice also have an abstract or hypothetical quality that may not focus the issues for determination as concretely as the adverse presentations of disputing parties. Such requests tend to come, moreover, in the heat of the moment, depriving the Court of the more detached perspective that the unfolding litigation process often affords. In any case, decisions by either the executive or legislative branches to ignore advice might put the federal courts in an awkward position, especially if the issue later came before them in litigation.

Apart from maintaining a formal ban on the provision of advice, the Court has often invoked anti-advisory rhetoric in other contexts. For example, some members of the Court have said that the inclusion of an alternative ground in support of a decision represents an improper advisory opinion, just as others have sometimes criticized the inclusion of dicta as unnecessarily advisory. (On this conception of the advisory opinion, much of what Chief Justice Marshall said in *Marbury* might be regarded as advisory.) In addition to these situations, the Court has sometimes characterized disputes in which one of the parties lacks standing or where the dispute lacks the necessary ripeness as calling for a prohibited advisory opinion. But the formal request for advice, rejected in 1793, differs from the rhetorical use of the term to describe parts of an opinion that some members of the Court may regard as unnecessary. What the Court chooses to say in a case properly before it differs importantly from what the Court might be compelled to say and do if it were subject to requests for advice from the other

---

3. In an interesting echo of the Court's position, by the early nineteenth century, the Attorney General of the United States had taken the position that the office would offer legal advice to the President and the heads of the executive departments but not to the general public or to Congress. See H & W I (1953).

branches. Moreover, the Court retains ultimate control over how it will treat portions of an earlier opinion that were unnecessary to the decision.

In contrast to practice in the federal court system, perhaps a dozen states and several foreign nations allow their courts to issue advisory opinions. In Massachusetts, for example, the state constitution has long provided the Supreme Judicial Court with authority to issue advisory opinions in response to requests from both the legislative and executive branches of government. Similar constitutional and statutory practices prevail in at least ten other states. In Europe, many constitutional courts provide abstract determinations of the constitutionality of proposed legislation during the pendency of the legislative process. Often set up outside the judicial department and exercising a reference (as opposed to an appellate) jurisdiction, these European constitutional courts operate as institutional hybrids with both legislative and judicial features.

2.5 Advisory Opinions and Declaratory Judgment Actions

The federal judicial code, 28 U.S.C. § 2201–02, authorizes the district courts, in a case of actual controversy, to declare the rights and liabilities of the parties. At the time of its initial adoption in 1934, the Declaratory Judgment Act was thought to present a potential advisory-opinion problem. A series of Supreme Court decisions had treated the execution of judgments (perhaps through the sale of property or the imprisonment of a party for contempt of an equitable decree) as an essential feature of the exercise of judicial power. Declaratory judgments simply specify legal rights, without actually awarding execution or enjoining the parties to take certain action on pain of contempt. Indeed, one purpose of the declaratory judgment was to enable the parties to obtain a resolution of their legal dispute even where they faced no threat of irreparable harm and had yet to take decisive steps in the face of legal uncertainty.

The useful features of the declaratory judgment proceeding are clearly illustrated in the case in which such proceedings were upheld against an advisory opinion challenge. In *Aetna Life Insurance Co. v. Haworth* (1937), the insurance company was involved in a coverage dispute with a policyholder who claimed a present right to disability benefits under the terms of certain insurance policies. The company claimed that the policies had lapsed for non-payment of premiums and sought a declaration to that effect. The Court agreed that such a dispute presented a case of actual controversy between disputing parties that satisfied the terms of the statute. The dispute required the federal courts to adjudicate a present legal right on established facts, and did not call for an advisory opinion on a hypothetical record. It thus satisfied the requirements of Article III.

Claim and issue preclusion provide a further key to understanding why the declaratory judgment proceeding in *Haworth* posed no advisory opinion problem. Under established law, once the district court declares the rights of the parties, the declaration becomes a final judgment subject to appellate review and enjoys the same preclusive effect as other federal judgments. Having lost to Aetna in the declaratory judgment proceeding, Haworth could not re-litigate the coverage question. If, some years later, he were to sue to establish Aetna's liability under the same policies, his action would be subject to dismissal as precluded by the prior declaratory judgment. Parties in the position of Aetna and Haworth thus understand that the declaratory judgment will control the outcome of their legal dispute; they have the usual incentives to press their claims vigorously.

Requests by the political branches for advisory opinions would not necessarily trigger similarly concrete adversarial presentations nor would the issuance of such opinions produce comparably preclusive effects. In a typical request for judicial advice (and some state constitutions authorize such requests), the executive and legislative branches of government do not formally join opposing parties as in an adversarial proceeding. With no right (or obligation) to participate in the proceeding leading up to the issuance of the advisory opinion, interested parties cannot fairly be bound by the result. While a court might choose to give effect to an advisory opinion in subsequent litigation under the doctrine of stare decisis, the absence of adverse parties would prevent the use of advisory opinions as a preclusive bar to future litigation.

The growing importance of amicus briefs at the Supreme Court, coupled with the Court's own conception of its role, may nonetheless create a model of decision making that today depends less on adversarial presentation by the parties. Amicus briefs appear with great frequency as the parties work to coordinate submissions from groups interested in the outcome of particular cases. Such briefs can be quite influential; certainly the support for affirmative action by institutions as different as the armed forces and the Fortune 500 is widely thought to have influenced the Court's decision to uphold an affirmative action plan in *Grutter v. Bollinger* (2003). By taking fewer cases and inviting broad amicus participation, the Court may have access to a range of views— competently presented—that lessens its dependence on adversarial presentation. For evidence that the Court perceives its role as less dependent on continuing adversity after a case has been fully briefed and argued, see *Pacific Bell Telephone Co. v. Linkline*

Communications, Inc. (2009) (declining to find that the mid-stream loss of adversity necessarily mooted the case).

If the participation of amici helps to ensure the presentation of a range of relevant considerations, the Court's control of its original and appellate dockets allows the Court to set its own agenda. The combination of Court's docket-setting authority and amicus submissions suggests a similarity to the legislative process, where members of Congress set their own agendas and schedule hearings on a broad range of public questions. But the judicial process differs in important ways from the legislative process. Courts focus on concrete problems, often reasoning from the bottom up within a settled legal framework. Requirements of adversity among parties continue to limit the scope of potential judicial intervention. The Supreme Court may today more frequently engage in the explication of legal norms that cannot be considered strictly necessary to the resolution of a particular dispute. But this law-saying function does not break with tradition, or with the pattern set in *Marbury v. Madison.*

2.6 The Standing Doctrine

Like the advisory opinion ban and the finality rule, the law of standing defines the "cases" and "controversies" that federal courts may hear. Standing law resembles other justiciability doctrines in its emphasis on the need for a concrete presentation of disputes by adverse parties and in its concern with limiting the role of the judiciary in a government defined by the separation of powers. Instead of operating as a doctrine of self-defense, however, standing typically acts as a form of judicial self-abnegation in which the federal courts decline to hear a particular case on the ground that one party (typically the plaintiff) lacks the requisite personal interest or stake in the dispute. Standing focuses on the interests of the parties to the dispute, but standing decisions invariably reflect judicial views about the fitness of the legal question for judicial resolution. Questions about fitness, in turn, often implicate the merits of the dispute, and open the Court to criticism that its standing doctrine lacks principle.

A few words may help introduce the material that follows. At its core, standing law reflects the widely held notion that only parties with a concrete stake in the case can bring a dispute before the federal courts. The common law writ system assured concrete interests; parties who suffered a cognizable legal injury to their person or property could bring a trespass action, but bystanders were barred from bringing suit on the ground that they had suffered no legal injury. So long as the writ system governed, questions of standing were incorporated into the general demurrer, the all-purpose motion to dismiss that put into issue the question whether the plaintiff's complaint articulated legally recognized rights and injuries. See Woolhandler & Nelson (2004). Today, under modern pleading rules, we would ask whether the plaintiff states a claim upon which relief may be granted.

Standing law performs somewhat the same function as the demurrer or motion to dismiss in determining whether the plaintiff may bring suit for the relief requested. But the inquiry differs in two important respects. First, standing law acts as a jurisdictional doctrine, so that the absence of standing deprives the district court of jurisdiction over the dispute. Like jurisdictional issues generally, standing issues remain open throughout the litigation and may be raised for the first time on appeal. Second, standing law features an intricate and somewhat artificial three-part test that focuses on the circumstances of the actual claimant. To establish standing, the plaintiff must show that she has suffered (i) an injury in fact; (ii) that is fairly traceable to allegedly illegal conduct; (iii) and that can be redressed through judicially manageable forms of relief. Each of these elements deserves separate consideration.

2.6.1 The Injury Requirement

To establish standing, plaintiffs must first show that they have suffered an injury to a protected legal interest. The Court has phrased this requirement in various ways, sometimes insisting that the injury be "distinct and palpable," sometimes that it not be "abstract" or "conjectural." The concrete injury requirement plays two roles in the Court's standing jurisprudence. First, it serves to ensure that the particular plaintiff has a genuine grievance or injury and is not acting in the "abstract" as a self-appointed guardian of the rule of law. Ideological considerations often influence the decision to sue, but the injury requirement means that an honest (and well-financed) desire to test a legal question in the federal courts will not alone justify litigation. These "test" cases additionally require an injured party to serve as the plaintiff.[4] Second, the injury requirement enables the Court to distinguish genuine injuries from what it has termed "generalized grievances," disputes over matters better left to the political branches. The interpretation of the injury requirement depends to some extent on which of these roles it performs.

An early case, *Sierra Club v. Morton* (1972), illustrates the role of the injury requirement in limiting the ability of ideologically motivated interest groups to challenge the legality of government action. There, the Sierra Club brought suit against the head of a

---

4. Ethics rules permit a third party to pay another individual's attorney's fees, so long as the individual bringing suit agrees to the arrangement. The attorney's duty of loyalty runs to the client, not to the third party financing the litigation.

federal agency to block development of a portion of the Sequoia National Forest, alleging that the Club's interest in the conservation of national parks was sufficient to confer standing. The Court disagreed, holding that clubs and organizations cannot sue to vindicate their own ideological preferences through the judicial process. Clubs and associations must instead point to some concrete injury to the legal interests of their members, perhaps by pointing to one or more members that had used the area in question and would be significantly affected by the proposed development. Only where an association identifies a member with a concrete stake in preserving an endangered species or wilderness area can it challenge action that would threaten the species or alter the area.

At first blush, the Court's approach seems counter-intuitive. Surely a well established group like the Sierra Club would often do a better job of framing an adversarial presentation of the issues than would an individual citizen acting alone. The individual may have a concrete injury by virtue of her relationship to the national forest, but she will not necessarily have the means to hire a lawyer or the experience to assess the legality of the government's policy. Justice Blackmun's dissent recognized as much in the *Sierra Club* case, arguing that the focus on individuals was misguided and should be replaced with a rule that permitted the association itself to pursue the claim in appropriate cases. But Blackmun's approach may have produced difficulties of its own by requiring the federal courts to distinguish between bona fide environmental groups and other groups that lack the same commitment to the cause of conservation. When faced with the task of choosing among associations, the Court's decision to focus on the situation of individual members may have avoided a problem of judicial administration.

Still, the Court's interpretation of the injury requirement can lead to a fairly artificial set of inquiries. While environmental associations finance and control the litigation, standing turns on the association's ability to identify members with the requisite connection to the site of the environmental controversy. *Lujan v. Defenders of Wildlife* (1992) provides the definitive example. The environmental group sought to challenge the failure of US government agencies to consult with the Interior Department as to the environmental impact of certain developmental projects that could threaten the habitat of the Nile crocodile and Asian elephant. Although the association's members had a professional interest in the species (as academics) and had actually traveled to observe the species in the sites affected by the development plans, the Court concluded that they failed to establish an injury in fact. The plaintiffs needed more than an intent to return; they needed a concrete plan to do so, such that the completion of the project could pose a threat of injury. As thus interpreted, the injury requirement may serve simply to require the association to purchase plane tickets as a way of showing that the scientists have concrete plans to return. What exactly these more concrete plans to return would add to the quality of the plaintiffs' presentation remains something of a mystery. Similar questions might be asked of the Court's decision in *Summers v. Earth Island Institute* (2009), where the failure of the member's affidavit to specify a more concrete plan to visit national forests proved fatal to the organization's standing to challenge regulations that proposed to streamline the sale of the timber from national park lands.

Apart from requiring a focus on the injury to individuals, the injury-in-fact requirement has been used to distinguish cognizable injuries from "generalized grievances" or claims based on a shared interest in government compliance with law. In *United States v. Richardson* (1974), the plaintiff sought to challenge the secrecy of the CIA's budget as a violation of Article I's requirement that Congress publish a "public account of the receipts and expenditures of all public money." The Court ruled that the plaintiff lacked standing; his claim was said to be a generalized grievance held in common with all other members of the public. Much the same conclusion was reached in *Schlesinger v. Reservists Committee* (1974). There, the Court denied the plaintiff standing to challenge the issuance of military commissions to members of Congress under Article I's Incompatibility Clause—a constitutional provision that seemingly bars the practice. By characterizing both claims as generalized grievances, the Court treated them as unfit for judicial determination and as better left to the political branches of government for enforcement (or neglect).

The generalized grievance cases resemble the *Sierra Club* decision in treating the interest in governmental compliance with law as insufficient alone to justify standing. But one important difference separates the cases. In *Sierra Club*, the Court pointed to the kinds of factors that would support an individual's standing to pursue an environmental claim, and thus enabled groups to overcome their own standing problems by acting on behalf of interested individuals or members. In the generalized grievance cases, by contrast, the Court apparently recognized that no individual would have standing to challenge the CIA's budget or the issuance of military commissions to members of Congress. In truth, the Court was not seeking a more concretely affected individual, but was foreclosing any judicial challenge to the constitutional practices at issue. The standing doctrine thus operated in effect as a barrier to relief on the merits.

Of course, not every action that injures a broad group of people will be treated as a generalized grievance. Wrongful conduct may inflict cognizable injuries on an entire class of victims. Inmates at a prison facility, for example, may share a common interest in their conditions of confinement. Such shared interests may enable the inmates to initiate a class action that would not be subject to dismissal as a generalized grievance; all the individuals in prison would be seen as having suffered an injury from unlawful prison conditions and would have standing to proceed with a claim. In contrast, the individual plaintiff in a generalized grievance case suffers no personal consequences or injuries at all and seeks to compel the government to comply with the law. Much may depend on whether the Court views the particular constitutional provision as one that structures government relations or as one that confers individual rights.

Taxpayer standing cases, a somewhat specialized subset of the generalized grievance category, illustrate the influence of judicial attitudes toward the constitutional right at issue. In an early case, *Frothingham v. Mellon* (1923), the Court rejected the notion that taxpayers could bring suit to challenge a government spending program as exceeding Congress's spending power under the Constitution. Even though the spending program might increase tax bills, the Court viewed the taxpayer's interest as minute and indeterminable, and held in common with the people generally. In a later case, *Flast v. Cohen* (1968), the Court allowed taxpayers to challenge a government spending program that furnished financial support for religious schools. Although the Court constructed an elaborate test to distinguish Establishment Clause challenges from other taxpayer claims, the Court's perception of the need to enforce the constitutional provision at issue rather than an evaluation of the individual taxpayer's interest apparently explained the differing results in *Frothingham* and *Flast*. In subsequent cases, the Court has cut back on the scope of taxpayer standing, even for claims under the Establishment Clause. See *Valley Forge Christian College v. Americans United for Separation of Church and State, Inc.* (1982).

The most recent such decision, *Hein v. Freedom From Religion Foundation* (2007), suggests that little remains of *Flast v. Cohen* (aside from its holding). In *Hein*, an organization and its taxpaying members brought suit to challenge a faith-based initiative housed within the executive office of President George Bush. The Court did not view the case as controlled by *Flast*: there was no federal statute actually conferring a financial benefit on religious organizations. Instead, the expenditures were made from a fund appropriated to the executive branch for its discretionary use. Any establishment of religion thus resulted from executive discretion rather than legislative fiat. In denying standing, the *Hein* Court nicely illustrated the influence of constitutional norms on the Court's use of standing doctrine. Taxpayers can challenge direct congressional spending for religious purposes (*Flast*) but cannot challenge the transfer of surplus property to religious organizations (*Valley Forge*) or the discretionary use of executive branch funds. None of these distinctions follows from the nature of the injury to taxpayers in the cases, whatever sense they may make as interpretations of the Establishment Clause.

2.6.2   Causation and Redressability

Apart from an injury in fact, plaintiffs must meet two other standing requirements. They must show that the wrongful conduct at issue *caused* their injury and that the federal courts have the power to remedy or *redress* their injury through a favorable decision. In general, the causation and redressability requirements invite the court's attention to the link between the alleged wrong and the injury and the likely impact of a favorable order. Will the decree actually improve the position of the plaintiff, or will it simply make it marginally more likely that the plaintiff will obtain some benefit or entitlement? The more indirect the chain of causation, the more likely a court will find a causation or redressability problem.

Causation and redressability problems frequently arise when the suit challenges government action and seeks to alter the manner in which the government regulates or processes claims involving third parties. Consider *Simon v. Eastern Kentucky Welfare Rights Organization* (1976). There, plaintiffs brought a class action against the Internal Revenue Service (IRS) to challenge the government's elimination of a requirement that hospitals provide indigent care to qualify for a charitable exemption from taxation. The plaintiffs argued that they could not afford to pay for hospital treatment and that the new rule would reduce the amount of available charity care. The Court dismissed the action for want of standing. Although the plaintiffs had alleged an injury (denial of needed hospital care), the Court viewed their claim that this injury resulted from the tax treatment of hospitals as "purely speculative." Nor would a change in the rule necessarily redress their injuries by producing charity care sufficient to meet their needs.

One can read the decision in *Simon* as reflecting the Court's suspicion of claims that seek to influence the manner in which the government regulates third parties. (Justice Stewart explained in his concurring opinion that he would rarely vote to permit a person whose own tax liability was not affected to challenge the tax liability of a third party.) Certainly, that suspicion has been in evidence on a number of occasions. *Linda R.S. v. Richard D.*

(1973) was a challenge to the state's policy of bringing prosecutions for the non-payment of support obligations against the fathers of *legitimate* children alone. The Court denied standing to the mother of an illegitimate child who sued under the Equal Protection Clause to compel the state to pursue the fathers of illegitimate children as well. The Court relied in part on the speculative nature of the claim: prosecution of the father would not necessarily produce support payments for the mother. The Court also emphasized its view that individuals lack a cognizable interest in the government's decision whether to prosecute another citizen.

Not all speculative claims defy standing, however, as the affirmative action cases reveal. In *Regents of the University of California v. Bakke* (1978), the Court agreed to hear Bakke's challenge to the use of an affirmative action quota in the medical school admissions process. The university argued that Bakke could not show redressability; his application was not strong enough to have assured his admission to the school even in the absence of an affirmative action program. But the Court found that Bakke had a cognizable interest in the ability to compete on an equal footing for all the positions in the class, free from a racially exclusive set-aside program. Such an approach transforms the redressability inquiry to focus not on the plaintiff's ability to gain the actual benefit (hospital care in *Simon*, support payments in *Linda R.S.*, and a place in the class in *Bakke*) but on the process by which the government determines who will receive the benefit.

Some have argued that other plaintiffs might use *Bakke*'s approach to re-characterize their injuries in terms that ease the task of showing redressability. The plaintiffs in *Simon*, for example, might have sought medical services under a system undistorted by unlawful tax incentives. See Sunstein (1988). So framed, the injury could arguably be redressed by an order that ends unlawful distortion. But it seems unlikely that a change in the way plaintiffs frame their claim of injury would alter the standing decision. Bakke was complaining about the way the University of California discriminated against him in denying him the benefit of admission to its medical school. In *Linda R.S.* and *Simon*, by contrast, the plaintiffs sought to gain benefits not from the government directly, but from third parties who were subject to government regulation. A decision compelling the government to change its regulatory approach would affect the plaintiffs only indirectly and only to the extent that the regulated third parties altered their behavior in response to new government policy.

More recent decisions on causation and redressability support the conclusion that re-framing the issue will not alter the standing analysis. In *Allen v. Wright* (1984), the parents of African-American school children brought a nation-wide class action against the

IRS to challenge its regulatory approach to racially discriminatory private schools. They argued that the IRS permitted discriminatory schools to obtain tax exempt status; that status was in turn said to encourage white parents to enroll their school age children in private schools instead of integrated public schools. (Exempt status means that the white parents can deduct charitable contributions to the private schools; tuition payments to private schools are not deductible. Exemption thus reduces the after-tax price of parental support of private education.) Plaintiffs asked for tougher regulatory standards to ensure a denial of charitable tax exemption to racially discriminatory private schools.

Although the Court found that the plaintiffs had adequately alleged a cognizable injury to their interest in a desegregated education, it found they lacked standing under the causation or "fair traceability" prong of the test. The IRS's treatment of private schools may have encouraged more parents of white children to leave the public schools; indeed, Justice Stevens' dissent argued that, as a matter of tax policy, economics, and common sense, reducing the price of private education through tax exemption will ordinarily increase private school enrollments. But the Court nonetheless viewed any impact on public education as too indirect to support standing. The injury to plaintiffs resulted not from the government's own actions but from "the independent action of some third party not before the Court."

With its suspicion of suits aimed at forcing the government to regulate third parties, the Court's 5–4 decision in *Massachusetts v. EPA* (2007) represents something of a departure. There, the Court found that the state of Massachusetts would suffer a cognizable injury from global warming that could result from the EPA's failure to regulate carbon dioxide emissions as a pollutant under the Clean Air Act. The injuries consisted of the threatened (but not impending) loss of coastal land following a global-warming-induced rise in sea levels and the injury to the state's quasi-sovereign status as a member of the Union. The Court also found that causation and redressability were satisfied, despite the lack of any demonstrable connection between EPA regulation and sea levels worldwide. Most observers agree that the Court adopted a more lenient standing doctrine for state plaintiffs than it has applied to private suitors. One can thus question the relevance of the precedent to the analysis of the standing of private litigants.

2.6.3 Congressional Control of Standing to Sue

In *Flast v. Cohen* (1968), Justice Harlan argued in dissent that the Court should not recognize a taxpayer's standing to pursue an Establishment Clause challenge to certain federal expenditures. Justice Harlan noted, however, that Congress was free to create a right of action and confer standing on individual taxpayers if it chose to do so. Harlan thus assumed that a judicial refusal to recognize standing would operate as a matter of prudential deference to the political branches and not as a constitutional barrier to Congress's power to authorize an individual suit. In assuming that Congress might go further in providing a right to sue, Harlan may have been influenced by the pattern of legislation that accompanied the New Deal and the rise of the administrative state. In many instances, administrative law had conferred rights of action on private individuals that were unavailable at common law.

In the past few decades, the Court's approach to standing has hardened somewhat. In *Allen v. Wright* (1984), the Court proclaimed that standing limits derive from Article III of the Constitution. While the Court also confirmed that standing law had a prudential component, it took the position that the core elements of standing—injury, causation, and redressability—were "derived directly from the Constitution." Much of this was dicta in *Allen* itself; the plaintiffs had not relied upon a right to sue conferred by an act of Congress, and the Court had no occasion to determine if the Article III standing requirements would invalidate such a statute.

Eight years later, though, the Court squarely held that Article III standing limits override a federal citizen suit statute that conferred standing on plaintiffs who failed to meet the doctrine's core requirements. The decision, *Lujan v. Defenders of Wildlife* (1992), involved a challenge by an environmental group to new regulations that altered the obligations of federal agencies to consult with the Interior Department on the environmental impact of overseas development projects. (Prior regulations had required federal agency consultation with the Secretary of Interior on all projects; the new regulations exempted projects on foreign soil.) Justice Scalia's opinion for the Court found that the plaintiffs had failed to satisfy the injury requirement (because the individuals had failed to establish any concrete plan to return to the sites in question). Justice Scalia also cast doubt on redressability (because other federal agencies would not be bound by any order directed to the Interior Department). He then considered the language of the citizen suit provision of the Endangered Species Act, which specifically authorizes "any person" to bring suit to enjoin anyone, including federal agencies and their officials, from committing a violation of the Act. The Court found that this broad language did not authorize plaintiffs to bring suit if they otherwise lacked standing under the injury and redressability prongs of the analysis.

Lujan not only disregarded the citizen suit provision, it articulated a new conception of the standing doctrine as restriction on the power of Congress. Under this new conception, the executive branch of government (and ultimately the president) enjoys a constitutional prerogative to determine how vigorously to enforce federal laws. According to the lead opinion of Justice Scalia, this prosecutorial discretion inheres in the Take Care Clause of Article II, which commands the president to "take care that the laws be faithfully executed." The Court portrayed the Endangered Species Act as interfering with this executive prerogative of law enforcement (or non-enforcement). By creating a citizen's suit provision, Congress was seeking to transform the executive power of prosecution into an individual right to enforce laws through suit in the federal courts. Such a transfer of enforcement oversight authority to the courts was seen as inconsistent with the rightful independence of the executive.

Lujan thus links standing doctrine to an ongoing debate over what has come to be known in constitutional and administrative law circles as the unitary executive thesis. Under the thesis, which has yet to win the support of a consistent majority on the Court, Article II of the Constitution vests the president with ultimate control over the executive branch of government. Such a constitutional vesting of ultimate control invalidates efforts by Congress to insulate the work of administrative agencies from executive oversight. The thesis draws on three provisions of Article II: the Vesting Clause (vesting executive power in the president); the Appointments Clause (empowering the president to appoint, and perhaps to remove, officers of the executive branch); and the Take Care Clause. Proponents of the unitary executive thesis seek to ensure greater political accountability to the president in matters of administrative law; they criticize independent agencies (agencies whose heads serve for a term of years and enjoy some protection from presidential discharge) and the independent counsel law (a Watergate-era statute, since repealed, that created a mechanism for an independent prosecutor to investigate and prosecute criminal activity by high government officials).[6]

Citizen suit provisions help to ensure some continuing oversight of the work of administrative agencies in a world where Congress has broadly delegated rulemaking authority. Citizen suit provisions thus provide one additional tool, along with many others, that Congress can use in overseeing the agencies. (Other mechanisms include oversight hearings, budget processes, and the adoption of clearer statutes that structure and confine the exercise of administrative discretion.) Indeed, citizen suit provisions resemble laws that limit the exercise of executive power by creating judicially enforceable rights in individuals; such laws have been a familiar

---

6. Justice Scalia, author of *Lujan,* also wrote the dissenting opinion in *Morrison v. Olson* (1986), urging the invalidation of the independent counsel law as an invasion of Article II executive power.

feature of the administrative state at least since *Marbury v. Madison* confirmed the availability of mandamus relief to protect an individual's rights under federal law.   Citizen suit provisions draw support from this tradition of congressional power to create rights that may be enforced against the government in federal court. Associated with environmental laws that date from the 1970s and 1980s, citizen suit provisions seek to ensure that both regulated industries and environmental activists will have a seat at the table when administrative agencies make decisions that affect the public interest.

Despite the doubts raised in *Lujan*, the Court's more recent decision in *FEC v. Akins* (1998) confirms the ability of Congress to create rights in members of the public that will satisfy the standing requirements of Article III.   A group of voters filed a complaint asking the Federal Election Commission to treat a lobbying group— the American Israel Public Affairs Committee (AIPAC)—as a political committee within the meaning of federal election law.   If adopted by the FEC, such treatment would have triggered disclosure of the sources of AIPAC's funding and the political figures and campaigns to which it made contributions.   When the FEC dismissed the complaint and declined to treat AIPAC as a political committee, the voters sued the FEC under a citizen suit provision that authorizes "any party aggrieved" by the dismissal of a complaint to seek review in federal district court.   The government argued, pointing to *Lujan*, that the plaintiffs lacked any cognizable injury in fact, but were suing on a generalized grievance held in common with all citizens of the United States.

In upholding the voters' standing (over Justice Scalia's dissent), the Court focused on the fact that the federal statute created a right in individual voters to obtain information from regulated parties like AIPAC.   The Court viewed this right to information as concrete and particular despite the fact that it was broadly shared with other voters around the country; it was not a generalized grievance of the kind that had failed to support standing in *United States v. Richardson* (1974).   Injuries might be widely distributed, as the Court explained by pointing to a hypothetical case involving a mass tort that injured large numbers of individuals, without becoming generalized grievances.   The Court also rejected arguments based on the causation and redressability prongs of the standing inquiry.   Although it acknowledged that standing to seek review of the FEC's decision would not guarantee disclosure of AIPAC information, the Court found that an order remanding for reconsideration would nonetheless redress the injury by providing the plaintiffs with an opportunity to argue that the FEC had erred in assessing AIPAC's status.

The *Akins* decision does not end constitutional scrutiny of individual standing under citizen suit provisions. It does suggest, however, that the Court will follow a more flexible approach to the injury and causation issues and will give effect to federal statutes that have been tailored to create specific rights (especially rights to information) in favor of individual claimants. As the Court explained, standing decisions must consider the substantive laws at issue and the extent to which they confer concrete and particular rights on individuals. In distinguishing *Richardson*, the Court noted that its analysis there had focused on the meaning of one provision of the Constitution and did not control the standing of litigants under other provisions that create more definite rights to the disclosure of information. Broad and diffuse citizen suit provisions, especially those (as in *Lujan*) that do not connect to relatively specific statutory rights, will continue to present standing problems.

2.7   The Mootness Doctrine

As we have seen, Article III's case or controversy requirement limits the federal courts to the adjudication of concrete disputes between adverse parties. If the decision will not affect the rights of litigants in the case before them, federal courts lack the power to proceed. Sometimes, a case or controversy that entered the federal courts as an appropriate subject for the exercise of judicial power may lose its status as such due to an intervening change in the situation or interests of the parties. When such changes occur, the controversy may cease to be definite and concrete, and its resolution may no longer affect the legal relations of adverse parties. The case may, in short, have become moot, and the mootness doctrine may require its dismissal.

Familiar cases illustrate the problem of mootness. In *Roe v. Wade* (1973), the plaintiff sought to challenge a Texas law that restricted her access to an abortion. By the time the case reached the Supreme Court, Roe had delivered the child and was no longer pregnant. The Court thus faced a question of mootness. Similarly, in *DeFunis v. Odegaard* (1974), the plaintiff claimed that he had been denied admission to the University of Washington law school as a result of an affirmative action program that discriminated against him on the basis of his race. The applicant ultimately gained admission to the law school through a lower court order. By the time the case reached the Supreme Court, the plaintiff had begun his third year, and the law school had agreed to permit him to graduate, whatever the outcome of the litigation. The agreement meant that the Court's decision could no longer determine the plaintiff's right to a legal education at the law school, thus presenting a mootness issue. In *Gerstein v. Pugh* (1975), a criminal defendant sought to challenge pretrial detention, but mootness issues arose when the criminal case went to trial (and the claimant was no longer held in pretrial detention.)

Although the mootness doctrine bears a strong family resemblance to standing and other justiciability doctrines, the Court does not treat mootness with the same rigidity that characterizes its standing analysis. While the Court has sometimes described mootness as a product of Article III limits on the power of the federal courts, it has developed a series of exceptions that introduce some fluidity into the doctrine's application. In *Roe v. Wade*, for example, the Court recognized an exception to the mootness doctrine and decided the case on the merits, whereas in *DeFunis*, the Court declined to apply an exception and dismissed the action as moot. No less a figure than Chief Justice Rehnquist cited such exceptions in arguing, though not without controversy, that mootness doctrine reflects prudential considerations rather than the more unyielding requirements of Article III. See *Honig v. Doe* (1988).

Moreover, the Court's recent decisions confirm that the mootness doctrine applies less rigidly than standing. In *Friends of the Earth v. Laidlaw Environmental Services, Inc.* (2000), the Court considered a suit brought under citizen suit provisions to enjoin a violation of the Clean Water Act and to collect a civil penalty. Midway through the litigation, the firm came into compliance with the Act (and then closed its facility) thereby mooting the claim for injunctive relief and leaving only the claim for a penalty. A lower federal court dismissed the action as moot, emphasizing that Article III required that each element of standing must remain in place throughout the litigation. (The plaintiff had no personal stake in the penalty, which was payable to the government. The lower court found that payment of the penalty would not redress any injury that the plaintiff had suffered.) On review, the Court rejected the position that a dispute becomes moot if it does not continue to satisfy the elements of standing throughout the litigation.

A certain pragmatism underlies the decision in *Friends of the Earth*. The Court had previously ruled that a defendant, when facing a threat of environmental litigation, might bring its activities into compliance with federal law and defeat the standing of a plaintiff to pursue prospective relief. See *Steel Co. v. Citizens for a Better Environment* (1998). But in *Friends of the Earth*, the Court applied a different calculus to a defendant that was out of compliance with federal law at the time of the commencement of litigation. As to such parties, the plaintiffs had standing at the outset to seek to compel future compliance and to seek a civil penalty (payable to the government) for past non-compliance. Once standing was established as a threshold matter, subsequent efforts on the part of the defendant to come into compliance during the course of the litigation did not moot the case in the Court's view (even though the same compliance efforts may have barred the suit initially). The decision recognizes that environmental groups would have little reason to invest in compliance litigation under the citizen suit provisions of the Act if a defendant, when sued, might procure the dismissal of the action by the simple expedient of bringing its operation into compliance. Standing established at the outset enables the suit to proceed even where the shape of the litigation changes.

Similarly practical considerations have long informed the Court's development of exceptions to the mootness doctrine. Thus, the Court has ruled that the defendant's voluntary cessation of wrongful conduct (as in *Friends of the Earth*) may not moot the action and that mootness may not require dismissal where the injury can be considered capable of repetition, yet evading review. These two exceptions merit separate treatment. (Note that mootness most often presents a problem when the plaintiff seeks prospective injunctive or declaratory relief; suits for damages would not ordinarily be mooted by changes in the defendant's conduct that take place after the events that gave rise to the claim.)

2.7.1 Mootness and Voluntary Cessation

When faced with litigation, defendants will sometimes voluntarily cease their allegedly illegal conduct in order to forestall any further litigation. On its face, such voluntary cessation may appear to moot the case by ending any live dispute or controversy. But under a long line of cases, the Court has recognized that voluntary cessation does not necessarily moot the case where it leaves the defendant "free to return to his old ways." *United States v. W.T. Grant Co.* (1953). Such a return to old ways might lead to another round of litigation and perhaps another voluntary cessation as the defendant tries to fend off adjudication of the legal question. To avoid such duplicative litigation, the Court has created an exception to the mootness doctrine driven by both the public interest in a definitive settlement of the legal question and concerns with gamesmanship.

Recent cases articulate a fairly strict standard for judging the claim by a defendant that its voluntary compliance with the law renders the dispute moot. In *Friends of the Earth*, as we have seen, the defendant came into compliance and sought dismissal on mootness grounds. To succeed, the Court noted that the defendant bears the burden to show that events make it "absolutely clear that the allegedly wrongful behavior could not reasonably be expected to recur." Having found that the defendant failed to meet this demanding standard, the Court declined to order a dismissal on mootness grounds.

Yet similarly strict standards have not been uniformly applied in the voluntary cessation context. In *DeFunis v. Odegaard*, the law school complied with an order to admit DeFunis and had voluntarily agreed to permit him to graduate, thereby bringing the voluntary cessation exception into play. But the Court refused to apply the exception, arguing that it was unlikely that DeFunis would ever again undergo the University's allegedly unconstitutional admissions policy. On the other hand, as the dissent noted, there was at least some possibility that DeFunis would fail to graduate as scheduled and would face the obligation to seek re-admission. Under the strict standard of "absolute clarity," even a modest prospect of recurrent behavior would justify a voluntary cessation exception to mootness. The argument for recognizing an exception was stronger, the dissent noted, in a case that presented a constitutional question of great significance and implicated the public interest in a prompt resolution.

Critics of *DeFunis* have argued that the decision does not reflect a fair application of the voluntary cessation exception but rests instead on the Court's own desire to avoid the merits of the affirmative action controversy. Section 2.10 will explore the debate over the use of the justiciability doctrines as tools of constitutional avoidance.

2.7.2 Mootness: Capable of Repetition, Yet Evading Review

Roe v. Wade represents a classic example of the mootness exception for issues that are capable of repetition, yet evading review. In *Roe*, the plaintiff was pregnant at the time she commenced her action to challenge abortion restrictions, but had delivered her child before the case reached the Supreme Court. Abortion was no longer an option, and her action to challenge the Texas law was arguably moot. But the Court found that the action fell within the mootness exception for disputes capable of repetition, yet evading review. There were two steps to the Court's analysis: it found that Ms. Roe might become pregnant again (capable of repetition) and that the reality of litigation through the state and federal courts could prevent any case from reaching the Supreme Court before the nine-month term of the pregnancy had passed. The dispute might thus evade review if the events recurred, leaving the parties without guidance on the legal question.

By its nature, the capable of repetition exception applies when the plaintiff challenges a matter of relatively short duration. States sometimes condition eligibility for government benefits, such as welfare payments, on the satisfaction of a durational residency requirement. Often, by the time challenges to such requirements reach the Court, the durational period will have passed, thereby entitling the plaintiff to the benefit in question and mooting the case. Other examples include challenges to the election laws, such as statutes that limit ballot access or the expenditure of funds during the campaign. Even where the election has occurred, mooting the dispute, the Court might regard the dispute as saved from mootness under the repetition exception.

In general, the Court has made clear that the event must be capable of repetition as to the plaintiff. In *Roe*, for example, the Court focused on the fact that the plaintiff was of child-bearing age and might once again wish to terminate a pregnancy. In *DeFunis*, by contrast, the Court found it unlikely that the plaintiff would ever have to seek admission to law school again. But the Court has been somewhat inconsistent in determining what sort of showing of likely recurrence or repetition must be made in order to trigger the exception. Sometimes, the Court appears to presume likely repetition and demands little by way of a concrete showing on this point. Other times, the Court has demanded a reasonable probability of recurrence and has refused to apply the exception. This variation in the standard suggests that, as with all justiciability doctrines, courts applying the mootness exceptions exercise judicial discretion.

2.7.3   Class Actions and Mootness

Plaintiffs who foresee a mootness problem during the course of extended litigation often choose to pursue their claims in the form of a class action. Governed by Rule 23 of the Federal Rules of Civil Procedure, the class action in federal court enables one or more plaintiffs to bring an action on behalf of members of a class of similarly situated individuals, provided that the claims bear a close family resemblance and that the named plaintiff (and the attorney) can fairly represent the interests of all members of the class. Once such an action has been certified (judicially approved for treatment as a class action), the Court has permitted the action to continue on behalf of the class, even where the named or representative plaintiff no longer has a live claim.

To see the importance of the class action as a procedural device to overcome mootness problems, consider an action to desegregate a public middle school. Parents of children of middle school age obviously have standing to bring such a claim (recall *Allen v. Wright* and the injury requirement). But the litigation may take more than the three years to complete, during which time the students will leave middle school and enter high school. At that point, the parents who brought the suit may face a mootness issue; they no longer have a live stake in middle school education. One can argue that such a dispute should be regarded as capable of repetition, yet evading review; other middle school children will have entered the system in the meantime and will face the same segregation. But any particular child will not likely face middle school again, just as DeFunis would never have to face the law school admissions process. So long as repetition as to the particular plaintiff remains a feature of the repetition exception, mootness might present a problem. (Of course, a parent with younger children might avoid the problem.)

Class actions overcome this mootness problem. In a series of cases, the Court has held that a named plaintiff may continue to represent the members of a certified class, even after the case becomes moot as to the representative plaintiff. The first step came in *Sosna v. Iowa* (1975), a class action challenging Iowa's requirement that individuals reside in the state for a year before seeking a divorce. After a year passed, the plaintiff satisfied durational residency requirement and no longer had a live dispute with the state. But the Court held that she could continue to represent the members of the certified class. Such an approach conceives of the class action as a fluid mechanism that takes on a life of its own. None of the unnamed members of the class at the time the litigation began would have a live controversy a year later, but the Court understood the members of the class as changing or floating. Old members of the class would be constantly replaced by new members who would face the same durational requirement.

Once the notion of a floating class action had been approved, the Court extended the class action exception to deal with other wrinkles. The first problem arose from the complexity of securing class certification; despite procedural rules that urge a certification decision at an early practicable date, it can sometimes take several months to conduct the discovery necessary to make a certification decision. Such delays mean, as a practical matter, that certain forms of litigation cannot possibly be certified before the passage of time presents a mootness problem. In *Gerstein v. Pugh* (1975), the plaintiff was held in pretrial detention, in circumstances that were alleged to violate his constitutional rights. But by the time any action could be brought and certified, the claimant would have been bailed or tried and no longer subject to *pretrial* detention. The Court accordingly approved an exception to mootness that permitted the named plaintiff to continue to seek certification on behalf of the class, even after the dispute had become moot as to him. Crucial to the Court's decision was its recognition that although their identify would change, a class of persons would constantly be subject to detention.

Recognition of a right to pursue class certification, notwithstanding the mootness of the named plaintiff's own claim, led to a further extension in *US Parole Comm'n v. Geraghty* (1980). There, the plaintiff brought a class action to challenge certain parole guidelines. The district court denied class certification and granted summary judgment for the defendant on all claims. After filing a notice of appeal, the plaintiff gained his release from prison on unrelated grounds, thereby mooting his parole challenge. The Court held, nonetheless, that he could continue to pursue his action and seek reversal of the class certification decision. The majority emphasized the practical reality of class action litigation, treating the individual plaintiff as gaining an interest in the certification of the class that was independent of his own claim on the merits. The decision was limited to appellate review of the certification issue; no further litigation of the merits was to be permitted until the class was certified on remand.

2.8   The Ripeness Doctrine

Like other justiciability doctrines, the ripeness doctrine seeks to limit the federal courts to the adjudication of disputes between adverse parties to a live controversy. Ripeness issues arise when the plaintiff may be said to have brought suit prematurely, before a threatened injury or consequence has actually occurred. In an illustrative case, *United Public Workers v. Mitchell* (1947), a group of federal government employees sought a declaratory judgment invalidating the Hatch Act—a then newly adopted federal statute that barred government employees from playing an active role in political campaigns. Several plaintiffs were merely planning to take part in campaigns in the future; the Court ordered the dismissal of their claims as unripe. One plaintiff, by contrast, had actually violated the Hatch Act and was the target of an administrative proceeding to secure his discharge. As to this plaintiff, the Court found that the dispute was ripe for decision and reached the merits. The Court in *Mitchell* thus drew a distinction between the unripe, hypothetical claims of most of the plaintiffs and the more concrete and therefore ripe claims of the plaintiff who faced discharge.

The ripeness issues in *Mitchell* reflect tension between the individual litigant's interest in pre-enforcement review and the government's interest in discretionary enforcement. Many observers share the view of Justice Douglas, dissenting in *Mitchell*, that the interest of the other plaintiffs in clarifying their legal obligations was sufficient to support pre-enforcement review. Denial of review on ripeness grounds may force parties to violate a law in order to secure a test of its constitutionality. On the other hand, too great a willingness to entertain pre-enforcement challenges may result in premature and perhaps unnecessary litigation. Prosecutors often exercise discretion in selecting cases for enforcement;

they prefer to target individuals at the core of a statutory prohibition and may decline to prosecute those on the periphery. Routine pre-enforcement litigation may encourage challenges from those on the periphery who face no realistic threat of prosecution. Prosecutors also invite courts, in the context of enforcement proceedings, to adopt narrowing interpretations of the scope of the statute in an effort to limit any possible infringement on constitutional values. Facial challenges to a statute in a pre-enforcement proceeding may prevent the development of these limiting interpretations. Finally, at least some pre-enforcement actions target criminal statutes that have grown stale through non-enforcement over many years. Allowing a pre-enforcement challenge to such statutes may awaken sleeping dogs that prosecutors would have otherwise let lie.

In light of these competing concerns, the federal courts doubtless enjoy a measure of discretion in deciding whether to regard pre-enforcement challenges as ripe for review. One leading case invites explicit consideration of two factors: the "fitness" of the issue for judicial determination and the hardship on the plaintiffs. In *Abbott Laboratories v. Gardner* (1967), the Court considered the ripeness of a drug company challenge to new labeling rules that were said to have exceeded the power of the Food and Drug Administration under the agency's organic statute. In concluding that the challenge was ripe, the Court emphasized that the case presented a pure question of law as to the meaning of the statute and thus was fit for judicial resolution in a pre-enforcement proceeding. (Had the legal issues depended on the particular facts, the dispute may have been seen as less fit for pre-enforcement resolution.) The Court also found substantial hardship to the plaintiffs. The drug companies had printed up a store of labels that complied with the old rule; the new rule required them either to incur the expense of printing new labels or to risk the threat of an immediate enforcement proceeding, with the prospect of criminal and civil penalties for distribution of misbranded drugs.

Although *Abbott Labs* does not explore the interplay between the two elements, a companion case made clear that a reduction in hardship could well alter the ripeness analysis. In *Toilet Goods Ass'n v. Gardner* (1967), an association of manufacturers brought a pre-enforcement proceeding to challenge a regulation that required firms to provide FDA inspectors with "free access" to their premises and threatened to suspend the marketing licenses of manufacturers who failed to comply. The Court found no immediate hardship. The regulation posed a potential threat of future inspections, but did not confront the manufacturers with any immediate inspections or with rules of conduct that would alter their day-to-day business operations. The Court found that judicial review could await the issuance of specific inspection orders, which would also improve the "fitness" by providing a surer footing for subsequent judicial review.

While many pre-enforcement suits seek to challenge government action, the Court has clarified that federal courts have power to entertain pre-enforcement suits in the context of private litigation. In *MedImmune Inc. v. Genentech, Inc.* (2007), the plaintiff brought suit to contest the validity of the defendant's patent. But in order to avoid potential liability and the threat of treble damages, the plaintiff chose to honor its license agreement and to pay royalties under protest until the patent dispute was settled. The lower court dismissed the action as unripe and unfit for federal judicial resolution. The Supreme Court reversed, reasoning that an actual controversy existed within the meaning of the Declaratory Judgment Act and that the plaintiff had a right to pursue such a claim as an alternative to "arguably illegal activity." The plaintiff need not "bet the farm" by engaging in doubtful activity as a condition of securing a test of legal rights.

Apart from ripeness issues that arise from pre-enforcement review of statutes and regulations, the Court has sometimes applied ripeness principles as a bar to a whole class of federal litigation. In *O'Shea v. Littleton* (1974), the Court rejected an attempt by a group of African-American plaintiffs in Cairo, Illinois to demonstrate a pattern or practice of racial discrimination in the administration of justice in that city. The plaintiffs claimed that they had previously been defendants in the criminal justice system and had been subjected to a pattern of discrimination in the setting of bonds, sentencing, and jury practices. The complaint sought injunctive relief against defendants involved in the criminal justice system, or what the Court described as an ongoing federal judicial audit of state criminal proceedings.

The rejection of the *O'Shea* litigation on ripeness grounds reflects a consistent reluctance on the Court's part to invite litigation aimed at securing federal district court oversight of state and local criminal justice systems. In *City of Los Angeles v. Lyons* (1983), the plaintiff sought to challenge the police department's practice of using chokeholds to subdue suspects. The plaintiff had been subjected to such a chokehold and sought both damages for his injuries and injunctive relief against the city's chokehold policy. Evidence showed that several people had died as a result of such chokeholds, a substantial majority of whom were (like the plaintiff) African–Americans. Although the district court granted an injunction, the Supreme Court reversed on ripeness grounds citing *O'Shea*. The Court acknowledged that Lyons had standing to seek damages for chokehold injuries he suffered in the past, but rejected his claim for prospective injunctive relief against the city's chokehold policy. To the Court, the prospect that Lyons might one day encounter another police chokehold was too speculative to support injunctive relief.

Unlike the situation with other state institutions, such as prisons and schools, *O'Shea* and *Lyons* make it difficult for an individual or a class of plaintiffs to challenge the constitutionality of the administration of state justice systems. By refusing to find the dispute ripe, *O'Shea* and *Lyons* permit a plaintiff to pursue constitutional claims only when actually caught up in the local justice system. (The ripeness holding does not foreclose all litigation. Recall *Gerstein v. Pugh*, in which the Court approved the use of a class action to challenge the constitutionality of pretrial detention brought by a named plaintiff who was, at the time of suit, subject to the challenged practice.) Ripeness combines with other doctrines of judicial restraint to ensure that federal judicial oversight of the state criminal justice system will typically occur, if at all, through review of state court decisions in the Supreme Court.[7]

To evaluate the effect of the ripeness decisions requires both a knowledge of remedial alternatives and a comparative assessment of the institutional competence of the federal district courts and Supreme Court. As for remedial alternatives, the *Lyons* Court assumed that the plaintiff could seek damages; prevailing law (42 U.S.C. § 1983) requires the plaintiff to establish that the city followed a policy of using chokeholds in an unconstitutional manner. But a successful suit for damages does not necessarily require the city to change its policy. Nor does such a suit provide an effective vehicle for challenges to police practices (such as racial profiling) that may be unknown to the victims and give rise to a dignitary injury. By rejecting injunctive relief on ripeness grounds, the Court may have foreclosed the only effective remedy for some police practices.

Similarly, the Court's rejection of the assertion of the pattern-or-practice claim in *O'Shea* effectively forecloses federal district court oversight of many state practices. How effective are the other forms of judicial oversight? Many features of the criminal justice system (bond, sentencing, jury selection) routinely come before the state courts for decision. One might view the Court's discretionary power to review such decisions through certiorari as an adequate federal judicial remedy. On the other hand, one can question the Court's ability to provide effective oversight of the thousands of decisions that take place each year in the state courts.

---

7. As explained in Chapter 8, federal judicial review of state criminal convictions may sometimes occur though a petition for habeas corpus in district court, but the doctrine of exhaustion requires that habeas petitioners first seek relief by pursuing available state court remedies. Similarly, the doctrine of equitable restraint (the subject of Chapter 9) bars many plaintiffs from seeking a federal injunction to stay pending state criminal proceedings.

As a practical matter, the rejection of the claims in *O'Shea* serves to entrust the state courts with primary responsibility for remedying problems with the administration of local justice. One's confidence in the capacity of state courts to perform this oversight function may shape one's attitude toward the ripeness doctrine in *O'Shea*.

2.9   The Political Question Doctrine

Dating from the Court's early years, the political question doctrine treats certain issues as non-justiciable on the ground that the Constitution assigns them to a coordinate department for determination. In *Marbury v. Madison* (1803), the Court first gave voice to the doctrine: it described its role as deciding on the rights of individuals and disclaimed any power to pass upon "[q]uestions in their nature political." Political questions—those that had been assigned to one of the political branches of government for final decision—could "never be made in this court." Several years later, in *Luther v. Borden* (1849), the Taney Court applied the political question doctrine in refusing to entertain a claim that the malapportioned assembly of the state government of Rhode Island violated the constitutional guarantee of a republican form of government. Without reaching the merits of the challenge, the Court concluded that the issue was to be resolved by Congress, not by the federal courts.

In the ensuing years, the Court has identified a number of non-justiciable political questions. For example, the Court refused to permit the federal courts to consider a challenge to the legality of the Senate's procedures for the trial of a federal judge impeached for the commission of high crimes and misdemeanors. See *Nixon v. United States* (1993). Similarly, the Court has sometimes treated issues that touch upon the president's power over foreign affairs as presenting political questions that the federal courts may not hear. See *Dames & Moore v. Regan* (1981); *Goldwater v. Carter* (1979). Many aspects of the war powers, including the determination of when war begins and ends and what powers the president may exercise, have been treated as political questions. Finally, the Court has refused hear challenges to the process by which constitutional amendments have been proposed and ratified, treating Congress as the department charged with determining the effectiveness of constitutional amendments. See *Coleman v. Miller* (1939).

By "political," the doctrine refers to questions that have been assigned to one of the political branches of government for final determination, and not to the question's tendency to excite political controversy or to influence the operation of the political process. In *Bush v. Gore* (2000), for example, the Supreme Court agreed to hear a challenge to the process by which the Florida Supreme Court had ordered the counting of ballots in that state's presidential election. The issues were political in several senses, but the Court concluded that they did not lie beyond judicial competence under the political question doctrine. Similarly, in *Baker v. Carr* (1962), the Court allowed individuals to mount a challenge on equal protection grounds to the apportionment of the Tennessee legislature. The right to vote has obvious political salience, but the Court found that the legal claims were amenable to judicial resolution.

The business of distinguishing non-justiciable political questions from claims that the federal courts may hear has proven complex and controversial. Beginning with *Baker v. Carr*, the Court has identified two important considerations in the analysis. A question may be deemed political if there is a "textually demonstrable constitutional commitment of the issue to a coordinate political department." Alternatively, a question may be treated as political if the courts "lack discoverable and manageable standards for resolving it." While these factors blend together to some extent, political question analysis often takes separate account of them.

Consider *Nixon v. United States* (1993), which nicely illustrates the blended nature of the two inquiries into constitutional text and manageable standards. There, the plaintiff sought to challenge his removal from office as a federal judge, arguing that the Senate had failed to "try" him as required in Article I. (Nixon argued that he was entitled to full-blown trial-type procedures before the full Senate, whereas the Senate rules for trying impeachments provided for a committee to collect evidence and hear testimony.) The Court ruled that judicial review was unavailable under the political question doctrine. As for textual commitment, the Court noted that the language of the Impeachment Clause provided that the Senate "shall have sole power to try all impeachments," language it read as committing the issue of what constitutes a proper trial to the Senate alone. As for standards, the Court noted the various meanings that one might ascribe to the word "try," and concluded that the courts could not develop a manageable standard with which to review any choice the Senate made about what sort of trial to provide.

Both conclusions were contestable. The Senate's "sole" power to try cases parallels a reference to the House's "sole" power to vote articles of impeachment; the language may have been chosen less to rule out any judicial role than to clarify the respective roles of the Senate and House in relation to one another. Similarly, as Justice White noted in his concurring opinion, the federal courts have broad experience in defining the basic elements of due process. Such basic due process norms could have provided standards with which to assess the fairness of Senate trial procedures. In the end, all of the Justices agreed that the trial in Nixon's case did not raise any fairness concerns. Instead, the debate centered on the breadth of the political question doctrine and the desire of the concurring Justices to preserve judicial review to address unfairness in a future case.

The concern of the concurring Justices with the preservation of a judicial role in future cases highlights an enduring puzzle about the breadth, durability, and function of any particular political question determination. Some aspects of the *Nixon* decision suggest that the Court meant to place the entire category of impeachment issues beyond the scope of judicial review. (At one point, the Court catalogued the reasons why the federal courts "were not chosen to have any role in impeachments." At another point, the Court cited the problems that might follow from judicial review of a presidential impeachment.) But the Court has not always embraced such a categorical approach to the political question doctrine. Indeed, the Court has indicated in other settings that the application of the political question doctrine requires a case-by-case inquiry. See *Baker v. Carr* (1962).

The Court's occasional emphasis on the need for careful interpretation and case-by-case application has led some observers to question the existence of the political question doctrine as a threshold barrier to the adjudication of the merits. As scholars have noted, the question whether to treat a particular issue as political requires the courts to interpret the Constitution. Final authority over the fitness of an issue for judicial determination will rest with the Supreme Court. See Henkin (1976). Thus, in *Powell v. McCormack* (1969), the Court reached the merits of and upheld a challenge to a decision by the House of Representatives to exclude a duly-elected member from the body. The Court considered a provision of the Constitution that made the House "judge" of the "Qualifications of its own Members." The Court narrowly construed this power to judge, finding that it applied only to the list of qualifications actually set out in the Constitution (age, residency and citizenship) and did not allow exclusion for the other reasons the House had cited in Powell's case. Rather than a textual commitment of final decision-making authority, the House's power to judge was said to operate within boundaries the Court itself would specify.

Much of the deference federal courts have paid to the executive branch in the course of litigating war-on-terror issues in the wake of the attacks on September 11, 2001 appears to bear some resemblance to the political question doctrine. Perhaps the clearest example of deference can be seen in lower court treatment of the so-called "state secrets" privilege. The privilege has roots in the common law, but received an important boost in *United States v.*

Reynolds (1953).   There, the families of civilians who died in the crash of a B–29 airplane filed suit for damages under the Federal Tort Claims Act.   In the course of the litigation, the plaintiffs sought discovery of the plane's flight records.   The government objected, invoking the privilege on the ground that the plane was involved in a highly classified mission at the time of the accident. Although the lower courts rejected the claim of privilege and entered judgment against the government as a sanction for non-compliance with the discovery rules, the Supreme Court reversed.

Drawing on the common law origins of the privilege and concluding that it had not been vitiated by the adoption of the FTCA, the Court set out the framework for evaluating the privilege.   As the Court explained:

> The privilege belongs to the Government and must be asserted by it. . . . It is not to be lightly invoked.   There must be a formal claim of privilege, lodged by the head of the department which has control over the matter, after actual personal consideration by that officer.   The court itself must determine whether the circumstances are appropriate for the claim of privilege, and yet do so without forcing a disclosure of the very thing the privilege is designed to protect.

In conducting this analysis, the federal courts were to give effect to the privilege when the government shows that "compulsion of the evidence will expose military matters which, in the interest of national security, should not be divulged."   The Court admonished that, when the plaintiffs make a strong showing of necessity, the claim of privilege should not be "lightly accepted."   But if military secrets are really at stake, "even the most compelling necessity cannot overcome the claim of privilege."   In the end, the courts were to recognize the privilege if there was a reasonable likelihood of serious injury to the interests of the United States.

A variety of state secret privilege issues have arisen in connection with national security litigation since 2001.   For example, the federal courts have considered state secret privilege defenses in connection with the extraordinary rendition program.   Under that program, as reported in the *New Yorker* and elsewhere, suspected members of Al–Qaeda have been flown to remote locations in other countries for interrogation, reportedly under harsh conditions.   See Jane Mayer, The Dark Side (2008).   In one well-known case, the CIA was said to have mistakenly subjected an innocent Canadian national to extraordinary rendition.   Although the Canadian government apologized for the incident and paid significant reparations, the government of the United States invoked the state secrets privilege.   The district court dismissed the action, citing the state secrets privilege and the absence of a remedy under *Bivens*.

A divided Second Circuit, sitting en banc, affirmed. See *Arar v. Ashcroft* (2d Cir. 2009). *See also El–Masri v. Tenet* (4th Cir. 2007) (state secrets privilege effectively bars suit to challenge extraordinary rendition).

In December 2005, the *New York Times* disclosed that the Bush administration and the NSA had expanded its foreign surveillance eavesdropping program to include conversations involving American citizens. President Bush acknowledged the program and defended the need for the information, some of which was obtained through the cooperation of the tele-communications industry without first obtaining warrants under the Foreign Intelligence Surveillance Act (FISA). Of the resulting litigation, two cases were dismissed on the basis that the plaintiffs could not establish standing without access to government information that was shielded by the privilege. As this edition went to press, the Supreme Court was poised to address the scope of the privilege in two cases where it was invoked to defeat a military contractor's claim against the government before the US Court of Claims.

In its focus on the disclosure of privileged information, the state secrets privilege obviously differs from the political question doctrine. Deciding on the scope of the privilege represents less an interpretation of the Constitution than an application of the common law. Yet the willingness of the federal courts to extend the privilege reflects the perception that federal judges lack judicially manageable standards with which to assess the government's interest in protecting classified information.

2.10 Justiciability Doctrines, the Merits, and Constitutional Avoidance

As with the political question doctrine, the Court's handling of standing, ripeness, and mootness often appears entangled with the Justices' own view of the merits of the dispute. The Court's disposition in *Allen v. Wright* (1984) effectively blocked a category of litigation against the IRS, just as the decision in *O'Shea v. Littleton* barred institutional reform litigation directed at state justice systems. While the doctrines of standing and ripeness that the Court deployed in those cases purport to embody a set of principles that exist independently of the merits of any particular dispute, many observers see the decisions as largely influenced by the Court's view of the merits. Thus, one scholar has argued that the Justices' views of the merits provide a better guide to the Court's standing decisions than doctrine. See Pierce (1999). Another scholar has argued that the Court should abandon standing as a threshold test, and make it part of a more avowedly merits-based inquiry into whether the plaintiff can state a claim for relief. See Fletcher (1988). Even the Court has acknowledged that the considerations that inform its justiciability decisions may "shade into" those that also determine the availability of equitable relief on the merits.

The influence of the merits on justiciability determinations poses a problem for the development of a consistent and neutral body of law. Doubts about consistency and neutrality also arise from evidence that the Court sometimes uses the justiciability doctrines to avoid the merits of a particular dispute. The decision of *DeFunis v. Odegaard* (1974), dismissing the claim of a third year law student on mootness grounds, provides a serviceable example. Many see the *DeFunis* decision as driven less by the Court's neutral application of mootness doctrine than by the Court's desire to avoid decision of the affirmative action controversy. The subsequent decision in *Regents of the University of California v. Bakke* (1978) revealed sharp divisions over the constitutionality of affirmative action, with four Justices voting to uphold such programs, four voting to strike them down, and one Justice adopting a middle position. Some scholars have speculated that these divisions emerged in *DeFunis*, and ultimately led to a mootness disposition that permitted the Court to dismiss without reaching the merits. Perhaps the same sort of merits-avoidance was reflected in the Court's decision to dismiss on prudential standing grounds a challenge to the Pledge of Allegiance. See *Elk Grove Unified School Dist. v. Newdow* (2004).

Use of justiciability doctrines as a tool of avoidance has occasioned a good deal of debate in scholarly circles. On one side of the debate, scholars have argued that the Court might properly exercise prudential and somewhat unprincipled discretion in deciding whether to reach the merits of particularly sensitive and divisive cases. See Bickel, (1962). By dismissing on some pretext, the Court might buy time for further deliberation in an effort to deliver a more principled and defensible resolution of the controversy. Others have been quite critical of Bickel's argument for unprincipled justiciability decisions. (Poking fun, one scholar described Bickel as advocating 100% principle 20% of the time. See Gunther (1964).) For these scholars, the Court should confine itself to developing a coherent body of justiciability law and should not use the doctrine to issue prudential avoidance decisions.

Attitudes toward Bickel's proposal for ad hoc avoidance may depend to some extent on the existence of other tools with which the Court can control its docket. At the time Bickel wrote, the Court enjoyed substantial but not complete discretion over its docket; in some matters, the parties could appeal to the Court as a matter of right (although the Court might limit access to full briefing and argument or dismiss for want of a substantial federal question). Today, the Court can almost always choose the cases it wishes to hear. It takes four votes to grant review by writ of certiorari and five votes to dismiss a case as one in which certiorari was improvidently granted. The Court does not justify its decisions to grant or deny review and does not treat such decisions as a disposition on the merits. With such tools of discretionary docket control readily available, one might ask why the Court needs additional powers of avoidance.

Attitudes toward avoidance may also depend on the degree to which the Court has succeeded in improving the quality, clarity, and persuasiveness of its constitutional decisions. If *DeFunis* represents an example of avoidance, it does not appear to have paid great dividends. While it did put off the decision for four years, during which time Justice Douglas retired and Justice Stevens was appointed to fill his seat, the Court's *Bakke* decision revealed a Court still deeply divided. On the other hand, the Court worked in the early 1950s to avoid any direct resolution of the continuing constitutionality of segregation under the separate-but-equal rule of *Plessy v. Ferguson* (1896). Historical accounts reveal a Court whose members were divided on the question whether to reaffirm *Plessy*. After a period of temporizing, the sudden death of Chief Justice Vinson brought Earl Warren to the Court. When the Court finally spoke, in *Brown v. Board of Education* (1954), it did so in a unanimous decision. Justice Frankfurter privately described the outcome as the only solid evidence he had ever seen of the existence of God.

But while Justice Frankfurter and others celebrated the unanimity that it eventually produced, the Court's *Brown* era avoidance strategy had its own unfortunate consequences. *Brown I* and *Brown II* declined to award any concrete relief; instead, the Court essentially acquiesced in a period of Southern resistance with its "all deliberate speed" formula for desegregation. Shortly after *Brown*, moreover, the Court struggled mightily to avoid any decision in a case challenging Virginia's law banning interracial marriage. Several years later in *Loving v. Virginia* (1967), the Court struck down Virginia's law as inconsistent with *Brown*'s principle. Avoidance may have helped to secure another unanimous decision, or it may have simply delayed the equal protection of the laws for another decade. See Pfander (2006).

Chapter Three

THE SUPREME COURT'S ORIGINAL JURISDICTION

3.1 Introduction

The deceptively straightforward words of Article III, section 2 provide that the Supreme Court shall have original jurisdiction in "all cases affecting Ambassadors, other public Ministers and Consuls, and those in which a State shall be Party." Despite its considerable historical importance, the jurisdiction does not account for a very significant share of the Court's modern docket. The Court issues some 80 full opinions each year in appellate cases, but may issue no more than one or two opinions in original cases. The tilt in favor of the appellate docket reflects the Court's own conception of how best to deploy its decisional resources. For much of past century, the Court has exercised a degree of discretion over the decision to hear a case originally or on appeal. Plainly, the Court regards its time as better spent on appellate matters.

At least two considerations help to explain the Court's preference for its appellate docket. Original cases can present complex factual disputes that require the appointment of a special master and some degree of judicial oversight. The fact-bound nature of the disputes makes them relatively time consuming and less effective as vehicles for the articulation of legal rules of national significance. Appellate cases, by contrast, do not require any further factual development; the Court chooses them on the basis of the legal issues they present and calls for briefs and oral argument. A second reason may inform the Court's appellate preference: with appellate cases, the Court can await the development of the legal issues in lower court litigation. In original matters, the Court provides both the initial and final resolution of the matter. What it gains in speed of decision, as when it heard original state challenges to voting rights legislation in the 1960s, *South Carolina v. Katzenbach* (1966), the Court may lose in terms of perspective.

This chapter provides a brief introduction to the Court's original jurisdiction. It first describes the modern function of the Court's original jurisdiction in state-party cases and then examines the jurisdiction's scope, historical origins, and implications. Questions relating to the Court's supervisory powers, exercised through petitions for habeas corpus and mandamus, are deferred to the chapter on the Court's appellate jurisdiction.

3.2   State–Party Disputes

Of the two categories of original jurisdiction, the number of state-party cases vastly exceeds that of foreign envoy cases on the Court's docket, and the total number of cases of both kinds remains remarkably modest.   One survey of the Court's original docket revealed that in its first two hundred years the Court had decided some 190 original cases through the issuance of a full opinion on the merits.   See McKusick (1993).   Of these, virtually all involved state parties.   Indeed, the Court has issued only two opinions on the merits in cases involving foreign envoys.   As a practical matter, then, the original docket has been dominated by cases involving state parties.

State-party litigation often involves a dispute between two or more states and can present a range of questions.   Most commonly, the cases seek to resolve a dispute over the precise location of an inter-state boundary.   One might suppose that the states would have resolved their boundary disputes by now, but the shifting course of inter-state rivers creates fertile ground for litigation. Early on, the Court decided that the inter-state border between states would lie directly above the deepest part of the river bed; changes in the river's flow invite litigation over boundary matters. Similarly, when a river jumps its old banks and flows along a new course, the Court must decide if the state borders change as well. Jurisdiction over an island, left high and dry by a shifting river, has occasioned litigation as have more prosaic changes.   During the 1990s, the Court heard a dispute between New York and New Jersey over Ellis Island, the historic site of the US immigration service in New York harbor.   In a poetic resolution, the Court found that New York would retain the original land mass and New Jersey would gain control over land that had been added to the Island over the years as landfill.   See *New Jersey v. New York* (1998).

Other forms of inter-state litigation have appeared on the Court's docket with some frequency.   Particularly in the West, the states often litigate their respective right to the waters flowing in inter-state rivers and streams.   One important decision allocates the flow of the Colorado River as between California and Arizona. In addition, the states have frequently invoked the Court's original jurisdiction to restrain other states from polluting the waters of an inter-state river.   Finally, in a relatively recent addition to the original docket, the Court has agreed to hear actions in the nature of interpleader to determine which of two or more states may impose taxes on the estate of wealthy decedents. (Although Howard Hughes in theory had but a single tax home, three different states sought to collect taxes on his estate.)

The next most important source of state-party litigation involves disputes between the United States and one or more of the states. Often these disputes involve border issues and thus resemble inter-state contests. For example, in a series of cases, the US successfully brought original actions against California, Texas, and other states to establish federal title to submerged lands beneath coastal waters. Suits involving the states and private individuals, though not unheard of, have been quite rare in recent years. The comparative rareness of such matters owes much to the exercise of the Court's discretion in choosing which cases to hear.

3.3   Discretionary Control of the Original Docket

Unlike other federal courts with original jurisdiction, the Supreme Court does not permit the parties to invoke its original jurisdiction as a matter of right. Rather, the plaintiff must petition for leave to file and can docket an original complaint only with the Court's permission. In a leading case, *Ohio v. Wyandotte Chemicals* (1971), the Court acknowledged the traditional understanding of original jurisdiction as available to the parties as a matter of right; it nonetheless found that changes over time made discretion essential. The Court pointed out that as-of-right access might interfere with its role as the final federal appellate court. Additionally, it noted that many of the cases that qualify for original jurisdiction do so on the basis of the alignment of the parties and might turn on questions of state common law. (Chapter 6 explores the *Erie* doctrine and its requirement that district courts, hearing cases on the basis of diversity jurisdiction, apply the law of the states in which they sit.) The Court explained that it had no particular expertise with such questions and would better devote its time to the exposition of federal law.

A variety of factors appear to shape the Court's selection of cases for original determination. One important factor has been the availability of an alternative forum. In 28 U.S.C. § 1251, Congress declared the Court's jurisdiction in controversies between two or more states to be both "original and exclusive." Exclusivity forecloses other courts from entertaining the claims and puts some pressure on the Court to grant leave to file. (Indeed, one might regard the predominance of state-state litigation on the Court's docket as an outgrowth of statutory exclusivity, rather than as a reflection of the Court's perception of the relative importance of such matters.) Congress has defined the remainder of the Court's original jurisdiction as non-exclusive, which permits lower federal (and state) courts to hear the claims concurrently (assuming they have jurisdiction). In such cases of non-exclusivity, the Court may refuse leave to file after assuring itself that another forum would be available. See *Ohio v. Wyandotte* (1971).

Apart from the presence of an alternative forum, the Court may consider the nature and significance of the claims and the need for prompt settlement of issues of national importance. In *South Carolina v. Katzenbach* (1966), for example, the Court granted the state leave to file a suit to enjoin the Attorney General from enforcing newly adopted voting rights legislation. Although the Court's jurisdiction rested (as in *Wyandotte*) upon the fact that the state had sued a nonresident, the Court's decision to grant leave reflected its perception of the national interest in an expeditious resolution of challenges to the law. Notably, the United States filed briefs in support of the state's assertion of original jurisdiction, emphasizing the need for a quick answer.

3.4 Special Masters and Jury Trials

In many cases within its original jurisdiction, the Court appoints a special master to assist with the preparation of the record. In a typical case, the master conducts a trial-like proceeding with testimony and evidentiary submissions from the parties; the master's report proposes findings of fact and conclusions of law. The parties file exceptions to the special master's report, inviting the Court's attention to legal or factual problems. The Court may set the matter for argument and will ultimately issue an order accepting or rejecting the master's recommended disposition. Reliance on masters enables the Court to avoid time-consuming hearings in original matters and to maintain its status as a court of review. (Of course, a special master may not be necessary in cases that involve no disputed issues of fact; the Court's rules permit the parties to seek summary judgment in such cases.)

Although much of the Court's original docket involves claims for equitable relief, such as a suit between states to determine sovereignty over disputed land or to determine rights to the flow of a river, disputes at law may occur. Both Congress and the Court have assumed that the right to trial by jury would attach to at least some legal proceedings. (For example, in the 1790s, the Court empanelled a jury to hear an individual's suit for damages against the state of New York. See *Oswald v. New York* (1795). The jury returned a verdict in favor of the individual and the New York legislature paid the judgment, before the ratification of the Eleventh Amendment swept such cases permanently from the Court's docket.) But the precise scope of the jury trial rights of litigants on the Court's original docket remains largely unsettled. One can debate from where the Court should draw its jurors, how it should instruct them, and whether the Seventh Amendment right to a jury trial attaches at all in suits brought against the states. (Interestingly, the Judiciary Act of 1789 provided for trial by jury in all actions against citizens of the US but not in actions against the states.)

3.5   Scope of the Original Jurisdiction

Defining the scope of the Court's original jurisdiction presents something of a challenge. On the one hand, the relevant statute grants original jurisdiction in a series of controversies defined by the alignment of the parties. Thus, 28 U.S.C. § 1251 provides for jurisdiction over disputes (a) between two or more states; (b) between the United States and a state; and (c) actions brought by a state against citizens of another state or aliens. (Jurisdiction also extends to cases involving foreign envoys. But this statutory grant of jurisdiction does not track the grant of original jurisdiction that appears in Article III of the Constitution). As noted above, the constitutional grant applies to cases affecting foreign envoys "and those in which a State shall be party." The potential universe of state-party litigation under Article III extends beyond the disputes specified in the statute, and the Court has often described the constitutional grant as mandatory and self-executing. Such statements suggest that the Court derives its jurisdiction directly from Article III and need not obey statutory provisions that expand or cut back on the scope of the jurisdiction. See *Marbury*.

To understand the uncertainty about what sorts of state-party "cases" qualify for original jurisdiction requires a brief tutorial about the difference for Article III purposes between cases and controversies. (Article III, section 2 describes the cases and controversies to which the judicial power shall extend. Most everyone agrees that this jurisdictional list or menu defines the outer bounds of federal jurisdiction.) In particular, Article III defines "cases" by reference to the subject matter of the dispute (e.g., "cases arising under this Constitution") and "controversies" by reference to the alignment of the parties (e.g., "controversies between two or more states"). State-party "cases" might include any case involving a state party that happened to present a claim under federal law; state-party controversies, by contrast, would include any dispute that happened to involve a state and one of the parties specified in Article III. Like diversity proceedings, such controversies appear on the jurisdictional menu not because they present questions of federal law (although they might) but because the framers distrusted the state courts in matters involving the United States, aliens, and nonresidents.

For the most part, the Supreme Court has construed the grant of original jurisdiction as if its reference to "those [cases] in which a State shall be party" confers jurisdiction over state-party controversies alone. See *California v. Southern Pacific* (1895); *Texas v. ICC* (1922). As the Court explained, the original jurisdiction "depends solely on the character of the parties, and is confined to the cases in which are those enumerated parties and those only." But the Court has not always adhered to this party-based interpretation. In *United States v. Texas* (1892), the Court agreed to hear a dispute over the location of the border between Texas and the federal territory that later became Oklahoma. Article III, section 2, however, does not specifically confer jurisdiction over controversies between the United States and a state. In defending its assertion of original jurisdiction, the Court noted that the case both presented a federal question and involved the United States as a party and was a proper subject for federal jurisdiction. The additional presence of the state as a defendant was seen as sufficient to ground the Court's original jurisdiction.

Perhaps because its rationale might considerably expand the Court's original jurisdiction to embrace any state-party dispute that presents a federal question, the federal question interpretation of *US v. Texas* has not taken hold. Both Congress and the Court have continued to treat the jurisdiction as party-based, and the Court has disavowed the broader implications of a federal question approach. One can understand this narrowing of the Court's original jurisdiction as reflecting the same docket worries that later drove the Court to claim a discretionary power to deny parties leave to file original suits. (Consider *Massachusetts v. EPA* (2007), a state-party case challenging the EPA's refusal to regulate greenhouse gases, as one example of the myriad federal question cases that might qualify for original jurisdiction.) But with such discretionary control now firmly in place, one can fairly question whether the Court should continue to adhere to an interpretation of its original jurisdiction that seems at odds with its plain meaning and that brings a mostly party-based diet of disputes to its original docket. See Pfander (1994).

Chapter Four

THE SUPREME COURT'S
APPELLATE JURISDICTION

4.1 Introduction

The Constitution provides for "one supreme Court" to hear a
largely appellate docket. While there was a good deal of debate at
the constitutional convention about the need for lower federal
courts and about the possibility that state courts might hear federal
matters in the first instance, few doubted the need for a single
federal appellate court. Two considerations shaped this consensus.
First, although the state courts were competent to hear some
federal matters, the various state courts might disagree as to the
meaning of federal law. A single federal court of appellate jurisdiction would unify these conflicting interpretations. Second, any
particular state court might favor state interests and fail to give
proper weight to federal law. Appellate review would prevent state
court hostility from undermining the enforcement of federal law.
Like the federal judicial department generally, then, the Court's
appellate jurisdiction was designed to address state court partiality
and to secure the uniform and effective enforcement of federal law.
This chapter describes the history and current operation of the
Court's appellate docket, as well as the complex collection of
doctrines that govern the Court's role.

4.2 Appellate Jurisdiction: An Overview

Today, the Court manages its appellate docket to emphasize its
role in unifying federal law. Since the nineteenth century, the
Court's docket has changed (with congressional acquiescence) from
one that the parties could claim as a matter of right, to one the
Court controls in its discretion. The Court receives some 8,000
petitions for appellate review each year and grants full review in
approximately one percent of the cases, or about 80 cases per year.
The Court chooses these cases on the basis of the significance of the
federal questions they present. Thus, when a question of federal
law has led to a division in lower court opinion, the Court may
grant review to resolve the conflict. Even absent a division of
authority, the Court may hear cases that it views as significant.
See *Bush v. Gore* (2000). But a simple claim that the lower court
erred on a question of federal law will rarely persuade the Court to

grant review. The Justices (and the law clerks who review petitions and draft memoranda to the Court's certiorari pool) often view such cases as fact bound or as presenting issues that do not warrant a full hearing.

Although the Court can review decisions from both systems, the Court has agreed to review many more federal court than state court cases in recent years. During a recent five-year period ending in 2002, the Court issued an average of 80 full opinions (decisions reached after briefing and oral argument). The Court also disposed of some 70 cases per year by memorandum order; such summary dispositions may occur without full briefing and argument. These cases include "GVRs," cases in which the Court will grant review, vacate a lower court opinion, and remand for further consideration, perhaps in light of its decision in a related case. Of the Court's full opinions, roughly 83% involved review of the decisions of the federal courts, and only 17% came from the state courts. This tilt in the Court's appellate docket cannot be explained by the distribution of state and federal petitions. During the same period, petitions for review of state court decisions accounted for nearly half (45%) of the Court's total petitions. The statistics suggest that the Court prefers to hear appeals from the federal courts.

Beneath the statistics, a variety of factors may help to explain the makeup of the Court's appellate docket. Many of the state court petitions seek review of state criminal convictions on behalf of petitioners too poor to afford counsel or to pay filing fees. These "in forma pauperis" or IFP petitions are often drafted by the litigants themselves or by jailhouse lawyers. The Court will occasionally take an IFP case—in *Gideon v. Wainwright* (1963), the Court granted review on the basis of the petitioner's handwritten letter. But in the vast majority of such cases, the Court denies review: IFP cases account for fewer than one percent of the cases in which the Court grants review. If one eliminates IFP petitions from consideration, then the makeup of the Court's docket looks somewhat different: relatively fewer petitions in "paid" as opposed to IFP cases come from the state courts. Still, the IFP factor does not explain the Court's preference for cases from the federal courts; the Court accepts review in a smaller proportion of paid state cases than of paid federal cases.

The Court's preference for cases that originate in federal court might appear to reflect its practice of reviewing only federal questions—questions of law that turn on the interpretation of the Constitution, laws, and treaties of the United States. But the practical importance of federal question cases does not explain the Court's selection of cases for review. The Court has always refused to exercise appellate jurisdiction in state court cases except where the decision of a question of federal law will decisively influence the outcome. See *Murdock v. Memphis* (1874) (continuing past practice). Today, litigants understand that the Court's jurisdiction turns on the existence of a decisive federal question. As a result, virtually all of the petitions—whether they seek review of state or federal court judgments—will attempt to identify a question of federal law in order to justify review. Thus, one cannot explain the Court's preference for review of federal court cases by assuming that the state court petitions present primarily issues of state law.

Perhaps the best way to explain the Court's appellate docket is to recognize that the Court bears ultimate responsibility for the entire corpus of federal law. While that body of law includes many constitutional issues (such as the criminal procedure protections of the Fourth, Fifth, and Sixth Amendments) that arise with equal frequency in state and federal court, it also includes a wide (and growing) range of federal statutory issues that arise in settings that virtually assure federal judicial review. Many federal statutes (such as those in the intellectual property arena) provide for exclusive federal court jurisdiction. Moreover, issues of federal administrative law and federal admiralty law almost invariably arise in the federal courts. When one recognizes that nearly half the Court's docket in any particular year will consist of questions of federal statutory law, one can better understand the predominance of federal court cases on its docket.

Apart from the Court's workload, the predominance of cases from the federal courts exerts a more subtle influence on the federal judiciary's role. The limited appellate capacity of the Court to correct errors in state court proceedings or to monitor such decisions closely may influence the distribution of federal jurisdiction among lower courts. Both the Court and litigants understand the lack of appellate capacity. For the Court, this often means that the issues about which it cares deeply must be assigned to the lower federal courts for determination. During the 1950s, for example, the Court grew concerned with the quality of Southern justice, particularly in criminal cases involving African–American defendants. In addition to expanding the rights of the accused throughout the 1960s (through interpretations of the Bill of Rights that applied to the states), the Court expanded access to the lower federal courts. It did so in *Brown v. Allen* (1953) by enabling those convicted of crimes in state court to file petitions for habeas corpus in federal court, challenging the constitutionality of state judicial proceedings. This expanded federal district court authority by way of habeas (or "collateral") review has been seen by many as a substitute for the Court's direct review of constitutional claims through its appellate jurisdiction.

If lack of appellate capacity shapes the Court's management of the jurisdiction of federal district courts, the same lack of capacity may influence the litigation choices of the parties. Parties may prefer a federal forum for any number of reasons. They may view federal judges as more independent than their state counterparts, or they may view federal courts as more willing to set aside state law to effectuate an unpopular or controversial federal right. (Debates over the relative competence and effectiveness of state and federal courts in effectuating federal rights have produced what scholars refer to the "parity" debate; section 9.5 discusses the debate.) Whatever the reason for preferring a federal court, litigants know that they cannot rely on the Court to review final state court decisions; if the case begins in state court, it will likely end there. Litigants who want a federal judicial determination must bring their claims into federal court at the outset, either by filing suit there or by removing the case from state to federal court. (Chapter 5 explores the rules that govern the jurisdiction of the federal district courts.)

4.3 Constitutional Roots

As with its original jurisdiction, the Supreme Court derives its appellate jurisdiction directly from Article III of the Constitution. After conferring original jurisdiction in foreign envoy and state-party cases, the relevant provision declares that the Court shall have appellate jurisdiction "in all the other cases before mentioned." By referring to the cases "before mentioned," the Appellate Jurisdiction Clause sweeps in all of the matters that appear earlier in the jurisdictional menu, including cases "arising under the Constitution, laws, and treaties of the United States." In addition to the constitutional grant, the Court also enjoys a statutory grant of appellate jurisdiction, and has since the adoption of section 25 of the Judiciary Act of 1789. The current statute, 28 U.S.C. § 1257, authorizes the Court to review final state court decisions that present federal questions, as well as all cases that originate within the lower federal courts.

The presence of a statute conferring appellate jurisdiction presents a jurisdictional puzzle. A statute that regulates and perhaps restricts the Court's docket may appear somewhat at odds with the accepted idea that the Court derives its appellate jurisdiction directly from the Constitution. But unlike its unadorned grant of original jurisdiction, Article III confers appellate jurisdiction "with such Exceptions, and under such Regulations, as the Congress shall make." This Exceptions and Regulations Clause contemplates a congressional role in organizing the Court's appellate docket, and may confer authority of uncertain scope on Congress to strip the Court of its appellate jurisdiction over specified issues of federal law. (Chapter 10 discusses the jurisdiction-stripping debate.) In most instances, the Court will simply exercise the affirmative grants of statutory jurisdiction and treat any gaps or omissions as implied exceptions. A wide range of exceptions has appeared over the years. For example, the Court's appellate jurisdiction over some civil cases that originated in the lower federal courts was subject to a substantial amount-in-controversy requirement. Moreover, early statutes made no provision for appellate review of final decisions in federal criminal cases.

Article III's grant of appellate jurisdiction in federal question cases has given rise to an important limit on the Court's appellate role. In general, the Court has refused to assert appellate jurisdiction over state law claims, and Congress has refused to make such jurisdiction available. (In both Canada and Australia, two nations with federal judicial systems that bear some resemblance to that of the United States, the high court enjoys appellate jurisdiction over provincial court dispositions of common law.) Even where the alignment of the parties in the state court would make the case a "controversy" within Article III (as in a dispute between citizens of different states), Congress has declined to authorize review in the Court. (The Court does have statutory power to review party-alignment or diversity matters that were first resolved by the lower federal courts, and it has occasionally exercised that authority. Since *Erie R.R. v. Tompkins* (1938) announced a regime of deference to state court formulations of the common law rules, the Court has seen little reason to grant review of a lower federal court decision on an issue of state common law.) This difference in treatment has made federal question cases the centerpiece of the Court's appellate docket, and has led to an important restriction on the scope of its jurisdiction to hear claims on appeal from the state courts.

4.4 Appellate Jurisdiction Over State Court Decisions

Two leading cases, *Martin v. Hunter's Lessee* (1816) and *Murdock v. Memphis* (1874), establish the doctrinal underpinnings and define the scope of the Court's appellate jurisdiction over state court decisions. In *Martin*, the Court upheld its own power to review decisions of the state courts. In *Murdock*, the Court narrowed the scope of its appellate jurisdiction. Additionally, the *Murdock* Court issued a considered dictum disclaiming jurisdiction even as to federal questions when state law furnished a sufficient basis on which to uphold the judgment below. *Murdock* gave rise to the adequate and independent state grounds doctrine, a doctrine that limits the Court's jurisdiction to review certain questions of federal law embedded in a state court judgment.

Martin v. Hunter's Lessee first arose as a test of the legality of legislation adopted by Virginia that proposed to take the lands of those who remained loyal to the British Crown during the War of Independence. Virginia adopted its forfeiture law in 1779, divesting loyalists of their property effective upon the completion of a proceeding known as an "inquest of office." Subsequent state legislation sought to confirm and perfect the transfer of the land into the hands of the Commonwealth, but much of it was enacted after the United States and Great Britain entered into the Treaty of Peace of 1783, ending the war and barring any further confiscations of loyalist property within the United States. (Jay's Treaty in 1794 confirmed the ban on forfeitures.) The *Martin* case centered on whether Virginia's confiscation of the property had been perfected as a matter of state law before the federal treaties of 1783 and 1794 intervened, foreclosing further takings. If the forfeiture was good, Hunter would keep the property as the grantee of Virginia; if not, title would remain in Martin and those claiming under him (including John Marshall, whose interest in the property led to his recusal in the case). When the case first arrived there, the Court ruled in favor of Martin's group, concluding that no inquest of office had been performed to perfect the forfeiture before the federal treaty took effect and barred any further forfeitures.

The court of appeals in Virginia refused to give effect to the Court's decision. Most importantly, the Virginia court simply denied that the Constitution empowered the Supreme Court to exercise an appellate jurisdiction over the decisions of the state courts. The grant of appellate jurisdiction in Article III was said to refer to appeals taken from the lower federal courts to the Supreme Court. State and federal judicial systems were portrayed as the creatures of two different sovereigns and were said to lack power to review one another's decisions, just as the courts in France lack revisory power over those in England. The separate sovereigns rhetoric took root during the antebellum period and certainly differed from earlier versions of the states' rights position; the anti-Federalists in the 1780s had assumed that the Supreme Court would review state court decisions on issues of federal law and argued that the availability of such review lessened the need for the establishment of lower federal courts. Now Virginia was switching ground and arguing for a state immunity from federal judicial oversight. (The argument may have owed something to a report on the Judiciary Act of 1789 prepared by Edmund Randolph, the nation's first attorney general and a leading member of the Virginia delegation to the constitutional convention of 1787. Randolph urged as a matter of policy that Congress should fully vest federal jurisdiction in federal courts so as to avoid as much as possible the need for direct federal review of state court decisions.)

Justice Story responded to the Virginia court of appeals with a powerful restatement of the Court's constitutional role. In a wide-ranging opinion, Justice Story argued that the text, structure, and history of Article III all supported the conclusion that the Court's appellate jurisdiction extended to cases originating before the state courts. Justice Story bolstered this argument by emphasizing the need for uniformity of decision, a goal that could only be achieved through the exercise of appellate jurisdiction. Story also noted that the historical practice since the Judiciary Act of 1789 had been to allow such appeals and pointedly observed that all the states had acquiesced in the exercise of the jurisdiction up to that time. Finally, Story demonstrated that Virginia was wrong to claim that federal courts could hear all federal claims without exercising a power of appellate review over state tribunals. Actions must be subject to removal from state to federal court to perfect such a system and Story portrayed removal itself as a form of appellate jurisdiction, albeit one exercised by the lower federal courts. Story also explained that defendants sued in state court might raise federal defenses that would evade federal judicial review unless an appeal to a federal court was allowed.

Most observers today regard Story's defense of the Court's appellate jurisdiction as entirely persuasive. But nineteenth century observers were less impressed. Attacks on the Court's appellate jurisdiction continued throughout the antebellum period, as states followed Virginia's lead in rejecting the Court's authority. Moreover, a number of bills were introduced in Congress to repeal the Court's statutory grant of appellate jurisdiction. Although the Court's appellate role now seems fairly secure, one can hear echoes of antebellum hostility in the reaction of Southern states to the Court's decision in *Brown v. Board of Education* (1954) and in recurrent congressional efforts to restrict the Court's appellate jurisdiction over certain divisive issues of constitutional law.

4.5 Appellate Jurisdiction Over Questions of Federal and State Law

Story also addressed Virginia's claim that the Court had exceeded the proper bounds of its appellate jurisdiction by considering issues of state law. Virginia argued that the effective date of the forfeiture was entirely a matter of state law, and did not present any federal question. Virginia further argued that the Court's appellate jurisdiction, if any, was limited by section 25 of the Judiciary Act to federal questions and other errors that "immediately respect[]" the interpretation and enforcement of federal law. Virginia claimed that even assuming the Court could hear an appeal to clarify the meaning of the federal treaties, it had no power to pass on the issues of state law that were involved in determining the effective date of the forfeiture. Story rejected these claims on the ground that the effective enforcement of the federal right necessitated federal judicial consideration of the issues of state law. Otherwise, as Story noted, state courts could undermine the enforcement of a federal right or title by simply rejecting the state law foundation of a federal right.

Scholars now describe the authority exercised in *Martin* as one to hear questions of state law when they are "antecedent" to the consideration of a federal question. The idea of antecedence is nicely illustrated in *Martin*; as a logical matter, one must first determine whether the forfeiture has taken effect (circa 1782) before determining if the Martin group enjoyed any property rights that came within the protection of the federal treaty (circa 1783). The Martin group, moreover, must prevail both on the state law issue and on their federal treaty claim to succeed in the litigation.

Other examples of antecedence appear in cases in which the Constitution protects property and contract rights grounded in state law. Thus, the Fourteenth Amendment's Due Process Clause protects individuals from a taking of their property without due process of law; state law creates and defines many of the property interests protected by this provision. Suppose that a state court were to deny the existence of any property right as a matter of state law and were to reject a due process claim on that basis. On appeal, the Court would have the power to review both the state court's interpretation of the Constitution and the antecedent question whether a property right existed that came within the ambit of due process protection. See *Demorest v. City Bank Farmers Trust* (1944). The same analysis would apply to claims that the state had violated the constitutional prohibition against any impairment of the obligation of contract; the Court has treated the question of contract formation under state law as antecedent to the federal question of impairment. See *Indiana ex rel. Anderson v. Brand* (1938).

Understanding the scope of the Court's appellate jurisdiction requires some ability to distinguish the "antecedent" state law issues in *Martin* and in the due process and contract-impairment examples, from situations in which state law provides a "distinct" basis for recovery. The second leading case in this area, *Murdock v. Memphis* (1874), helps to clarify the difference between antecedent and distinct questions of state law. Murdock made essentially two claims against the city of Memphis, both of which sought to perfect his title to riverfront property that had been owned by his predecessors before it was transferred to the city and then to the federal government for use as a naval depot and later returned to the city by federal statute adopted in 1854. First, as a matter of state law, Murdock argued that the deed in which his predecessor conveyed the land to the city contemplated its use as a naval depot; when the land ceased to be used for that purpose, Murdock argued that ownership returned to him. Second, Murdock argued that the federal statute created a trust in his favor. Although the state and federal claims were clearly related, in the sense that they both grew out of the same dispute over title to the property, they represented "distinct" grounds for recovery. Murdock could win on either the state or the federal ground, and he would own the land.

Some have difficulty in seeing why the state law question is regarded as antecedent in *Martin* and distinct in *Murdock*. After all, in both cases, the dispute centers on property ownership issues in which state law plays an important role. The key lies in the relationship between the state and federal claims. In *Martin*, the federal treaty claim could succeed only if the plaintiff first established the antecedent point that he retained title to the land (due to the absence of an inquest of office). The state law issue did not provide an independent basis for recovery but served as a necessary predicate for the assertion of the federal treaty claim. In *Murdock*, by contrast, the plaintiff could win title on the state ground alone (assuming he could prove the elements of a trust or condition subsequent under state law). He could also win title on the federal ground, assuming he could prove a federal statutory trust. While the federal ground may have depended to some extent on the interpretation of deeds to property (matters typically governed by state law), the federal claim was not formally based upon an antecedent showing that the plaintiff was entitled to the property in trust as a matter of state law. It was the formal independence of the federal ground from the state ground that makes the state and federal claims "distinct" in *Murdock*, rather than "antecedent."

Murdock thus presented a question concerning the scope of the Court's appellate jurisdiction that differed from that in *Martin*. In *Murdock*, the Tennessee Supreme Court rejected Murdock's state and federal claims, ruling in favor of Memphis on both issues. Murdock appealed under section 25, and sought to persuade the Supreme Court to hear both the state and federal issues. He was aided in this endeavor by an amendment to section 25, adopted in 1867, in which the Reconstruction Congress deleted a provision that had limited the scope of appellate jurisdiction to errors that "immediately respect[]" claims of federal right. Justice Story had concluded that the antecedent state law question in *Martin* satisfied this test of immediacy. Murdock argued that, by eliminating the immediacy requirement, Congress had broadened the Court's jurisdiction to encompass less immediate matters, including perhaps the distinct state law ground on which Murdock relied. Murdock's appeal thus confronted the Court with questions concerning the meaning of the 1867 amendment and the constitutionally permissible scope of its appellate jurisdiction.

The Court took a narrow view of the scope of its authority over distinct issues of state law. Hinting that a power to review distinct state law claims would exceed constitutional limits, the Court refused to read the 1867 statute as expanding its appellate jurisdiction. It thus asserted jurisdiction over the federal claim (ruling on the merits that the federal statute failed to create a trust in favor of Murdock), but it refused to reach the state law ground. Today, the Court continues to follow this narrow conception of its appellate jurisdiction and will refuse to hear issues of state law other than those antecedent to, or bound up with, the enforcement of a federal right.

The Court's refusal to hear related but distinct issues of state law represents a sensible limit on its appellate role, particularly in our post-*Erie* world of state court primacy in the articulation of rules of state law. The decision in *Murdock*, however, anticipated *Erie* by some sixty years, during the regime of *Swift v. Tyson* (1842) when the Court regarded the federal courts, sitting in diversity, as free to ignore state court decisions on questions governed by the common law. (For a discussion of *Erie*, see chapter 6.) To be sure, *Murdock* differed from *Swift* in important respects: *Murdock* involved title to real property, a matter that would have been regarded as governed by local or state law even under the *Swift* regime, and *Murdock* arose as an appeal from state court in which a claim arising under federal law, rather than the alignment of the parties, provided the predicate for federal jurisdiction. Despite these differences, however, the *Murdock* Court may have found *Erie*-like concerns relevant in thinking through the propriety of the proposed expansion of its appellate jurisdiction. Although its decision on the state law issue would have necessarily controlled the disposition of the particular case, it would not necessarily have established a binding precedent for future state court litigation, and might have contributed to the creation of a "spurious" body of state law similar to that the *Erie* Court later condemned.

The analogy to supplemental jurisdiction at the trial court level furnishes the strongest argument against viewing the limited scope of appellate jurisdiction in *Murdock* as constitutionally compelled. Today, original jurisdiction would presumably extend to the federal statutory claim in *Murdock*. (In contrast to the situation at the time, the federal courts now enjoy jurisdiction over all claims arising under federal law.) If so, then supplemental jurisdiction would extend to a state law claim so related to the federal claim that the two claims together form a single constitutional case. See 28 U.S.C. § 1367(a). (The test for relatedness focuses on the nature of the claims and the underlying factual basis of the litigation, and differs conceptually from the analysis of whether state law claims should be regarded as "antecedent" or "distinct." As a practical matter, many supplemental claims today would be regarded as "distinct," but could still satisfy the test of relatedness for supplemental jurisdiction purposes. For a discussion of supplemental jurisdiction, see Chapter 5.) The *Murdock* dissenters argued that, just as Congress has freedom to confer supplemental jurisdiction on the federal trial courts over related state law claims, so too may Congress confer supplemental appellate jurisdiction over related state and federal claims, thereby enabling the Supreme Court on appeal to adjudicate the whole constitutional case.

Whatever the strength of this "whole case" argument at the time of the *Murdock* decision, it has a good deal less force today. In federal trial court, supplemental jurisdiction operates as a tool of efficiency that enables the parties to secure a single judicial determination of all the claims in dispute, including both federal anchor claims and related (but distinct) state law claims. When the federal courts pass on state law issues in this context, the *Erie* doctrine applies and the federal courts must give effect to state court interpretations of state law. The *Murdock* doctrine (barring a supreme judicial role as to matters of state law) does not apply to the Court's review of such federal court dispositions of state law issues in the supplemental jurisdiction context, however. As a consequence, the Court could review the entire case (and correct an erroneous lower federal court determination of state law). One might justify such intervention on the theory that the federal judiciary has an obligation, ultimately enforced at the highest level, to ensure that federal court dispositions pay appropriate respect to state court definitions of state law. But the argument for review to ensure respect for state law has a good deal less force in the *Murdock* context, which concerns the Court's power to review *state* court decisions. When the state courts speak on state law issues, they do so with finality under the *Erie* doctrine. The Court would have no occasion to correct a *state* court's resolution of a state law issue.

In any case, once a judgment has been entered at trial, the focus shifts on appeal to the determination of discrete claims of error. Arguments based on efficiency and on the need to resolve the entire dispute do not apply with the same force on appeal. The Court's refusal to consider issues of state law on appeal does not burden the enforcement of federal rights in quite the same way that a refusal to permit federal trial courts to hear related state law claims could burden the plaintiff's right to invoke original federal jurisdiction over federal question claims. For both reasons, one can question the dissenters' argument in *Murdock* that the analogy to supplemental jurisdiction at the federal trial level should inform the scope of appellate jurisdiction.

4.6   The Adequate and Independent State Grounds Doctrine

Once the *Murdock* Court concluded that it lacked power to hear distinct questions of state law, it next considered the possibility that the presence of state law grounds for the judgment might bar the exercise of appellate jurisdiction over the federal claim. The Court's discussion of the problem, though dicta, provides the foundation for the "adequate and independent state grounds" doctrine. Under the doctrine, the Supreme Court will not exercise appellate jurisdiction over a federal issue where the judgment below was supported by an adequate and independent state ground. In other words, if the Court concludes that its disposition of the federal claim cannot affect the ultimate resolution of the dispute, it will refuse to exercise appellate jurisdiction.

The doctrine did not apply in *Murdock*, so the Court proceeded to reach and resolve the federal question. But if we alter the posture of the *Murdock* case on appeal, we can see how such a bar to review might arise. Suppose that Murdock brought his case in state court today and that he won on both the state and federal grounds. If Memphis appealed to the Supreme Court, the Court would as an initial matter seem to have jurisdiction to consider the federal claim but would lack jurisdiction over the distinct issue of state law. But, on further reflection, the Court's inability to consider the state ground might deprive the Court of jurisdiction even as to the federal claim, so long as the Court viewed the state ground as an adequate and independent ground for upholding the judgment below. After all, the Court's decision of the federal issue would not affect the ultimate disposition of the case. Even if Memphis were to succeed in overturning the federal statutory trust, the property would still go to Murdock on the basis of a state law determination that the Supreme Court would lack power to review. Because our hypothetical plaintiff won on both state and federal grounds, disposition of the federal issue could not affect the outcome of the dispute, and the Court would accordingly decline to hear the issue.

The key to the application of the adequate and independent state grounds doctrine lies in considering the posture of the case on appeal, and in asking whether the Supreme Court's reversal on the federal ground could affect the judgment below. In *Murdock*, reversal on the federal ground would have changed the outcome, resulting in a ruling in favor of Murdock and a reversal of the disposition below. Even though the Court could not review the state ground, it had jurisdiction to consider the federal statutory trust claim that Murdock presented on appeal. (It did so, and rejected the federal claim.) By contrast, in a case like the one hypothesized above in which Murdock won on both state and federal grounds below, appellate review of the federal ground could not change the outcome.

Although the adequate and independent state grounds doctrine has become a well-established feature of the Court's appellate jurisdiction, the doctrine continues to pose important puzzles for litigants. For starters, the Court has displayed some uncertainty about whether to regard the doctrine as a prudential limit on its exercise of appellate jurisdiction or as a firm statutory or constitutional restriction on its jurisdiction. In the early years, the Court seemingly treated the doctrine as prudential. (Originating at a time when parties could invoke the Court's appellate jurisdiction over state court decisions as a matter of right, the doctrine enabled the Court to exercise some control over its docket.) But some later cases have apparently viewed the doctrine as constitutionally compelled by the Court's obligation under Article III to avoid the issuance of advisory opinions. See *Herb v. Pitcairn* (1945).

Apart from how to characterize the doctrine, questions persist as to what constitutes "adequacy" and "independence" for purposes of determining that a state ground bars appellate review. As for adequacy, the Court must consider whether the state ground will suffice as a basis for upholding the judgment. One can test adequacy by asking whether, in the posture of the case, a reversal of the federal ground would leave the judgment below adequately supported on non-federal grounds. If so, then the non-federal ground meets the test of adequacy. Yet there may be a variety of situations in which an apparently adequate state ground suffers from some infirmity that makes it inadequate to sustain the judgment and bar federal review.

Issues of the adequacy of state grounds frequently arise when the state court has found that the party asserting a federal claim has committed a procedural default that bars consideration of the merits. Procedural defaults occur in a variety of situations. Suppose the state offers a confession at the trial of a criminal charge and the lawyer representing the defendant fails to make a contemporaneous objection to its introduction into evidence; the state court may treat that failure as barring any challenge to the jury's consideration of the evidence at trial, including a challenge based on a claim that the confession was obtained in violation of the Constitution. Similarly, lawyers may fail to raise certain federal claims on appeal with the result that the state may treat the issues as procedurally defaulted and foreclosed from review. Questions concerning the adequacy of these procedural grounds arise when a state court relies upon them as a bar to its own review of the merits of a federal claim.

In general, the Court has held that procedural grounds can provide an adequate basis on which to uphold a state judgment, thus barring review of federal claims. (In the old days of as-of-right appellate review, such a finding would have required dismissal of the appeal for want of jurisdiction; today, the Court might simply refuse to grant review by certiorari.) But while procedural grounds may be adequate to foreclose review of federal questions, the Court has also expressed a willingness to scrutinize state procedural grounds in a range of cases to ensure their adequacy. Thus, if the state court's procedural rule itself violates due process by failing to give one of the parties an adequate opportunity to be heard, it will not bar review of a federal claim. See *Reece v. Georgia* (1955). Similarly, the state ground may prove inadequate if the state court applies an unduly burdensome procedural rule, see *Lee v. Kemna* (2002), or a novel procedural rule that a party could not have anticipated through a fair review of the statutory and judge-made rules. See *NAACP v. Patterson* (1958). Finally, if the state court applies its procedural rule inconsistently or exercises discretion in deciding whether to forgive a procedural default, the Court may find the ground inadequate to bar federal review. See *Sullivan v. Little Hunting Park* (1969). Cf. *Beard v. Kindler* (2009) (concluding that some procedural defaults imposed in the exercise of judicial discretion may be adequate to block post-conviction review).

Apart from questions of adequacy, the Court will consider whether the state ground rests on an independent basis such that a reversal of the federal ground will not influence the outcome of the case. Issues of independence arise in a variety of settings in which the state court's resolution of the state law question may appear to be interwoven with or dependent upon its interpretation of federal law. The facts underlying the Court's decision in *Michigan v. Long* (1983) provide a serviceable example. There, the defendant was convicted of possession of marijuana that the police had discovered in a search of his car. Long moved to suppress the evidence on the ground that the search violated both the Fourth Amendment and a similar provision of the Michigan state constitution. The Michigan supreme court agreed with Long and invalidated the conviction on both the state and federal grounds. In this posture, the state ground would appear to bar appellate review; even if the Supreme Court reversed on the Fourth Amendment issue, its decision would not affect the outcome so long as the state court adhered to its decision that the Michigan constitution also invalidated the search.

In assessing whether the state constitutional ground would survive a reversal of the Fourth Amendment issue, the question of *independence* arose. Many state courts have consciously based the interpretation of their state constitutions upon the decisional law the Supreme Court has developed in interpreting related provisions of the federal Constitution. In cases of conscious decisional dependence, the state court's view of state law may depend on its understanding of what federal law requires or permits. When the state law determination appears to rest on, or to be interwoven with, federal law, a reversal on the federal law ground may have a decisive impact on the outcome of the case. In *Michigan v. Long*, the Michigan supreme court had relied upon federal law in defining the scope of the state constitutional guarantee; its view of state law might change if the Supreme Court were to cut back on the scope of the Fourth Amendment. There was, as a consequence, some reason to doubt the state ground's independence of federal law and to doubt whether it would bar appellate review.

Michigan v. Long illustrates the importance of a state ground's independence and highlights the difficulty the Court faces in deciding whether to treat the state ground as truly independent. On the one hand, there was some reason to suspect that the state ground depended on federal law considerations. On the other hand, the Michigan supreme court had based its decision on both the state and federal constitutions. How should the Supreme Court determine in such a case whether the state ground enjoys the independence necessary to bar review of the federal ground? As the Court observed, it had developed at least three approaches to such problems in the past. In some cases, the Court had vacated the decision and remanded the case to state court for clarification of the nature of the state ground. In other cases, the Court itself had carefully parsed state law to determine whether the state ground rested upon an independent body of law or depended on federal law considerations. In still other cases, the Court had simply refused to exercise jurisdiction, taking the position that doubts about the independence of a state ground should be resolved against the exercise of appellate review.

After criticizing each of these options, the Court in *Michigan v. Long* adopted a new approach. In cases where the state court appears to have relied upon federal law, such that doubts arise about the state ground's independence, the Court adopted a presumption in favor of its own appellate jurisdiction. Such an approach was said to avoid the cumbersome alternatives of remanding to state court or of reviewing state law for signs of independence. It was, moreover, said to leave the state courts free to develop their own independent bodies of law. As the Court explained, the presumption in favor of appellate jurisdiction would apply only in cases of uncertainty, where the state ground fairly appeared to be dependent on, or interwoven with, federal law. The state court could overcome the presumption by clearly stating that it was basing its decision on an independent state ground; such a clear statement would bar appellate review.

One might criticize the Court's approach from three perspectives. First, one might argue that the approach will result in a series of unnecessary rulings on issues of federal law. In *Michigan v. Long*, the Court asserted jurisdiction and overturned the Michigan court's decision on the Fourth Amendment issue. On remand, the state court adhered to its view that the search violated the state constitution. Thus, Long's conviction was overturned, and the Court's decision of the Fourth Amendment issue did not actually influence the ultimate disposition of the case. Some might go so far as to argue that the Court's resolution of the Fourth Amendment issue was merely advisory in the sense that it failed to control the outcome of the case. But a ruling on a question of federal law that the Court has found to be fairly interwoven with state law and potentially dispositive should not necessarily be deemed advisory based upon what happens in subsequent litigation after remand.

A second criticism focuses on the Court's decision to expand its jurisdiction to reach cases involving what it perceives as state court overprotection of constitutional rights. After concluding that it had jurisdiction, the Court reached the merits in *Michigan v. Long* and cut back on the scope of Fourth Amendment protections, part of a consistent pattern of restrictive decisions in the area of criminal procedure by the Burger and Rehnquist Courts. Justice Stevens argued in dissent that the federal system had no substantial interest in correcting errors in cases like Long; overprotection of an individual's rights in the state of Michigan does not freeze the law or establish a precedent applicable throughout the nation. Rather, it simply imposes certain restrictions on police behavior in one state and does so in the interest of individual liberty.

But one can question Justice Stevens's view of overprotection as constitutionally benign. Expansion of individual liberties may impede society's ability to pursue law enforcement goals that many would support. More subtly, state courts may have incentives to issue fuzzy constitutional decisions that rely upon federal law in the protection of individual rights; by resting in part on federal grounds, such decisions may shift political responsibility to the federal government for unpopular decisions to expand the rights of accused criminals. (State judges remain more accountable politically than their federal counterparts; they may be subject to recall or removal from office, and state constitutions are typically much easier to amend.) One can imagine the state judge saying, in effect, that federal law compelled the result and left the state court with no choice in the matter. *Michigan v. Long* may counter this tendency toward fuzziness and buck-passing. It enables the state courts to fashion an independent state ground, but requires them to do so openly. It thus requires state judges to take responsibility for the individual protections they discern in state law, and subjects resulting state law decisions to the state political process for possible correction. See Althouse (1987).

Finally, some critics have argued that the Court's approach was result oriented, defining jurisdiction expansively in a case in which it clearly wanted to reach the merits. These critics have expressed doubt that the Court would remain true to its stated goal of developing a consistently applicable body of law in dealing with state grounds of doubtful independence. Subsequent decisions tend to support the critics' view. The Court not only has occasionally reverted to its past practice of vacating and remanding for clarification, but also has sometimes declined to apply the *Michigan v. Long* presumption in favor of federal jurisdiction, despite the appearance of a state ground that arguably lacked independence from a federal constitutional claim.

4.7 Some Procedural Aspects of Appellate Review

Just as the Court reviews only dispositive issues of federal law, it limits review to such issues that have been fairly presented to the state courts for decision and have been finally decided in a judgment of the highest state court in which review could be had. This section explores these requirements of fair presentation, finality, and exhaustion of available high state court remedies.

The requirement of fair presentation operates to foreclose Supreme Court review of federal questions that were not fairly presented to the state courts for decision. As a consequence, the Court will decline to review federal questions that have been raised for the first time in a petition to the Court for appellate review. The requirement of fair presentation may derive from the language of the relevant statute, 28 U.S.C. § 1257, which now provides for review of state court decisions involving federal questions that have been "drawn in question" or "specially set up and claimed." (Similar language in section 25 of the Judiciary Act of 1789 provided for review of federal questions that had been raised and decided adversely by the state court.) The requirement also draws support from policy considerations. According to the Court, the fair presentation requirement facilitates the development of a proper record below and provides the state courts with an opportunity to pass on the issue in the first instance. See *Cardinale v. Louisiana* (1969).

The Court has not specified either the precise basis for the fair presentation requirement or the degree to which policy considerations influence the requirement's application. The result has been some inconsistency in application. On the one hand, the Court has required the party seeking review of a federal question to present a claim that identifies federal law; a general invocation of notions of due process or fundamental fairness may be regarded as referring to the state constitution and may not fairly present claims based upon the federal Constitution. See *New York v. Zimmerman* (1928). On the other hand, in cases where the party does identify a federal law claim, such as the Due Process Clause of the Fourteenth Amendment, the Court has permitted the party to make new arguments in support of the claim that had not been presented to the state court. See *Yee v. City of Escondido* (1992). The state court may have developed an adequate factual record for assessing such a new argument, but it will not have had an opportunity to pass upon the argument in the first instance.

Although both doctrines govern the Court's appellate jurisdiction, issues of fair presentation should be distinguished from those involving the adequate and independent state procedural ground. Federal law requires a fair presentation of issues to the state courts as a condition of federal appellate review; in cases such as *Cardinale*, the petitioner has failed to present any federal claim to the state court. State procedural rules, in contrast, govern the manner in which the petitioner presents a federal law claim to the state court for resolution; a failure to comply with state procedural rules may bar review under the adequate state grounds doctrine even though the claim was fairly presented within the meaning of federal law. One might regard fair presentation as necessary, but not sufficient, to ground appellate jurisdiction; presentation of the federal claim must also comply with state procedural rules (unless some exception casts doubt on the state procedure's adequacy to bar review).

Federal law provides for review of "final" decisions of the state courts, 28 U.S.C. § 1257, and has been construed to bar review of most cases that remain pending in the state system. During the nineteenth century, the Court rigidly applied the finality requirement; only where the state court had entered a final judgment was the proceeding ripe for appellate review in the Supreme Court. In the last century, however, the Court recognized a number of exceptions in which the state court decision might be regarded as practically final for purposes of appellate review. The key to analysis of these cases lies first in identifying them as non-final within the traditional rule, and then in considering whether the Supreme Court might nonetheless resolve the federal issue in a way that could be considered to have a dispositive effect on the remainder of the state court litigation.

The Court's decision in *Cox Broadcasting v. Cohn* (1975) illustrates both aspects of the problem of finality. There, the plaintiff brought a civil action against a media firm, seeking damages for the publication of the name of a rape/murder victim in apparent violation of state law. Among other defenses, the media firm invoked the First Amendment, arguing that it enjoyed a constitutional right to publish the information (which was available to the public in the police report). The Georgia Supreme Court rejected the argument that the First Amendment established an absolute defense to civil liability in the circumstances of the case and remanded for trial before a jury. The case thus remained pending in the state trial court; no final judgment had been entered. Under a strict application of the final judgment rule, review in the Supreme Court would have had to await both the jury's verdict and state appellate review of the ensuing judgment.

Notwithstanding the lack of formal finality, the *Cox Broadcasting* Court upheld its appellate jurisdiction. In effect, the Court ruled that the First Amendment issue could dispose of the entire case, thereby making unnecessary any return to state court for a jury trial of other issues. Moreover, the Court noted that a refusal to provide immediate review could seriously threaten federal policy as embodied in the First Amendment. The Court's own view of the merits of the federal claim thus informed its decision to fashion a pragmatic exception to the finality rule. Justice Rehnquist dissented, arguing against pragmatic exceptions and observing that the final judgment rule serves to protect the role of the state courts in a federal system. Recognition of the exception in *Cox Broadcasting* was also said to undermine the policy of avoiding the unnecessary determination of constitutional issues; had the Court denied review, the case would have returned to state trial court where the media firm might have won a verdict on a non-federal ground that would have rendered decision of the federal question unnecessary.

As noted in *Cox Broadcasting*, the Court has recognized other exceptions to the final judgment rule. First, the Court has agreed to review the federal issue when it will prove dispositive of the whole case and effectively end the litigation. Second, the Court has recognized practical finality when the federal question will necessarily survive any further proceedings that may occur in state court. Third, the Court has permitted immediate review when the federal issue might evade review if further proceedings were to occur. Consider, for example, a state supreme court decision that reverses a state criminal conviction on federal constitutional grounds and remands for a new trial. Despite the lack of formal finality, the Court has agreed to review the federal question on a petition for certiorari by the prosecutor, reasoning that an acquittal of the defendant at trial could effectively foreclose review of the constitutional issue. See *California v. Stewart* (1966). (The bar to effective review follows from the rules governing appeal from a jury verdict of acquittal. When exclusion of the state's evidence at trial leads to an acquittal, the prosecutor cannot appeal the decision even to challenge the trial court's resolution of pure questions of law.)

A number of factors may have influenced the Court's decision to recognize pragmatic exceptions to the final judgment rule. First, in reviewing the judgments of federal courts, the Court faces no final judgment rule. The Court has, moreover, fashioned a series of exceptions to the strict rules of finality that apply to federal circuit court review of federal district court decisions. Though obviously inapplicable to the interpretation of the statute that governs appeals from the state courts, these federal exceptions to strict finality may have influenced the Court's approach to state decisions.

Perhaps of greater significance, the switch from a mandatory to discretionary appellate docket may have influenced the Court's willingness to recognize pragmatic finality. During the nineteenth century, when appellate review of state court decisions was available to litigants as a matter of right, strict application of the final judgment rule would enable the Court to maintain some control over its sizable mandatory appellate docket. Congress's decision to switch to a discretionary docket reduced the importance of the final judgment rule as a tool of docket control. Notably, the first exception to the final judgment rule appeared in 1914, the same year Congress introduced the discretionary writ of certiorari as a mode of appellate review. Moreover, discretionary review has led to closer attention to the merits of the dispute at the time the Court agrees to grant review and may invite the recognition of merits-based exceptions like that in *Cox Broadcasting.*

In addition to providing for review of final judgments, the relevant statute provides for review of judgments of the highest court of the state in which review could be had. This highest-court requirement effectively requires the petitioner to exhaust all available avenues of state appellate review before filing a petition for review with the Supreme Court. This includes an obligation to exhaust discretionary modes of review, such as a petition for leave to appeal to a higher court or to an en banc court sitting to review decisions made by a division or panel of that court. It does not, however, require the party seeking review to file a petition for rehearing to the same court that had previously denied the claim. In some cases, the highest state court rule may permit Supreme Court review of relatively low-level state tribunals if state practice makes the decision of such tribunals final and not subject to further state review.

4.8 Appellate Review of Federal Court Decisions and the Supervisory Power

In addition to a power to review final decisions of the highest state courts, the Supreme Court has long had power to review decisions of the lower federal courts. Indeed, as noted earlier, the great majority of cases on the Court's appellate docket come from the federal courts. As with the state courts, the Court's review of federal decisions has evolved into a largely discretionary exercise, with only small pockets of as-of-right review remaining (as in the provisions for direct appellate review of the decisions of three-judge courts comprised of district and circuit judges and convened to hear special challenges to state laws). This represents a substantial change from the nineteenth century, during which the Court's appellate jurisdiction in matters coming from the lower federal courts was available to litigants as of right in economically significant cases. (As-of-right review persisted until 1988 for cases in which the lower federal court invalidated state laws on federal grounds.)

Congress moved from a mandatory to discretionary docket with the passage of the Judges' Bill of 1925. This legislation capped a thirty-year period of reform during which Congress established the three-tiered federal judiciary that we know today, with district courts as courts of original jurisdiction, circuit courts as appellate bodies, and the Supreme Court at the top of the judicial hierarchy. Previously, the circuit courts had exercised both original and appellate jurisdiction, and had been staffed to some extent by Justices of the Supreme Court, serving as circuit judges. (It was circuit-riding duty that Congress restored in its repeal of the Judiciary Act of 1801.) By transforming the circuit courts into full-time appellate bodies, and eliminating the Justices' circuit judgeship duties, Congress sought to address the Court's appellate backlog. It did so by shifting as-of-right review of federal trial court decisions to the circuit courts and by staffing those courts with their own circuit judges. Congress also freed the Court to concentrate its resources on an appellate docket of its own choosing.

The Court's jurisdiction to review decisions of the circuit courts now extends quite broadly. The relevant statute provides for the issuance of the writ of certiorari in any civil or criminal case before or after rendition of the judgment or decree. See 28 U.S.C. § 1254. This broad grant of appellate jurisdiction effectively does away with the final judgment rule, freeing the Court to grant review before judgment has been rendered in the circuit court. It also permits the Court to review any case in the lower federal courts, without first identifying a dispositive federal question as the basis for the exercise of its authority, as it must do in reviewing state court matters. Cf. *Murdock v. Memphis* (1874) (limiting the Court's appellate jurisdiction to state court cases that present dispositive federal questions). Thus, the Court has power to review decisions in cases brought to the lower federal courts on the basis of diversity of citizenship. (Chapter 5 explores the diversity jurisdiction of the federal district courts.) Diversity disputes do not necessarily present a federal question; the jurisdiction depends on the alignment of the parties rather than the subject matter of the dispute, and many diversity disputes turn entirely on state law. While the Court has the power to grant review in such cases, it would clearly decline to do so simply to correct a perceived error in the lower court's interpretation of state law.

The Court also retains the power to pass on questions certified to it by the federal circuit courts, although the Court has indicated a sharp aversion to the practice. See 28 U.S.C. § 1254(2). (Federal statutes make no provision for state courts to certify questions of federal law to the Supreme Court.) This certification power survives as a vestige of an earlier day; it was first adopted in the early nineteenth century to enable circuit courts to request a dispositive ruling from the Court when the judges of the circuit were divided among themselves about the proper interpretation of federal law. Today, the Court no longer welcomes certified questions. It has ample authority to grant review before judgment and thus to expedite consideration of any federal questions it deems worthy of expedited treatment. Moreover, it prefers to retain control of its own docket rather than to place control in the hands of a lower federal court. As a consequence, the Court often carefully scrutinizes any certified question and may find, for any one of a variety of reasons, that the question has not been properly framed for its consideration.

Apart from a formal power to review decisions of, and certified questions from, the lower federal courts, the Supreme Court may use its supervisory powers to oversee the exercise of judicial authority throughout the federal judicial department. The assertion of supervisory jurisdiction grew controversial during the twentieth century, as the Court relied upon such authority to impose rules of criminal procedure on the lower federal courts. Critics questioned the wisdom of these decisions as well as their legitimacy, noting that the judiciary's role in promulgating rules of evidence, practice, and procedure had usually been based on power delegated from Congress, rather than on a claim of inherent authority. See Beale (1984). Critics thus portrayed the supervisory power, which they view as having arisen in *McNabb v. United States* (1943), as a break with a historically more circumscribed judicial role.

Despite the force of this critique of the Court's role in fashioning judge-made rules of criminal procedure, the Court's power to exercise some supervisory authority over the proceedings of the lower federal courts rests on a relatively firm textual and historical foundation. As for text, the Constitution declares that there shall be but one Supreme Court and that all other federal courts must remain in an inferior relationship to that Court. At the time of the framing, supreme courts exercised a power of supervision over inferior courts through the issuance of a variety of supervisory writs, including the writs of mandamus, habeas corpus, prohibition, and the like. These writs enabled a supreme court to oversee the work of its judicial inferiors and to prevent lower courts from exceeding the boundaries of their jurisdiction. Supreme courts in the common law tradition also enjoyed broad authority over rules of practice and procedure. The degree to which such powers of supervision may inhere in the Supreme Court of the United States (perhaps by virtue of its supremacy) has divided commentators. Some argue that federal courts may claim only a narrow core of inherent authority and must defer in all other cases to congressional power over practice and procedure. See Pushaw (2001); Burbank (1982).

Whatever the scope of the Court's inherent authority, it has long enjoyed statutory authority to issue the supervisory writs. Since the enactment of sections 13 and 14 of the Judiciary Act of 1789, the Court has had power to issue writs of mandamus and habeas corpus in accordance with the principles and usages of the common law. Today, the Court's supervisory powers survive in the form of the All Writs Act, 28 U.S.C. § 1651, which provides the federal courts, including the Supreme Court, with power to issue all writs necessary to the exercise of their respective jurisdictions. The statute empowers the Supreme Court to entertain interlocutory (non-final) petitions for supervisory review in a variety of situations in which one might doubt its authority to hear an appeal under its formal statutory grants of appellate jurisdiction. In *Ex parte Republic of Peru* (1943), for example, the Court invoked the All Writs Act in entertaining a petition for a writ of mandamus directed to the judge of a federal district court in Louisiana who was said to have exceeded his jurisdiction in entertaining a claim against an ocean-going vessel owned by a foreign sovereign. See also *Chandler v. Judicial Council of the Tenth Circuit* (1970) (posing question of the scope of the Court's authority under the All Writs Act in circumstances where doubts arose about the amenability of a circuit judicial council's decision to formal appellate review); *Hollingsworth v. Perry* (2010) (using mandamus to overturn district court order allowing Internet coverage of same-sex marriage trial in California). The *Peru* Court did so despite Justice Frankfurter's argument that the Court lacked statutory power to review district court decisions and thus lacked the jurisdictional predicate for reliance upon the All Writs Act. On Frankfurter's account, the "in aid of" language of the All Writs Act authorizes mandamus and other writs not on a freestanding basis, but only where those writs would facilitate the exercise of appellate jurisdiction conferred elsewhere by statute.

One might solve the All Writs problem in cases such as *Peru* and *Chandler* by treating the Act as permitting the issuance of writs in aid of the exercise of the Court's appellate jurisdiction as conferred in Article III of the Constitution. Such an interpretive approach would appear consistent with the breadth of supervisory powers conferred in the Judiciary Act of 1789, and would address Justice Frankfurter's doubts about the Court's power to proceed under the All Writs Act in the absence of some other statutory source of appellate jurisdiction. The approach would also cohere with the traditional recognition of the supervisory writs as free-standing sources of authority that do not depend on the existence of some other statutory grant of authority. So long as the petition sought review of a lower court, it would qualify as permissibly appellate within the meaning of Article III, and the Court would have authority to provide appropriate supervision. See Pfander (2000). Only if a party were to invite the Court to issue mandamus to an executive branch official would the petition appear impermissibly original within the rule of *Marbury v. Madison* (1803).

Marbury's functional distinction between mandamus jurisdiction over executive officials (prohibited as an expansion of the Court's original jurisdiction) and broad supervisory oversight of lower federal courts (permitted as an exercise of appellate jurisdiction) can be quite confusing. One key to better understanding lies in recognizing that only the Court operates under the *Marbury* disability; other lower federal courts may issue mandamus or its modern equivalents to executive branch officials. Another key lies in recalling *Marbury's* formula: so long as the petition seeks to revise or correct the work of a lower court, it seeks review of a permissibly appellate character. Thus, in *Ex parte Bollman* (1807), the Court agreed to entertain what has come to be known as an "original" petition for a writ of habeas corpus, directed to the custodian of individuals who were suspected of involvement with Aaron Burr in a conspiracy to lead southwestern states out of the Union. It did so despite the government's argument that the petition sought action of an impermissibly original character inasmuch as the writ would direct an executive officer to release the petitioners. The Court found that the writ fell onto the appellate side of its docket because similar relief had first been sought from another federal court in the District of Columbia. Although the proceeding originated with the submission of a petition to the Court, the Court treated the petition as seeking the functional equivalent of appellate review of the other court's denial of relief.

Petitions for writs of habeas corpus may still be submitted to the Court under the All Writs Act. (The Court continues to characterize such petitions for supervisory writs as "original" proceedings, but this classification means only that the petitioner files the petition with the Court as an original matter. It remains an appellate proceeding within the meaning of Article III.) But the Court has other methods to review the work of the lower federal courts and generally requires petitioners to pursue those standard routes of appellate review as an initial matter. Indeed, the supervisory writs usually operate as a residual source of appellate jurisdiction that comes into play only when other avenues of review are unavailable. Thus, the Court has occasionally reaffirmed its power to issue the "original" writ of habeas corpus following legislation that restricts other modes of review. See *Ex parte Yerger* (1868); *Felker v. Turpin* (1996). The prospect of relief may prove more theoretical than real. Although the Court granted relief in *Bollman* (the petitioners, who attended the proceeding, reportedly walked out of the courtroom as free men), it has not granted similar relief on an original petition since the early years of the twentieth century. Today, with changes in habeas practice, petitioners no longer routinely appear in court and relief often takes a less dramatic form. Even in *Boumediene v. Bush* (2008), following its decision to invalidate statutory restrictions on the habeas rights of detainees at Guantanamo Bay, the Court remanded for further proceedings in the district court.

Chapter Five

ORIGINAL JURISDICTION OF THE FEDERAL DISTRICT COURTS

5.1 Introduction

This chapter examines the subject matter jurisdiction of the federal district courts as courts of original jurisdiction. The two most important statutory sources of original jurisdiction are the grant of jurisdiction over cases arising under the constitution, laws, and treaties of the United States, 28 U.S.C. § 1331 (commonly known as federal question jurisdiction), and that over disputes between citizens of different states, 28 U.S.C. § 1332 (commonly known as diversity jurisdiction). In addition to discussing these sources of judicial power, this chapter will explore supplemental jurisdiction (which permits the district courts to hear additional claims that bear a close relationship to those already within the original jurisdiction) and removal jurisdiction (which authorizes defendants to remove actions from state to federal court). The chapter begins with a discussion of the origins of the district courts, their role as courts of limited jurisdiction, and the constitutional limits on their power.

5.2 The Origin of the Federal District Courts

Under the Articles of Confederation, Congress had only the most limited power to create a federal court system. Congress could (and did) appoint the state courts to serve as federal courts to hear maritime felonies (such as mutiny), and it could (and did) establish a federal appellate court to hear appeals from the state courts in a narrow range of cases (those in which citizens captured the vessel of an enemy power and sought to establish title through a forfeiture proceeding). But Congress had no general authority to create a set of lower federal courts in which federal claims might be brought in the first instance or to establish an appellate tribunal with jurisdiction that extended beyond disputes over the legality of "prizes," vessels taken in the war with Great Britain.

The Constitution takes a different approach. Article III vests the judicial power in one Supreme Court, and in such inferior courts as Congress may from time to time ordain and establish. This language reflects the Madisonian compromise, which empowers, but does not require, Congress to create lower federal courts. When deliberations began at the Philadelphia convention of 1787, one preliminary draft of the Constitution (known as the Virginia plan after the state delegation that introduced it for initial consideration) provided for the establishment of one or more supreme tribunals and of inferior tribunals. Delegates objected to the provision for inferior tribunals, arguing that the state courts could serve as federal courts of first instance, subject only to review in a supreme court to secure federal rights and uniformity of decision. The convention agreed and struck the provision for the establishment of inferior tribunals. Thereafter, James Madison moved to confer on Congress a discretion to establish lower federal courts, and the motion carried.

A second debate over lower federal courts took place during the drafting of the Judiciary Act of 1789. Most Federalists supported the creation of a federal court system, expecting such courts to favor the interests of the creditor class and to insist upon a strict enforcement of federal revenue measures. Opponents viewed the proposed federal courts as expensive and unnecessary, given the availability of state courts. Federalists responded by questioning the ability of Congress to appoint state courts to hear federal causes of action; state courts employed judges who lacked life tenure and whose appointment did not comport with the requirements of the federal Constitution (nomination by the president and confirmation by the Senate). (As noted in Chapter 10, state courts might hear federal claims as tribunals constituted under Article I rather than as Article III courts.) In the end, the Federalists carried the point, and the Judiciary Act established federal district (and federal circuit) courts to exercise original jurisdiction. (Congress also gave the Supreme Court original jurisdiction over disputes involving ambassadors and state parties.)

Along with the power to establish lower federal courts, Congress also apparently enjoys the power to disestablish them. That power might not seem obvious from the text. The Constitution does not expressly confer a power of disestablishment, and it requires life tenure for all federal judges, thereby providing the basis for an argument that federal courts, once established, become relatively permanent features of the government. But the party of Thomas Jefferson rejected permanence in 1802 when Congress repealed the Judiciary Act of 1801 (controversial legislation that expanded the federal judiciary). Federalists argued against the repeal on constitutional grounds, but the Jeffersonians were determined to rid themselves of both the intermediate appellate courts and the new Federalist judges that President Adams had appointed to staff them in the waning days of his administration. (Today, presumably, Congress would provide other judicial assignments for any federal judges whose courts were disbanded.)

The combination of the Madisonian compromise and the early experience with the creation and destruction of lower federal courts has persuaded most observers that Congress enjoys broad control over the existence and jurisdiction of the lower federal courts. (A similar consensus views the Supreme Court as constitutionally established and as impervious to congressional destruction. Thus, the Judiciary Act of 1789 established federal district courts, but simply assumed the existence of the Supreme Court and provided for the appointment of six justices to serve on the bench.) A vocal minority has argued that the Constitution mandates the creation of lower federal courts to hear some matters within federal jurisdiction, usually federal criminal cases and cases of admiralty and maritime jurisdiction. See Collins (1995) (collecting examples). Others have contended that practical changes in the operation of the federal judiciary may necessitate lower federal courts, either as (1) substitutes for a Supreme Court that no longer hears appeals from state courts as a matter of right, (2) substitutes for state courts that lack power to hear certain claims, or (3) essential overseers of the work of the nation's many administrative agencies. See Eisenberg (1974); Redish (1990); Pfander (2004). On the whole, though, most accept a broad degree of congressional control over lower court jurisdiction as a constitutional given.

As a consequence, much of the debate in jurisdictional circles focuses on how broadly Congress may expand the scope of original federal jurisdiction. Article III, section 2 addresses that question, specifying the cases and controversies to which the judicial power of the United States shall extend. Federal district courts thus operate as courts of limited jurisdiction in two respects: they may hear only the matters that Congress has assigned to them and only to the extent permitted by the Constitution. Consideration of the scope of the district courts' subject matter jurisdiction thus requires an analysis of both the constitutional and statutory limits on that jurisdiction. The next section begins with an introduction to the constitutional limits of federal question jurisdiction.

5.3 Federal Question Jurisdiction: Constitutional Limits

In perhaps its most significant grant of jurisdiction, Article III authorizes the federal courts to hear cases arising under the Constitution, laws, and treaties of the United States. This federal-question grant of jurisdiction was designed to ensure that the federal judiciary would have power to hear and decide disputes that turned on the meaning federal law. The emphasis on federal law operates in turn to restrict the power of the federal courts to hear claims based upon state law. Only where state law claims include federal ingredients or involve parties that satisfy the requirements of alienage or diversity jurisdiction may the federal courts entertain the suit. Thus, the task of defining the scope and limits of federal-question jurisdiction boils down to a sorting process: courts and litigants must distinguish their state law claims from those that present federal law issues and support federal jurisdiction.

One can begin by identifying the body of law (state or federal) that creates the claim or cause of action. As a general rule, the great majority of state-created claims will stay in state court just as the great majority of federal claims will be proper subjects of federal question jurisdiction. This rule does not work perfectly as we shall see; some state law claims include federal ingredients that will justify an assertion of federal question jurisdiction. But the simple distinction between claims created by state and federal law does provide an essential starting point for sorting out the scope of federal question jurisdiction.

Consider, for example, the various claims that Rodney King might have brought against officers of the Los Angeles police department. (King's beating by police officers in 1991 was captured on videotape; the officers' acquittal on state criminal charges led to rioting. The officers were later convicted on federal criminal charges, and King sued both the city and the officers for damages in a civil lawsuit. He eventually recovered $3.8 million.) King might have brought a state tort claim against the responsible officers. King suffered a battery at the hands of the LA police, and the law of California provides victims of battery with a right to sue for resulting damages. If King invoked California tort law, he would be asserting a state law claim or right of action. Both the right (the right to freedom from unjustified invasions of bodily integrity) and the right of action originate in state law. Without more, such a claim would arise under state law—the law that creates the cause of action. (We can ignore for present purposes any defenses the officers might raise.)

In addition to this state law claim, King might sue under a federal law for damages resulting from a constitutional tort. Federal law, 42 U.S.C. § 1983, provides that any person who suffers a violation of his rights under the Constitution and laws of the United States by persons acting under color of state law may bring suit for appropriate relief, including damages and injunctive relief. In a section 1983 claim, King would assert a violation of his Fourth Amendment right to freedom from an unreasonable seizure. Both the Fourth Amendment right and the federal statutory right of action derive from federal law. Federal law, in short, creates both the right and the right of action. The claim thus arises under the

Constitution and laws of the United States, and no one would doubt the existence of federal question jurisdiction. Congress may, therefore, constitutionally confer jurisdiction on the federal district courts to hear such a claim (as it has done). (Again, we will ignore federal defenses such as the officers' qualified immunity defense.)

Now consider a different sort of claim. Suppose that California passed a statute like section 1983 that entitles individuals as a matter of state law to sue for any damages they suffer due to a violation of their rights under the federal Constitution and laws. In such a case, state law creates the cause of action. But the right at issue derives from federal law. In such a case, we would say that the state law right of action incorporates a federal ingredient; the cause of action would necessarily include allegations that the defendants violated King's right to freedom from an unreasonable seizure under the Fourth Amendment. Such state law claims—claims with embedded federal ingredients or issues—can sometimes present difficult issues of federal jurisdictional law. (They also tend to produce rhetorical flights; Justice Cardozo once referred to the need for care in choosing between a "kaleidoscopic" array of possibilities.) One cannot simply describe the claim as the creature of state or federal law; it's something of a hybrid with both state and federal elements.

The Supreme Court first struggled with the proper treatment of such hybrid claims—state law claims that include a federal element or ingredient—in *Osborn v. Bank of United States* (1824). In *Osborn*, the Bank sought an injunction directing officers of the state of Ohio to return money they had seized to satisfy the Bank's state tax obligations. (The Bank plausibly contended that the state tax was invalid under the Constitution; *McCulloch v. Maryland* (1819) found that, as a creature of federal law, the Bank enjoyed an immunity from state taxation.) The *Osborn* Court based its finding of statutory jurisdiction on the terms of the Bank's federal charter of incorporation, which gave the Bank the right to sue or be sued in the courts of the United States. (There was no general provision for federal question jurisdiction until 1875.) Reading this provision quite generously as a grant of jurisdiction to the federal courts (rather than a simple declaration of the Bank's capacity to sue as an artificial person), the Court concluded that Congress had authorized the federal courts to hear virtually any claim the Bank chose to make.

Having concluded that the statute conferred jurisdiction on the federal trial court, the Supreme Court next considered whether such a broad grant of jurisdiction exceeded constitutional boundaries. Was the Bank's case one arising under the Constitution and laws of the United States or did the case arise under state law? To answer that question, the Court acknowledged that state law created the cause of action; it was a state law claim for trespass that gave rise to the suit for injunctive relief. (The state officials were alleged to have trespassed on the Bank's property when they came on the premises to enforce the state tax lien. Trespass allegations against government officers were a standard form of pleading in nineteenth century litigation over the legality of government action. Chapter 7 explores the officer suit as a tool of government accountability in greater detail.) It was also obvious that the case would present federal questions. The case would turn on whether the officers could justify their trespass under state law as lawful tax collection or whether the federal Constitution invalidated both the state tax and the immunity that state law conferred on its tax-collection officials. The challenge for the Court lay in determining whether these federal issues, or others, would support *original* jurisdiction in federal court.

The distinction between federal questions that will support original jurisdiction and those that will support appellate jurisdiction was pressed most vigorously in the dissenting opinion of Justice Johnson. (Chapter 4 explored the original-appellate distinction in connection with *Murdock v. Memphis* (1874).) Justice Johnson argued against original jurisdiction essentially on the ground that the Bank's claim was a creature of state law. Johnson understood that constitutional issues could appear in the course of the litigation, but these federal issues were not an essential part of the Bank's statement of its initial claim. For Johnson, the fact that the Bank was pressing a state-law claim meant that the Bank was required to bring suit in state court as an initial matter. Only those rights of action that were themselves creatures of federal law would support the exercise of original jurisdiction. If dispositive federal questions entered the litigation after the initial complaint was filed, these were proper subjects for appellate, but not original, jurisdiction.

The Court, however, chose a different path. Speaking through Chief Justice Marshall, the Court rejected the notion that the common law origins of the Bank's claim necessarily foreclosed the assertion of original jurisdiction. (Today, after *Erie R.R. v. Tompkins* (1938), we would regard the cause of action as a creature of state law; at the time, the Court spoke of the matter as one of general law. Both then and now, claims arising under such common law principles do not, in themselves, present federal questions.) Rather, the Court explained that federal jurisdiction would be available, even over state-created (common law) claims, so long as federal law formed an "ingredient" of the original cause. In justifying the availability of jurisdiction over claims involving federal ingredients, Marshall emphasized that Article III sought to ensure that the judicial power of the federal courts would be co-extensive with the legislative power of Congress (co-extensivity implies that federal jurisdiction would extend to disputes over any piece of federal legislation Congress might enact.) He also argued that Congress might extend the federal trial court's original jurisdiction to any claim within the Court's appellate jurisdiction. Some have viewed this equation of original and appellate jurisdiction as empowering Congress to assign jurisdiction to the federal trial courts any time a potential federal issue exists, however remote the likelihood that such an issue would be actually drawn into litigation in the case. See *Textile Workers Union v. Lincoln Mills* (1957) (Frankfurter, J., dissenting).

One can question, however, whether Marshall meant to embrace the broadest implications of his argument for an equivalence of original and appellate jurisdiction. After all, one can easily imagine federal issues that might be injected into the course of a pending state law proceeding at a stage in the process that would make the assertion of original federal jurisdiction quite awkward. (Consider a statute that authorizes removal of an action from state to federal court following a due process challenge to a jury instruction.) Moreover, when the Court actually got down to the business of identifying a federal ingredient in *Osborn*, it focused not on the constitutional issues that might arise in the course of the litigation but on the Bank's capacity to sue under its federal charter of incorporation. Under the pleading rules of the day, corporations typically included allegations about their capacity to sue. See Bellia (2004). The Bank's right to sue, the Court ruled, provided an original federal ingredient in every claim the Bank might bring.

The *Osborn* Court's ingredient test has provided an enduring and quite expansive definition of the scope of arising-under jurisdiction. Whatever the pleading norms, the Bank's recitation of its status as a federal corporation with capacity to sue under federal law would not necessarily present a *disputed* issue of federal law in every case the Bank brought. In many cases, the defendant would not bother to challenge the legality of the Bank's incorporation (a matter settled in *McCulloch*) and would simply focus on the merits of the Bank's claim. For example, in a companion to the *Osborn* case, the Bank had brought a simple breach of contract claim against Planter's Bank, a state-chartered bank in Georgia. There were apparently no contested issues of federal law in the case, but the Court nonetheless upheld jurisdiction on the basis that the Bank's federal charter provided an original federal ingredient under which the claim would arise.

Justice Johnson's dissent highlighted the expansive nature of the Court's approach. According to Johnson, the *Osborn* test would enable Congress to provide for the assertion of original jurisdiction over state law claims brought by a naturalized citizen (on the theory that citizenship originated in federal law) and over similar claims to any tract of land that was first acquired by grant from the federal government. In both cases, Johnson argued, federal law would provide an original ingredient in the claim, even though the resulting litigation would rarely present questions concerning the legality of the plaintiff's citizenship or the lawfulness of the original land grant. The Court attempted to distinguish these hypothetical cases and to limit the apparent scope of its ruling. It did so by contrasting the relatively complete specification of rights and duties in the Bank's corporate charter with the bare bones approach of the naturalization laws of the day, which simply conferred citizenship and left other provisions of law to define the incidents of that status. While the Court may have been correct that the more complete specification of rights in the corporate charter might increase the likelihood that suits by the Bank would present a disputed federal question, such completeness does nothing to ensure that such a question will arise in the course of litigation of the Bank's common law claims.

Since *Osborn*, the Court has sometimes pressed the decision to its logical conclusion in upholding jurisdiction on the basis of initial incorporation or appointment. One early case, the *Pacific Railroad Removal Cases* (1885), concluded that the federal courts could hear (state) common law actions against a federally chartered railroad, even where the corporation was privately owned and did not act as a federal instrumentality. The federal charter was treated as an original ingredient in any suit by or against the railroad. Similarly, the Bankruptcy Act of 1898 provided for federal jurisdiction over any claim brought by the trustee in bankruptcy (the individual charged with collecting and administering the assets of the bankrupt estate), including claims based entirely on state law. In upholding this grant of jurisdiction, the Court pointed to *Osborn* and the trustee's initial appointment under federal bankruptcy law. See *Williams v. Austrian* (1947).

More recent cases may cut back somewhat on the broadest implications of *Osborn*. In *Verlinden B.V. v. Central Bank of Nigeria* (1983), the plaintiff brought suit under the Foreign Sovereign Immunities Act, a federal statute that codifies the law of foreign sovereign immunity from suit but authorizes suit in federal court against foreign nations in certain circumstances. Although the claim itself was one for breach of contract (arguably a creature of non-federal law), the plaintiff was required to show that one of the FSIA's exceptions to foreign immunity applied to the claim. This requirement necessitated the application of "detailed federal law standards" and sufficed to make the claim one arising under federal law. (The lower court had treated the standards as defenses and had accordingly concluded that they did not form an ingredient of the original cause.) In *Mesa v. California* (1989), the Court considered a state court proceeding, removed to federal court on the basis that the defendants were employed in the US postal service at the time they were cited for a violation of state traffic laws. Although the relevant statute permits removal by federal officers, acting under color of their office, 28 U.S.C. § 1442(a)(1), the Court took a narrow view of the provision. Only where the defendant officers were tendering a defense based upon federal law was this statutory provision brought into play. In the absence of such a federal issue, and none was presented in *Mesa*, removal of the state law proceeding would pose "grave" constitutional issues.

Some scholars have proposed a theory of protective jurisdiction to explain and perhaps justify an expansive view of federal jurisdiction. In brief, these scholars contend that Congress may have the power to protect an area of federal interest from the vagaries of state court litigation by providing for federal jurisdiction over litigation that touches an identified area of federal concern. Consider the problem presented by section 301 of the Labor Management Relations Act (LMRA), 29 U.S.C. § 185, which provides for federal jurisdiction over suits for violations of collective bargaining agreements, but fails to specify any substantive federal law to govern the resulting litigation. Questions arose after the statute's passage as to its constitutionality under Article III; such doubts rested upon the assumption that state law would govern any breach of contract actions. Scholars defended the statute on protective jurisdiction grounds, emphasizing the power of Congress over labor relations. Congress had enacted a substantial body of federal law to govern the collective bargaining process, and it clearly enjoyed power under the Commerce Clause to enact a detailed code for the enforcement of labor contracts. With power to regulate commerce and displace state control with federal standards, Congress might take the less dramatic step of shifting litigation from state to federal court for the application of state law principles. Such a grant of federal jurisdiction could be seen as protecting the federal interest in the collective bargaining process from possibly hostile state court interpretation.

These issues came to a head in *Textile Workers Union v. Lincoln Mills* (1957). Although the majority upheld the statute, it did not reach the issue of protective jurisdiction. Instead, it concluded that the statute directed the federal courts to fashion a body of federal common law to govern all breach of contract actions under section 301. (Under the majority's approach, breach of labor contract claims would be regarded as creatures of federal law and would obviously arise under federal law, thereby obviating any concerns under Article III.) The Court might have adopted a less sweeping approach by emphasizing the elements of federal law necessarily drawn into issue with breach of labor contract claims. Federal labor law established that labor organizations, acting within an industry affecting commerce, were to be treated as corporation-like entities with the power to negotiate and sign collective agreements and to sue and be sued in federal court. (Later legislation, the Labor Management Reporting and Disclosure Act of 1959, sets forth a detailed federal code that regulates the internal affairs of labor unions.) On the theory of the *Osborn* and *Verlinden* cases, these federal capacity issues might have been regarded as establishing an original ingredient in any action the organization brought for breach of a collective agreement. *Osborn's* ingredient approach, in short, creates protective possibilities for a Congress concerned about the fairness or effectiveness of state courts.

Justice Frankfurter declined to follow the majority's approach, concluding that the breach of contract actions arose under state law. However questionable that conclusion, see Pfander (1991), Frankfurter went on to deliver a sharp attack on the idea of protective jurisdiction. He argued that Article III itself had conferred a limited form of protective jurisdiction by authorizing Congress to protect aliens and citizens from outside the forum state (commonly known as alienage and diversity jurisdiction). These were, Frankfurter argued, the only instances in which Article III permitted Congress to assign state law matters to the federal courts on the basis of a distrust in the fairness or neutrality of the state courts. To justify federal jurisdiction other than on the basis of party-alignment required a substantial federal question. While he did not doubt that Congress could adopt governing standards under which labor-contract claims would arise, Frankfurter found that it had not done so.

Frankfurter's extended critique of protective jurisdiction remains the leading judicial opinion on the subject. More recent opinions of the Court simply suggest a reluctance to develop the doctrine of protective jurisdiction any further. Thus, in the *Verlinden* case noted above, the Court specifically declined to reach a protective jurisdiction issue, having found that the *Osborn* ingredient test was satisfied. More revealing perhaps, the Court in *Mesa* refused to permit the exercise of federal jurisdiction over an action removed from state court unless the federal defendants tendered a federal defense. The government had argued that protective jurisdiction might support removal, even without the assertion of any federal defense; such jurisdiction was said to be necessary to prevent state court hostility from impeding the ability of federal officers to perform their jobs. The Court quite pointedly refused to go along, indicating that it had seen no reason to adopt a theory of protective jurisdiction in the past and saw no reason to do so now to uphold federal jurisdiction over a state criminal proceeding.

The *Mesa* Court's evident discomfort with protective jurisdiction leaves Congress with two options: It may confer jurisdiction on the basis of an original federal ingredient that satisfies the *Osborn* test, or it may expand the scope of federal jurisdiction over state law claims by broadly conferring jurisdiction on the basis of diversity of citizenship. A later section explores the constitutional limits of diversity jurisdiction, an under-theorized corner of jurisdictional law, and then examines the options available to a Congress bent on expanding federal judicial power to hear state law claims.

5.4 Statutory Federal Question Jurisdiction: The Well–Pleaded Complaint

Having explored the constitutional scope of federal question jurisdiction, we now examine the interpretation of the statute that confers federal question jurisdiction on the federal district courts, 28 U.S.C. § 1331. (Note that federal law authorizes federal question jurisdiction in many other settings. See, e.g., 28 U.S.C. § 1333 (conferring original jurisdiction on the district courts in cases arising under an Act of Congress regulating commerce); § 1338 (conferring original and exclusive jurisdiction over claims arising under federal laws relating to patents and copyright); cf. 28 U.S.C. § 1257 (conferring appellate jurisdiction on the Supreme Court in cases involving state court interpretation of dispositive issues of federal law).) In general, the federal question statute has been construed more narrowly than has the analogous constitutional provision; not every case that presents a federal question can be brought in a federal district court. In brief, claims must stay in state court unless a relatively substantial federal question appears on the face of the plaintiff's complaint. This section will discuss these rules for sorting cases between state and federal court and then offer a brief critique and analysis.

Although the jurisdictional focus on the face of the plaintiff's well-pleaded complaint began much earlier, students commonly trace the rule today to the Court's decision in *Louisville & Nashville R. Co. v. Mottley* (1908). In *Mottley*, the plaintiffs brought suit in federal court, alleging that the Louisville & Nashville railroad had breached its contract with them to provide annual passes for free travel. The Mottleys had paid good consideration, having given up tort claims against the railroad for their passes some thirty years earlier. But Congress, seeking to root out its corrupting influence, had banned free rail travel. The railroad cited the statute in denying the Mottleys' request to renew their pass. The Mottleys argued both that the statute did not apply to them (because they had paid for their passes) and, if it did, it violated the Fifth Amendment's prohibition of the taking of property without just compensation. Their complaint in federal court referred to the statutory and constitutional issues.

The lower federal courts asserted jurisdiction over the claims and granted relief to the Mottleys. But the Supreme Court reversed on jurisdictional grounds, emphasizing the well-pleaded complaint rule. Federal courts may hear original claims under the general federal question statute only where a claim arising under federal law appears on the face of the well-pleaded complaint. Although the dispute between the Mottleys and the railroad would present federal questions, and although those questions were set forth in the complaint, under prevailing rules of pleading and practice, the federal matters would actually enter the case as defenses to the Mottleys' breach of contract claim. Since a "well-pleaded" complaint does not anticipate defenses, but simply sets forth an affirmative claim for relief, the federal issues would not have appeared on the face of the Mottleys' well-pleaded complaint. Such a well-pleaded complaint would have presented only a state law contract claim, a claim that does not arise under federal law, and would have left the railroad company to invoke the federal statute as a defense.

After suffering this jurisdictional defeat, the Mottleys refiled their claims in state court and won again. The state court obviously had jurisdiction, and it agreed with the Mottleys that the railroad could not justify its breach of contract by reference to the Act of Congress. On direct review of this decision, the Supreme Court reversed again. This time it reached the merits of the federal questions and ruled in favor of the railroad on both the statutory and constitutional issues. The subsequent history of the *Mottley* case highlights an important truth: the *Mottley* litigation presented federal questions and those federal questions were sufficient to support federal adjudication by way of appeal. But the federal issues arose in a defensive posture that the Court viewed as failing to support an assertion of original federal question jurisdiction in the lower courts.

One can make at least two arguments in favor of the Court's well-pleaded complaint rule. First, it makes sense to base jurisdiction in the federal district courts on the state of affairs that exists at the time the plaintiff initiates the action. Both plaintiffs and defendants need to know if a lawsuit qualifies for federal jurisdiction; plaintiffs must determine whether to file in state or federal court, and defendants must determine if they can remove a state court proceeding to federal court or challenge the jurisdiction of the federal forum if the plaintiff has lodged the case there. In addition to the interest of the parties in relatively clear jurisdictional rules, society has an interest in avoiding unnecessary jurisdictional wrangling. The first *Mottley* action wasted the resources of the federal courts, resulting in a jurisdictional dismissal. Clear rules available to the parties and the court to shape decisions at the outset can reduce the threat of similarly wasteful litigation in the future.

Second, a focus on the complaint to identify federal questions sensibly avoids the jurisdictional expansion that might result if plaintiffs or defendants were able to claim a federal forum through the anticipation or assertion of federal defenses. In the modern world, it can be quite easy to assert affirmative defenses of all sorts, including defenses based upon federal law. A jurisdictional rule that allowed the parties to base federal jurisdiction on the assertion of such defenses could result, as one jurist noted, in a relatively modest federal tail wagging an otherwise largely state law dog. See Posner (1995). If the case truly centers on issues of state law, and the federal defenses simply serve as jurisdictional hooks, one can question the need for a federal forum. State courts can weed out insubstantial federal defenses as effectively as the federal courts.

Despite these arguments, critics have identified problems with the well-pleaded complaint rule. First, the rule can result in an improper allocation of cases between state and federal court, locking a particular dispute into state court even though the dispute actually turns entirely on federal law. Consider the situation in *Mottley*. The state law contract provided the formal source of the Mottleys' affirmative claim, but was unlikely to generate controversy in either a state or federal forum. The case turned entirely on the railroad's proffered federal law justification for refusing to give effect to the contract and on the applicability of the Mottleys' constitutional reply to that defense. If jurisdictional rules seek to assign state law issues to state court and substantial questions of federal law to federal court, then one can easily argue that the *Mottley* case deserved an original federal forum.

Second, the *Mottley* rule came at a time when the consequences of denying an original federal forum were less dramatic. At the turn of the twentieth century, the Supreme Court closely monitored state court decisions involving the denial of a claim or defense based upon federal law; parties could appeal from a state court's denial of a federal claim as a matter of right. By denying original jurisdiction, the *Mottley* Court simply chose to treat federal defenses as matters to be resolved by it upon appellate review, rather than by a lower federal court in the first instance. Today, the parties no longer have a right to appellate review of state court decisions; the Court exercises discretion over its appellate docket and often turns away petitions seeking review of state court decisions. With this change, the *Mottley* rule no longer simply shifts the first instance determination to state court for ultimate review on the Court's appellate docket, but operates to foreclose federal jurisdiction altogether in virtually all cases.

Third, the well-pleaded complaint rule interacts with the rules governing removal of cases to federal court to produce jurisdictional allocations that some see as illogical. In general, as we will see in section 5.11, only *defendants* can remove an action to federal court and only if the action was one that the *plaintiff* could have brought there in the first instance. The well-pleaded complaint rule thus enables defendants to remove a federal claim that the plaintiff has chosen to submit to a state court for resolution but prohibits removal when defendants raise a substantial federal question in a defensive posture. Removal thus operates to open the federal courts to defendants only when the federal right-holder (the plaintiff) has been willing to forego the federal forum and has filed in state court. Some argue that a more sensible approach to original and removal jurisdiction would be to enable only the party invoking federal law, whether the plaintiff or defendant, to invoke federal jurisdiction for its determination. See Wechsler (1965). If adopted, such an approach would preclude removal by defendants on the basis of claims in the complaint (which by hypothesis the plaintiff agreed to submit to state court) but would allow removal on the basis of newly asserted federal defenses. In the *Mottley* context, such an approach would allow the railroad (as holder of the federal defense) to remove when it invoked the federal statute and would allow the Mottleys (assuming the railroad had not already done so) to remove when they tendered a constitutional reply to that defense.

Whatever the force of such criticisms as a logical matter, the Court has made it quite clear that it has no intention of judicially abrogating the well-pleaded complaint rule. Recent decisions take the rule as their point of departure and apply the rule in new contexts. Indeed, after describing criticisms of the well-pleaded complaint rule and its corollaries, the Court long ago indicated that any adjustment in the rules must come from Congress. See *Franchise Tax Board v. Construction Laborers Vacation Trust* (1983). So far, Congress has not budged.

5.5 Statutory Federal Question Jurisdiction: State Law Claims With Federal Ingredients

The well-pleaded complaint rule establishes a sorting device for claims appearing on the face of the complaint depending on whether they rest on state or federal law. In general, state law claims must remain in state court (absent diversity), and federal law claims may be brought in federal court, or removed there by the defendant. While the rule may seem simple to apply, it has grown vastly more complicated by virtue of the Court's willingness to permit the assertion of jurisdiction over a state-created claim that includes a federal ingredient. Just as the existence of a federal ingredient has been seen as crucial to upholding the constitutionality of an assertion of federal question jurisdiction over state-created claims under the *Osborn* test, so too has the presence of a federal ingredient sometimes (but not always) been regarded as a sufficient basis for the assertion of federal jurisdiction under the general federal question statute, 28 U.S.C. § 1331.

One early case, *Smith v. Kansas City Title & Trust* (1921), illustrates the operation of the federal ingredient rule. There, the plaintiff brought a shareholder's derivative action to enjoin the defendant corporation from investing in certain kinds of financial instruments. The right of action was a creature of state law, but the complaint alleged that the investment instruments in question had been issued by a federal agency that lacked power under the Constitution to do so. Thus, the case put into issue the constitutionality of Congress's power to provide for the issuance of investment instruments. Although the claim and proposed remedy (injunctive relief) were creatures of state law, the question at the center of the litigation was plainly federal. The federal issue, moreover, properly appeared on the face of a well-pleaded complaint to enjoin the investment. It did not arise as a defense. Accordingly, the Court held that the action arose under federal law; the plaintiff's right to relief was seen as depending on "the construction or application of the Constitution or laws of the United States."

But not all federal ingredients will suffice to establish federal-question jurisdiction. In *Moore v. Chesapeake & Ohio R. Co.* (1934), the plaintiff brought suit under a state tort statute, seeking damages for personal injury. Most observers have viewed the state-created claim in *Moore* as having included a federal ingredient; the plaintiff alleged that the railroad had violated a federal statute governing the safety of railroad coupling devices. One could characterize this alleged violation of federal law as constituting negligence per se within the meaning of state tort law. On such a view, the state tort claim would include a federal ingredient, and the claim would seem to turn upon the construction of laws of the United States within the meaning of *Smith*. Despite the straightforward lesson of *Smith*, the Court refused to treat the claim in *Moore* as one arising under federal law, noting that virtually all of the determinative considerations involved in the litigation were matters of state law. Scholars have long viewed *Smith* and *Moore* as in "irreconcilable" conflict with one another. See Redish (1980).

The Court had an opportunity to address the conflict in *Merrell Dow Pharmaceuticals v. Thompson* (1986). There, the plaintiffs brought suit in Ohio state court, seeking damages for personal injuries that they claimed were the result of exposure to the drug

Bendectin. Count IV of the complaint set up a claim of negligence per se, alleging that the manufacturer had marketed the drug without the warnings required by federal law. On this basis, the defendant removed, contending that the negligence per se claim incorporated a federal ingredient within the meaning of the *Smith* rule, and thus arose under federal law. The Court rejected the argument and ordered a remand of the case to state court. The Court acknowledged the tension between the *Smith* and *Moore* decisions but suggested that disparities in the nature of the federal interest might harmonize the two cases. Thus, the Court contrasted the important constitutional claim at issue in *Smith* with the mostly state-law issues involved in *Moore*. Scholars have suggested an additional ground for distinguishing the cases: docket impact. Assertion of federal-question jurisdiction over state-law claims for personal injury in *Moore* might have brought more claims to federal court than did the decision in *Smith* to take jurisdiction over the shareholder's derivative action. See Shapiro (1985).

One can criticize the *Merrell Dow* Court's emphasis on the nature of the federal interest as a relevant inquiry in federal ingredient cases. First, as the dissent pointed out, consideration of the strength of the federal interest could result in the use of an ad hoc balancing test to determine the existence of federal jurisdiction. Such a balancing test could result in uncertainty and the prospect of wasteful jurisdictional litigation. Apart from the problems with interest balancing, the *Merrell Dow* Court failed to perceive that the *Moore* case might be best regarded as one in which the state law claim failed the well-pleaded complaint test. Kentucky state law created tort liability and incorporated a federal standard by referring to federal statutes that regulate rail safety. But the Kentucky statute, which was fully quoted in the complaint and repeated in the lower court opinion, did not incorporate the federal standard into its definition of liability. Rather, state law provided that the railroad could not assert claims of contributory negligence or assumption of the risk so long as the railroad was shown to have violated any federal standard governing the safety of rail equipment. Most pleading regimes, then and now, have treated contributory negligence and assumption of the risk as affirmative defenses. See, e.g., Fed. R. Civ. P. 8(c). Under such a regime, references to federal law would properly appear not in plaintiff's well-pleaded complaint but in a response to affirmative defenses. With the claims so characterized, the federal question in *Moore* might be seen as having failed the *Mottley* test. See H & W (2009).

Apart from its attempt to distinguish *Smith* on the basis of the federal interest at stake, the *Merrell Dow* Court gave a fair amount of weight to the failure of Congress to create a federal right of action for drug purchasers who suffer injury due to a violation of their federal right to proper drug labels. In recent years, the Court has treated the creation of a federal right of action as a matter of special congressional expertise; it has accordingly declined to recognize implied, or judge-made, rights of action except in very narrow circumstances. (Chapter 6 discusses the Court's approach to express and implied rights of action in greater detail.) In *Merrell Dow*, both parties agreed that the federal statute failed to create a right of action, either express or implied. The Court treated the presumed absence of an implied right of action as an argument against the recognition of federal-question jurisdiction over a state claim with a federal ingredient. If, by hypothesis, Congress declined to create a federal action, it must have also preferred to avoid federal adjudication of state law claims to enforce the federal standard.

One can question the Court's reliance on the absence of a federal right of action from several perspectives. First, the argument may prove too much. In virtually every case in which a state claim incorporates a federal standard, Congress will have failed to have fashioned an explicit federal right of action to enforce that standard. That was certainly the case in *Smith* and in other cases in which jurisdiction has been based upon federal ingredients. Strict adherence to the negative implication analysis could foreclose federal ingredient jurisdiction altogether (except in those rare cases where Congress created a right of action but the plaintiff preferred to proceed under state law; even there a preemption problem might arise). It may be necessary, as a result, to give some attention to the context in which Congress declines to create a right of action. Second, the argument assumes that Congress's failure to fashion a federal right of action may reveal something about its jurisdictional preferences. But even when Congress declines to fashion a federal right of action, it may well expect enforcement of federal standards through other available processes of law.

Judged solely by the degree to which it brought clarity to jurisdictional law, one might consider the *Merrell Dow* decision a failure. A prominent commentator has suggested that conclusion, based on reports that of some 69 district court decisions applying the *Merrell Dow* criteria, 45 were overturned on appeal. See Meltzer (2004). The decision also spawned a division in the circuits as to whether the failure of Congress to fashion an explicit right of action should always be regarded as fatal to the recognition of jurisdiction over a federal ingredient embedded in a state law claim. This combination of considerations may have persuaded the Court to address the issue again in *Grable & Sons Metal Products v. Darue Engineering* (2005).

In *Grable*, the embedded federal ingredient appeared in a state law quiet title action to recover property that the IRS had seized and later sold to satisfy a tax obligation. Grable & Sons, the tax delinquent, argued that the IRS notice was defective; instead of providing personal service as the statute contemplated, the IRS had sent the notice by certified mail. (The IRS was not a party to the case, but the government filed a brief in the Supreme Court on the jurisdictional issue.) Grable & Sons dutifully pleaded the defective notice in contending that the IRS had no title to pass along to the purchaser, Darue Engineering. The quiet title action thus presented a question of federal law, namely, whether literal compliance with the federal statutory requirement of personal service was necessary to make the IRS's seizure and sale of property legally effective.

In a unanimous opinion, the Court found that federal jurisdiction extended to the quiet title action. The action satisfied the well-pleaded complaint rule, as the Court noted, and it would necessarily "raise a stated federal issue, actually disputed and substantial." Moreover, the Court found that a federal forum could entertain the action "without disturbing any congressionally approved balance of federal and state judicial responsibilities." The Court thus undertook a two-part inquiry, focusing first on the substantiality of a disputed federal question, and second on any signals Congress may have sent as to the proper jurisdictional allocation. On the first question, the Court found the defective notice issue to be substantial and actually in dispute; on this basis, it distinguished earlier decisions in which jurisdiction had been denied when federal law issues were merely in the background of the case. On the second question, the Court found a fairly significant federal interest in the assertion of jurisdiction over issues relating to the IRS's power to conduct tax sales of real property.

The Court distinguished *Merrell Dow*. There, jurisdiction was said to have threatened to federalize a tremendous number of state tort claims; the *Grable* Court noted that state negligence per se complaints incorporate federal standards with monotonous regularity. In addition, the *Grable* Court corrected what it saw as *Merrell Dow's* over-emphasis on the absence of a federal right of action; while Congress's failure to create such an action may have some continuing relevance in assessing congressional intent, it should not be viewed as dispositive. In *Grable* itself, for example, Congress had failed to create a federal quiet title right of action, but the Court ascribed little significance to that legislative omission. Most quiet title proceedings go forward under state law and Congress may have assumed the effectiveness of those remedial schemes in failing to adopt a federal scheme. The Court thus distanced itself from any implication in *Merrell Dow* that the absence of a federal right of action was fatal to the exercise of federal ingredient jurisdiction.

Grable & Sons thus revives the embedded federal ingredient as a potential source of federal question jurisdiction. But the Court's emphasis on the need for a *substantial* and *disputed* question of federal law may give rise to new questions in the future. Suppose a new plaintiff today were to set up precisely the same challenge to the sufficiency of IRS notice in a quiet title proceeding in Michigan. Such a claim might fail the *Grable & Sons* test for want of a substantial and disputed federal question. The Sixth Circuit ruled in *Grable & Sons* that certified mail substantially complied with the statutory requirement of personal service, at least where the owner received actual notice of the tax seizure and sale. With such a ruling on the books, a plaintiff's challenge to the IRS notice might be regarded as failing to present a substantial and disputed question.

The example illustrates the potential flexibility of the *Grable & Sons* approach. A question of federal law might be regarded as substantial and disputed when it appears as a matter of first impression, but not when the issue has been settled. Federal question jurisdiction might vary over time, expanding to permit the resolution of disputed embedded issues, and then contracting to foreclose federal adjudication when the issues no longer meet the substantial and disputed test. Recall that in *Osborn*, the Court noted the potential controversy over the legality of the bank's charter as a justification for the assertion of jurisdiction over any claim the bank might bring. Surely today, the bank's legality would be regarded as settled (notwithstanding the views expressed in President Andrew Jackson's veto message). Under the *Grable & Sons* approach, the bank's legality might no longer present a disputed and substantial question. Similarly, once resolved, the constitutional issue in *Smith v. Kansas City Title* might no longer justify an assertion of federal jurisdiction.

With the flexibility of the *Grable & Sons* approach might come a degree of uncertainty. Jurisdiction might turn in part on what other courts have said about the federal question; if all the circuits have rejected the plaintiff's contention (or accepted it), the federal issue may not justify an assertion of jurisdiction. If the federal courts have divided, however, the embedded federal issue may be seen as both substantial and disputed. Alternatively, the *Grable & Sons* test might treat the defendant's answer (or removal petition) as relevant for purposes of determining whether the federal issue would qualify as disputed. Such an approach seems hard to square with the well-pleaded complaint rule, which requires the court to focus on the complaint in determining jurisdiction and to ignore what appears in the defendant's response.

Apart from the nature of the federal question, the *Grable & Sons* Court emphasized the importance of the congressional "balance of federal and state judicial responsibilities." While Congress had failed to enact an explicit federal quiet title right of action, the Court reasonably concluded that such an omission was, in contrast to the situation in *Merrell Dow*, entitled to little weight as an argument against the assertion of jurisdiction. In weighing the import of congressional silence, the Court focused on the nature of the federal legislative process, noting that Congress would have had little reason to adopt a quiet title procedure in connection with the creation of rules to govern IRS tax sales. Other congressional signals might be more meaningful. Consider the Court's decision in *City of Chicago v. Int'l College of Surgeons* (1997), upholding the assertion of federal ingredient jurisdiction over a state law claim under the Illinois Administrative Procedure Act. The federal ingredients in the *City of Chicago* case—alleged violations of federal due process and equal protection assurances—were proper subjects of an action under 42 U.S.C. § 1983. Since Congress had already authorized the federal courts to hear such constitutional claims under section 1983, the assertion of jurisdiction over similar claims embedded in a state right of action would not upset the congressional balance.

5.6 Federal Question Jurisdiction: Declaratory Judgment Proceedings

Declaratory judgment actions can present difficult jurisdictional questions. Congress adopted the Declaratory Judgment Act, 28 U.S.C. § 2201, in 1934, and many states have authorized similar proceedings. In brief, declaratory judgment actions ask the court to declare the rights and liabilities of the parties. Such actions can often help the parties better plan their affairs by enabling them to determine the legality of a proposed course of action. Thus, an insurance company may file a declaratory judgment action to resolve a dispute over the coverage of an insurance policy. Similarly, a plaintiff who wishes to protest government policy at a local mall may bring a declaratory judgment action to determine whether his first amendment rights must give way to local trespass laws. The actions proceed upon the assumption that an actual dispute exists between the parties and that the determination of their legal rights will govern any future litigation on the same claims.

Complaints in declaratory judgment proceedings typically recite the history of the dispute between the parties and the nature of the legal issue that the parties wish to have the court determine. Consider, for example, the dispute in *Louisville & Nashville R. Co. v. Mottley* (1908) over the continuing legality of the Mottleys' free railroad passes. Either party might bring an action, seeking a declaration as to the validity of the contract. Such an action would typically recite the existence of the contract, and the dispute over the applicability of the new Act of Congress and the Fifth Amendment. In requesting a declaration of rights, the complaint would place both the state law contract claim and the federal statutory and constitutional issues before the court. A well-pleaded declaratory judgment complaint by the Mottleys might anticipate defenses in order to show that an actual dispute exists between the parties; one brought by the railroad might recite both the Mottleys' demand for recognition of the contract and the existence of federal defenses. Either way, the complaint's inclusion of the railroad's defenses to the contract's enforcement would seemingly present a federal question.

The prospect of jurisdictional expansion persuaded the Supreme Court to modify the well-pleaded complaint rule for declaratory judgment complaints. In *Skelly Oil Co. v. Phillips Petroleum Co.* (1950), the Court held that a district court must unwind the allegations of a declaratory judgment action in order to determine the existence of subject matter jurisdiction. Rather than looking at the face of the declaratory judgment complaint, the Court ruled that one must consider what a hypothetical complaint would have included had one been filed before the legislative creation of a declaratory judgment action. The Court's rationale for considering a hypothetical complaint was to prevent the declaratory judgment procedure from expanding the jurisdiction of the federal courts. In the case of the Mottleys, then, the district court would consider only the Mottleys' contract claim and would ignore any issues the railroad might raise as defenses to such an action. This unwinding or unpacking of the action applies irrespective of which party actually initiates the action; thus, the *Skelly Oil* rule would foreclose federal jurisdiction over the Mottley case whether the declaratory proceeding was initiated by the Mottleys or the railroad.

The hypothetical exercise required by *Skelly Oil* can be difficult to perform. Consider *Franchise Tax Board v. Construction Laborers Vacation Trust* (1983). There, a California state tax agency sought to collect individual tax obligations by levying on assets held in the Trust. The Trust argued that ERISA, a federal statute regulating employment benefit plans, preempted any such state law and immunized the trust funds from levy. To settle the dispute, the state agency brought suit in state court, seeking to enforce its levy and to obtain a declaration that federal law did not preempt the state levy rules. The Trust removed, arguing that the state declaratory judgment action presented a federal question (preemption) on the face of the well-pleaded declaratory judgment complaint. The Court ultimately held that the federal district court lacked original and removal jurisdiction of the action.

Yet the rationale of the *Franchise Tax Board* decision remains somewhat obscure. The defendant trust fund might have been entitled to bring an action under federal law to seek an injunction prohibiting the application of the state tax levy scheme to trust funds created in compliance with ERISA (an issue the Court declined to resolve). Unlike the usual situation in which preemption issues arise as a defense to a state law proceeding, the *Franchise Tax Board* case was treated as a situation in which the preemptive effect of federal law might have given rise to an affirmative right to federal relief. If one performed the unwinding exercise decreed in *Skelly Oil*, one might have concluded that the defendant's coercive claim was a creature of federal law. Yet the Court nonetheless denied federal jurisdiction, citing comity concerns. An apparently significant factor in the Court's thinking was its view that the state courts should be open to hear claims by a state agency to determine the legality of state regulatory action.

As the result in *Franchise Tax Board* makes clear, preemption claims often present difficult jurisdictional puzzles. In general, the supremacy clause displaces state laws that conflict with the Constitution, laws, and treaties of the United States. But preemption typically operates as a federal defense to state law claims and does not appear on the face of the well-pleaded complaint for jurisdictional purposes. Nonetheless, in a long line of cases culminating in *Verizon Maryland, Inc. v. Public Serv. Comm'n of Maryland* (2002), the Court has authorized the assertion of original jurisdiction over suits seeking injunctive and declaratory relief against allegedly preempted state regulatory schemes. One might try to justify this line of cases by noting that complaints seeking injunctive relief often will include an account of the preemptive force of federal law. But such actions for injunctive and declaratory relief closely resemble the suits that the Court in *Skelly Oil* evaluated not at face value but by imagining the content of a well-pleaded complaint in a coercive proceeding based on state law. If the Court were to unwind the *Verizon* action, as it had done in *Skelly Oil*, no federal question would appear on the face of the coercive state regulatory proceeding. *Verizon* thus exemplifies a judge-made exception to the well-pleaded complaint rule for suits seeking relief from preempted state regulatory schemes. It must be kept analytically distinct both from *Skelly Oil* and from the so-called complete preemption removal doctrine (considered in Section 5.11).

5.7 Diversity and Alienage Jurisdiction: Constitutional Scope

Apart from jurisdiction over federal questions, Article III extends the judicial power to controversies between various parties based upon their alignment in the litigation. These party-alignment grants of jurisdiction (all of which Article III defines as controversies, rather than cases) include a variety of disputes.

Thus, Article III brings disputes between citizens of different states within federal power (diversity), as well as disputes between a citizen of the United States and a citizen or subject of a foreign nation (alienage). (Other grants of party-alignment jurisdiction in Article III empower the federal courts to hear disputes between a state and a citizen of another state or foreign nation. These grants provided the jurisdictional predicate for the Court's decision in *Chisholm v. Georgia* (1793) and were superceded in part by the ratification of the Eleventh Amendment.) Party-alignment jurisdiction reflects distrust of state courts; creditors from other states and from Europe were thought to a series of hurdles in attempting to enforce their debts in the post-revolutionary state courts.

Congress implemented these grants of party-alignment jurisdiction in the Judiciary Act of 1789. Indeed, that statute was notable for conferring diversity and alienage jurisdiction on the lower federal courts and for failing to confer any similar grant of general federal question jurisdiction. (The first general grant of federal question jurisdiction, in the Judiciary Act of 1801, was repealed a year later. A second such grant in 1875 has remained on the books ever since.) Under the 1789 Act, a citizen of one state could bring suit in federal court against a citizen of another state, but only if one of the parties would face bias in state court. A New Yorker could file suit against a Virginian, invoking the diversity jurisdiction of the federal court in Virginia, but the federal forum was unavailable under the terms of the statute if the state court's neutrality rebutted concerns of bias. Thus, a New Jersey federal court would have lacked diversity jurisdiction over a dispute between a New Yorker and a Virginian; as between two out-of-staters, the statute regarded the New Jersey state court as a neutral forum.

The statute's concern with situations involving a risk of state court bias may have helped to produce the venerable complete diversity rule. In *Strawbridge v. Curtiss* (1806), plaintiffs from Massachusetts brought suit jointly against defendants from Massachusetts and Vermont in a Massachusetts federal court. In an opinion by Chief Justice Marshall, the Court ruled that such partial diversity of citizenship would not suffice. All of the plaintiffs must be citizens of a state different from that of all the defendants; that remains the rule of complete diversity today. Marshall's opinion was short on analysis, but it may have reflected the statute's focus on citizenship-based bias. With Massachusetts citizens on both sides of the litigation, the Massachusetts state court would have no reason to discriminate against the interests of the Vermont citizen on the basis of state citizenship, at least where the Vermonter's legal interests were held in common with those of citizens of

Massachusetts.[1] Later decisions built complete diversity into a hard and fast rule, and it has remained a part of jurisdictional law ever since.

Less clear, at least for 150 years or so, was whether the Court would treat the complete diversity rule as constitutionally compelled. A negative answer came in *State Farm v. Tashire* (1967). There, an insurance company brought an interpleader action to force claimants to present claims to the proceeds of an insurance policy in a single proceeding. (Interpleader actions seek to avoid the possibility of inconsistent judgments that might result if there were more than one proceeding to establish rights to a limited fund.) The interpleader statute, 28 U.S.C. § 1335, explicitly authorizes the federal district courts to hear the competing claims of two or more adverse claimants from different states. The Court interpreted the statute to authorize jurisdiction on the basis of minimal diversity between adverse claimants (which was present in *Tashire*), finding that it did not require complete diversity among all competing claimants. (A decision to require complete diversity would have lessened the effectiveness of statutory interpleader.) Having so construed the statute, the Court had little trouble in upholding its constitutionality. *Tashire* makes clear that while the complete diversity rule continues to control the interpretation of the general diversity provisions of 28 U.S.C. § 1332(a), it does not prevent Congress from using minimal diversity as the basis of jurisdictional expansion in other statutes.

Building on the result in *Tashire*, Congress has come to rely with increasing frequency on minimal diversity as the basis for broadening federal jurisdiction. In 1999, Congress adopted the Y2K Act to provide for federal jurisdiction over litigation arising from computer failures that some feared would occur with the arrival of the new millennium. In 2002, Congress enacted the Multiparty Multiforum Trial Jurisdiction Act, conferring jurisdiction on the federal district courts to hear claims arising from mass torts that cause the deaths of more than seventy-five people. See 28 U.S.C. §§ 1369, 1441(e). A few years later, Congress adopted the Class Action Fairness Act of 2005 authorizing the federal district courts to hear state law class actions that involve plaintiffs and defendants from more than one state and involve aggregate claims worth in excess of $5 million. See 28 U.S.C. § 1332(d), 1441, 1711–15. In all three cases, Congress based jurisdiction on minimal diversity.

---

1. If the interests of the Vermont defendant were distinct (not shared with those of the Massachusetts defendants), a prospect of bias may have existed. Interestingly, Marshall reserved judgment on the jurisdictional issue in a case involving distinct interests.

The increasing reliance on minimal diversity raises important questions about the limits, if any, to Congress's power to expand this source of federal jurisdiction. Consider *Bank of the United States v. Deveaux* (1809), where the Bank brought suit through its officers and members, all of whom were alleged to be citizens of Pennsylvania, against citizens of Georgia who were alleged to have trespassed on the Bank's property in Georgia. The Court concluded that the alignment of parties satisfied the requirements of diversity, and then went on to opine that the corporation was irrelevant to its analysis. The decision indicated that only the citizenship of the corporation's owners as natural persons was relevant and suggested that the corporation could not become a citizen within the meaning of the diversity provision.

The Court's early decision to analyze the citizenship of the owners or members of the corporation no longer controls today. (The Court came to treat the corporation as a citizen of its state of incorporation; Congress made its principal place of business an additional state of citizenship. See 28 U.S.C. § 1332(c). Section 5.8 explores these statutory elements of modern diversity jurisdiction.) But a focus on shareholder citizenship, if authorized by Congress, would enable virtually any modern business corporation or labor organization to bring state law claims in federal court on the basis of minimal diversity. So analyzed, the Bank's claims in *Osborn* would surely satisfy a test of minimal diversity, as would those of the labor union in *Lincoln Mills*. Minimal diversity challenges the idea that Article III imposes limits on the scope of federal judicial power. Any corporation with shareholders from more than one state (even one that was chartered under state law and failed the federal ingredient test of *Osborn*) could presumably litigate all its claims in federal court if Congress saw fit to confer jurisdiction on the basis of minimal diversity.

Consider also the implications of a minimal diversity theory for the jurisdictional issue presented in *National Mutual Ins. Co. v. Tidewater Transfer Co.* (1949). In the *Tidewater* case, the Court upheld the power of Congress to define citizens of the District of Columbia as state citizens for purposes of diversity jurisdiction. In doing so, the *Tidewater* Court had to work around an early Marshall Court opinion that had held, apparently on statutory grounds, that the District was not a state and that its citizens could not invoke diversity jurisdiction. See *Hepburn v. Ellzey* (1805). The rationale chosen in the *Tidewater* decision for avoiding a conflict with its earlier opinion enjoys a certain infamy in jurisdictional circles. The three-Justice plurality decision of Justice Jackson argued that Congress might use its powers under Article I to confer jurisdiction on Article III courts, thereby empowering them to hear matters not included in the jurisdictional menu. The six other

Justices objected strenuously to this claim, but two believed that Congress had the power to treat the District as a state, and thus joined in voting to uphold the statute. Four Justices dissented, with Justice Frankfurter giving voice to the classic view of Article III as defining the outer limits of federal jurisdiction and as blocking any attempt by Congress to confer statehood on the District for purposes of diversity.

A variety of solutions to the *Tidewater* problem have appeared in the literature. One body of thought holds that Congress might confer protective jurisdiction on the district courts, perhaps in exercise of its power to regulate the interests of citizens of the United States residing in the District of Columbia. (Everyone agrees that Congress may create territorial courts within the District of Columbia, and assign them power to hear disputes between District citizens and the citizens of other states. The *Tidewater* controversy arose from a suit brought in an Article III court in Maryland.) A second theory would treat Congress as exercising its power under section 5 of the Fourteenth Amendment to protect citizens of the United States resident in the District of Columbia from a state court violation of their privileges and immunities. See Pfander (2005). Rather than conferring expanded diversity jurisdiction, then, Congress might be seen as having conferred federal question jurisdiction to protect citizens of the United States from the possibility of biased state court decisions. None of this elaborate theorizing would be necessary under a minimal diversity approach; it would be enough to point to minimal diversity between the shareholders of the two corporate parties.

Yet despite the expansive potential of minimal diversity, one cannot easily define limits on the constitutional scope of diversity jurisdiction. The *Strawbridge* decision involved an interpretation of the diversity statute; it does not provide any rationale for limiting the constitutional scope of the jurisdiction. The *Tashire* Court treated the constitutional question as unworthy of analysis; it simply referred in a footnote to relevant lower court decisions. One might return to the roots of the party alignment provisions of Article III in suggesting that the Constitution limits diversity jurisdiction to situations in which litigation of the dispute in state court would present a threat of bias against a non-citizen. But no requirement of threatened bias appears in the Constitution; Article III speaks only of jurisdiction over controversies between citizens of different states. It may be that any controversy or dispute between adverse claimants from different states will ground the jurisdiction, clearing the way for additional disputes involving non-diverse parties that bear an appropriately close relationship to the diversity dispute at hand. In this way, one might view diversity between two adverse claimants as the foundation for the exercise of federal diversity jurisdiction. For an examination of possible constitutional limits on the aggregation of separate controversies between non-diverse claimants, see Pfander (95 Cal. L. Rev. 2007).

5.8 Diversity Jurisdiction: Statutory Elements

Two elements comprise the classic test for determining the existence of diversity jurisdiction under 28 U.S.C. § 1332(a). (Other statutory regimes, such as those governing jurisdiction over interpleader and class actions, alter these rules.) First, as we have seen, the venerable complete diversity rule of *Strawbridge v. Curtiss* requires that the citizenship of the plaintiffs differ from that of the defendants; no plaintiff and defendant can be citizens of the same state. Second, the statute requires that the value of the controversy exceed a specified figure, now set at $75,000. Determining the existence of diversity jurisdiction thus requires an assessment of the parties' citizenship and of the value or amount in controversy.

The definition of citizenship under the diversity statute depends on the status of the party, with the rules differing for natural persons, corporations, and unincorporated associations. For natural persons, a simple test has emerged: citizens of the United States will be treated as citizens of their state of domicile. (Individuals who lack US citizenship cannot become citizens of a state for diversity purposes, except through the operation of an inexpertly drawn provision that deems permanent resident aliens to be citizens of their state of domicile for certain diversity purposes.) See 28 U.S.C. § 1332. Domicile, in turn, has been defined as one's permanent home, the place where an individual has established a permanent residence and intends to return when away. Both elements—actual physical presence and an intention to make the place one's home—must be present to establish domicile (and citizenship).

Domicile analysis often identifies a person's original state of citizenship, and then considers whether a change in domicile has occurred. In a typical case, a person will assume the domicile of her parents at birth and will remain a citizen of her parents' state of citizenship until she establishes a domicile of choice. That typically occurs when she moves away from home to support herself and establish her own permanent residence. Domicile issues often turn on particular facts. A woman who leaves her home state to attend college may lack the intent to make the new state her permanent home; she would remain a citizen of her home state. But a woman who leaves her home state to begin her working life, and later supports herself as she attends college there may have established a new domicile.

Volition plays a role in domicile analysis. A prisoner in the federal prison system does not choose his place of incarceration; the Bureau of Prisons may shift him from place to place. Such changes would not produce a change in domicile because they do not reflect the individual's own choice about where to live. Similarly, a member of the Armed Forces may be deployed to bases throughout the United States and around the world. Such changes in deployment do not reflect the service member's own choice and would not ordinarily produce a change in domicile. In contrast, a person working for a global business may be expected to accept a transfer to a new state or give up prospects for advancement in the firm. Such transfers would typically produce a change in domicile, if the individual actually moved to a new locale. After all, the individual could have given up the job and stayed home, an option that was unavailable to either the prisoner or the service member.

Courts base the citizenship determination on the situation at the time the litigation begins, ignoring changes in domicile that have taken place before and after the lawsuit was filed. This rule as to the timing of the domicile determination makes it possible for a party to move to a new state in advance of litigation and file suit in federal court on the basis of the citizenship of the parties on the date of filing. The district court, in such cases, must determine if the party has established a new permanent home in good faith, and has no present intention to live elsewhere. If such bona fides are present, and an actual move has occurred, then the district court will uphold the change in domicile even if the sole or a central reason for the move was to obtain (or defeat) access to a federal forum.

The resident alien proviso complicates the determination of citizenship for those natural persons who are citizens or subjects of foreign states. The proviso states that an alien admitted to the United States for permanent residence shall be deemed a citizen of the state in which such alien is domiciled. The proviso apparently sought to curtail jurisdiction over disputes involving aliens; under § 1332(a)(2), jurisdiction exists over any dispute between a state citizen and a citizen or subject of a foreign state. By deeming permanent resident aliens (those who hold green cards from the federal immigration service) as citizens of their home state, the proviso would foreclose the assertion of jurisdiction over such citizen-alien disputes. Unfortunately, the deeming proviso may expand jurisdiction in unanticipated ways and create other problems. For example, a dispute between a resident alien and a nonresident alien would apparently satisfy the statutory terms of § 1332(a)(2) (as a dispute between a deemed state citizen and an alien), but Article III has long been interpreted to bar the assertion of jurisdiction over disputes between aliens. See *Hodgson v. Bow-*

erbank (1809). Courts might deal with the threat of jurisdictional expansion most effectively by treating the resident alien's deemed citizenship as an additional basis for foreclosing or narrowing jurisdiction. See *Intec USA v. Engle* (7th Cir. 2006).

Federal jurisdictional law defines corporate citizenship, deeming a corporation to be a citizen of its state of incorporation and of the state where it has its principal place of business. See 28 U.S.C. § 1332(c). The origins of this dual citizenship idea deserve brief mention. Recall that the Court first denied corporations any citizenship at all; it regarded the citizenship of the shareholders or owners as controlling. Later, the Court switched course, creating a firm (if fictional) presumption that all such owners lived in the state of incorporation. See *Louisville R. Co. v. Letson* (1844). The Court's rule effectively made the corporation a citizen of its state of incorporation and may have helped to spur the Delaware incorporation movement. A firm doing business in Illinois could obtain access to federal court for most of its legal disputes with Illinois citizens by the simple expedient of incorporating in Delaware. The perceived absence of any justification for a federal forum in such cases (due to the absence of any genuine risk of out-of-state bias to the corporation) persuaded Congress to make the change in 1958. The provision now treats the corporation as a citizen of both its state of incorporation and its principal place of business.

After years of uncertainty, the Supreme Court finally defined the statutory phrase "principal place of business" to mean the corporation's nerve center or headquarters. The case, Hertz Corp. v. Friend (2010), began in California as an action brought by an individual against Hertz, the rental car company. Hertz was incorporated in Delaware, had its corporate headquarters in New Jersey, and did business throughout the country. In refusing to assert federal diversity jurisdiction over the dispute, the lower courts reasoned that Hertz was a citizen of California; that was the state from which the corporation derived the bulk of its business revenues. In reversing, the Court rejected this focus on the source of corporate revenues, choosing instead to treat the corporate nerve center in New Jersey as its principal place of business. The Court emphasized that such a nerve center test would be easy to administer: parties can identify the corporate headquarters with relative ease. The Court might have been influenced in part by the perception that many national corporations do the bulk of their business in California, not because they have a special connection to California in particular but because California has the nation's largest state economy.

In defining the citizenship of unincorporated associations and partnerships, jurisdictional law focuses not on the entity but on the citizenship of the individual members or partners. This has long been the rule, and the Supreme Court has repeatedly declined invitations to depart from it. See *United Steelworkers v. RH Bouligny Inc.* (1965). Even for a limited partnership, where the general partners manage the business and the limited partners resemble corporate shareholders, the Court has continued to insist that the citizenship of all the partners be considered in determining the partnership's citizenship for diversity. See *Carden v. Arkoma Assocs.* (1990).

Diversity requires both a determination of the parties' citizenship and a finding that the amount in controversy exceeds the statutory threshold, now $75,000. In general, the Supreme Court has treated the amount claimed in the plaintiff's complaint, if claimed in good faith, as establishing the amount in controversy. See *St. Paul Mercury Indemnity v. Red Cab Co.* (1938). Only where it appears to a legal certainty that the plaintiff cannot recover the amount demanded will the district court refuse to assert jurisdiction. Claims for liquidated amounts pose few problems but personal injury claims can present complications. Under the legal-certainty test, most serious personal injury claims will easily satisfy the threshold; even if out-of-pocket losses do not reach the threshold, the inclusion of claims for emotional or dignitary injuries, pain and suffering, and punitive damages will satisfy federal jurisdiction. Only where the injuries seem modest or the damages can be calculated as a liquidated amount or have been formally capped by the legislature can a court conclude to a legal certainty that the plaintiff cannot recover the statutory threshold.

Virtually all amounts that the plaintiff seeks in the complaint, except interest and costs, will be included in the calculation of the amount in controversy. Thus, the amount includes lost wages, pain and suffering, punitive damages, out of pocket losses, and so forth. Attorney's fees generally do not appear in the calculation, unless applicable substantive law creates a right to recover them. Valuation problems can arise, especially in cases where the plaintiff seeks injunctive relief or other remedies that do not translate easily into a dollar figure. Courts disagree about how to perform such a valuation exercise; some ask about the value of the relief from the perspective of the plaintiff, while others examine the cost to the defendant of compliance.

Complex rules govern the aggregation of claims. In general, the plaintiff can aggregate the value of different claims against a single defendant. The rule of aggregation applies even where the claims bear no relationship to one another; unlike the rules of supplemental jurisdiction that we explore below, aggregation does not depend on a transactional relationship among claims. On the other hand, the plaintiff cannot aggregate claims against two or more different defendants to reach the threshold. (Nor can two or more plaintiffs aggregate their various claims against a single defendant to reach the threshold.) The claims by each plaintiff against each defendant must satisfy the statutory threshold. One very slight exception permits the plaintiff to aggregate claims against multiple defendants, but only where the claims satisfy the definition of a common and undivided claim. Thus, the plaintiff might bring an action to quiet title to real property worth $100,000, and include claims against two defendants, A and B, who own a common and undivided interest in the property. Courts would value the case at $100,000, aggregating the value of the undivided interests of the two defendants.

Class action litigation frequently presents citizenship and aggregation issues. Established law defines the citizenship of the class by reference to the citizenship of the named plaintiff or plaintiffs. See *Supreme Tribe of Ben Hur v. Cauble* (1921). Depending on the geographic breadth of the action, attorneys for a plaintiff class may enjoy some discretion in selecting named plaintiffs that either establish or defeat diversity. As for aggregation, the traditional rule required the claims of each member of the plaintiff class to satisfy the amount in controversy; the Court refused to permit aggregation of claims across the class as a whole. See *Zahn v. International Paper Co.* (1973). This aggregation rule has now been twice modified. The supplemental jurisdiction statute, 28 U.S.C. § 1367, has been interpreted to authorize jurisdiction over related class action claims below the threshold, so long as one claim meets the statutory figure. See *Exxon Mobil Corp. v. Allapattah Servs. Inc.* (2005). The Class Action Fairness Act of 2005, codified at 28 U.S.C. §§ 1332(d), 1453, goes further, eliminating the $75,000 figure and providing for jurisdiction if the aggregate value of all class claims meets a threshold of $5,000,000.

5.9 Judicial Control of Devices to Create or Defeat Diversity

Federal courts frequently describe plaintiffs as the masters of their complaints, free to structure claims so as to invoke federal jurisdiction or not. At the same time, defendants often challenge the forum choice of plaintiffs, removing actions that the plaintiffs might prefer to litigate in state court, or challenging the jurisdiction of the federal forum. Empirical evidence suggests that this wrangling over forum choice can have a significant impact on the outcome of the litigation; plaintiff win rates are lower in cases that have been removed or transferred than in cases where the plaintiff's choice of forum was left undisturbed. Courts often face the task of monitoring partisan wrangling over forum selection.

Some of the issues have been addressed legislatively, as Congress has taken steps to prevent the plaintiffs from engaging in devices to create diversity of citizenship. One longstanding rule, now codified at 28 U.S.C. § 1359, prohibits the assertion of jurisdiction over an action to which a party has been improperly or collusively joined. Such improper or collusive joinder may occur when a one party assigns a promissory note or other valuable instrument to another party for the purpose of manufacturing diversity. See *Kramer v. Caribbean Mills* (1969). A second rule, now codified at § 1332(c)(2), attempts to deal with the strategy of naming a representative party (a guardian or trustee, for example) solely for the purpose of obtaining access to a federal court. The statute simply treats the representative party as a citizen of the same state as the infant, incompetent, or deceased person whose interests are at issue in the litigation.

Plaintiffs also engage in tactics designed to defeat diversity. In one common tactic, the plaintiff restricts the amount of damages claimed to a figure below the statutory threshold. To the extent the plaintiff has authority under state law to limit the recovery, the restriction should operate to prevent removal. (After all, if the plaintiff chooses to give up a recovery in excess of $75,000, that choice will be respected, and the case will not qualify for federal adjudication.) In another tactic, the plaintiff may add an additional defendant of non-diverse citizenship. Such jurisdictional spoilers keep the case in state court, at least so long as they remain parties to the litigation. Defendants may attempt to counter these tactics, either by showing that the true amount in dispute exceeds the threshold, or by showing that the plaintiff has no substantial or colorable claim against the jurisdiction spoiler.

5.10 Supplemental Jurisdiction

In *Osborn v. Bank of the United States* (1824), the Court laid the constitutional foundation for the assertion of supplemental jurisdiction. There, the Court recognized that every matter in dispute between the parties need not present a federal question in order to permit a federal trial court to assert original jurisdiction. Jurisdiction attaches to the entire case, including federal claims (that ground the court's jurisdiction) and accompanying questions of general or state law. A central question since *Osborn* has been to determine how closely the incidental questions of state law must relate to the federal issues to bring them within federal power. Another question, ignored in early decisions, was whether Congress had adequately authorized the assertion of jurisdiction over incidental state law matters. Congress supplied the missing grant of statutory authority in 1991, adopting the supplemental jurisdiction statute, 28 U.S.C. § 1367. One can best understand the statute against the backdrop of the cases that came before it.

Those cases developed along parallel tracks, giving rise to the doctrines of pendent and ancillary jurisdiction, doctrines that Congress codified together under the single rubric of supplemental jurisdiction. Pendent jurisdiction received its definitive treatment in *United Mine Workers v. Gibbs* (1966). In *Gibbs*, the plaintiff alleged that the union had committed two civil wrongs: a secondary boycott in violation of federal labor law and a state law tort of interference with advantageous economic relations. We refer to the federal claim as jurisdictionally sufficient to capture the idea that the district court had an express grant of federal question jurisdiction over the secondary boycott claim. (Such jurisdictionally-sufficient claims are also sometimes known as anchor claims or freestanding claims.) In contrast to the federal anchor claim, the district court lacked any independent basis for asserting jurisdiction over the state tort claim. (The claim presented no federal question and diversity was absent; as an unincorporated association, the union would have been regarded as a citizen of every state in which it had members.) The question in *Gibbs* was whether, given its obligation to adjudicate the federal anchor claim, the district court could also hear a related state law claim (sometimes known as a pendent or supplemental claim).

The *Gibbs* Court approved the exercise of federal jurisdiction, rejecting the more restrictive approach of earlier decisions as unnecessarily grudging. The Court held that district courts may exercise pendent jurisdiction over a state law claim so long as it arises from the same "common nucleus of operative facts" as the federal claim. Although different bodies of law gave rise to the claims, they both grew out of a single dispute over labor relations at a coal mine in Tennessee. Under modern pleading rules, the parties would ordinarily expect to try such related claims in a single proceeding. So long as the federal claim has sufficient substance to confer jurisdiction and the state claim forms a part of the same constitutional case, the district court has power to hear the whole proceeding.

Having defined the potential scope of pendent jurisdiction in broad terms, the Court was quick to note that the power need not be exercised in every case. Rather, district courts were to exercise discretion in deciding whether to hear pendent claims and to consider various factors in doing so. For example, a district court might decline to hear a pendent claim where the state law issues were difficult or unsettled or where they seemed to present issues of greater importance than the federal claim. Moreover, district courts would presumably dismiss pendent claims if the federal anchor claim were dismissed early in the litigation. Later on, a different result might obtain. On the eve of trial, the district court might decide to proceed with the pendent claims, even after the dismissal of the federal anchor claim. In such a case, considerations of efficiency and judicial economy would argue against a jurisdictional dismissal that would require the parties to start over in state court.

The Court's emphasis on efficiency and judicial economy may well explain its willingness to define the doctrine of pendent claim jurisdiction in relatively expansive terms. The presence of an anchor claim based upon federal law strengthens the argument. A plaintiff with such a claim has a right to a federal forum; if pendent claim jurisdiction were unavailable, the plaintiff would have to choose between litigating the entire case in state court in a single proceeding or dividing the case into two proceedings and pursuing the federal claim in federal court and the state claim in state court. Pendent claim jurisdiction avoids the burden that splitting related claims would otherwise impose on the plaintiff's right to a federal forum.

Following *Gibbs*, the Court has taken a progressively less expansive approach to supplemental jurisdiction. In *Owen Erection Co. v. Kroger* (1978), the Court considered the operation of the doctrine in the context of diversity litigation. Kroger sued Omaha Power in federal court on the basis of diversity, seeking damages for a workplace accident that resulted in the death of her husband. Omaha Power in turn filed a third-party complaint against Owen Erection, contending that Owen was responsible for a portion of any award of damages entered against Omaha. Following Owen's impleader, Kroger amended her complaint to add a claim against the new defendant. Although diversity was lacking as to Owen, Kroger argued that the district court might exercise a form of supplemental jurisdiction known as ancillary jurisdiction. The federal courts had previously upheld the assertion of ancillary jurisdiction over a variety of claims in which defendants sought to protect themselves by expanding the scope of the litigation to include additional claims and parties. In an important footnote, the Court seemingly approved the exercise of ancillary jurisdiction over cross-claims, third-party impleader claims, and counterclaims. The question was whether ancillary jurisdiction also extended to the affirmative claim by Kroger against Owen.

The Court said no, essentially drawing a line between defensive claims that would qualify for ancillary jurisdiction and affirmative claims by plaintiffs like Kroger that were to remain subject to the complete diversity rule. One can certainly argue that Kroger's claim had a protective or defensive element. Had she not sued Owen, following its impleader, the jury might have assigned much of the responsibility for Kroger's loss to Owen, and that might have resulted in a reduction in the amount of any verdict against Omaha without the possibility of any corresponding judgment against Owen. Despite this defensive element, the Court treated the claim as a threat to the complete diversity rule. The Court feared that plaintiffs like Kroger might withhold their claims against nondiverse defendants, await the predictable third-party complaint, and then assert ancillary claims against them in derogation of the complete diversity requirement. The Court recognized that the goal of judicial efficiency would be best achieved by resolving the claims in a single proceeding, but noted that the state courts were available to hear the whole case.

The Court took a further step in narrowing the scope of supplemental jurisdiction in *Finley v. United States* (1989). There, the plaintiff sued the US government under the Federal Tort Claims Act (FTCA), a federal statute that confers exclusive jurisdiction on the district courts to hear tort claims against the federal government. The plaintiff joined two additional defendants, asserting state law tort claims that derived from the same common nucleus of operative fact (a plane crash in San Diego). Unlike the situation in *Kroger*, the state courts were unavailable as an alternative forum to hear the whole case; the exclusive jurisdictional grant deprived state courts of power to hear the FTCA claim. Nonetheless, the Court ruled that the district court could not exercise pendent party jurisdiction over the two state tort defendants. The Court noted that pendent party jurisdiction differed from the pendent claim variety it had approved in *Gibbs* in the sense that it brought defendants into the case against whom no claim within federal jurisdiction had been asserted. Without an explicit grant of statutory authority, the Court refused to permit the district courts to assert such jurisdiction.

Finley posed a significant threat to pendent and ancillary jurisdiction, at least where the assertion of jurisdiction involved (as it had in *Kroger*) the joinder of new parties. Congress responded by adopting the supplemental jurisdiction statute, 28 U.S.C. § 1367, supplying the written grant of statutory authority that the *Finley* Court had identified as missing. Though designed to codify the status quo and overrule the result in *Finley* itself, the statute produced controversy among scholars, some of whom viewed it as having failed to define jurisdiction with the requisite clarity. But aside from a circuit split over the continuing vitality of the *Zahn* decision—a split the Court later resolved—the statute has functioned fairly well. A brief overview follows.

Section 1367(a) begins with a broad grant of supplemental jurisdiction, making clear Congress's aim to authorize the assertion of such jurisdiction over claims so related that they form a part of a single constitutional case within the meaning of Article III of the

Constitution.　Many view this provision as codifying the *Gibbs* test and as extending supplemental jurisdiction to the constitutional limit.　In addition, section 1367(a) specifies that the jurisdiction so conferred extends to claims involving the joinder or intervention of additional parties.　The provision thus authorizes pendent party jurisdiction in a case such as *Finley*, and ancillary jurisdiction in cases involving party joinder (such as the impleader of third-party defendants that the Court implicitly approved in *Kroger*).

Section 1367(b) seeks to prevent the expansive definition of supplemental jurisdiction from undermining the complete diversity rule.　It provides a special rule for diversity matters, declaring that supplemental jurisdiction shall not extend to cases involving the assertion of claims by plaintiffs against persons made parties under certain specified rules of procedure, at least when the exercise of supplemental jurisdiction would undermine the complete diversity requirement.　For example, the statute mentions Rule 14 by name, and thus forecloses a claim by a plaintiff in the position of Kroger against a party joined in a third-party complaint.　Subsection (b) forecloses the exercise of supplemental jurisdiction over claims by plaintiffs against parties joined for a just adjudication (Rule 19), parties joined as defendants on related claims (Rule 20), and parties seeking intervention as defendants.　It also forecloses supplemental jurisdiction over claims by persons seeking to intervene as plaintiffs.

The last two provisions of the statute govern the district court's decision to retain or dismiss supplemental claims.　Subsection (c) codifies the *Gibbs* factors, authorizing the district court to decline to exercise supplemental jurisdiction over state law claims in cases where the state law issue is novel or complex, where the issue substantially predominates over the federal claim, and where the federal anchor claim has been dismissed.　Subsection (d) deals with the statute of limitations, establishing a tolling rule that enables a party who suffers dismissal of state claims in federal court to re-file in state court within thirty days.　The Court upheld the application of this thirty-day tolling rule to state law claims brought against cities or counties, reasoning that its adoption was an appropriate exercise of Congress's power to regulate procedure in federal court.　See *Jinks v. Richland County* (2003).

Confusion over the meaning of section 1367 has mainly centered on the interpretation of subsection (b) and its provision restricting the operation of supplemental jurisdiction in diversity.　Critics of the statute, and many federal appellate courts, read the statute as overturning the rule in *Zahn v. International Paper Co.* (1973), which had foreclosed the exercise of diversity jurisdiction over claims by members of a plaintiff class that did not themselves meet the amount-in-controversy threshold.　These decisions rested on the assumption that subsection (a) had conferred supplemental jurisdiction over such below-threshold claims (so long as they bear the requisite relationship to another above-threshold claim that confers jurisdiction). Without any Rule 23 restriction on supplemental jurisdiction in subsection (b), the broad grant of jurisdiction in (a) was seen as controlling. See Arthur & Freer (1991).

Not all courts and commentators shared this "literal" view of section 1367(a). Application of such an interpretive approach would threaten not only the rule in *Zahn*, but also the familiar complete diversity requirement of *Strawbridge v. Curtiss*. Consider a claim by Plaintiff 1 from Illinois against Defendant 1 from New York. Now suppose Plaintiff 1 added claims by Plaintiff 2 from New York. If the claims of Plaintiff 2 were related to those of Plaintiff 1 such that they comprise a single constitutional case, the literal interpretation would hold that supplemental jurisdiction applies to the claim. Because subsection (b) does not include an exception for claims by plaintiffs joined under Rule 20, one could argue that the statute overturns *Strawbridge* in this and perhaps other contexts. Critics of the literal view sought to preserve *Strawbridge* and *Zahn* by reading the aggregation and citizenship rules of diversity jurisdiction back into the requirement in subsection (a) that original jurisdiction first attach to the civil action, before supplemental jurisdiction comes into play. See Pfander (1999). Such an approach would mean that, in diversity, supplemental jurisdiction would not expand original jurisdiction, but would operate primarily to protect defendants as a source of what the *Kroger* Court called ancillary jurisdiction.

The debate over these two views produced a deep circuit split and eventually divided the Supreme Court. See *Exxon Mobil Corp. v. Allapattah Services* (2005). Rather than adopt either the literal or alternative interpretation, the Court borrowed something from each approach. As for rules governing the determination of the amount in controversy, the Court proclaimed itself a literalist. It thus concluded that *Zahn* had been abrogated and a class action could proceed with members of a plaintiff class whose claims failed to meet the threshold (so long as one claim did). As for citizenship rules, however, the Court held that *Strawbridge* continued to govern. Supplemental jurisdiction will come into play in diversity only where the parties' alignment first meets the requirements of complete diversity as an original matter. In treating citizenship, but not amount, as essential to ground the district court's authority, the Court drew a distinction not from the face of section 1332 (which defines original jurisdiction in terms of both considerations), but from an unspoken assessment of the relative importance of the two requirements.

5.11 Removal of Actions From State to Federal Court

Beginning with the Judiciary Act of 1789, federal law has provided for the removal of certain actions from state to federal court, and no one today doubts the constitutionality of the practice. To determine which actions may be removed, and through what sort of procedure, one must consult provisions of the judicial code, 28 U.S.C. §§ 1441 et seq. In general, the code provides for the removal of actions only by defendants and only on the basis that the claims asserted by the plaintiffs come within the original jurisdiction of the district courts. The availability of removal thus depends on whether the claim was one that the plaintiff could have brought in federal court. (Congress has the power to allow defendants to remove if they assert a defense to the action grounded in federal law, but it has largely declined to do so. A few exceptions permit removal on the basis of federal law defenses by federal officers, members of the Armed Forces, and those who can establish their inability to secure enforcement of their federal civil rights in state court.) A plaintiff can thus avoid removal in many cases, either by forgoing the assertion of any federal question claims or by ensuring that the configuration of parties and claims in the complaint does not satisfy the requirements of diversity.

Removal requires both that the complaint assert claims within the district court's original jurisdiction and that the defendants follow the proper procedures. In general, defendants must act promptly to effect removal, typically within thirty days of their receipt of the complaint. If they fail to do so, they will be treated as having forfeited their right to remove. (Removal can occur after the thirty-day period runs if the action first became subject to removal at a later point in the litigation, as when the plaintiff amends the complaint to assert a claim arising under federal law. For claims newly removable on the basis of diversity, the same rules apply, except that the statute bars removal more than one year after initial filing.) In a case involving more than one defendant, all defendants must join in the notice of removal; if one defendant declines to go along, the case must be remanded to state court.

The propriety of removal typically arises on a motion by the plaintiff to remand the action to state court. The statute allows remand if the action lies beyond the district court's jurisdiction or if there were some defect in removal procedure. Other provisions authorize remand of actions in special circumstances, and the Court has occasionally recognized relatively narrow judge-made rules, such as the rule permitting remand of pendent claims following dismissal of federal anchor claims. See *Carnegie–Mellon University v. Cohill* (1988). Appellate review of removal decisions can present problems; if the district court upholds the removal, the case remains pending and review may have to await entry of a final judgment. If the district court remands the action, the statute restricts appellate review, although the Court has recognized some exceptions. See *Thermtron Prods. Inc. v. Hermansdorfer* (1976) (upholding mandamus to review remand order in which the district court acted without statutory authority); *Quackenbush v. Allstate Ins. Co.* (1996). Recent decisions suggest that the Court might revisit its approach to appellate review of remand orders. See Carlsbad Technology Inc. v. HIF Bio, Inc. (2009) (upholding appellate review of Cohill remand orders but expressing doubt about the wisdom of judge-made exceptions to the statutory ban on appellate review); see generally Pfander (159 U. Pa. L. Rev. 2010).

Two odd jurisdictional puzzles arise in the removal context, and both deserve brief discussion. The first grows out of § 1441(c), which authorizes removal of the entire action whenever a separate and independent federal question claim has been joined with one or more otherwise non-removable claims. The idea of the statute seems straightforward; it permits removal of a federal claim where separate state law claims have been joined with the claim in state court and protects the defendant's right to a federal forum on the federal claim. The statute becomes puzzling when considered in light of supplemental jurisdiction, which applies to actions removed from state to federal court, and enables the federal courts to hear related state law claims. If the claims are so unrelated as to fall outside of supplemental jurisdiction, then the assertion of jurisdiction over them may exceed the limits of Article III. Critics thus question whether the district courts may exercise the distinctive jurisdiction conferred by a separate and independent claim removal statute without exceeding constitutional limits. Most courts will deal with the problem by simply remanding the unrelated state law claims to state court, as authorized in the statute, and proceeding with the federal question claim.

A second puzzle grows out of a line of cases that authorize what has come to be known as complete preemption removal. Preemption defenses typically assert that federal law displaces or defeats a state law cause of action; as defenses, they do not give rise to original federal jurisdiction and do not make an action removable. (Sometimes, as noted in section 5.6, defendants can secure access to a federal forum by invoking the Verizon preemption exception to the well-pleaded complaint rule.) In a quirky exception to the rule, however, the Court has recognized that some federal regimes exert so strong a preemptive force as to transform a nominally state law claim into a federal claim for removal purposes. In theory, then, the only well-pleaded complaint possible would be one that asserts a federal question claim. It thus becomes necessary to distinguish defensive preemption doctrines (which do not transform the state law action) from the complete preemption doctrine (which performs the transformative alchemy necessary to bring a state law claim within federal removal jurisdiction.)

The leading case, *Beneficial National Bank v. Anderson* (2003), identifies two factors needed to support complete preemption removal. First, federal law must establish a federal preemption defense to any state right of action. Second, federal law must establish an exclusive federal cause of action. In such a situation, federal courts will treat any claim that the plaintiff attempts to assert as one that necessarily arises under federal law. In *Anderson*, the Court found that both factors were present and accordingly held that a usury claim against a national bank, though nominally grounded in state law, arose under federal law for removal purposes. The usury claim joins a modest collection of additional claims that have been treated as subject to complete preemption removal. See *Avco Corp. v. Machinists* (1968) (permitting removal of nominally state law claim for breach of a labor contract); *Metropolitan Life Ins. Co. v. Taylor* (1987) (permitting removal of a benefit claim under ERISA).

Some might wonder why a defendant would bother to invoke complete preemption removal. After all, the federal defense of preemption would seemingly defeat the state law claim in state court without the need for any additional assertion that the claim really arises under exclusive federal law. Indeed, complete preemption removal may appear to provide the plaintiff with a viable federal substitute for a defective state law claim. The answer no doubt lies in the defendant's preference for a federal forum and in the defendant's expectation that federal law provides a defense to the transformed federal law claim once it reaches federal court. For example, after removing an individual's suit for breach of a labor contract, the defendant may argue that the parties must first exhaust arbitral remedies under the contract. Such a defense may be easier to establish in federal court. Complete preemption removal will likely be a popular gambit among defendants and could become available under a variety of federal statutes. See *Aetna Health Inc. v. Davila* (2004) (allowing complete preemption removal under ERISA of a state law tort claim).

Given its likely popularity among removal-minded defendants, the question remains why the Court has chosen to fashion a complete preemption exception to the well-pleaded complaint rule. Cf. *Rivet v. Regions Bank* (1998) (refusing to recognize an exception for a claim preclusion defense). The *Anderson* majority failed to explain the exception, despite having been pressed on the point by a dissenting opinion that challenged the Court to distinguish complete preemption defenses from others that failed the well-pleaded complaint rule. Earlier decisions had rested on legislative intent to provide for removal, but the *Anderson* Court moved away from such a focus. Instead, the Court viewed the legislative desire to provide an exclusive federal action as the centerpiece of its analysis.

The key to understanding complete or transformative preemption removal lies in the recognition that the doctrine differs from the ordinary preemption doctrine. Ordinary preemption defeats a state law cause of action or the exercise of state regulatory authority on the basis of a conflict with federal law. Often, in such cases, the finding of preemption operates to protect a federal administrative scheme from state interference. Complete or transformative preemption, by contrast, operates to protect an exclusive federal judicial right of action (and the associated body of federal law) from the risk of improper characterization in state court and the associated possibility that the state court will apply state, rather than federal, law. Transformation to ensure application of related federal law helps to account for the *Anderson* Court's emphasis on the fact that the federal usury statute provided both an exclusive federal cause of action and a number of additional federal provisions that regulate entitlement to relief. The regulatory authority protected is not that of a federal agency but that of the federal courts.

Chapter Six

THE *ERIE* DOCTRINE(S) AND FEDERAL COMMON LAW

6.1 Introduction

Once a federal court establishes that it has jurisdiction over a case, it must decide what law to apply. That process, inevitably, requires interpretation and the resolution of conflicts of law. In *Marbury*, for example, the Court faced what it saw as a conflict between an ordinary act of federal legislation and a constitutional provision limiting the Court's original jurisdiction. In such a case, the higher law prevails. Conflicts may also arise between laws of equal dignity, such as a treaty and a federal statute, or two federal statutes; in such cases, the more recent or specific enactment will control. Finally, conflicts may arise between rules of state and federal law. In general, federal law will control under the Supremacy Clause if the Court finds an unavoidable conflict. But the Court may work to accommodate state and federal law in order to prevent the needless displacement of state rules.

The *Erie* doctrine, the converse-*Erie* doctrine, and federal common law all represent attempts to resolve conflicts between state and federal law. One can group these doctrines together under the rubric of vertical choice of law. Vertical choice of law refers to a choice between state and federal law, with federal law understood as the higher law (under the Supremacy Clause). Vertical choice of law differs from horizontal choice of law, which typically involves the choice between two (or more) rules of state law of equal dignity. (This book does not address the horizontal choice of law process, except to the extent relevant to the *Erie* doctrine.) Vertical choices can arise in a variety of different contexts and can involve a range of competing interests. This section will examine these various contexts with some care, exploring the range of considerations that the Court has deemed relevant to the resolution of vertical conflicts. The section will thus explore the substance and procedure distinction that arose in the wake of the *Erie* decision, the converse-*Erie* doctrine (which addresses substance and procedure conflicts in state court); and the rules of federal common law that empower federal (and state) courts to fashion a uniform body of judge-made law in certain areas. The section begins with a review of the *Erie* case itself, which eliminated one source of conflicting law and gave rise to a second.

6.2 *Erie R. Co. v. Tompkins*

The story begins, as it did so vividly in the Court's opinion in the case, with an injury that Tompkins sustained one dark night while walking along the Erie's right of way near Hughestown, Pennsylvania. (Testimony at trial indicated that Tompkins was struck by something that protruded from a passing train.) Tompkins brought suit in federal district court in New York, the state where Erie had its corporate home, invoking diversity of citizenship jurisdiction. Tompkins was twice a forum shopper; he preferred federal court over state court and New York courts over those of Pennsylvania. His preferences were the product of perfectly good strategic thinking; Pennsylvania state law would have apparently treated Tompkins as a trespasser and would have denied him any compensation, whereas the law of New York and of the federal system apparently regarded Tompkins as a licensee, permitting him to recover damages on a showing that the railroad failed to use ordinary care in preventing an injury. Tompkins won a jury verdict at trial, and the Court granted review to consider if the "oft-challenged" doctrine of *Swift v. Tyson* (1842) was to be disapproved.

In *Swift v. Tyson*, the Supreme Court had ruled in an opinion by Justice Joseph Story that the federal courts were free to determine the common law rules that would govern disputes brought into federal court on the basis of diversity of citizenship. In *Swift* itself, the plaintiff sued to recover the value of a bill of exchange that had been accepted in New York. The defendant argued a failure of consideration, and pointed to New York decisions that treated such a failure as a valid defense to a collection proceeding. The *Swift* Court concluded that it was not bound by New York decisional law; such decisions did not make up a part of the "laws" of the state that the federal Rules of Decision Act, now codified at 28 U.S.C. § 1652, required the federal courts to respect. Rather, state court decisions on questions of common law were the products of the same decision-making process that federal courts followed in elaborating rules of common law. As Story saw matters, then, the law of commercial transactions was part of a national (or indeed international) body of commercial law to which state and federal courts were equally competent to contribute. (Today, something similar goes on, as the courts of Canada, Australia, England, and other Commonwealth nations work together to refine the rules of the common law.) On the merits, Story felt little hesitation in rejecting the New York rule; he viewed litigation over the sufficiency of consideration as posing a threat to the negotiability of commercial paper.

If *Swift* accurately reflected the jurisprudential understandings of its day, its provision for federal courts to fashion rules of common law in diversity actions gave rise to mischievous results. For one thing, the *Swift* doctrine enabled the federal courts to issue decisions on divisive issues of social policy in a context in which the sole basis for judicial involvement was the existence of diversity of citizenship. Such policy decisions, unconnected to any controlling provision of federal law, came to be seen as particularly controversial during the Progressive era. Progressives decried both the Court's willingness to recognize new constitutional protections for property owners and business enterprises, and the Court's use of diversity jurisdiction to free private enterprises from state regulations that it viewed as onerous. In *Gelpcke v. City of Dubuque* (1863), for example, the Court ignored state court decisions as to the interpretation of the Iowa constitution and ruled in a diversity case that certain state bonds had been validly issued under state law.

As state and federal law persistently diverged on matters within the scope of Story's general commercial law, *Swift* also created new opportunities for forum shopping. At the dawn of the nineteenth century, travel was slow, law books were a scarce commodity and many state systems lacked a hierarchical judicial system. In such a horse-and-buggy world, one would struggle to locate a distinctive body of decisional law for any a particular state. Lawyers like the young Abe Lincoln (riding circuit in Illinois at about the time of *Swift*) would look for the common law in Blackstone's and Kent's Commentaries, and in abridgments (the concise hornbooks of the day). By the end of the nineteenth century, all that had changed. State courts with a supreme appellate jurisdiction regularly issued decisions in bound volumes, and the West Reporter system made these volumes available to lawyers searching for the law of a particular jurisdiction. The resulting disparities between state and federal law created forum-shopping opportunities of the kind most famously exploited in *Black & White Taxicab v. Brown & Yellow Taxicab* (1928). There, a corporate party successfully evaded Kentucky law by reincorporating under Tennessee law and entering into an exclusive dealing arrangement; although exclusive arrangements were invalid where the service was to be performed in Kentucky, the contract was nonetheless deemed valid by the federal courts in a case brought in diversity.

It was to these mischievous results that the *Erie* Court pointed in disapproving the *Swift* doctrine. The opinion of the Court, written by Justice Louis Brandeis, cited the problems of the inequitable administration of the laws that resulted from forum shopping of the kind on display in *Black & White Taxicab*. It also cited research on the original meaning of the Rules of Decision Act, which supposedly revealed an intention on the part of the First Congress to subsume judicial decisions within its reference to the laws of the state that were binding on the federal courts. But fundamentally, the Court concluded that the federal courts simply lacked power under the Constitution to render decisions on the content of the substantive law that governed common law disputes. Such substantive law was state law, not general common law, and the federal courts were bound to apply the rules pronounced by the highest state court. Times had changed. Rather than a brooding omnipresence in the sky (in Justice Holmes's pungent phrase), common law was now seen in positive terms as the voice of the sovereign, reflected in authoritative decisions of the state courts. Unless the federal courts were applying the Constitution, laws, and treaties of the United States (or, as we shall see, elaborating a specific body of federal common law within an area of federal interest) they were to apply the laws of the states as rules of decision. "There is no federal general common law."

Much has been written about Brandeis's decision to base his decision on the Constitution, which he said required a re-interpretation (not an invalidation) of the Rules of Decision Act. According to one prominent commentator, the constitutional portion of the Brandeis opinion rests on a finding that Congress lacks power to enact rules of decision to govern disputes in diversity. See Friendly (1964). Such rules of decision would have a spurious quality; they would apply to disputes that happen to satisfy the requirements of diversity but would not apply to other similar disputes where diversity was lacking. Such spurious rules of decision for diversity give rise to forum-shopping problems and make little sense, especially where Congress has ample power to fashion nationally uniform rules in the exercise of its power under the Commerce Clause. The *Erie* decision arrived just one year after the Court had taken a broader view of the Commerce Clause (after the switch-in-time in 1937). While Congress may regulate railroad safety on a national basis under the Commerce Clause and while any such rules would govern in both state and federal court, *Erie* establishes that Congress cannot do so on a hit or miss basis by establishing rules to govern diversity disputes. It follows that the federal courts should not presume to do so themselves in diversity proceedings.

Viewed from within the Legal Process paradigm, the *Erie* case presents a classic problem in the proper distribution of law-making power. From the perspective of federalism, the *Erie* decision can be seen as restoring the proper role of state governments and state courts as the primary source of governing law. *Erie* also speaks to the proper allocation of authority between the legislative and judicial branches of the federal government; the decision invalidates an exercise of judicial authority that was said to have exceeded constitutional limits and to have defied the specific instructions of Congress as expressed in the Rules of Decision Act. From an institutional perspective, *Erie* rooted out a spurious body of federal judge-made law that had often led to forum shopping and to uncertainty about governing legal norms.

The case remains a subject of great interest to scholars. Historians who view the *Erie* decision as the product of progressive and New Deal politics have criticized the Legal Process paradigm for obscuring with talk of institutional competence the populist, pro-worker impulse that underlay the decision. See Purcell (2000). Other scholars have examined sources from the eighteenth and nineteenth centuries and have found striking parallels between the *Swift* regime and the approach to the determination of legal questions in other cases, such as disputes over the meaning of maritime contracts. See Fletcher (1984). Still other scholars doubt that courts can agree on how to choose a single body of state law to govern disputes that implicate the interests of more than one state. *Erie* applies to disputes brought to federal court on the basis of diversity of citizenship, disputes that, essentially by definition, involve citizens and interests from different states. The next section considers how *Erie* and its progeny address the problem of choosing between the competing laws of more than one state in a diversity action.

6.3 *Erie* and the Horizontal Choice of Law Process

In *Erie*, the Court simply overturned the rule of *Swift* and sent the case back for the application of state law. Although the Court did not address the issue, it apparently assumed (as did the lower courts) that Pennsylvania law would apply. Such an assumption was consistent with the prevailing choice-of-law rules of the day; most courts followed what was called the "vested rights" approach, applying the law of the place where the last act occurred that was necessary to give rise to liability. (Today, the vested rights approach has fallen into disfavor, and courts often apply policy analysis to determine which of the competing states has the most significant interest in the application of its law to the disputed question.) In a tort case, courts treated the injury as the last act, and looked to the law of the place of injury to determine the rights and liabilities of the parties. (In a contract case, courts would often look to the law of the place where the contract was made or to the place where it was to be performed.) The *Erie* decision left unresolved whether a federal court should fashion its own choice of law rules or look to the law of the state of New York, where the federal action was pending, to determine what law to apply.

The Court answered that open question in *Klaxon Co. v. Stentor Mfg. Co.* (1941), ruling that federal courts were obligated to apply the choice of law rules of the state in which they sit. In justifying its requirement that federal courts apply state choice of law rules, the Court emphasized vertical uniformity of result and the primacy of state courts in fashioning choice of law rules. Federal courts were not to second-guess state choice of law rules (except to the extent that they may violate constitutional limits). They were instead simply to give them effect in a diversity proceeding. Such an approach might give rise to some lack of uniformity as between federal courts; different outcomes might obtain, depending on the content of the underlying state choice of law rule. But such differences in result were the legitimate product of permissible variations in the law-making choices of the state courts, and were simply to be tolerated as the price of a federal system.

Many have criticized the rule of *Klaxon*, arguing that the federal courts might have played an effective role as the neutral arbiter between two potentially conflicting bodies of state law. On such a view, closely associated with early editions of the Hart & Wechsler casebook, federal courts would develop rules for the uniform selection of applicable state law that would apply irrespective of the forum chosen by the parties. But such a model of uniformity depends first on the ability of the federal courts to fashion a set of choice-of-law rules that will yield a degree of clarity and predictability. (Many students of the choice-of-law process in the courts of the United States would doubt that such a goal will soon be achieved.) Even if the federal courts were to work out the necessary rules, their effective application would depend on the ability of parties to remove all multi-state disputes to federal court on the basis of diversity. Students who recall the many ways in which parties can evade removal through the addition of jurisdictional spoilers or by suing defendants in their home-state may question the prospects for consistent removal. Choice of law rules for diversity proceedings, and for them alone, may thus have the same spurious quality that led the Court away from *Swift* in the first place. A less spurious solution, federal choice of law rules that would govern in both state and federal court, has yet to emerge either from Congress or from the Court.

6.4 *Erie* and the Substance/Procedure Distinction

Confronting an issue of substantive law (duty of care owed to those walking on the right of way), the *Erie* Court did not face the question whether its insistence on the application of substantive state law would interfere with the ability of the federal courts to develop and apply uniform federal procedural rules. Yet as many have noted, the Federal Rules of Civil Procedure took effect in the same year (1938) that *Erie* came down. The new rules ushered in an era of federal procedural uniformity after a century and a half during which federal courts applied a mish-mash of state and federal procedural rules depending on whether cases presented issues of law or equity. The drafters plainly expected that the new federal procedural rules would apply to all disputes in the federal system, including those that present questions of state and federal law and of law and equity. *Erie* and federal procedural uniformity set the stage for a new body of vertical conflicts of law: conflicts between state substantive law and federal procedural law.

Similar conflicts had arisen in the past in the horizontal choice of law context. States apply their own laws of procedure to the disputes before their courts. While the law of the forum governs procedural matters, state courts apply choice of law rules (such as the old place-of-injury rule or some modern variant) to determine what body of substantive law to apply. In a case like *Erie*, therefore, a New York court might apply its own procedural rules and look to Pennsylvania for substantive law. While this substance/procedure distinction makes sense as a conceptual matter, issues of procedure shade imperceptibly into matters of substance. Consider the role of a statute of limitations: it encourages timely litigation (when recollections are fresh), clears dockets of stale claims, and fosters a sense of repose among potential targets of litigation. Of these functional justifications for a statute of limitations, the first two have a procedural thrust but the third has a more substantive feel. No wonder, then, that the challenge of characterizing questions of timeliness as substantive or procedural has presented recurring difficulties in both the horizontal and vertical choice of law contexts.

The Supreme Court first faced the timeliness issue in *Guaranty Trust v. York* (1945). There, plaintiffs brought a class action for breach of trust, seeking equitable relief in federal court on the basis of diversity. Although *Erie* required that substantive state law control, the federal courts had a long tradition of developing and applying their own rules of equity procedure. In the *Guaranty Trust* case, the plaintiffs argued that the federal equitable rule of laches should apply to determine the timeliness of their action. (In a laches analysis, the court must determine if the passage of time has prejudiced the defendant's ability to mount a defense.) The corporate defendant argued instead that the case was barred by the hard-and-fast terms of New York's statute of limitations. The lower federal court applied the federal laches rule, noting the distinctiveness of federal equity procedure and appealing to the substance/procedure distinction. As we have seen, matters relating to the timing of suit have often been regarded as matters of procedure to be governed by the law of the forum.

The *Guaranty Trust* Court reversed, making two contributions to the development of the *Erie* doctrine. First, the Court refused to treat the substance/procedure distinction from horizontal choice of law as the proper starting point for analysis in the *Erie* context. As the Court observed, the various policies that inform the development of the substance/procedure distinction in the horizontal setting do not invariably apply in the vertical context, where the allocation of state and federal lawmaking authority hangs in the balance.   The Court's refusal to import a prefabricated substance/procedure distinction remains good law today.

Second, and somewhat less enduringly, the Court developed what has come to be known as the outcome-determinative test for deciding when federal procedural law must give way to a state rule. Under this approach, the Court treated a federal court, sitting in diversity, as "only another court of the State." If the rule would significantly affect the outcome, federal courts were bound to apply the same rule that would control a dispute between the same parties in state court. Such an approach was said to require the application of the New York limitations period, and would (presumably) require the dismissal of the action. While the holding remains sound, and the Court continues to treat issues relating to the timeliness of state law claims as controlled by state law, the outcome-determinative test has been limited and refined by subsequent decisions.

The first important limitation was announced in *Byrd v. Blue Ridge Rural Electric Co-Op* (1958). Byrd sued in federal court for damages due to personal injury; the viability of his claim depended on his establishing that he was not an "employee" within the meaning of the South Carolina worker's compensation act. (As with many worker's compensation schemes, South Carolina required injured employees to accept scheduled compensation under the act and immunized employers from tort damages.) Such an inquiry would ultimately turn on the facts surrounding Byrd's employment status; in federal court, the strong policy favoring the preservation of the jury trial supported the determination of such issues of fact by the jury. In South Carolina state court, by contrast, such fact questions were heard by the judge on review of the decision of an administrative tribunal. In the *Byrd* case, the employer/defendant argued that the *Erie* doctrine required the federal court to follow the state court's practice of submitting such questions to a judge for determination.

In a decision admired in some corners for its articulation of the factors that guide the *Erie* analysis (and criticized in others for its lack of determinacy), the *Byrd* Court first considered the values that underlay the state court rule. Examining the relevant cases, the Court found no reason to conclude that the state supreme court viewed its rule of judicial determination as bound up with the definition of the substantive rights and obligations of the parties. The rule of judicial determination thus appeared to be no more than a form or mode of enforcing the employer's immunity from tort liability. To be sure, the Court acknowledged that the identity of the decision-maker could have an impact on the outcome of the dispute (presumably, a jury would be more likely to resolve a close factual question in favor of the plaintiff and to award damages). But the Court pointedly observed that impact on outcome was not the only relevant consideration, particularly in a case in which there were affirmative countervailing considerations.

For the Court, the federal interest in the preservation of a independent system of justice argued for the application of the federal rule on the division of work between judges and juries. As the Court noted, the Seventh Amendment contributed to a policy favoring jury determination, even if the Amendment did not itself compel the submission of the particular question to a jury. (Had the Court found that the Seventh Amendment compelled a jury trial, it would have had no occasion to balance state and federal interests but would have simply applied controlling federal constitutional law.) The federal policy in favor of jury trial was entitled to some weight, especially when considered in relation to a state rule that the Court viewed as procedural and as not bound up with primary rights and obligations. In the end, the Court held that federal law controlled, and entitled to the plaintiff to a jury trial.

Although *Guaranty Trust* and *Byrd* identify a set of relevant considerations, they provide little guidance as to whether a more evident impact on outcome or a different balance of state and federal interests would have produced a different result. The resulting uncertainty cast continuing doubt on the degree to which the Federal Rules of Civil Procedure would control in a case of conflict with state law. The struggle of the lower court in *Hanna v. Plumer* (1965) nicely illustrates the predicament. *Hanna* began as a suit brought in federal court on the basis of diversity against the administrator of an estate. The dispute centered on what law governed the determination of how to serve the defendant with process at the outset of the litigation. State law specified personal (or in-hand) service on the administrator, but the plaintiff, relying upon what was then Rule 4(d) of the Federal Rules of Civil Procedure, had left the suit papers with a responsible adult at the defendant's home. The defendant argued that the plaintiff's failure to serve process in accordance with applicable state rules barred the action under the state statute of limitations. The lower federal court agreed, concluding that state law would plainly affect the outcome (in keeping with *Guaranty Trust*) and that the state had a strong interest in timely notice to the estate's administrator (in keeping with *Byrd*).

The *Hanna* Court reversed, and in the process developed a conceptual approach that divides the *Erie* doctrine into two theoretically separate categories. (In practice, courts do not always preserve an airtight distinction between the two compartments.) On the one hand were cases, like *Hanna* itself, in which a controlling provision of positive federal law (drawn from the Constitution or laws or from the procedural rules validly promulgated pursuant to federal statute) actually speaks to the question at hand. In such cases, the Constitution's supremacy clause requires that valid federal law control in a case of conflict with state law. The task for courts in such cases thus boils down to one of determining if the federal law has been validly issued and whether it really conflicts with state law. If the court answers both questions affirmatively, then the state rule must give way. (Note that in *Erie* itself, there was no conflict between a validly issued federal law and a state rule; the Court concluded that judge-made general federal common law was invalid.) For as the Court noted in *Hanna*, it has never invalidated a federal rule of procedure on the basis of conflict with state law or policy.

On the other hand, the Court acknowledged the existence of cases in which a rule of state law comes into apparent conflict with a federal judge-made rule that has an arguably procedural justification. Such conflict had occurred in the case of *Guaranty Trust v. York*. While the *Hanna* Court did not cast any doubt on the result in *Guaranty Trust*, it did offer a considered gloss on the outcome-determinative test. The twin aims of *Erie*, according to the *Hanna* Court, were to end the inequitable administration of the laws and the forum shopping to which such inequities could give rise. Not all differences in the rules of federal and state procedure would implicate such concerns. While application of state law in *Hanna* might influence the outcome at the time the defendant moved to dismiss the action in federal court (after the passage of time prevented the plaintiff from altering the mode of service to comply with state law), the Court found that the difference in the two rules was unlikely to have influenced the plaintiff's choice of forum at the outset of the litigation. *Hanna* thus refined the outcome-determinative test, focusing on the question whether the difference in state and federal law was likely to have influenced the parties' choice of forum.

Applying its new approach, the *Hanna* Court found that Rule 4(d) governed the manner of service in federal court. This was not a case governed by the Rules of Decision Act in which a federal judgemade rule came into conflict with state law; as a consequence, it was not a case in which *Erie* and the newly refined outcome-

determinative test of *Guaranty Trust* would apply. Rather, it was a
case controlled by the Rules Enabling Act, 28 U.S.C. § 2021, under
which the rules of federal procedural law were promulgated. As
the Court noted, Congress had adopted the Enabling Act in the
exercise of its power to regulate the practice and procedure of the
lower federal courts, power that the Constitution had amply conferred. The Enabling Act, in turn, validates federal procedural
rules so long as they have an arguably procedural justification.
Even rules that might appear to implicate state law rights and
obligations have been upheld under the Enabling Act. Here, the
Court cited *Sibbach v. Wilson & Co.* (1941), which upheld federal
procedural rules that authorized a medical examination of the
plaintiff in a personal injury case. Such an exam might invade the
plaintiff's privacy to some extent, but it had a procedural justification in facilitating the more accurate determination of the claim for
damages. Applying *Sibbach's* deferential arguably-procedural test,
the *Hanna* Court found that Rule 4(d) had been validly promulgated as a rule of procedure and applied in a case of conflict with a
state rule.

   Hanna thus establishes a firm constitutional foundation for the
power of Congress to regulate federal procedure and treats federal
statutes and rules that regulate procedure as virtually immune to
challenge. Conceivably, a federal statute regulating procedure
might exceed congressional power, but the Court's broad view of
congressional power makes such a conclusion unlikely. Similarly, a
federal rule might exceed the scope of the Rules Enabling Act.
That Act creates a rule-making process that begins with an advisory committee on civil rules housed within the judicial department
and culminates in the issuance of rules by order of the Supreme
Court; it forecloses the issuance of any rules that "abridge, enlarge,
or modify a substantive right." Debate continues about its purpose; some see the no-abridgement provision as protecting state
substantive law in keeping with *Erie* values while others view it as
seeking to preserve congressional primacy in making rules that
affect substantive rights. Whatever the merits of that debate, the
provision does suggest limitations on the rule-making power of the
federal judiciary that could call into question the validity of a
federal rule. Indeed, the Court has suggested that the promul-
gation of civil rules governing the preclusive effect of federal
judgments would lie beyond the rule-making power. See *Semtek
Intern. Inc. v. Lockheed Martin Co.* (2001).

   In a case involving a federal procedural rule or statute, the
Hanna approach validates federal law and shifts the focus to the
question whether the federal rule actually conflicts with state law
so as to require its displacement. The Court found such a conflict
in *Hanna* itself; state law required personal service, while federal

law authorized service on a responsible adult in the same house-
hold. Subsequent cases make clear that the analysis of conflict can
be quite tricky; apparently applicable federal rules can be broadly
or narrowly construed. A broad interpretation will produce a
conflict that requires state law to give way; a more narrow reading
will avoid the conflict and leave state law intact and applicable to
the problem. The challenge lies in articulating the factors that
influence the determination of how broadly or narrowly to read
federal law.

The strategy of narrowing was nicely illustrated in the post-
Hanna case of *Walker v. Armco Steel Corp.* (1980). There, the
Court avoided an apparent conflict between Rule 3 of the Federal
Rules (which specifies that an action in federal court will commence
with the filing of the complaint) and state commencement rules.
State law treated the service of the complaint on the defendant as
the relevant event for purposes of the action's commencement and
the satisfaction of the state statute of limitations. Emphasizing
that it had previously resolved a similar case in favor of state law,
the Court invoked the doctrine of stare decisis. The Court also
viewed Rule 3 as governing commencement only for certain federal
procedural purposes; the federal rule did not purport to supply a
uniform federal rule to govern compliance with state limitations
periods. Absent conflict, the Court found no justification for displacing state law.

In contrast to its approach in *Armco Steel*, the Court has
occasionally taken quite a broad view of the application of a federal
procedural statute. In *Burlington Northern R. Co. v. Woods* (1987),
the Court considered a potential conflict between Rule 38 of the
Federal Rules of Appellate Procedure, which authorizes the appellate court to exercise discretion in imposing sanctions for a frivolous appeal, and Mississippi state law, which imposed a 10% penalty
on all defendants who filed an unsuccessful appeal. The discretionary federal and mandatory state sanction schemes could have co-
existed; the mandatory sanction would apply quite without regard
to any judgment as to the frivolousness of the arguments on appeal,
and might be analogized to an award of interest to protect the value
of the plaintiff's recovery. Nonetheless, the Court found there to
be a conflict and displaced state law.

Similarly, in *Stewart Organization, Inc. v. Ricoh Corp.* (1988),
the Court took a broad view of 28 U.S.C. § 1404(a)'s provision for
the district court to exercise discretion in deciding whether to
transfer an action. Despite the fact that the federal statute speaks
of the convenience of the parties and the interests of justice and
does not specifically address the treatment of forum-selection agreements, the Court found that the federal law expressed a policy
favoring the enforcement of such agreements. This federal prefer-

ence for enforcement was said to grow out of the statutory emphasis on mutual convenience and was said to apply instead of Alabama state law, which (like the law of some other states) then regarded forum-selection clauses as unenforceable. The Court could have preserved the discretionary federal transfer regime and given effect to state law; it would simply have been required to consider a range of other convenience factors, and to discount the contract, in making any transfer decision.

Many observers have expressed frustration with these post-*Hanna* decisions because they display some inconsistency in determining whether the federal rule displaces state law. In both *Burlington Northern* and *Stewart Organization*, one can easily fashion arguments to narrow the federal rule. One can also make arguments that the state law at issue bears some relationship to what the *Byrd* Court referred to as the definition of primary rights and obligations. The Mississippi appeal penalty might have been characterized as protecting the value of the plaintiff's judgment and the Alabama bar to the enforcement of forum-selection clauses might have been seen as protecting the interests of local parties in the local determination of their contract disputes. While the appellate penalty does not seem likely to influence the plaintiff's choice of forum at the outset of the litigation, the federal refusal to give effect to Alabama's policy on the enforcement of forum-selection clauses might well induce forum shopping. Whatever values informed the Court's analysis of how broadly or narrowly to construe the federal law thus appear to have played little consistent role in the decisions.

Uncertainty remained after the Court's decision in *Gasperini v. Center for Humanities* (1996). The case, brought in federal district court in New York on the basis of diversity, resulted in a substantial verdict ($450,000) for the loss of 300 photographic slides. The litigation presented two questions: what standard of review should govern the defendant's claim that damages were excessive, and what judicial body should apply that standard. In New York, recent legislation had specified reversal of a verdict that "deviates materially" from what a reasonable jury would award; federal law had traditionally upheld verdicts so long as they did not "shock the conscience" of the court. Under state law, the task of applying this new standard fell to the appellate court; federal law allocated the primary role to the trial court, subject to review for an abuse of discretion.

With the breadth of interpretation that it had displayed in *Stewart Organization*, the Court could have treated the case as governed by the *Hanna* prong of its *Erie* analysis. The Seventh Amendment not only guarantees a right to trial by jury, it specifically forbids the re-examination of jury verdicts on appeal. Rules that govern the appellate review of jury verdicts in the federal system have long evolved under the shadow of the constitutional prohibition of verdict re-examination. Moreover, Rule 59 of the federal rules specifies a historical standard for the appellate review of jury verdicts. Together, the Seventh Amendment and Rule 59 could have been cited as the source of the "shock the conscience" standard. Such an approach would have enabled the Court to treat those federal rules as valid and binding and as displacing conflicting rules of state law. But the Court chose to treat the case as one that was governed by neither the federal Constitution nor a federal procedural rule. This narrow construction of available federal laws enabled the Court to analyze the case under the *Erie* prong instead of the *Hanna* prong.

The Court first turned to the deviates-materially standard, asking if it had some connection to the state's definition of primary rights and obligations. The Court had little doubt that a cap on damages should be treated as substantive for *Erie* purposes; it drew an explicit analogy between such a cap and the state's more searching standard of appellate review. The Court also suggested that a difference in the applicable standard could induce forum shopping, although one might reply that rules of appellate practice would not often figure prominently in decisions about where to file a complaint. Having concluded that the state standard would apply in federal court, the Court next considered what tier of the judicial system should apply that standard. On this question of who decides, the Court followed its approach in *Byrd*. It thus chose to apply the federal rule, assigning responsibility to the district court for initial application of the new standard.

The judicial perception of a state rule as substantive for *Erie* purposes can dramatically influence the Court's approach to vertical choice of law. In *Gasperini*, the perception of New York's deviates-materially standard as substantive helped to persuade the Court to treat the case as one involving the *Erie* prong rather than the *Hanna* prong. A similar calculus apparently informed the Court's approach in *Armco Steel*, a *Hanna*-prong case, where a substantive conception of rules governing the timeliness of suit helped to produce a narrow interpretation of the federal rule. The challenge lies in identifying the factors that may induce the Court to regard the state rule as sufficiently substantive to warrant the interpretive maneuvers necessary to protect the rule from federal displacement. Those factors may include *Hanna's* refined test for forum-shopping and outcome-determination and some attempt to gauge whether the action implicates the state's definition of primary rights and obligations. Strong state interests may induce efforts, like those in *Gasperini,* to craft a compromise if that can be accomplished without too great a perceived sacrifice of federal procedural uniformity.

In a recent attempt to sort out the conflict between federal procedural uniformity and state policy, *Shady Grove Orthopedic Assocs. v. Allstate Ins. Co.* (2010), the Court delivered a deeply divided set of opinions. Shady Grove, the plaintiff and class representative, sued in federal court on the basis of diversity, seeking to recover a statutory penalty of $500 on behalf of several thousand class members. (Under the Class Action Fairness Act of 2005, minimal diversity jurisdiction attaches to claims valued in the aggregate at more than $5,000,000.) The defendant argued that applicable New York state law forbade the collection of penalty claims through class litigation. The plaintiff argued that Rule 23 alone governed the question whether the plaintiff can maintain the suit as a class action. Speaking for a four-Justice plurality, Justice Scalia adopted the plaintiff's broad view of Rule 23: it was a procedural device that governed the joinder of claims into a class action in federal court and displaced conflicting state law. Justice Ginsburg dissented, adopting the view (much like her position in *Gasperini*) that state policy could be accommodated through a narrow interpretation of the federal rule. Justice Stevens cast the deciding vote, joining Justice Scalia's conclusion on different grounds. While the opinions do little to alter the fundamental tools of analysis, they certainly demonstrate that the Court remains divided as to how broadly or narrowly to read federal procedural rules. Students of this subject might plausibly argue (though not in a brief or on an exam) that they can hardly be expected to master an analysis that the Court has done so little to clarify.

6.5   The Converse–*Erie* Problem

Converse–*Erie* problems arise when state courts entertain federal rights of action. Like federal courts, sitting in diversity, state courts may generally apply their own procedural rules in determining such claims. And like federal diversity courts, state courts must respect the rules of decision that define the substantive rights and obligations of the parties. In an *Erie* case, federal courts look to the substantive law of the states, whereas in a converse-*Erie* case, state courts must follow federal substantive law. The problem arises with monotonous regularity; state courts may exercise jurisdiction over most federal rights of action (except for the relatively modest number that Congress has exclusively assigned to the federal district courts). State court concurrent jurisdiction over federal claims opens a wide field for clashes between state rules of procedure and federal substantive law.

One such clash occurred in *Dice v. Akron R. Co.* (1952). The plaintiff brought suit in state court under the Federal Employers'

Liability Act (FELA), alleging injury in connection with employment on a railroad. The employer defended by pointing to a signed release of liability. The plaintiff contended that the company had procured the release by fraudulent misrepresentations about the document. The case presented two questions: what standard governs the resolution of the fraud claim, and who should decide the claim. The state supreme court applied a state law standard (holding the employee responsible for supine negligence in signing the release without reading it carefully) and followed state practice (which assigned the determination of the issue to a judge). On review, the Supreme Court reversed.

On the matter of what standard to apply to the release, the Court unanimously ruled that federal common law must control. (Section 6.6 considers other examples of federal common law that have persisted in the wake of *Erie*). Federal law had created the right of action and was thought to control the circumstances in which a party may surrender a federal claim. The standard for such a surrender of rights was not to vary from state to state as it might if state law were to control. On the matter of who was to decide, the Court split more narrowly. The majority held that individuals have a right to trial by jury of issues of fact in federal court, a right that the Court viewed as "part and parcel" of the remedy afforded railroad workers under FELA. The Court ruled that the state court was obliged to follow federal law, and submit the fraud issue to a jury. The dissent argued that the state had a strong interest following its own rule of practice, under which issues of fraud were characterized as equitable and assigned to the judge for decision.

The case bears an interesting resemblance to *Byrd v. Blue Ridge Rural Electric Co-op.* (1958), an *Erie* case in which the Court faced a similar question about the allocation of responsibility between judge and jury. In *Byrd*, federal law favored jury determination, and appeared to conflict with the state practice of assigning the decision of issues of fact to a state judge. The Court applied the federal rule, after concluding that the federal system had an interest in the integrity of its procedural system and that the state rule of determination by the judge was not bound up with the definition of primary rights and obligations. A cynic might conclude that the federal interest always wins, and there may be some truth to that conclusion particularly in a world of federal supremacy, where the federal court has the last word. One can nonetheless harmonize the two decisions by noting that the Court regarded jury determination as bound up with substantive rights and obligations in the *Dice* case, but did not similarly regard judicial decision-making in *Byrd*. Unfortunately, the *Dice* Court did not provide much by way of guidance to state courts that face converse-*Erie* problems.

Converse–*Erie* problems often arise from disputes over the statute of limitations. One interesting problem has arisen under the Jones Act, which creates a federal right of action for employees who suffer injury while working in maritime commerce. Federal law defines a period of limitations for such suits, and also permits individuals to pursue such claims in state court. State courts have sometimes applied their own shorter limitations periods, and dismissed the claim. Although states might argue that their shorter period does not bar the claim entirely, but only excludes from state dockets a claim that state law has defined as stale, the Court has repeatedly held that states must follow the federal rule of timeliness. See *McAllister v. Magnolia Petroleum Co.* (1958). Thus, the conclusion in *Guaranty Trust v. York* that issues of timeliness of suit are to be treated as substantive for *Erie* purposes also holds in the converse-*Erie* setting.

Tolling questions analogous to those in the *Erie* context also arise in the converse-*Erie* setting. Although *Walker v. Armco Steel* holds that the state law governs the tolling of limitation periods for state law claims, the Court has since held that federal law governs the tolling of limitations periods for federal rights of action. Indeed, the Court fashioned the federal tolling rule, which looks to the filing date of the action, from Rule 3 of the Federal Rules of Procedure—the very source it had rejected for state law claims in *Walker*. See *West v. Conrail* (1987). In the converse-*Erie* context, where federal law controls the limitation period, state courts face the question whether to apply their own tolling rule (such as the state rule of tolling on the date of service that the state of Oklahoma followed in *Walker*) or to look to federal law. At least one state court has looked to federal law, despite the fact that the federal tolling rule has its origins in a rule of procedure. See *Hurley v. Shinmei Kisen K.K.* (Ore. App. 1989).

6.6 Federal Common Law

Federal common law complicates the vertical choice of law process. Despite *Erie's* rejection of "general federal common law" to govern in diversity cases, the Supreme Court has continued to fashion judge-made rules in areas of federal interest. The resulting federal rules of decision make up what has come to be known as federal common law. Federal common law arises in a field where the Constitution and laws of the United States establish a federal interest but fail to specify a particular rule of decision. Courts fashion rules of federal common law to advance and protect such federal interests, and do so without much useful guidance from Congress. The resulting body of federal law operates, like other federal rules of decision, to displace conflicting state law under the Supremacy Clause. It also applies in state court, obligating state judges to give effect to federal common law rules and providing the basis for Supreme Court review. Federal common law thus lacks the spurious quality that defined general federal common law under the regime of *Swift v. Tyson.* Rather than applying only in diversity cases, federal common law applies in both state and federal court and offers the prospect of national uniformity through the exercise of Supreme Court oversight.

While the legal consequences of the Court's decision to fashion federal common law seem clear enough, a range of factors can influence the creation of such rules and make outcomes less predictable. Among other factors, the Court has focused on the nature of the federal interest, constitutional implications, relevant congressional actions or silences, the likely impact of a proposed federal rule on the interests of the states and the workability of relying on state law as an alternative. The resulting decisions do not form a predictable pattern but have something of a episodic quality; federal common law arises here and there for reasons that one can rationalize in retrospect but cannot often predict in advance. Within the enclaves in which federal common law has been established, lower federal courts (and state courts) will simply work out answers to new questions. In fields to which federal common law has not been applied, courts will proceed with greater caution and greater deference to state interests.

Note an important distinction at the outset. Federal courts doubtless have authority to interpret controlling provisions of the federal Constitution and laws. Obviously, this interpretive process may shade into the creation of federal common law, depending on one's view of the clarity of the constitutional or statutory command and the breadth of one's preferred theory of interpretation. The discussion that follows will distinguish the interpretive process, which grounds the resulting rule of decision in some controlling provision of federal law, from the somewhat less clearly grounded exercise of federal common lawmaking power. Indeed, such a distinction may seem to emerge from the Rules of Decision Act, which obliges the federal courts to apply state law except where the constitution, laws and treaties "otherwise require or provide." The Act authorizes federal judges to interpret the Constitution and laws, but may cast doubt on the legitimacy of federal common law that lacks a similar textual warrant. Recognizing some blurriness on the edges, the discussion that follows will focus less on the interpretive process and more on the creation of federal common law.

Scholars point to at least four separate fields or enclaves in which federal common law has arisen. See Hill (1967). These enclaves include cases involving the proprietary interests of the United States, interstate controversies, cases of admiralty and maritime jurisdiction, and cases involving international relations. In each of these areas, Article III and the judicial code have long authorized federal courts to exercise jurisdiction. But neither the Constitution nor the Congress has set forth a detailed code to govern the merits of disputes falling within these enclaves. During the era of *Swift v. Tyson*, the federal courts had no obligation to justify their exercise of common lawmaking authority; jurisdiction over disputes within these enclaves (as within diversity) carried with it the authority to find, fashion, and apply rules of law. After *Erie*, jurisdiction alone would no longer justify an exercise of lawmaking authority, and the Supreme Court was obliged to explain the extent to which federal common law remained valid within other established enclaves and to justify the creation of new ones.

6.6.1 Government Proprietary Interests

Consider disputes that implicate the proprietary interests of the United States. The federal government owns property, enters into contracts, and often brings suit to protect its interests. Jurisdiction presents no difficulties; Article III authorizes the federal courts to hear controversies to which the United States shall be a party and the judicial code has long provided jurisdiction over actions by the United States as a plaintiff. See 28 U.S.C. § 1345. (Suits against the United States implicate the doctrine of sovereign immunity, the subject of chapter 7.) One might argue that the availability of party-based jurisdiction may itself imply certain power in the federal courts to fashion federal common law. After all, party-based jurisdiction applies even where state (or other) common law creates the government's cause of action; it extends federal judicial power beyond those situations in which the government's action arises under the federal law within the scope of federal question jurisdiction. Had the framers of Article III expected the federal courts to hear only cases brought by the United States in which a controlling federal statute creates a right of action, they would have had seen no reason to confer party-based jurisdiction on the federal courts. Party-based jurisdiction bespeaks an awareness that federal courts were to find, fashion, and apply the law.

Yet in tackling the problem of justifying federal common law in the wake of *Erie*, the Court has placed little weight on the simple fact of jurisdiction. Consider *Clearfield Trust v. United States* (1943), the Court's first confrontation with claims involving the government's proprietary interests. There, the government invoked US/plaintiff jurisdiction in an action to recover the value of a forged check. The check, issued in connection with a Depression-era government program (the WPA), had been cashed at a JC Penney store in Pennsylvania, deposited in Penney's bank, Clearfield Trust, and then deposited with the Federal Reserve. Within a year or so, the government realized the check was forged; two years later, the government brought suit to enforce Clearfield's guarantee of the validity of prior endorsements, a standard feature of the law of commercial paper. Clearfield argued that the government's suit came too late, after the Pennsylvania statute of limitations had run. (The case thus bore some resemblance to *Guaranty Trust v. York* (1945), in which the Court later ruled that matters of timeliness in an equitable diversity proceeding were governed by state law.)

The *Clearfield Trust* Court rejected state law, and ruled that federal common law should control the timeliness issue. As for the content of federal law, the Court turned to the judge-made commercial law that it had previously created under the discredited decision in *Swift v. Tyson*, ruling that Clearfield Trust must establish that it has suffered some prejudice due to the passage of time. In explaining its decision, the Court noted that the government issues commercial paper on a vast scale and needs to refer to a single body of nationally uniform law. In addition, the Court noted that the government's check writing operations took place in an established field of federal interest, pursuant both to constitutional provisions that empowered Congress to act, and legislation that established the program that led to the issuance of commercial paper. The federal interests in uniform rules for the issuance and enforcement of rights in government-issued commercial paper were said to justify federal common law.

Having established that federal common law governed the proprietary interests of the federal government, the Court next faced the question of how far that body of common law would extend in displacing the state law that would otherwise control the rights of private parties. One can immediately see the importance of such a question. If Clearfield Trust faces suit by the United States, it will presumably bring suit against JC Penney (perhaps by way of impleader) to recover for that company's breach of its guarantee of prior endorsements; as between Clearfield Trust and JC Penney, the loss should fall on Penney as the company that accepted the instrument from the forger. But that may depend on whether the federal common law rule of timeliness will also govern the private dispute between Clearfield and Penney; if state law controls, then Penney may gain a limitations defense and Clearfield may be left holding the bag.

That possibility reveals the importance of saying where federal law ends and state law begins, and it led to the Court's decision in *Bank of America v. Parnell* (1956). Bank of America was the victim; it brought suit to recover the value of government bonds that had disappeared in suspicious circumstances. Parnell and others looked suspicious; they had obtained the bonds and cashed them in. A central issue in the case was the good faith of Parnell and the other defendants; a central factor bearing on their good faith was the degree to which the bonds were overdue at the time they were cashed. State law apparently cast the burden of proof on the issue of good faith on the defendants, but the federal appellate court concluded that federal common law controlled under *Clearfield Trust* and required the plaintiff to prove that the defendants acted without good faith.

The Court rejected the idea that federal common law extended to the burden of proof issue, ruling that state law should control. In justifying this deference to state law, the Court emphasized that the dispute arose between private parties, was brought in federal court on the basis of diversity, and did not directly implicate the interests of the federal government. The Court acknowledged that the federal interest in defining the rights and obligations of parties to a transaction in government securities may "radiate" outward from disputes in which the government itself appears as a party to those involving private parties. But the Court denied that the burden of proof involved such a radiating federal interest. Some have criticized the decision as posing a threat to federal uniformity, and for increasing the likelihood that a party like Clearfield Trust may be left without a remedy after losing to the government. See Friendly (1964). Certainly, the Court offered little by way of guidance for lower courts to use in drawing the line between federal and local law in such cases.

Despite these criticisms, the *Parnell* decision may not poke too important a hole in the edifice of federal uniformity. As the Court explained, its decision was limited to the burden of proof question; a second crucial question, bearing on good faith, was whether the bonds were overdue at the time they were cashed. The Court explicitly noted that the definition of overdueness was to be controlled by federal law, in keeping with the *Clearfield Trust* decision. Perhaps the Court recognized that it could not apply a federal standard of timeliness to disputes involving the federal government, and a different standard to disputes between private parties; such an approach could create a problem of fairness for private parties caught between the two standards. Although one can imagine scenarios in which a party (like Clearfield Trust) loses to the federal government in a dispute over commercial paper, but cannot win against a private party (like JC Penney) due to a change in the burden of proof, such cases will surely be quite rare.

More recent cases continue the *Parnell* trend in looking to state law to define many of the legal rules that govern disputes over the government's proprietary interests. *United States v. Kimbell Foods* (1979) offers a serviceable example. The federal government brought suit to enforce contract-based security interests in certain property; the government claimed that federal common law gave its liens priority over those of other private creditors. Under state law, by contrast, the federal government would get into line along with other creditors in accordance with the nature of its interests and the date on which the liens were perfected. While the Court acknowledged that federal common law applied to the dispute as one involving the government's proprietary interests, it nonetheless applied state law to govern the particular dispute over priority. Its reasons for doing so seem quite sound; the government was seeking an advantage in priority that could well upset the expectations of other private parties who had presumably looked to state law to determine priority issues and make their lending decisions. What emerges from the decision is a two-step process, in which the Court first determines if federal interests justify the creation of federal law, and only then considers whether to fashion a nationally uniform rule or to look to state law instead.

This two-step process has been described as dividing the analysis into questions of federal competence and discretion. See Mishkin (1957). At the first stage, the federal courts consider whether federal interests (from whatever source) make it competent for federal courts to fashion rules of federal common law. At the second stage, the courts exercise discretion in deciding whether to fashion a nationally uniform federal rule or one that looks to state law. Some criticized the *Clearfield Trust* decision for having considered only the competence issue and for having slighted the interests of the states. *Kimbell Foods* responds to this critique to some degree, and conducts an explicitly two-step analysis. Other decisions question the need for a two-step approach. Thus, in *Boyle v. United Technologies* (1988), the Court took the highly adventuresome step of fashioning a government contractor's defense as a rule of federal common law. In the process, the *Boyle* Court framed the inquiry in terms of the preemption of state law, and cast doubt on the need for an explicitly two-step analytical process.

In *Boyle*, the plaintiff alleged that the improper design of a helicopter led to the death of a member of the Marine Corps. The defendant, United Technologies, argued that it had designed the helicopter in accordance with government specifications, and was entitled to immunity from a state law tort claim based on a theory of negligent design. Although the dispute involved private parties, the Court found that two federal interests radiated into the private sphere. First was the government's interest in the relatively inexpensive procurement of military hardware; government contracts had long been a subject of federal common law. Second was the discretionary function doctrine of the Federal Tort Claims Act, under which individuals may not recover damages from the federal government for actions taken in the exercise of discretionary functions. The Court viewed the specification of a design for helicopter construction as unquestionably discretionary, and as immune from tort liability under the FTCA had the government performed the design and construction task itself. If state law were permitted to impose liability on the contractor, it would lead to a pass through of costs to the federal government, thereby raising contract prices and imposing indirect liability for discretionary functions. These federal interests were said to preempt state law to the extent of requiring the recognition of a nationally uniform government contractor's defense.

The *Boyle* decision raises questions about the scope of the Court's power to fashion federal common law, and about the relevance of congressional silence. Government contractors had worked the halls of Congress for years, seeking the legislative creation of a government contractor's defense. Justice Brennan detailed these failed legislative efforts in his dissenting opinion, arguing that the issue was one that the Court should have left to Congress to resolve. Legal process arguments might bolster such a contention; there's no obvious defect in the legislative process that would preclude the federal military and its contractors from obtaining a fair hearing on the need for such a defense. Yet it can be difficult to ascribe interpretive significance to a legislative failure to act; Congress has a variety of competing issues to address, and limited time and energy to work on specific bills. If the absence of explicit legislative authority were a compelling argument against federal common law, very little such law (which almost by definition lacks an explicit statutory predicate) would be adopted.

6.6.2   Federal Common Law for Cases of Admiralty and Maritime Jurisdiction

Article III extends federal jurisdiction to cases of admiralty and maritime jurisdiction in keeping with the framers' understanding that issues involving seagoing warfare and commerce were matters of federal concern. Congress in turn broadly conferred federal jurisdiction over such claims. Relying on these jurisdictional grants, the Court built up a body of law in the nineteenth century that governs maritime employment, contract, and tort disputes, among others. The Court also took a broad view of maritime jurisdiction as extending to events on all navigable waterways (including freshwater rivers and lakes and not just the salty water that laps at the nation's coastlines). Much of the law arose before the *Erie* decision re-shaped thinking about federal common law, at a time when courts were primarily responsible for developing rules of commerce. One finds a good deal of overlap between the content of the general law merchant that applied under *Swift v. Tyson* and the law of maritime commerce.

If the legal rules overlapped, however, the consequences of their application differ in important ways. Most importantly, the Court came to insist that federal admiralty and maritime law applied on a uniform basis throughout the country. This conclusion produced straightforward results as to matters within the exclusive jurisdiction of the admiralty courts, such as prize cases and in rem proceedings. (Prize cases arose during wartime, when enemy ships were captured and brought into port for a determination that the captors had obtained title to ship and cargo. In rem proceedings were brought by instituting a seizure of the vessel itself; owners typically posted a bond to secure the vessel's release. Ultimately, the bond would satisfy any claim of the successful litigant seeking wages or payments of other kinds.) Uniformity was more difficult in situations in which a common law remedy might be pursued in the state courts, as in an action for tort damages. The federal jurisdictional grant qualified its regime of exclusivity with a saving-to-suitors clause that preserved a "common law remedy" in cases "where the common law was competent to give it."

The saving-to-suitors clause blurs the line between federal and state law. In *Chelentis v. Luckenbach SS Co.* (1918), the plaintiff brought suit in state court, seeking damages for injuries received during work on board the Luckenbach steamship. The action was removed to federal court on the basis of diversity, and the plaintiff sought to ground his claim on state law and disclaimed any interest in recovery under such established federal maritime doctrines as unseaworthiness and maintenance and cure. The Court held that federal maritime law displaced state law and furnished the sole basis for the recovery of damages for injuries sustained on board ship. The savings clause thus allowed the petitioner to seek remedies at common law (perhaps through trial by jury), but preserved the rules of federal common law that govern the substantive rights of employees at sea. To much the same effect was *Southern Pac. Co. v. Jensen* (1917), in which the Court reversed a state court worker's compensation award on the ground that the application of state law to a maritime worker would impede the harmony and uniformity of maritime tort law. These doctrines of federal uniformity survive today, although they have been qualified in various ways as the Court has occasionally acted to import state law remedies and Congress has attempted to fill the gaps in compensation law.

Today, these statutes create a patchwork of rules that sometimes threaten the supposed harmony and uniformity of federal maritime law. In addition, federal courts face questions about the continued legitimacy of past exercises of federal common law authority. For example, in the nineteenth century, the Court applied the common law in ruling that negligent actions resulting in death do not give rise to an action for damages. See *The Harrisburg* (1886). The common law rule apparently reflected a punitive conception of tort law; it was thought to make no sense to punish a tortfeasor on behalf of a person who has died. The common law rule became increasingly anachronistic as tort law came to serve a compensatory function; many states passed wrongful death statutes that enabled the decedent's dependents to recover damages. Maritime law evolved as well, incorporating these state statutes where applicable to permit the recovery of damages for wrongful death. But the patchwork still created a risk that certain claimants, though more or less similarly situated, might fall through the cracks and enjoy no right to damages.

The Court faced such a problem in the well-known decision of *Moragne v. States Marine Lines* (1970). There, the claim for wrongful death fell within a gap in the existing scheme of compensation law. Although maritime workers could claim compensation for wrongful death under state and federal law in various situations, none of the established compensation schemes applied to the widow of a longshoreman who had been killed while working in navigable waters. Instead of denying relief, and putting the onus on Congress to re-write the rules, the Court overruled its own prior decision in *The Harrisburg*. In the process, the Court drew persuasively on a range of enactments as evidence of a change in the legal treatment of claims for wrongful death compensation. Rather than giving legal significance to the gaps in federal statutory law, the Court asserted a power to fill those gaps by drawing upon the policies of the federal statutes in revising its own rules of federal common law. In effect, then, the Court honored the equity of the statutes in a decision about the content of the common law.

6.6.3   Federal Common Law for Interstate Disputes and Customary International Law

Disputes between states have given rise to another enclave or field of federal common law. The Supreme Court's original jurisdiction extends to such disputes, and the Court early held that it was free to develop substantive rules to govern their resolution. For example, the Court has held that state laws on the rights of riparian land owners do not control the Court's own resolution of a dispute between states over the diversion of waters from an interstate river. See *Connecticut v. Massachusetts* (1931). Similarly, the Court has fashioned a federal rule to govern the location of the boundary line between two states that share a river as their common border. (The Court followed international law in selecting the line along the river's surface that lies directly above the deepest part of the river's channel.) On the same day *Erie* came down, the Court reaffirmed the existence of this body of federal common law. It ruled that non-state parties may be bound by the federal common law that arises to resolve disputes between the states. See *Hinderlider v. La Plata River Ditch Co.* (1938). Thus the rule of apportionment that the Court had developed for interstate disputes was said to apply to an action brought by a private party against a state official. The radiating influence of federal common law that we witnessed in *Clearfield Trust* and *Parnell* can be seen as explaining the decision in part.

Customary international law may define yet another field or enclave of federal common law, though the question has grown quite controversial. Here again, the initial role of the federal courts arose from jurisdictional grants; Article III provides for federal jurisdiction over cases affecting ambassadors, other public ministers and consuls, and over controversies between a citizen of the United States and a foreign nation or a citizen or subject of a foreign nation. Although the ambassador grant has given rise to only a sparse collection of decided cases, federal courts have often asserted jurisdiction over disputes involving foreign nations and foreign nationals. Before *Erie*, the federal courts were free to develop a judge-made body of law to govern such disputes, and could draw upon customary international law in formulating rules of decision. After *Erie*, jurisdiction no longer suffices to confer lawmaking authority and scholars now doubt the power of the federal courts to formulate a body of federal common law that incorporates customary international law.

Analysis of this question often begins with *Banco Nacional de Cuba v. Sabbatino* (1964), a case growing out of Cuba's decision to expropriate sugar owned by an American firm. The Cuban government transferred ownership of the sugar to its national bank, which arranged for its export and sale. Instead of paying the bank, however, the buyer paid the purchase price to original American owner. The Cuban bank sued in federal court for the value of the sugar, a winning claim if the bank had obtained good title to the sugar. The bank's title, in turn, depended on the legality of the Cuban expropriation under customary international law and the willingness of the district court to scrutinize the issue. Under the act of state doctrine, itself a creature of international law, courts may not examine the legality of the acts of a sovereign government taken within its own territory. If applicable, the doctrine would immunize the Cuban expropriation from judicial scrutiny, and clear the way for the bank to recover.

Although the lower court reached the issue and found that the expropriation violated customary international law, the Court held that the act of state doctrine applied. Justifying the conclusion proved more difficult. The Court acknowledged that the doctrine was compelled neither by the text of the Constitution nor by controlling principles of international law. Instead, the Court traced the act of state doctrine to constitutional structure and the separation of powers. In particular, the Court viewed the executive branch as primarily responsible for the formulation of foreign policy, and saw the judicial department as playing a relatively neutral role in the enforcement of legal claims. Emphasizing the need for nationally uniform judicial response in both state and federal court, the Court justified federal common law on practical terms.

As for the content of the rule, the Court worried that judicial scrutiny of the legality of an expropriation could upset diplomatic relations. It thus held that the courts of the United States would decline to scrutinize a taking of property by a sovereign government, and would simply apply standing legal principles, leaving the executive branch free to negotiate a different resolution if it saw fit. The Court's decision shows the imprint of Cold War considerations (as shaped by such events as the Bay of Pigs invasion and the Cuban missile crisis) and a practical recognition that the development of standards for measuring the legality of expropriations under international law was unlikely to succeed in an ideologically riven world.

The *Sabbatino* decision can be seen as relatively successful in explaining why state law could not control. Subsequent decisions have continued the trend of viewing the federal interest in foreign relations uniformity as preempting state law. Thus, in *Zschernig v. Miller* (1968), the Court found that federal common law preempted a state law that barred inheritance by foreign legatees unless the law of their country of origin extended reciprocal inheritance rights to US legatees. This regime of reciprocity was said to impair the effective exercise of foreign policy. Similarly, in *American Insurance Ass'n v. Garamendi* (2003), the Court considered the application of a California statute that required insurance companies to disclose information about any policies they sold in Europe during the period 1920–45. The avowed purpose of the disclosure regime was to generate information that Holocaust survivors and their dependents might use in attempting to recover compensation due under the terms of such policies, perhaps by pressuring or suing foreign governments. Again, the Court found that federal law preempted the state disclosure rule.

As for making an affirmative case for the proposition that federal common law incorporates customary international law, the *Sabbatino* decision has not been viewed as definitive. To be sure, leading commentators have often taken such an incorporation view, and it has since been enshrined in the Restatement (3d) of Foreign Relations Law. But critics have mounted a serious challenge to the claim, based both on an analysis of *Erie* and on their skepticism about the direction in which customary international law has evolved. See Bradley & Goldsmith (1997). Customary international law increasingly includes human rights norms, some of which conflict sharply with state laws on the use of the death penalty. Critics fear that application of such international principles could displace state control over criminal justice.

Similar questions concerning the scope of customary international law arose in connection with the interpretation of the alien tort statute (ATS), 28 U.S.C. § 1350, which provides the federal courts with jurisdiction to hear claims by an alien for a tort in violation of the law of nations. At the time of the statute's adoption in 1789, torts in violation of the law of nations included a fairly narrow range of misdeeds: violation of safe conducts, infringement of the rights of ambassadors, and piracy. Customary international law has grown some in the meantime. In the last generation, lower federal courts breathed new life into the ATS by treating it as the basis for recovery of damages for other violations of customary international law, such as torture. See *Filartiga v. Pena–Irala* (2d Cir. 1980). Congress lent important support with the passage of the Torture Victim Protection Act (TVPA), which allows an action for damages for torture or extra-judicial killing committed under color of the law of any foreign nation. Depending on the scope of customary international law, and the degree of federal judicial creativity in the fashioning of federal common law, the ATS could provide the foundation for a somewhat expansive judicial role.

The Court narrowed the scope of the judicial role in *Sosa v. Alvarez–Machain* (2004). The plaintiff, a Mexican citizen, brought suit in federal court, alleging that he had been abducted in Mexico and brought to the United States in violation of international norms governing lawful arrest and detention. The Court recognized that the ATS provided jurisdiction on the assumption that at least some torts in violation of the law of nations were actionable under the statute. In addition to the three listed above, the Court embraced the possibility that some additional tort claims might join the list if sufficiently well grounded in international norms. As for torture, the Court noted that Congress's enactment of the TVPA tended to confirm the result in *Filartiga* by supplementing it in considerable detail. But the plaintiff's claim of illegal arrest and detention did not qualify, despite the existence of sources of customary international law (such as the Universal Declaration of Human Rights and the International Covenant on Civil and Political Rights) that bore on the question. These sources were said to lack the specificity and universality necessary to give rise to federal common law obligations that would support a tort claim under the ATS.

6.7 Implied Rights of Action for Statutory Violations

Federal courts often face the question whether to recognize the existence of a cause of action to enforce certain rights that have their origin in federal law. Congress can, of course, create such rights of action itself, authorizing individuals to bring suit for a violation of the right in question. Thus, by enacting 42 U.S.C. § 1983, Congress empowered individuals to sue any person who violates their constitutional rights under color of state law. In such a case, the right has its origin in the Constitution, and the right of action can be considered an express or explicit creature of congressional action. In other cases, however, Congress might create a right and fail to create an express or explicit right of action. For example, in adopting the Civil Rights Act of 1964, as amended in 1972, Congress established a right on behalf of all persons to freedom from discrimination on the basis of sex and race in the operation of programs that receive federal funds. But Congress did not specify (as it had in section 1983) that any individual who suffers a violation of the nondiscrimination right can bring suit for appropriate relief. Congressional silence requires the courts to decide whether to recognize an "implied" right of action, or what might be called a judge-made right to sue in federal court to enforce the right in question. (Note the language; the act of judicial recognition would normally be described as an *inference* drawn from congressional action. But the courts prefer to speak of *implied* rights of action, as if the establishment of a right implies the existence of a right of action. Referring to an implied right of action makes the judicial role sound less creative or active.)

Beginning in the 1960s, the Court expressed a certain willingness to recognize implied or judge-made rights of action. Under the prevailing standard of that day, the federal courts were to consider four factors in deciding whether to permit a private party to sue for the violation of a federal right. See *Cort v. Ash* (1975). These factors were whether the statute was enacted for the benefit of a special class of persons that includes the plaintiff; whether the legislative history of the statute sheds light on the question of a private remedy; whether a private action would frustrate some feature of the statutory scheme; and whether the recognition of an action would intrude into an area of basic concern to the states.

Applying such factors, the federal courts recognized a number of implied rights of action, especially in the securities and civil rights arenas. For example, in *Cannon v. University of Chicago* (1979), the Court recognized an implied federal right of action to enforce the provision in title IX that "no person shall, on the basis of sex, be excluded from participation" in an educational program that receives federal funds. The Court found that the right in question, freedom from discrimination on the basis of sex, operated for the special benefit of women in the position of Ms. Cannon. This, coupled with its assessment of the other factors, persuaded the Court to recognize a private right to sue.

At least in theory, other options may have been available to enforce the right in question. As we have already seen, Congress will sometimes create a federal right in the expectation that the state courts will enforce the right through common law causes of action. In such a situation, the federal right may be taken up as an ingredient of the state law action. (If so, federal question jurisdiction may extend to the claim. Chapter 5 discusses the jurisdictional issue and the leading cases, *Merrell Dow v. Thompson* (1986) and *Grable & Sons v. Darue Engineering* (2005)). Alternatively, Congress may create a federal agency and charge the agency with enforcing the right in question. For example, in the *Cannon* case, federal law had given the responsible agency the right to deny federal funds to any entity that was found to have violated the prohibition against sex discrimination. Depending on the statute, one might conclude that Congress meant such an agency remedy to serve as the only remedy for a violation of the federal standard. Such agency exclusivity might counsel against the recognition of an implied federal right of action, just as it might preempt any private state law remedy. The various tools for the enforcement of a federal right—a private federal right of action (as in *Cannon*), a private state right of action, and an agency remedy of some sort—explain why analysis of remedial options must pay close attention to the statute and the intent of Congress.

Since the *Cannon* decision, the Court has been far more reluctant to recognize implied rights of action. The trend began in *Cannon* itself, with the issuance of Justice Powell's dissenting opinion. Powell argued that the business of creating rights of action to enforce federal rights was properly left to Congress, and was not a proper task for the judicial branch. The claim rested in equal measure on an argument that courts lacked the tools necessary to fashion rights of action, and on the claim that doing so might disrupt the legislative process. For Powell, plaintiffs in the position of *Cannon* had simply failed to obtain the necessary legislative authorization for their federal claims, and should be remitted to Congress to secure it. Similarly, defendants may have lobbied to defeat the legislative adoption of any express provision for suit and now faced judge-made suits nonetheless. Judicial recognition of private rights of action was thus said to denigrate the legislative process. On this view, the legislative process operates as a forum for the clash of competing interest groups; judicial recognition may award an interest group something it lacked the clout to obtain from Congress.

The rise of textualism as a mode of statutory interpretation has lent additional force to Powell's critique of implied rights of action. Textualists like Justice Scalia view the use of legislative history with great suspicion, and rely instead on the text of the statute as the primary focus of the interpretive process. For textualists, the idea of an implied right of action makes no sense. Congress may include such a right of action in the text of the statute or not as it sees fit; federal courts cannot add a right of action that Congress has omitted. Strong textualists thus go beyond Powell, who recognized in his *Cannon* dissent that particularly persuasive evidence of legislative history might give rise to an implied right of action. Thus, in *Alexander v. Sandoval* (2001), with Justice Scalia writing the majority opinion, the Court took the view that the creation of rights of action, like other elements of substantive federal law, was a task for Congress, and not one for federal courts. "Raising up causes of action ... may be a proper function for common-law courts, but not for federal tribunals." The *Sandoval* Court refused to approve an implied right of action to challenge discriminatory practices that excluded a disproportionate number of minorities from participation in a federally funded program. (The Court reaffirmed the right of action in *Cannon* for intentional discrimination, but ruled out private claims on the theory of disparate impact.)

Despite the Court's embrace of the anti-implication views of Justice Powell, one can fairly question the claim that judicial recognition of an implied right of action will invariably interfere with the legislative process. Legislation gets written against the backdrop of the rules of interpretation followed in the federal courts at the time of enactment. A background rule against the judicial recognition of implied rights of action notifies all actors in the legislative process that the parties seeking to obtain private federal judicial enforcement must obtain an explicit provision to that effect in the statute. (For example, supporters of the Americans with Disabilities Act, which became law in 1991, may well have understood that private enforcement would depend on their securing an explicit right to sue.) Such an interpretive rule allocates the risk of legislative silence to the proponents.

A different interpretive rule need not disable the legislative process; it simply reverses the background rule. In the world of

Cort v. Ash, where the federal courts were willing to imply rights of action, opponents of legislation presumably knew that they must either block the legislative recognition of a right or obtain explicit language in the statute foreclosing the enforcement of a new right through private federal suit. (This explains why some members of the majority in *Cannon* stressed that the law had been enacted at a time when the federal courts were willing to imply rights of action; participants in the legislative process presumably understood the likely implications of the legislative creation of the federal right in question and opponents were on notice that the right's creation could give rise to private enforcement actions.) Under either interpretive approach, in sum, interest groups can fairly contend for the outcome they prefer. Justice Powell's portrait of implied rights of action as an affront to the legislative process seems overblown.

Once we recognize that neither approach, consistently applied, will disable the legislative process, we can consider issues of comparative institutional competence. In other words, the decision about implication of rights of action might turn on which branch— the legislative or the judicial—can best determine how to fit the enforcement of new federal rights into the overall scheme of state and federal law. Justice Powell assumes that Congress does a better job, and so assigns the task to the legislature. But Congress may not foresee the many circumstances in which disputes over the enforcement of a federal right may arise. As we have seen, the state courts may take up a federal right and make it enforceable as an element of a state cause of action. Alternatively, Congress may create a federal agency with some responsibility for the enforcement of a federal right. Courts must determine whether agency enforcement excludes private enforcement, and whether private enforcement should proceed in state or federal court. All such determinations will influence what we might call the remedial potency or salience of the federal right, and one can argue that courts have traditionally considered such issues as part of the law of remedies.

Indeed, the Court appeared to embrace such the arguments for judicial competence in *Franklin v. Gwinnett County Public Schools* (1992). There, the Court faced the question whether the private right of action recognized in *Cannon* as applied to a claim of sexual harassment would support an action for money damages, in addition to an action for injunctive relief. The federal government, as amicus, argued that Justice Powell's approach to judicial implication required that federal courts decline to recognize a damages remedy except in circumstances where Congress had expressly authorized one. The Court unanimously rejected the argument. Once a private right of action exists (whether by congressional creation or judicial implication), the general rule was said to be that the federal courts have the power to award any appropriate relief, "absent a clear direction to the contrary by Congress." In *Franklin*, then, the Court adopted the view that Congress may exclude a damages remedy by legislative text or implication, but need not expressly authorize such a remedy in order for courts to award the remedy in an appropriate case. A similar approach to private rights of action would leave Congress in charge of the creation of federal rights, and recognize that federal courts may recognize rights of action to make such rights effective, absent a clear direction to the contrary.

Just as the Court has reaffirmed its exercise of remedial discretion against arguments for deference to Congress, so too has it continued to treat issues relating to the preemption of state remedies as a matter for judicial determination. Consider the preemption problems presented by the federal law that required warning labels on boxes of cigarettes. Congress may not have foreseen the rise of products liability litigation at the time it created a "right" to such labels; it certainly included nothing in its federal warning law that addressed the degree to which federal warnings would displace state tort claims for personal injuries resulting from cigarette warnings that state courts judged to be inadequate. Despite congressional silence, the Supreme Court ruled that the federal warning law preempted state tort remedies for smoking-related injuries, except in situations involving relatively gross misconduct. See *Cipollone v. Liggett Group* (1992).

A textualist might argue that federal courts should deny preemptive effect to a federal statute except in circumstances in which Congress says by clear text or overwhelming implication that preemption must follow. Indeed, Congress sometimes includes language in a statute that purports to specify its preemptive effect. But neither Justice Scalia nor the Court has adopted a broad prohibition against the judicial determination of preemption issues. But Justice Thomas has expressed precisely that view. In *Wyeth v. Levine* (2009), the Court faced a preemption question that grew out of Congress's adoption of the Food Drug and Cosmetic Act (FDCA). The plaintiff, a violinist, received an improper injection of a drug, developed gangrene, and eventually had her arm amputated. The drug company argued that her successful state law claim for improper warning labels on the drug in question was preempted by the federal scheme, which explicitly regulated the content of warning labels. In concurring with the majority's rejection of the preemption claim, Justice Thomas gave voice to the textualist argument. Preemption was proper, he argued, only when Congress said so.

While Justice Thomas deserves credit for consistency, his textualist view might be consistently wrong. Strict insistence on textual clarity for every question under a statute may disable Congress just as surely as unprincipled interpretive modifications of a federal statute. Congress may not anticipate the specific conflicts that later arise, as the law continues to evolve in the wake of an enactment. Sometimes, Congress cannot reach agreement on the resolution of questions it does anticipate. If courts can help with preemption issues that Congress did not resolve, it makes little sense to assign the task to Congress through a clear-statement rule.

6.8　Implied Rights of Action for Constitutional Violations

Most observers agree that the federal courts have greater freedom to recognize implied rights of action when the right in question originates not in a federal statute but in the Constitution itself. One can understand this broader judicial role as resting upon a variety of possible foundations. For one thing, the Constitution was adopted on the assumption that an existing body of common law rights and remedies would be available in the state and, perhaps, lower federal courts to make its provisions effective. Perhaps this presumed availability of common law remediation explains why the Constitution itself says very little about the sorts of remedies it has in mind for the violation of constitutional rights. Article I's justly famous reference to habeas corpus assumes the existence of a functioning common law writ, and simply protects against its suspension except in times of rebellion or invasion. Similarly, the Fifth Amendment's reference to payment of just compensation for the government's taking of property does not specify the judicial mechanism, if any, by which the justness of such payments shall be assessed or the payment be compelled.

In addition to the presumed availability of common law remedies, the distinctive role of Article III courts in our scheme of government provides support for judicial implication of constitutional remedies. *Marbury v. Madison* claims a role for the Article III courts in making constitutional rights and government restrictions effective through the litigation process. So long as the federal courts retain their role in enforcing constitutional rights against the political branches of government, the courts may sensibly claim some freedom to make such enforcement effective through the recognition of implied rights of action. Otherwise, the political branches might defeat constitutional limits by declining to adopt (or by repealing) the laws needed for their judicial enforcement. Judicial independence in the enforcement of the Constitution may thus necessitate a degree of judicial creativity in the development of appropriate remedies. Statutory rights, by contrast, often depend entirely on legislative action, and may be qualified or strengthened as Congress sees fit. A more modest judicial role may be appropriate in such a context.

One can see both the presumed availability of common law remedies and the perceived need to provide a judicial remedy for unconstitutional action at work in leading cases on the implication of rights of action for constitutional violations. Consider *Ward v. Love County* (1920), an action in state court to secure a refund of state taxes that the plaintiffs had paid under a threat by the state that a failure to pay would result in foreclosure sales of their property. The Court had previously ruled that the taxes violated the federal Constitution by taxing property that a federal statute had lawfully immunized from state taxation. At issue was the plaintiffs' right to a remedy in the face of the state court's finding that they had paid the taxes voluntarily and lacked any right to recover them back. At common law, individuals had a right to bring suit to recover back the value of government exactions and taxes paid under protest by suit against the collecting officer. The Court in *Love County* found that something similar must be made available as a remedy for the plaintiffs. "As the payment was not voluntary, but made under compulsion, no statutory authority was essential to enable or require the county to refund the money." The reference to the absence of any need for statutory authorization indicates that the Court viewed the obligation as constitutionally compelled.

Constitutional compulsion also seems to underlie more recent tax refund decisions. In *McKesson Corp. v. Division of ABT* (1990), the Court held that a state court must afford a litigant a meaningful opportunity to obtain a refund of taxes paid under protest by a party who claimed that the tax violated the dormant Commerce Clause. The Court grounded the state's obligation in Fourteenth Amendment due process, but the case was complicated by the fact that the state had required the litigant to pay first and litigate later. Similarly, in *Reich v. Collins* (1994), the Court held that due process requires that states afford a litigant a "clear and certain" remedy for taxes collected in violation of federal law. The Court acknowledged that either pre-deprivation relief (injunctive and declaratory relief) or post-deprivation relief (damages) would suffice. A later case may limit the force of these decisions by suggesting that they require the availability of a damages remedy in state court only where the state has held out such a remedy in collecting taxes and later ruled that such a remedy does not exist. See *Alden v. Maine* (1999).

Apart from holding that state courts owe a constitutional obligation to make remedies available for certain constitutional violations, the Court has also recognized the existence of an implied federal right of action for damages for certain constitutional torts. Such an action has come to be known as a *Bivens* claim, after the leading case, *Bivens v. Six Unknown Named Agents of the Federal Bureau of Narcotics* (1971). A *Bivens* claim arises under federal law for jurisdictional purposes, and alleges a constitutional violation by *federal* officers. (When *state* officials are alleged to have committed constitutional torts, section 1983 provides an express right of action and eliminates the need for any implied right of action. Section 1983, a Reconstruction-era statute, makes no provision for suit against federal officials.) *Bivens* thus provides an important example of the Court's willingness to create the rights of action needed to enforce the Constitution.

The circumstances of the *Bivens* case vividly illustrate the need for such a remedy. Agents of the federal bureau entered his house without a warrant, arrested Mr. Bivens on narcotics charges, and searched the premises. After handcuffing him, the agents took him to a station house in Brooklyn, NY where he was booked and subjected to a strip search. Ultimately, the drug charges were dismissed. The circumstances thus denied Mr. Bivens any obvious way to challenge the constitutionality of the agents' actions. Had he been charged with a crime, he could have moved to suppress the evidence as having been obtained in violation of the Constitution. Had he known of the proposed raid on his house in advance, he might have brought an action for injunctive and declaratory relief. Had the officials been state officers, Mr. Bivens could have sued under section 1983. None of these avenues were available.

One alternative remained. Bivens could sue for damages in tort under the law of New York. Much of what government does, from searches and seizures to the taking of property to satisfy a tax obligation, would (unless justified) be considered a tort at common law. Individuals who wished to challenge government action in the nineteenth century would often file a trespass action, perhaps coupled with claims of assault, battery, or false imprisonment. In the course of such litigation, courts would often consider whether the government officer acted within the boundaries of law and applicable constitutional limits. Such litigation would enable the common law courts to reach the constitutional issue, and to award damages against the responsible officer in cases of constitutional violation. (*Osborn v. Bank of the United States* (1824) provides one example of such officer suit litigation, although the bank in that case sought injunctive relief from state officers.) In the *Bivens* case, the government contended that such a common law claim in state court provided the only remedy. Although it candidly admitted that it would remove such an action to federal court (invoking the federal officer's removal statute), the government argued against the recognition of an implied right of action that would enable Mr. Bivens to bring suit in federal court in the first instance.

Rather than remitting Mr. Bivens to his state common law remedy, the Court found that the Fourth Amendment itself gave rise to an implied federal right of action. The Court noted the potential mismatch between the official conduct that the Fourth Amendment prohibits and the scope of conduct made actionable by a common law trespass action. Before *Erie*, such a mismatch would have presented less of a problem; indeed, in *Osborn*, the Court shaped the Bank's right to injunctive relief against trespass to ensure that the legal regime adequately protected the federal interest. After *Erie*, and the loss of federal control over common law rights of action, the Court could no longer assume the power to reshape common law claims. The Court also considered the surrounding legislative framework, and found "no special factors counseling hesitation." In particular, the Court noted that, while Congress had not in so many words authorized the claim (as it had suits against state officials), neither had it explicitly prohibited the remedy.

A much admired concurring opinion by Justice Harlan elaborated on the justification for recognizing an implied right of action. Justice Harlan noted that the right in question derived from federal law, and did not depend on state considerations. He also rejected the claim that the federal courts were barred from recognizing a right to sue in the absence of express congressional authority. In part, Harlan drew on then-recent (and now discredited) decisions recognizing implied rights of action in the statutory context. But Harlan placed greater weight on the acknowledged existence of a right to seek equitable relief from unconstitutional government action. Harlan found that the right to sue *already existed* and the only question was one of whether the range of appropriate remedies included an action for damages. (Harlan thus framed the issue somewhat the way the Court framed the issue in the statutory case of *Franklin v. Gwinnett County Public Schools*, above.) On that issue, Harlan argued that the range of policy considerations for the courts to consider was at least as broad as those a legislature would consider. Harlan placed special emphasis on the absence of an effective equitable remedy, noting that for people in Mr. Bivens' shoes, it is "damages or nothing."

Although the dissenting justices expressed concern with the docket impact of recognizing this new right of action, they also challenged the propriety of doing so without legislative authority. Justice Black, for example, cited the example of section 1983 in arguing that Congress had authorized similar rights of action in the past, at least for state official misconduct. But one can question the relevance of the section 1983 example. While the failure of

Congress to address federal official misconduct may have reflected a judgment that nineteenth century state court remedies were adequate, it may have also reflected a desire to protect the federal fisc and federal employees. Congress may be less inclined to provide monetary remedies for federal misconduct if it will eventually confront an obligation to pay any such judgments. The prospect of such payments was not purely theoretical; even though the federal government retained its sovereign immunity from direct suit in such matters, Congress often agreed to pay certain tort judgments by way of a private bill that indemnified officers for their losses. See Pfander & Hunt (2010).

Self-interested motives on the part of Congress may help justify a judicial role in fashioning a remedy that Congress deliberately omitted. Consider the *post-Bivens* decision in *Davis v. Passman* (1979). There, the plaintiff brought suit against a former member of Congress after losing her job due to what she alleged was sex discrimination. The relevant federal statute, Title VII of the Civil Rights Act of 1964, covered discrimination on the basis of sex, and applied to certain federal employees, but deliberately excluded the personal staff of Congress from its coverage. Nonetheless, the Court found that the plaintiff could pursue a private claim directly under the equal protection component of the Fifth Amendment. (Although the equal protection clause of the Fourteenth Amendment applies only to the states, the Court had previously held in *Bolling v. Sharpe* (1954) that due process imposes similar limits on the federal government.) The Court treated the availability of a right of action as more or less presumptive in the wake of *Bivens*, and did not view the omission from Title VII as a special factor counseling hesitation. A similar, matter of fact extension of *Bivens* to claims for cruel and unusual punishment followed in *Carlson v. Green* (1980).

More recent decisions take a narrower view of the availability of a *Bivens* remedy (just as the Court has more recently cut back on the implication of private suits for statutory violations). Some of the more restrictive decisions emphasize the availability of alternative remedies as special factors counseling hesitation. In *Bush v. Lucas* (1983), a federal employee sought damages for a violation of his first amendment rights. The Court declined to permit such an action, pointing to the fairly elaborate administrative protections that civil service employees enjoy under federal law. Similarly, in *Schweiker v. Chilicky* (1988), the Court declined to permit a claimant to challenge the denial of disability benefits under the Social Security Act as a violation of due process. Again, the Court found administrative remedies for a denial of benefits to be adequate, even though they did not duplicate the remedies that would have been available through a *Bivens* claim.

Other decisions deny a *Bivens* remedy, even in the absence of an effective alternative. In *Chappell v. Wallace* (1983), the Court refused to permit enlisted men to sue their commanding officers for racial discrimination in the US Navy. Such litigation would interfere with the disciplinary structure of the military, and disrupt the comprehensive (but not necessarily effective) system for the adjustment of military grievances. In *United States v. Stanley* (1987), a former member of the Army brought suit for damages, alleging that he had been given experimental doses of LSD without his knowledge or consent. Again, the Court found that the military setting created "special factors" that required denial of the claim. While the plaintiff may have been entitled to some medical care as a veteran, the Army offered no system of compensation for people in the plaintiff's position.

These cases, and other more recent decisions, suggest that the Court will think long and hard before expanding the range of constitutional provisions that individuals can enforce through *Bivens* claims. In *Wilkie v. Robbins* (2007), for example, the Court voiced continuing *Bivens* skepticism. There, the plaintiff resisted Interior department requests for an easement across his land. Government officials responded by taking a series of retaliatory actions, aptly described as death by a thousand cuts. While some of the particular actions were subject to administrative review, applicable law provided no remedy for what the plaintiff characterized as retaliation aimed at undermining his Fifth Amendment right to freedom from an uncompensated taking of his property. The Court first evaluated alternative remedies and assumed the viability of state common law remedies for some of the conduct at issue. See also *Correctional Servs. Corp. v. Malesko* (2001) (assuming existence of state tort remedies against private firm that operated a prison under contract with the federal government). Next, the Court considered the wisdom of extending constitutional litigation into a new arena, one that it characterized as the highly contentious world of federal government land negotiations. It decided that the courts should stay out, and thus rejected the *Bivens* claim. See also *Ashcroft v. Iqbal* (2009) (treating as an open question the availability of a *Bivens* remedy for detention policies said to discriminate on the basis of national origin and religious affiliation in violation of the First and Fifth Amendments).

The *Bivens* line of cases has inspired much head-scratching on the part of constitutional theorists. Although the cases that authorize a remedy draw their inspiration from the Constitution, the more restrictive later decisions suggest that the Constitution does not inflexibly require a *Bivens*-style remedy in every case. How then can we account for the disparity in treatment of various claims? Some contend that the Constitution should be regarded as affording individuals an opportunity to recover damages for every violation of their rights, invoking Marshall's dictum in *Marbury* to the effect that there must be a remedy for every wrong. See Amar (1987). Others argue that remedial law should be seen as creating a sub-constitutional body of "constitutional common law." See Monaghan (1975). On such a view, the remedial law operates less as a matter of constitutional obligation than as a body of federal common law rules, inspired by the Constitution but subject (like other bodies of federal common law) to judicial and congressional modification in appropriate cases.

In an important contribution to this literature, two scholars argue that the law of constitutional remedies does not and cannot afford a remedy for every constitutional violation. See Fallon & Meltzer (1991). Rather, the law sets out to keep the government mostly within the bounds of the law, most of the time. Fallon & Meltzer note an array of doctrines (apart from the limits of the *Bivens* remedy) that prevent the ideal of completely effective individual remediation from ever being achieved. Prominent among these doctrines are the rules of sovereign immunity (which bars suit against the government, except in accordance with its consent) and official immunity (which shields an officer from liability in tort, so long as the action does not violate clearly established law). But other remedies come into play to supplement the suit for damages, including the action for injunctive and declaratory relief, the motion to suppress unlawfully obtained evidence, and the invocation of federal constitutional law as a defense to the imposition of criminal and civil liability. According to Fallon & Meltzer, this web of remedies may effectively constrain government, even if particular remedies fail in particular cases.

While the Fallon & Meltzer paper captures an important truth about the need to think systemically about constitutional remediation, one can question some of its assumptions. For starters, the doctrine of sovereign immunity provides scant support for the assumption that some kinds of constitutional violations may go unredressed. Consider a federal benefit program, like Social Security. While the government has no obligation to establish a benefit program or to allow itself to be sued for benefits due, it cannot establish such a program on terms that violate the Constitution. Thus, a program that discriminates on the basis of race or sex would be subject to judicial invalidation. Congress could not sidestep such invalidation by simply proclaiming that it intended to retain its sovereign immunity with respect to such claims. See *Bartlett v. Bowen* (D.C. Cir. 1987). The presumptive viability of constitutional claims also argues for a more capacious conception of the availability of the *Bivens* action. Not only has Congress taken steps to preserve the action from displacement by the Federal Tort

Claims Act and Westfall Act, in many cases the *Bivens* action provides the only mode by which an individual can test allegedly unconstitutional government conduct. For many victims of government misconduct, as Justice Harlan recognized in Bivens, it has been damages or nothing. Now, with the adoption of the Westfall Act in 1988, Congress has displaced state common law suits against federal officials and eliminated a mainstay of federal government accountability. For many folks seeking a constitutional remedy, we now live in a world in which it's *"Bivens* or nothing." See Pfander & Baltmanis (2009).

6.9 Self–Enforcing Treaties

The Supremacy Clause of the Constitution expressly includes treaties as part of supreme federal law and requires state courts to give them effect notwithstanding anything to the contrary in state law. By giving treaties binding force in the domestic legal order, the Constitution departed from the treaty-enforcement model in Great Britain, where treaties were negotiated and signed by the Crown but took effect only after the adoption of implementing legislation by Parliament. Early decisions nicely illustrate how the regime of self-enforcement operated. But recent developments suggest that the notion of the self-enforcing treaty might not survive in a world where the proliferation of international agreements produces a growing number of conflicts with strongly held views about local policy. In these recent cases, federal (and state) courts face familiar questions about how far they should go in fashioning law to effectuate treaty obligations without first obtaining guidance from Congress.

In the early republic period, the Supreme Court had little doubt about the enforceability of federal treaty obligations, even those that were most unpopular. In Clause 4 of the Treaty of Peace of 1783, the United States agreed with Great Britain that creditors on both sides would meet with no lawful impediment to the enforcement of the obligations of their debtors in hard currency. While this provision was nominally even-handed, the creditors were predominantly English and the debtors were predominantly American. The Constitution was framed against the backdrop of this obligation; the Supremacy Clause encompasses all federal treaties, including treaties that had taken effect before the Constitution became law in 1788. In addition, the judicial article provides for jurisdiction over controversies between English subjects and American citizens, thus transferring debt litigation to the federal system. Southern states looked with some suspicion on these provisions; state legislatures had allowed their debtors to discharge these debts during the Revolutionary War by making substitute payments to the state treasuries with depreciated money. The combined force of the Treaty and Article III threatened to revive these old (and possibly discharged) debts and make them payable in specie.

In *Ware v. Hylton* (1796), the Court addressed the impact of the 1783 Treaty on the right of British creditors. It concluded that the Treaty invalidated state laws that would impede the collection of the debts, including laws that were enacted prior to the adoption of the Treaty. While the Court acknowledged that some treaties were addressed to the legislative and executive branches of the government, others were specifically addressed to the judicial branch. The provisions in Clause 4, invalidating impediments to British debt-collection, were clearly addressed to the judicial branch and they controlled. The combination of the creditors' common law right to recover their debts and the Treaty's invalidation of state impediments to recovery meant that the actions were viable without any need for implementing legislation by Congress.

Not all treaties enjoy this self-executing quality. (Indeed, one can question whether the Treaty of 1783 can be fairly described as self-executing; after all, it took the adoption of the Constitution with its supremacy clause and its provision for jurisdiction over the claims of British creditors to make its guarantees effective.) Some treaties, for example, contemplate the payment of money from the treasury; these require an appropriation bill. As the appropriation example illustrates, treaties impose obligations on the political branches that may not be judicially enforceable. In a useful summary, Professor Vazquez has identified the following four situations in which treaties require further action:

1) The parties intended that legislation would be adopted to effectuate treaty

2) The treaty norm was addressed to the legislature

3) The Constitution requires a statute (or constitutional amendment) to effectuate the treaty

4) The plaintiff has a right under the treaty but lacks a private right of action.

Vazquez (2008). Deciding in any particular case whether a treaty creates rights enforceable without further legislation can present the same ticklish problems of interpretation that we have encountered elsewhere in this chapter.

The Court's decision in *Medellin v. Texas* (2008) illustrates the ticklish quality of the interpretive process. Medellin, a Mexican national, had been sentenced to death in Texas state court. On review, he challenged the failure of Texas to afford him his right to a consular visit as required by the Vienna convention to which both the United States and Mexico were parties. Texas refused to reach the merits, asserting that the claim had been procedurally defaulted by virtue of Medellin's failure to raise it at trial. Then, Mexico espoused (or took on as its own) the claim of Medellin and others, and brought suit against the United States before the International Court of Justice. The ICJ ruled that the treaty obliged the United States to afford Medellin (and others) an opportunity to press consular claims without regard to any default. The Bush administration responded to this decree by directing the Texas state courts to revisit Medellin's case. (It also withdrew the United States from the relevant treaty, thus depriving the ICJ of compulsory jurisdiction over such claims in the future.) Texas refused to reconsider the death sentence and the case went to the Supreme Court.

The case presented the Court with a difficult set of problems. It had previously ruled that the consular convention did not create rights in Mexican nationals that overrode procedural defaults. The ICJ had, in a sense, rejected that decision. But the ICJ's decision did not involve a direct reversal; foreign courts do not sit as a court of errors to review decisions of the Supreme Court. Rather, the ICJ judgment came in a case involving the United States and Mexico and did not occasion any direct consideration of the claims of individuals. As a result, the ICJ judgment established that the US, as a nation, owed an obligation to respect consular rights but it did not specify how that obligation was to be effectuated. The relevant treaty language said that the US "undertakes" to comply with ICJ judgments. One might read that language (as the dissent did) to indicate that the US owes an existing obligation enforceable in judicial proceedings. For the majority, in contrast, the language was seen as contemplating the taking of future steps to ensure compliance. As a result, the judgment was not self-executing but required the adoption of implementing legislation. (In an interesting aside, the Court also refused to give any binding legal effect to the President's directive to the state courts; such directives were not law.)

The Court's approach views the treaty itself as the best source of information about whether its obligations should be regarded as self-executing. The treaty, in this instance, was notably silent about the judicial enforcement of ICJ judgments. In effect, then, the Court has created a regime of presumptive non-self execution that can be overcome either by treaty language or by the passage of implementing legislation. Such an approach should help to protect decisions of the courts of the United States from the influence (seen as corrupting in some circles) of international adjudication. (Indeed, Chief Justice Roberts' opinion in *Medellin* sounded themes of judicial self-protection in invoking the Court's power to explicate federal law.) By temporizing, the Court could refrain from incorporating international views of the death penalty into its habeas jurisprudence. Yet one might question (as the dissent did) the effectiveness of the political branches, as an institutional matter, in fashioning a regime for the effective enforcement of ICJ judgments.

Chapter Seven

GOVERNMENT ACCOUNTABILITY

7.1 Introduction

Chief Justice Marshall issued a famous dictum in *Marbury v. Madison* (1803), proclaiming that the essence of civil liberty consists of the right of an individual to claim the protection of the laws "whenever he receives an injury." This broad assurance of remediation was thought to extend to rights that individuals held against the government. While Marshall disclaimed any general power to oversee the executive branch, he reaffirmed the importance of individual rights and portrayed the courts as the instrument through which such rights were to be enforced.

Despite Marshall's proclamation, however, *Marbury's* vested legal right to his position as a justice of the peace was not enforced, and he had to look for work elsewhere. Similar gaps in the regime of government accountability developed during the nineteenth and twentieth centuries, as our inherited system of common law remedies interacted with jurisdictional limitations to foreclose remedies in a range of cases. Some of the jurisdictional gaps resulted from judicial interpretation, as with the denial of jurisdiction in *Marbury* itself. Others resulted from legislative decisions, such as Congress's failure to confer federal question jurisdiction (until 1875) or to create a mechanism for the judicial determination of claims against the federal government (until 1855). As a result, some divergence has always existed between the rhetoric of assured remediation in *Marbury*, and the reality of rights-enforcement in the courts.

Beginning with the New Deal, Congress has steadily expanded government accountability by adopting statutes that provide for judicial enforcement of the rights of individuals. Most of the organic statutes that created new administrative agencies during the New Deal (such as the National Labor Relations Act) made explicit provision for federal judicial review of agency action. Eventually, this presumptive availability of judicial review made its way into the Administrative Procedure Act, a cornerstone of government accountability and the focus of law school classes on administrative law. In addition to provisions for judicial review of agency action, Congress adopted the Federal Tort Claims Act (FTCA), allowing individuals to bring tort claims against the federal government.   Before the FTCA, individuals could sue only the officials themselves, and had no remedy against the government.   Similar statutes allow individuals to bring breach of contract claims and quiet title actions against the federal government.

Developments at the state level parallel those at the federal level.   State legislatures have authorized state courts to hear tort claims against the state, they have created state administrative agencies and subjected them to judicial review, and they have established courts of claims to hear individual contract and property claims against state government.   In many garden variety situations, this body of state law provides individuals with a reasonable chance to enforce their rights.   Although a few states retain their immunity from suit on state law claims, such as contract or property claims, most permit individuals to seek ordinary remedies in state court.

As a consequence, much of the attention in discussions of government accountability focuses on the ability of individuals to enforce their constitutional and federal statutory rights.   Inevitably, such enforcement actions blend together issues of jurisdiction and remediation with issues of what substantive rights the individuals actually enjoy under federal law.   The issues grow especially contentious when individuals bring suit against the states in federal court to enforce federal rights.   Such litigation has occupied the Supreme Court for much of the last generation, and has led to an expansive and controversial conception of the states' sovereign immunity from suit under the Eleventh Amendment.

This chapter explores the remedial tools available to individuals who seek to enforce their federal rights.   It begins by sketching the common law remedial system, which did a fair job of securing government accountability in certain areas (trespass actions against responsible officials) and functioned rather poorly in others (contract and property claims against the government).   It then considers modern rules of government accountability as they apply to the federal government.   Finally, it takes up the range of actions available against the state governments.

7.2   Common Law Foundations of Remedies Against the Government

For two related reasons, our analysis of government accountability begins with an overview of the common law remedial framework of the late eighteenth and early nineteenth centuries.   First, the Constitution says very little about judicial remedies for government wrongdoing.   Instead, the document assumes that common law actions would secure the enforcement of the new constitutional limits on government power.   One can see this presumptive reliance on common law remedies in the judicial article itself, and in the sparseness of remedial references in the Constitution. Article III invests federal courts with "judicial power" to decide specified "cases and controversies" and extends jurisdiction to controversies involving the United States, foreign nations, and the states. But Article III does not necessarily require Congress to provide the federal courts with jurisdiction over suits against government bodies and officials, and thus leaves open the question of how individuals may enforce rights against government actors. (Chapter 10 returns to the question of congressional control over the jurisdiction of the federal courts.) The common law framework best explains government accountability assumptions that the framers left unspoken.

Second, the common law scheme provides a baseline with which one can understand and assess the sufficiency of our current system of government accountability. Over the past two centuries, Congress has built upon or superseded common law remedies in many instances by enacting statutory provisions for suit against the government. These statutory schemes respond to perceived problems with the common law approach. More subtly, one can assess the sufficiency of the new statutory framework by considering it in comparison to the remedies available at common law. Although the rhetoric of sovereign immunity suggests that Congress can freely withhold remedies against the federal government, the common law tradition provides a basis on which the federal courts might claim remedial authority in the absence of explicit legislative authorization. Gaps in the statutory scheme may lead to the revival of common law remedies, rather than a denial of all relief.

7.2.1 Actions Against the Government Itself

At common law, individuals who wished to initiate an action would select one of the many forms of action (trespass, assumpsit, debt) as the predicate for their claim for relief. Proceedings often began with the arrest of the defendant, who was held in jail by the sheriff or the marshal until bond was posted. But such actions could not proceed at common law against the government, which was identified in various ways with the personal authority of the king or queen. The idea of the "Crown" came to embody both the king or queen as an individual and royal government as a whole; the maxim "the king can do no wrong" reflected the simple but profound fact that litigants could not name the king or queen as a defendant in the courts at Westminster and could not have them arrested or served with process. This immunity from suit came to be known as "sovereign immunity."

Sovereign immunity could lead to grave injustice, as when litigants held rights in property or contract against the Crown and had no way to assert those rights in court. With typical ingenuity, the common law developed a fictional solution. Instead of naming the Crown in a coercive action brought before the common law courts, litigants could bring their suit by filing a "petition of right" in Chancery. Subjects of the Crown had long enjoyed a right to petition for a redress of their grievances, and petitions might request anything from the passage of favorable legislation, to the grant of royal lands or titles. The common law thus conceptualized the petition of right as a non-coercive process (one that did not involve the arrest of the defendant) that enabled the petitioner to press a claim founded upon a legal right. If the Crown allowed the petition, then the action proceeded to trial against the government on common law principles.

By Blackstone's day, the petition of right was described as a relatively routine legal process through which individuals could secure legal rights in litigation with the government. Although the petition of right might appear to invoke the sovereign's grace or pleasure, it had become conventional for the government to grant leave to litigate anytime the claim appeared to be well grounded in law. To supplement the petition of right, Parliament adopted a range of statutory proceedings that enabled individuals more readily to interplead with the government. As a consequence, remedies against the Crown developed as a body of law somewhat separate from the common law forms of action that governed litigation between individuals. See Pfander (1997). Recent scholarship suggests, moreover, that Parliament had established relatively complete control over the payment of money claims, rendering the remedy by petition of right more theoretical than real. See Figley & Tidmarsh (2009).

The absence of a common law remedy against the government left its mark on the practice of Britain's North American colonies. Money claims against the colonial governments were typically handled through a process of legislative petitioning. Individuals would petition the assembly for the payment of certain funds, and the claims were assigned to a committee on petitions that served somewhat like an adjudicative body in assessing the claim and recommending payment. If the assembly agreed with the committee's report, it would vote an appropriation to pay the claim in question. Claims against the government thus inevitably implicated the power over the purse and the acknowledged constitutional reality that the payment of money from the treasury required action by the assembly. The tradition of legislative control over the appropriations process, coupled with a distrust of royal judges, helps to explain why colonial assemblies tended to retain control over claims against the government. It was not an argument against government accountability but one for the primacy of the assembly in passing upon the claim and determining the extent of any payment. See Desan (1998).

7.2.2 Actions Against Government Officials

In contrast to its failure to develop a form of action for claims against the government (aside from the petition of right), the common law regarded its forms of action as readily adaptable to suits against government officers. Perhaps the two most important such actions were the trespass action, and the action in debt or assumpsit for money had and received. An early trespass action, *Little v. Barreme* (1804), illustrates the way in which such claims might proceed. During the Quasi–War with France, an officer of the US navy, acting on the basis of presidential orders, intercepted a vessel that was involved in a form of trade that was thought to violate federal law. The vessel's Danish owner brought suit for trespass against the official, challenging the seizure's legality. The officer justified his action both by pointing to the presidential order and to the relevant statute. The Court, however, construed the statute as foreclosing the seizure in question and treated the president as lacking the power to legalize a seizure made invalid under controlling law. Since the proffered justification had failed, the officer was viewed as a liable in trespass for the losses suffered.

The common law trespass action imposed a fairly rigid discipline on officers who carried out government orders. The naval officer in *Little* had apparently acted in good faith, a factor that Chief Justice Marshall initially viewed as providing a defense. But Marshall explained that his colleagues had persuaded him to abandon that view. The Court accordingly found that the officer, acting beyond the scope of his authority, was subject to personal liability. Similar personal liability might be imposed upon a US marshal if she were to seize persons or property without proper legal authority. Moreover, the government official would face personal liability if the Constitution invalidated the authority under which the official acted. Individuals might recover damages on the basis of a trespass claim if a US marshal carried out a search on the basis of a warrant or precept that violated the Fourth Amendment. As paramount law, the Fourth Amendment would override the officer's defense of due authority and leave the officer subject to liability.

The apparent strictness of this common law liability scheme was ameliorated somewhat by the possibility of congressional indemnification. Officers could petition Congress for the adoption of a private appropriations bill; if the bill became law, it would indemnify the officer for the losses suffered. For example, the naval officer in the *Little v. Barreme* litigation was successful in securing a private bill to pay the judgment against him. See

Pfander & Hunt (2010). Such a system of personal liability, followed by requests for indemnity, made a certain amount of sense. It protected the officer from ruinous personal liability, and shifted the loss to the government. At the same time, it enabled Congress to consider the officer's good faith as a factor in its indemnification decision. (Perhaps the relevance of good faith at the indemnification stage explains why the Court refused to treat the issue as a defense to liability.) But the system did not work perfectly. If the official lacked private resources, or Congress refused to grant indemnity, the loss might fall on a comparatively blameless victim of government wrongdoing.

Common law claims also enabled individuals to contest the collection of taxes. So long as the individual paid the tax under protest, the individual could sue the officer for money had and received. Such an assumpsit action would require the officer to justify the tax under applicable law, and could result in an order directing the officer to refund the payment. In the early years, the federal government's budget depended heavily on the collection of taxes (or customs) on items imported from foreign lands. The collector of customs in each port (a federal government official working in the Treasury Department) was charged with collecting these taxes and paying them over to the government on a regular basis. Collectors were frequently named as defendants in actions to recover allegedly unlawful taxes. When these actions succeeded, the collector simply returned the money. Unlike the trespass claim, collection suits did not impose personal liability on the officer, so long as the Treasury Department allowed the officer a credit for the payment.

Officer suits worked tolerably well to test the legality of government taxes and actions that, if unjustified, would constitute a common law tort. Such suits worked far less well to provide a remedy for government breaches of contract. Government officials, acting as agents of the federal government in contractual matters, did not incur any personal liability for the government's breach of contract. Only the government itself, as the principal, was subject to liability for breach. The absence of official liability meant that the victim of a government breach of contract was required to petition for payment of the claim. In the United States, the petition of right did not take root, and most petitions were submitted to the legislature. Depending on the scope and complexity of the government's affairs, the process of legislative petitioning could become quite cumbersome. Moreover, political considerations that would have no role in a judicial decision might influence the determination of a legislative petition.

7.2.3 The Common Law or Supervisory Writs

The supervisory writs contributed a final element to the common law's scheme of remedies for government wrongdoing. These writs include two that remain well known today—the writs of mandamus and habeas corpus—and others that have lapsed into a comfortable obscurity (such as the writs of quo warranto, prohibition, and scire facias). The purpose of these writs was to enable a superior court, such as King's Bench in England, to oversee and correct the work of inferior officers and tribunals. Thus, the writ of mandamus would issue to require an inferior officer to conform her actions to the clear dictates of law. It provided an effective remedy in cases where the inferior officer had failed to act, or had acted in the teeth of clearly established law. (Recall that Marbury relied upon the writ of mandamus in seeking to compel the government to honor his appointment as a justice of the peace.) The writ of habeas corpus would issue to require a warden or jailer to explain why an individual was being detained. If the petition was supported by an adequate showing, the jailer was required to bring the detained person into court along with the rationale for confinement. If the rationale was judged inadequate, the court would, in dramatic fashion, order that the individual go free.

Writs of mandamus and habeas corpus enabled superior courts to oversee much of the work of the government, keeping government officials within the bounds of the law. Government inaction would often evade review through the use of common law forms of action; inaction did not constitute a trespass on rights of property or person. But a local government's failure to hold an election, for example, might well violate the charter of the village or town, making mandamus an appropriate remedy. Habeas corpus performed a different function, testing the legality of confinement. To be sure, trespass was an available remedy, but it came after the fact. The great feature of habeas corpus was that it provided a relatively quick procedure and actually led to a release from unlawful confinement. It thus played an important role in the constitutional struggles of seventeenth century England.

The common law writs shared a number of common features. First, they typically operated through what was called summary process: that is, the petitioner initiated the action by submitting motion papers and supporting affidavits for determination by the court itself. No jury was impaneled to hear the claim. Second, common law writs typically resulted in an order by the court that was enforced by the threat of contempt sanctions. An inferior officer thus faced the threat of imprisonment if she failed to comply with a supervisory writ. Third, supervisory writs issued in the exercise of a court's discretion, meaning that the court would first consider the application before issuing the writ. Fourth, the supervisory writs would not invariably issue if some alternative remedy were available at common law. Thus, the decision to provide a remedy (except in habeas, where the right to freedom from unlawful confinement was seen as more absolute) might turn on equitable considerations.

Much of modern administrative law, with its presumption of judicial review, derives from the robust presumption of supervision that developed at common law in the early eighteenth century. Inferior officers, whether acting in a judicial or administrative capacity, were required to explain and justify their official conduct to superior courts. (If the inferior court was a court of record, then review by writ of error was available. Less formal courts and tribunals did not produce a record, and were subject to review through other modes, such as common law trespass actions and writs of mandamus and prohibition.) Inferior officers might justify their actions by arguing that they were acting within the range of discretion afforded them by law. But the supervisory writs would issue in cases where inferior officers overstepped the bounds of their discretion. Thus, Chief Justice Marshall emphasized that Marbury's legal right to his office had vested, and all that remained was the ministerial (non-discretionary) act of putting him in his place.

7.3   Federal Government Accountability: The Constitutional and Early Statutory Framework

The common law background played a significant role in shaping the tools of federal government accountability in the antebellum years, adding flesh to a fairly skeletal set of jurisdictional provisions. Article III extends federal jurisdiction to cases arising under the Constitution and laws of the United States, and thus potentially reaches all claims in which an individual alleges that the government or its officers have violated rights grounded in federal law. Article III also extends jurisdiction to controversies involving the United States as a party, and thus authorizes the federal courts to hear a claim by and against the United States itself (even where the claim rested on the general common law of contract or property and thus failed to present a federal question under the regime of *Swift v. Tyson*). Article III thus creates a jurisdictional framework for broad judicial involvement in the determination of claims against the federal government and its officers.

Despite Article III's provision for broad federal judicial involvement, government accountability legislation got off to mixed start. In the Judiciary Act of 1789, Congress declined to confer federal jurisdiction over claims against federal government officials as such; many tort claims against federal officers were thus left to the state courts (subject, of course, to review in the Supreme Court). On the other hand, the separate law that regulated the collection of customs authorized an officer suit in federal court to challenge government exactions. As for the common law or supervisory writs, the Judiciary Act conferred relatively generous authority on the federal courts. Section 13 of the Act conferred mandamus power on the Supreme Court (power that reached both inferior officers and inferior courts), and gave the Court power to issue writs of prohibition to federal courts in admiralty cases. All federal judges were given the power to issue writs of habeas corpus in cases challenging federal confinement.

Congress took a more cautious approach to suits against the federal government, limiting federal jurisdiction to suits brought by the United States as plaintiff. This choice apparently reflected Congress's preference for legislative control over the payment of money claims against the government, and indeed such control continued throughout much of the antebellum period. (An early draft of the short-lived Judiciary Act of 1801 included a provision authorizing the Supreme Court to hear money claims against the federal government, but the provision was deleted before the bill became law.) It was not until 1855 that Congress first created the Court of Claims, a court charged with hearing a limited number of claims against the federal government. Later, the Tucker Act expanded the mandate of the Court of Claims to include claims arising under the Constitution (such as takings claims).

7.3.1 Federal Sovereign Immunity: Functional Justifications

In keeping with Congress's apparent decision to retain control over money claims, most observers assumed that the federal government enjoyed sovereign immunity from suit in federal court. For example, in *Chisholm v. Georgia* (1793), an early case upholding the right of individuals to sue the states in federal court, Chief Justice John Jay expressed the view in dicta that the federal government could invoke such an immunity (even though the states could not). The Court eventually formalized its acceptance of the government's claim of sovereign immunity in *United States v. McLemore* (1846). Since that decision, the Court has generally assumed that suits against the government may proceed in federal court only where Congress has waived the government's immunity through the adoption of a statute clearly specifying the right of individuals to sue.

While many have questioned the appropriateness of sovereign immunity in a country that has no sovereign and operates on a theory of government accountability, the doctrine may help to maintain a healthy working relationship between the legislative and judicial branches of the federal government. See Jackson (2003); Krent (1992). For even if it lacks a textual foundation in the Constitution, the doctrine of sovereign immunity ensures congressional primacy in the appropriations process and helps to protect the finality and integrity of the federal judicial process. Recall the legislation that the circuit courts invalidated on finality grounds in *Hayburn's Case* (1792) (discussed in chapter 2). Congress had called upon the federal courts to make initial rulings on the pension claims of disabled veterans, subject to review by both the executive and legislative branches of government. Legislative review made a certain functional sense; Congress understandably preferred to know the magnitude of its pension liability as it considered bills to appropriate the necessary money. At the same time, the federal courts understandably worried about the implications of being assigned a preliminary role; the possibility of review by Congress and the executive was inconsistent with the necessary finality that inhered in the judicial function. As a result, when Congress created a specialized Court of Claims to hear claims against the federal government, and continued to retain a degree of legislative oversight, the Supreme Court regarded the tribunal as a non-Article III court.

Sovereign immunity helps to resolve the tension between the congressional role in the appropriations process and the need for judicial finality. By encouraging Congress to enact legislation that clearly establishes a judicial role, the doctrine helps to assure the federal courts that Congress will appropriate the funds needed to pay any judgments. Indeed, the Court has long since recognized that Congress may enlist the federal courts in the determination of money claims against the government by making an adequate provision for the payment of claims. In *Glidden Co. v. Zdanok* (1962), the Court concluded that the Court of Claims (as redesigned during the twentieth century) had been lawfully constituted as an Article III court. (Congress has since re-configured the US Court of Federal Claims as an Article I tribunal.) In the course of its opinion, the *Glidden* plurality noted that Congress had established a standing appropriation, known as the Judgment Fund, for the payment of judgments against the federal government up to $100,000. The plurality concluded that such an appropriation, coupled with evidence that Congress had a pretty good payment record, established a sufficiently firm prospect of payment to satisfy any requirement of finality. Today, the Fund has no limitation, and judgments against the government require no separate appropriation bill. For an account of an early decision, *Maley v. Shattuck* (1806), that seemingly anticipates the result in *Glidden*, see Pfander & Hunt (2010).

If the desire to ease inter-branch conflict helps to explain the doctrine of sovereign immunity, it may do little to define the form of legislation or degree of specificity that Congress must achieve in articulating its waiver of immunity. As part of a general revival of sovereign immunity in the last few decades, the Court has taken to demanding an exceptionally clear statement to waive the government's immunity from suit. For example, in *Lane v. Pena* (1996), the Court found that the Rehabilitation Act of 1974 authorized victims of discrimination to sue the federal government for reinstatement but not for damages. Such clear statement requirements may frustrate the legislative process by demanding a set of magic words that the drafters of the legislation could not have anticipated at the time of enactment. Such specificity has not always been required as a condition of making damages relief available. Recall that in *Franklin v. Gwinnett County* (1992) (a case that presented no issues of sovereign immunity), the Court upheld the right of the federal courts to fashion a damages remedy once the cause of action itself had been firmly established either by enactment or implication. Instead of demanding a clear statement of Congress's intent to make a monetary remedy available, as in *Lane v. Pena*, the *Franklin* Court treated the creation of a right of action as the main event. Such an approach, if extended to the sovereign immunity context, would enable the federal courts to contribute to the development of a sensible body of remedial law and allow Congress to foreclose a damages remedy in appropriate cases.

Yet one might defend the clear statement rule after recognizing that the Judgment Fund makes the payment of damages essentially automatic. (Few defendants have pockets as deep as the federal government.) The clear statement rule enables the Court to make doubly sure that Congress intends to allow an award of damages before permitting essentially unlimited judgments to expend themselves on the federal treasury. Such a focus on the potential extent of liability might help to explain why the Court rejected the claim for damages in *Lane v. Pena* but allowed a claim for damages in *West v. Gibson* (1999). In *West*, the Court found a sufficiently clear statement of Congress's desire to permit the EEOC (the federal agency charged with administration of workplace discrimination law) to fashion an award of compensatory damages against another federal agency for employment discrimination under Title VII. Unlike the Rehabilitation Act, Title VII defines with some care the extent of damages available and imposes some limits on the amount of judgments.

7.3.2   The Party-of-Record Rule and Suits Against Government Officers

Although sovereign immunity bars suits against the federal government itself, the common law tradition supports the right of individuals to bring suit against government officials. Government officers do not share the sovereign's immunity from suit. As a consequence, federal courts have long exercised mandamus authority over officials of the executive branch, compelling such officials to take action required of them by law. See *Kendall v. United States* (1838) (concluding that mandamus would issue to compel the US postmaster to perform the ministerial act of granting the plaintiff a financial credit); cf. *Decatur v. Paulding* (1840) (denying mandamus on the ground that the relevant statute had conferred discretion on the executive officer to decide on what basis to pay pension claims). Strikingly, the decisions uphold the issuance of mandamus to the treasurer of the United States, compelling payment of funds upon a finding that the law clearly imposes a duty to make the payment in question. See *Roberts v. United States* (1900). Similarly, the Court has allowed mandamus to compel the land office to issue a patent reflecting the petitioner's ownership of the property in question. See *Lane v. Hoglund* (1917).

In many of these cases, mandamus operated much like equitable relief in permitting the parties to seek a remedy for government wrongdoing in situations where alternative remedies were unavailable. Not surprisingly, then, the federal courts have permitted the parties to secure through a mandatory injunction much the same relief that they had traditionally obtained through mandamus. See *Houston v. Ormes* (1920) (allowing a mandatory injunction to issue against the secretary of the Treasury on the basis that mandamus relief was clearly justified). The Court has not offered an entirely satisfactory explanation as to why these actions against federal officers for equitable relief do not implicate the doctrine of sovereign immunity. But the Court has concluded with fair consistency that the actions do not present a sovereign immunity problem, at least where they seek to compel ministerial action within the mandamus tradition. See *Houston v. Ormes* (1920); *Minnesota v. Hitchcock* (1902).

The line between permissible suits against government officers and impermissible suits against the government itself grows a bit fuzzier outside the mandamus context. Consider *United States v. Lee* (1882), an ejectment action brought by General Robert E. Lee's son to recover possession of the Lee estate in Arlington, Virginia. The federal government had taken over the estate following General Lee's failure to pay a modest property tax during the Civil War. It had since become Arlington National Cemetery. Lee's ejectment action challenged the legality of the estate's forfeiture and named the two federal government officers responsible for oversight of the cemetery; the United States (though not a party) argued on immunity grounds that the court lacked jurisdiction over a suit involving title to property in the government's possession. When that argument failed below, the government sought review in the Supreme Court.

The *Lee* Court applied the party-of-record rule in rejecting the government's claim of sovereign immunity. Under the party-of-record rule, the government enjoys immunity from suit only where the government itself has been named as a party in the litigation. The rule invites the plaintiff to evade the immunity by naming a government officer who has possession of disputed property. Thus, the Court noted that it had permitted the Bank of the United States to bring suit against Osborn, a state official who had possession of certain specie that had been taken from the Bank in payment of Ohio state tax obligations. See *Osborn v. Bank of the United States* (1824). Similarly, the party-of-record rule enables individuals to challenge a government tax by suit against the collecting officer; money in the officer's hands can be paid to a successful litigant. So long as property, wrongfully taken, remained in the hands of an official and had not been deposited in the treasury, the *Lee* Court held that the mere suggestion of title in the federal government could not arrest the proceeding.

The party-of-record rule reflects the Court's view that the doctrine of sovereign immunity should not operate to bar litigation to enforce an individual's constitutional rights. The majority clearly viewed Lee's son as the victim of a government taking of property without due process of law. Unless the plaintiff could secure a test of the government's title, he could not compel the government to institute proceedings for the payment of just compensation. The party-of-record rule thus served to facilitate a test of title that the Court viewed as essential to the protection of constitutional rights. Sovereign immunity was an inevitable part of legislative primacy in the payment of money claims, on this view, but it should not be expanded by judicial interpretation to produce failures of justice.

In circumstances where constitutional rights are less clearly implicated and the failure of justice less obvious, the Court has indicated that it may relax the party-of-record rule and bar the litigation on sovereign immunity grounds. Thus, in *Larson v. Domestic & Foreign Commerce Corp.* (1949), the Court ruled that the doctrine of sovereign immunity barred a suit brought by a corporation to secure equitable recognition of its title to coal in the hands of a government official. The Court noted that the requested injunction would "stop the government in its tracks" and thus required a finding of sovereign immunity. (Consider whether such a claim makes sense in light of the routine availability of mandamus and equitable relief against government officers.) The Court's decision can better be explained by noting that the plaintiff could sue for just compensation or breach of contract before the Court of

Claims (and did not need injunctive relief to compel the government to pay compensation). The *Larson* exception to the party-of-record rule applies less as a threshold barrier to recovery than as a tool to coordinate remedies and effectuate the apparent congressional preference for an after-the-fact damages remedy.

7.3.3 Federal Government Waivers of Sovereign Immunity

As indicated above, most litigation against the federal government proceeds under the terms of statutes that explicitly waive sovereign immunity. This section will briefly survey three of the most important waivers of immunity, the Tucker Act of 1887, the Federal Tort Claims Act of 1946, the Administrative Procedure Act. The statutes create explicit rights to pursue a special category of claims against the federal government. In addition to these special purpose statutes, Congress often includes provisions in other regulatory schemes that subject the federal government to suit along with other institutional defendants. For example, both Title VII (prohibiting employment discrimination on the basis of sex and race) and the federal bankruptcy law (authorizing the trustee to bring suit to collect the assets of a debtor) allow suits to be brought against agencies of the federal government.

The discussion begins with the Tucker Act, which confers jurisdiction on the Court of Claims to hear claims based upon the Constitution, laws, and regulations of the United States, and claims, "not sounding in tort," in which the United States would bear liability if it were subject to suit. As the jurisdictional grant makes clear, Congress took the position that the United States already owed a legal obligation to claimants; the Tucker Act simply conferred the necessary jurisdiction to enable those obligations to be heard by a court instead of by the claims committee of Congress. For the first several decades of its existence, the Court of Claims was treated as an Article I tribunal, and its decisions were subject to a degree of legislative oversight. The Court of Claims briefly became an Article III court during the middle of the last century but in 1982, Congress re-designated it the US Court of Federal Claims and returned it to Article I status. (On the distinction between Article I tribunals and Article III courts, see chapter 10.) Today, the US Court of Federal Claims (CFC) sits in Washington, D.C., and its judges serve for a term of years, renewable at the pleasure of the president.

The grant of special jurisdiction to the CFC creates a variety of jurisdictional difficulties, and has been criticized as unwieldy. While federal district courts often hear constitutional challenges to federal government activity in the form of suits for injunctive and declaratory relief, the district courts lack power to hear most money claims for a violation of the Constitution and laws of the United States. (The jurisdiction of the district courts over such matters extends only to relatively modest claims of less than $10,000.) Meanwhile, the CFC lacks the power to hear suits for injunctive and declaratory relief. This complimentary set of jurisdictional limitations creates what some have called the Tucker Act shuffle. Litigants who wish to challenge a government taking of their property must shuffle back and forth between the CFC and the district courts to gain complete relief. Some propose an expansion of CFC power to address the problem.

A more sensible approach, and one that has gained some support in legislative circles, would end the Tucker Act shuffle by closing down the CFC and transferring its jurisdiction to the federal district courts. One study of the docket impact of such a transfer concluded that the CFC's caseload could be distributed to the various federal district courts around the country without imposing a significant burden. See Schooner (2003). Such a move would have added advantages; it would secure an independent Article III judicial determination of an individual's claims against the federal government and would transfer the locus of such litigation away from the relatively inconvenient CFC forum in Washington, D.C. to the more convenient docket of the litigant's local district court.

As the jurisdictional language of the Tucker Act makes clear, the CFC has no authority to hear claims sounding in tort. As a result, the federal government remained immune from tort claims (unless it chose to adopt the cumbersome solution of providing indemnity to its officers by private bill). Congress remedied this situation in 1946, with the passage of the Federal Tort Claims Act. The Act waives immunity from suit for injuries to person or property resulting from the acts of employees of the federal government, "where the United States, if a private person, would be liable to the claimant in accordance with the law of the place where the act or omission occurred." The Act thus incorporates the law of the state in defining the extent of the government's tort liability, and authorizes the federal district courts to hear the resulting claims.

Congress apparently adopted the FTCA to deal with ordinary tort claims, such as those for simple negligence. The Act deals less effectively with complex claims of responsibility. Indeed, an explicit exception excludes liability where the claim is based upon the performance of a discretionary function or duty on the part of an agency or employee of the government. This "discretionary function" exception has given rise to a series of uneven and controversial decisions. Although the cases defy easy summary, the better reasoned decisions suggest that the exception applies to situations in which an agency exercises discretion in regulating some third party. For example, in *United States v. Varig Airlines* (1984), the Court ruled that the discretionary function exception immunized the Federal Aviation Administration from liability for accidents that allegedly resulted from the agency's failure to inspect the work of airplane manufacturers.

Two other exceptions deserve brief mention. The first—a judge-made exception—excludes liability for any injury that a member of the armed services receives in the course of or incident to military service. See *Feres v. United States* (1950). According to the Court, the military already made some provision for the care, rehabilitation and compensation of those who suffer service-related injuries; the imposition of liability in such a situation was thought to undermine military discipline. A second statutory exception excludes liability for a broad range of intentional torts, including assault, battery, false imprisonment, false arrest, malicious prosecution, libel, slander, deceit, misrepresentation, and interference with contractual relations. In 1974, however, Congress qualified the intentional tort exception by permitting many such actions to proceed against federal investigative and law enforcement officers (but not those for libel, slander, misrepresentation, and deceit).

The FTCA thus overlaps to some extent with the right of individuals to bring a *Bivens* claim (discussed in chapter 6). Many claims under the Fourth Amendment, like that of Mr. Bivens himself, arise from federal police conduct that would also give rise to a claim for assault, battery, false arrest, or false imprisonment. Where state law affords a right of action for such claims, the individual could presumably proceed against the government under the FTCA and against the individual officer under *Bivens*. (Note that the FTCA excludes liability for punitive damages.) Congress addressed the problem of overlapping liability in 1988, making the FTCA the exclusive remedy for torts committed by federal officers whenever the attorney general certifies that the employee was acting in the course of her employment. A certification has the result, if accepted, of transforming the action into one against the federal government.

If garden-variety contract and tort claims typically proceed under the Tucker Act and the FTCA, a somewhat broader array of possibilities beckons the litigant who wishes to challenge administrative action. Many organic statutes make an explicit provision for judicial review of agency action. Administrative lawyers refer to judicial review under these provisions as "statutory review." In addition, litigants can mount challenges to administrative action even in the absence of any provision for statutory review by invoking the tradition of mandamus and injunctive relief that has provided the foundation of federal agency accountability. In such actions, known as "non-statutory review," the litigant simply brings suit under the general federal question jurisdictional grant, seeking injunctive and declaratory relief from agency action. Non-statutory review provides a remedy in circumstances where the litigant cannot otherwise secure relief from agency action, and thus plays the same role as mandamus in furnishing a kind of backstop.

The Administrative Procedure Act, a comprehensive statute that governs administrative law-making and adjudication, gives an explicit boost to the institution of judicial review. The APA first appeared in 1946, establishing a presumption in favor of judicial review. In 1976, Congress adopted a series of measures designed to make judicial remedies more effective. For one thing, Congress removed the amount-in-controversy requirement from the federal question statute, thereby enabling the federal courts to hear suits against the government without regard to their monetary value. Second, Congress expressly waived the federal government's sovereign immunity in all suits seeking relief other than money damages. See 5 U.S.C. § 502. Third, Congress empowered the federal courts to enter judgment against the United States, so long as the official responsible for compliance with the decree was also identified. These provisions essentially overturn government immunity, making specific relief generally available against government agencies (at least outside the government contract context in which *Larson* arose).

7.4 State Government Accountability

This section focuses on the rules that enable individuals to enforce their federal rights (both constitutional and statutory) against state and local governments through civil litigation. (The section defers to chapter 8 consideration of the right of individuals to seek review, by federal habeas corpus, of federal constitutional issues that arise in the course of state criminal proceedings). By focusing on claims by individuals, this section puts to one side the fact that the federal government has sometimes brought suit to compel state compliance with federal law. By focusing on federal rights, this section pays scant attention to the fact that state governments have adopted statutory waivers of sovereign immunity that permit individuals to pursue many tort, contract, and property claims in state court. The focus of the section on individual enforcement of federal rights, particularly rights under the Constitution, leaves a wealth of government accountability out of the picture.

Yet the section's emphasis on federal rights, and the role of federal courts in their enforcement against the states, focuses attention on the issues that have proven consistently difficult throughout the nation's history. One of the country's first constitutional crises arose from the Supreme Court's decision in *Chisholm v. Georgia* (1793) to assert jurisdiction over money claims against the states. Congress's response, to propose the Eleventh Amendment as a restriction on the manner in which the federal courts were to construe their judicial power, was one that indebted states enthusiastically ratified. Two hundred years later, the Court breathed new life into the Eleventh Amendment as a bar to suits in federal court. See *Seminole Tribe v. Florida* (1996). The Court's revival of state sovereign immunity raises profound questions about the meaning of the Eleventh Amendment, and the adequacy of the many other tools with which the federal courts oversee state compliance with federal law. This section explores these many issues, beginning with the Eleventh Amendment and then examining the right of individuals to sue state government officials under *Ex Parte Young* and section 1983.

7.4.1 The Eleventh Amendment: Original Understanding

The Eleventh Amendment was declared effective in 1798, restricting the scope of the judicial power conferred in Article III of the Constitution. The history of ratification has been canvassed on numerous occasions, both by scholars and by the Court, and two schools of thought have emerged. On one view, known as the diversity account, the Eleventh Amendment operates quite narrowly to curtail only two sources of jurisdiction over suits against the states, those brought by diverse citizens and aliens. On another view, known as the profound-shock thesis after its articulation by the Court in *Hans v. Louisiana* (1890), the framers recoiled from state suability and meant to curtail virtually all federal judicial power to entertain suits against the states, even though the Amendment itself did not say so. The Court has made the profound-shock thesis the law of the land, with some exceptions.

Our story begins with Article III, which included a variety of provisions that more or less explicitly appeared to contemplate suits against the states. Article III provides for the assertion of jurisdiction over controversies between "two or more States," between "a State and the Citizens of another State," and between "a State, . . . and foreign States, Citizens or Subjects." While the provision does not expressly say that a state may be sued in federal court, one has difficulty imagining a suit between two or more states that does not involve the appearance of one of the states as a defendant. Indeed, the Articles of Confederation had included a provision for the resolution of boundary disputes between the states; Article III's provision for jurisdiction over inter-state litigation operates in part as the successor to that provision. The subsequent provisions empower federal courts to hear disputes between states and diverse citizens, foreign states and aliens, again without specifying that the states shall only appear as plaintiffs in such litigation.

The original jurisdiction clause of Article III complemented these provisions for suits against the states by conferring original jurisdiction on the Supreme Court over "those [cases] in which a State shall be Party." The grant of original jurisdiction may have reflected a desire to provide the states with a dignified tribunal in which to litigate; it may also have reflected a distrust of the alternatives. At the time, most state constitutions did not provide for the judicial determination of money claims, but assigned the task to the state legislature. While some state legislatures (notably those in New York, Pennsylvania, Virginia and Georgia) had adopted provisions for the judicial determination of money claims, building on the model of the petition of right in England, most had not done so. In addition, under the terms of the Madisonian Compromise, the framers of Article III could not be sure that Congress would create lower federal courts or empower them to hear claims against the states. With few assured alternatives, the grant of original jurisdiction can be seen as an integral part of the Constitution's plan for ensuring the availability of a federal forum for claims against the states.

The possibility of state liability was not lost on critics of the Constitution. Brutus, writing in opposition to ratification in New York, argued that Article III would subject the states to suit in federal court for the full amount of their outstanding debts. These, of course, were substantial. Not only had the states borrowed heavily from foreign governments to pay for the War of Independence, but they had borrowed from their own citizens both formally through debt instruments and less formally by printing gobs of paper money to pay off current obligations. (These state debts and bills of credit were in addition to the federal debts Congress had incurred and federal currency Congress had emitted.) Patrick Henry made the same point in Virginia, arguing that Article III would subject the state to suit on outstanding debts and land claims. At the time, Virginia was embroiled in a long-running land dispute with citizens of Pennsylvania over land purchased from the Native Americans.

Defenders of the Constitution responded to these critics in one of two ways. Some (like Governor Edmund Randolph of Virginia) simply admitted that Article III did in fact contemplate suits against the states, and argued that it was a good thing. Others, like Alexander Hamilton and James Madison, temporized. Hamilton acknowledged that Article III seemed to contemplate suits against the states, but then issued a carefully hedged statement in Federalist No. 81, denying that the jurisdiction would divest the states of "the privilege of paying their own debts in their own way, free from every constraint but that which flows from the obligations of good faith." Hamilton's statement thus seemingly rules out only the collection of existing debts, and leaves open the possibility of asserting jurisdiction over future state action. Madison and John Marshall, speaking in favor of the Constitution in Virginia, took a different approach. They denied that the provisions of Article III would apply to suits against the states, arguing that the provisions permitted states to sue, but not to be sued.

Following ratification, Congress included in the Judiciary Act of 1789 a provision authorizing the Court to assert original jurisdiction over "controversies of a civil nature" involving the states. A range of such suits were quickly filed. In *Chisholm v. Georgia*, the plaintiff sued in assumpsit for money the state owed for supplies it had acquired to fight the war. Similar claims against South Carolina and Virginia sought to enforce loans that the states had procured from foreign creditors. An action brought against Massachusetts sought to recover the value of prime real estate on Beacon Hill that the state had taken from a British loyalist during the war. A New York printer brought suit against that state for the value of his printing services. And the land claim that Virginians feared, one brought by Pennsylvania citizens, also appeared on the Court's docket.

The *Chisholm* Court responded to this litigation by confirming its jurisdiction, and its ability to proceed to trial on claims against the state. In a lengthy set of opinions, four Justices upheld the Court's jurisdiction over Chisholm's claims against the state of Georgia. Most of the Justices contented themselves with a reference to the plain language of the statute, and constitutional provisions. Justice James Wilson, a strong supporter of the Constitution from Pennsylvania, went further, offering a lengthy and to modern eyes somewhat opaque discussion of the nature of sovereignty (one that notably included the Court's first reference to "political correctness"). Only Justice Iredell dissented, and he did so not to argue that the Court necessarily lacked jurisdiction but to argue that it could not entertain suits against the states until such time as Congress fashioned a right of action and furnished remedial details, such as rules governing service of process and enforcement of judgments. As Justice Iredell emphasized, the states were not subject to suits at the time they had incurred their debts. To recognize a judge-made action in assumpsit and apply it to states for the first time to enforce old debts was to engage in retroactive judicial lawmaking.

States, particularly those with substantial outstanding indebtedness, reacted with little enthusiasm to the ruling. Some supporters of state sovereignty argued for a constitutional amendment that would entirely bar all claims against the states. A rejected version of the Eleventh Amendment would have done just that. Others took a more nuanced view. While they opposed the use of Article III as a mechanism with which to enforce the states' previously incurred debts, they acknowledged the possibility that suits against the states might be appropriate to enforce the obligations that the states had incurred under the new federal Constitution. After all, the great bulk of the state debts and obligations that formed the subject of suits on the Court's original docket had been incurred before the Constitution had taken effect. Many who participated in the framing had denied that the Constitution would reach back to alter the rules previously applicable to state conduct. (Thus, a delegate to the North Carolina ratifying convention had explicitly reassured his colleagues that the ban on the issuance of paper money would not affect the legality of paper money *previously* issued; Justice Iredell was from North Carolina and participated in the ratification debate there.) The framers of the Eleventh Amendment could foreclose suit on previously incurred obligations and leave in place the rules that permitted suit to enforce state obligations under the new Constitution.

Such a temporal compromise apparently informed the drafting of the Eleventh Amendment. The distinction between old claims and new also corresponds to a distinction between claims against the states based on general common law and claims based on federal law. Before the Constitution was ratified, and took effect, the states were not subject to federal restrictions; all of their debts would have been contracted on the basis of the remedial systems in place within the states themselves and no federal court or cause of action would have been available to enforce them. This, in essence, was Justice Iredell's point. After ratification, by contrast, federal restrictions on the states would take effect and would have been judicially enforceable through the exercise of federal question jurisdiction. The Eleventh Amendment could curtail jurisdiction on the basis of party-alignment and thereby foreclose the imposition of liability for all debts previously incurred, while leaving intact the power of the federal courts to hear federal question cases against the states for purposes of securing state compliance with their federal obligations.

The language of the Eleventh Amendment nicely fits with the proposed distinction between old claims based upon common law and new claims based upon federal law. The Amendment reads as follows:

> The Judicial power of the United States shall not be construed to extend to any suit in law or equity, commenced or prosecuted against one of the United States by Citizens of another State, or by Citizens or Subjects of any Foreign State.

On its face, the text affects only two kinds of suits, those in law or equity, and only suits brought by two disfavored litigants, diverse citizens and foreign subjects. The provision thus apparently leaves intact the judicial power over suits brought by other claimants (including the federal government, the states, and foreign states) as well as judicial power over cases of admiralty and maritime jurisdiction that happened to involve the states as defendants. Law and equity cases were understood as categorically distinct from admiralty cases.

The text has given rise to a debate in the literature between the so-called diversity theory of the Eleventh Amendment and the literal theory. Under the diversity theory, the Amendment operates to narrow the affirmative grants of jurisdiction in Article III and does so only where Article III jurisdiction would have been based on the alignment of the parties. Diversity theorists note that Article III fails to confer party-alignment jurisdiction over claims by individuals other than the two disfavored parties identified in the Eleventh Amendment. They conclude from this that the Amendment set out to deny the federal courts any diversity jurisdiction in litigation against the states. On this theory, the Amendment would deny jurisdiction over general common law claims but would leave Article III jurisdiction unaffected as to suits based on federal question and admiralty jurisdiction. In other words, the diversity theory views the Eleventh Amendment as leaving federal question and admiralty jurisdiction fully intact. See Fletcher (1983); Gibbons (1983); Pfander (1998). Not so the literal theory. For literalists, the Eleventh Amendment bars all suits by the two disfavored plaintiffs no matter what sort of claim (diversity or federal question) they present. See Marshall (1989); Massey (1989).

The debate between diversity theorists and literalists can be viewed as a friendly debate. See Amar (1989). Diversity theorists and literalists agree that a citizen of a state such as Illinois can bring a federal question claim against the state of Illinois under Article III. Moreover, they agree that the Eleventh Amendment does not affect federal jurisdiction over such a claim. But consider a federal question suit by an Illinois citizen against the state of Iowa. Literalists would interpret the Eleventh Amendment as a bar to the suit (in view of the parties' alignment) whereas diversity theorists would not (in view of the presence of a federal question). Since most individuals with claims based upon federal law will be seeking to enforce them against their own state, both theories of the Eleventh Amendment would leave federal question jurisdiction largely unimpaired.

The temporal wrinkle mentioned above makes the diversity theory more persuasive. Literal theorists view the Eleventh

Amendment as having been framed to place claims held by out-of-state creditors entirely beyond the jurisdiction of the federal courts, whether such claims were to be based upon state or federal law. Literalists posit a variety of theories under which common law debt claims might be transformed into federal question claims so as to pose a continuing threat to the state treasuries.   But once one recognizes that the claims on the Court's docket at the time of the Eleventh Amendment's ratification virtually all arose from conduct that pre-dates the effective date of the Constitution, one cannot easily see on what basis those claims could be re-stated in federal law terms.   Without a threat of restatement, literalists have difficulty in explaining why debt claims posed a threat that would require a restriction of federal question jurisdiction.   See Pfander (1998).

Despite the fact that the Court's Eleventh Amendment jurisprudence has reached something of a resting point, scholars continue to comb through the historical records for insight into the Amendment's original meaning.   One particularly valuable account emphasizes the likelihood that the Amendment was adopted as a compromise between contending forces, some of whom wanted to foreclose all state suability and others of whom wanted to preserve suability and the assurance of accountability it would provide.   See Manning (2009).   On this view, close attention to the text of the Amendment makes sense; relying on the intention of either one of the two opposing camps would threaten to undermine the compromise.   Yet this argument for narrowing the Amendment has met stern resistance.   Some view the Amendment as restoring a widespread ratification-era understanding of state immunity under Article III.   Others view the prospect of state suability as essentially unthinkable, at least at the suit of individuals.   See Clark (2010). Both accounts thus portray the Amendment as restoring a lost world threatened by *Chisholm* rather than as a narrow and rather technical response to an interpretation of Article III that many had anticipated, criticized, and defended.

7.4.2 The Eleventh Amendment: *Hans v. Louisiana*

Whatever the comparative merits of the scholarly debate over the impact of the Eleventh Amendment on admiralty and federal question claims, the Court has taken a broad view of state sovereign immunity.   Under the Court's approach, the Eleventh Amendment bars all individual claims against the states, no matter what the parties' alignment or on what jurisdictional basis they rest. The Court's has justified its departure from the Amendment's text by offering a combination of history and policy.   Its historical argument emphasizes the framers' desire to erect a relatively absolute immunity for the states and its policy argument emphasizes the need to protect state treasuries from liability based upon federal law. The Court's approach has often been informed by a certain antipathy to the federal rights that individuals have been seeking to enforce against the states. This section sketches the origins of the Court's approach, and then examines the officer suit alternative as a prelude to its consideration of such modern cases as *Seminole Tribe v. Florida* (1996).

The Court's departure from the Amendment's text began in *Hans v. Louisiana* (1890), an action brought by a resident of the state of Louisiana to recover the value of repudiated state bonds. Hans based his claim on federal law; he argued that the state's repudiation violated the Constitution's prohibition against state impairments of the obligation of contract. (The Contract Clause has not been an especially important restriction on state power since the 1930s, but it played a more significant role in regulating state legislation in the nineteenth century.) Hans argued that he was not embarrassed by the Eleventh Amendment; he was not one of the disfavored plaintiffs mentioned in the Amendment's text and his claim arose under federal law and thus did not depend on the alignment of the parties. The Court nonetheless ruled that the Eleventh Amendment barred his claim.

The Court's decision discounted the text and focused on the perceived purpose of the Amendment. According to the Court, the framers of Article III had expressly assured the several state ratifying conventions that the provision would pose no threat to state treasuries. (Actually, of course, the historical record reveals a wide range of comments.) Despite these assurances and Justice Iredell's prescient warning, the *Chisholm* Court had agreed to assert the jurisdiction in question. When the decision issued, it was said to have fallen upon the country with a "profound shock." In response, Congress promptly proposed and the states promptly ratified the Eleventh Amendment. The Amendment was meant to deal with all of the suits then pending, and should be interpreted in keeping with its purpose to offer relatively absolute protection against such suits. The fact that Hans's claim was outside the text of the Amendment was of no moment; literalism had previously led the *Chisholm* Court astray in interpreting Article III.

Two factors suggest that *Hans* was born of judicial weakness. First, historians have noted that the decision occurred after the North had ended military Reconstruction in the South and no longer had the means to compel compliance with a decree directing the state legislature to honor the bonds. See Orth (2000); Purcell (2003). Second, Congress had done little to facilitate or support the claims of bondholders like Hans. To be sure, the plaintiff had relied upon the general federal question grant of jurisdiction that Congress had adopted in 1875. But that jurisdictional provision said nothing about suits against the states. Nor did any act of Congress speak to the right of individuals to enforce their bond claims against the state. If the political branches were willing to permit the South to repudiate their bonds on a massive scale, perhaps the Court concluded that it could not resist effectively and simply needed a plausible excuse to stand aside. (It may have done less longstanding damage to the law had the Court chosen to place its decision on statutory grounds.) Perhaps, then, we can find some similarities between *Hans* and the experience that led to the Eleventh Amendment. In both situations, indebted states had decided to repudiate or re-finance their indebtedness after a war. The *Chisholm* Court had attempted to prevent such repudiation on its own authority without enlisting the congressional support that Justice Iredell's approach would have secured. Even if it misread the text of the Eleventh Amendment, perhaps the *Hans* Court did a fair job of reading the political lessons of its ratification.

After *Hans*, the Court continued to interpret the Eleventh Amendment not by reference to its text but as a general prohibition of suits against the states. In *Ex parte New York* (1921), the Court found that the Eleventh Amendment barred suits against the states in admiralty jurisdiction, notwithstanding the rather pointed omission of any reference to admiralty in the text. Similarly, in *Monaco v. Mississippi* (1934), the Court found that the Amendment barred suits by foreign states, even though such parties were not included among the text's two disfavored plaintiffs. In *Monaco*, the Court acknowledged the lack of textual support but pointed out that "behind the words of the constitutional provisions are postulates which limit and control." Presumably the Court had in mind structural factors and functional considerations that it viewed as tending to support the recognition of sovereign immunity.

7.4.3 The *Ex Parte Young* Exception

As they have with the federal government, officer suits provide an important vehicle for keeping the states within constitutional limits. Indeed, with the *Hans* rule in place as a flat barrier to suits against the states, the federal courts have relied increasingly on suits for injunctive and declaratory relief against state officers. Although it was not the first such decision, the leading case, *Ex parte Young* (1908), came down within several years of the *Hans* decision and has produced a world in which litigants can more or less routinely pursue claims against responsible state officers, so long as the complaint refrains from naming the state itself as a party of record. Section 1983 has given a boost to such litigation; it authorizes suits against state and local government officials for both damages and injunctive relief.

Sec. 1983 diff.

Ex parte Young began with the adoption of state legislation that proposed to regulate the rates that railroads could charge in Minnesota. Not only did the law fix the rates, it also threatened fairly stiff criminal sanctions for a violation. Shareholders of various railroads brought suit in Minnesota federal court, seeking an injunction that would bar the state's attorney general, Edward Young, from enforcing the new law, which was said to have taken the property of the railroads in violation of the substantive due process protections then perceived in the Fourteenth Amendment. (The complaint also alleged equal protection and dormant commerce clause claims.) The trial court agreed, granted the injunction, and imposed contempt sanctions when Young refused to comply. The action reached the Supreme Court on a petition for a writ of habeas corpus in which Young sought release from custody.

Note that at the time the litigation began, Young had done nothing that would have violated any common law duty owed to the railroad. As attorney general, Young was free to insist on compliance with state law, and free to threaten to enforce the law in accordance with its terms (at least until the injunction was issued). If the company violated the law, Young would presumably begin a state prosecution in which the defendant (with the assistance of the company's lawyers) would raise constitutional defenses to the new state law. Ordinarily, courts of equity (both state and federal) would decline to interfere with such a pending state criminal proceeding. The railroad company would obtain its day in court on the constitutional issue, subject to ultimate review in the Supreme Court on appeal from any unfavorable state court decision. The shareholders who commenced the *Young* litigation on the railroad's behalf sought to upend this established mode of proceeding, and shift to a model in which the action began in federal court as a suit for relief in advance of the commencement of any criminal proceeding. In other words, the action sought to transform the protections of the Fourteenth Amendment from a shield (defending the company from state criminal liability) into something like a sword (enabling the company to pursue its own constitutional claims affirmatively rather than defensively).

In *Ex parte Young*, the Court ratified this proposed switch from a defensive conception of constitutional rights to a more affirmative conception. It was quite an important change in the structure of constitutional litigation, and one that remains important today. See Dellinger (1972). By enabling the railroad to institute an anticipatory challenge to the state law in federal court, the Court made a forum available that may have been better disposed to the enforcement of the federal rights at issue. In addition, such affirmative or anticipatory litigation had the consequence of denying the state court (and state prosecutor) the important opportunity to address the breadth and applicability of the state law in the first instance. A concerned prosecutor might decline to bring charges on the fringe of a statute's constitutional applicability; a friendly state court might trim overbroad sections of the statute, enabling a problematic piece of legislation to withstand constitutional scrutiny. Federal courts may be less willing to re-interpret a statute troublesome on its face and more willing to address the constitutional problems directly. The shift to an affirmative litigation regime thus has important consequences for the state's ability to work out constitutional kinks in the course of a statute's administration.

The *Ex parte Young* Court displayed little concern for the transformative implications of its decision. Instead, the Court emphasized that it would be unfair to require the railroad to violate the state law in order to secure a test of its constitutionality. For the Court, the harshness of the punishment served to make clear the propriety of injunctive relief; remedies at law were viewed as inadequate. But even today, at a time when the irreparable harm test for injunctive relief applies with reduced force, see Laycock (1990), the concern with clarifying legal obligations remains legitimate. We generally take the view that the parties should be able to secure a test of their legal claims and should not be required to act at their peril. Congress's adoption of the Declaratory Judgment Act reflects the view that the courts should be open to determine genuine disputes so that parties can conform their conduct to the law. See Chapter 2.5 above. Actions for injunctive and declaratory relief help to clarify legal obligations for parties disposed toward complying with the law.

In order to accomplish its switch to an anticipatory model of constitutional litigation, the Court had to decide two questions. First, it concluded (implicitly but unmistakably) that the Fourteenth Amendment gave rise an implied right of action for injunctive relief. Congress had not created an express right of action to permit suits to challenge rate regulations and the Court did not rely upon section 1983 (a then-moribund Reconstruction-era statute that the Court revived in *Monroe v. Pape* (1961)). Moreover, the Court could not rely upon a common law trespass claim as the vehicle for the railroad's right to pursue its claim; Young had not committed a trespass at the time suit was brought. (Compare *Osborn*, where the Ohio state officials came onto the Bank's property and carried away specie from the vault.) In the end, then, the Court could permit the action to proceed only by finding that the effective protection of the constitutional rights at issue required the recognition of a federal cause of action. Today, of course, the federal courts would rely on section 1983 as the source of the plaintiff's right to pursue the claim. But the *Ex parte Young* Court did not do so. By engaging in an act of judicial creation, the Court built an important conceptual foundation for the recognition of a federal right of action in *Bivens*.

A second question for the Court was how to square its willingness to permit an action for injunctive relief with the dictates of the Eleventh Amendment. Here was the puzzle. Young was clearly viewed as acting for the state of Minnesota within the meaning of the Fourteenth Amendment; his actions brought into play the constitutional protections of due process, equal protection, and so forth. Yet the Eleventh Amendment had been interpreted to block suits against the state. How could Young act for the state under the Fourteenth Amendment without triggering the state's immunity from suit under the Eleventh Amendment? After all, as Young noted, the injunction purported to bind him in his official, not his personal, capacity and thus appeared to view him as acting for the state.

The Court dealt with the Eleventh Amendment objection by invoking an authority-stripping rationale. In brief, the Court found that Young's violation of the federal Constitution stripped him of his official capacity and left him, like any other private party, subject to the decree of a federal court. One has difficulty explaining this rationale on other than fictional grounds, and indeed the rule that the Eleventh Amendment does not bar suits for injunctive and declaratory relief against state officers has come to be known as the "*Ex parte Young* fiction." In effect, the Court found that the importance of securing the enforcement of the constitutional rights at issue, given the barrier that *Hans* had erected to a direct suit against the state, justified a finding that immunity did not apply to the action.

The fundamental inconsistency of the pro-immunity rule of *Hans* and the pro-accountability rule of *Ex Parte Young* casts a long shadow over this area of the law. Indeed, one prominent observer has described the law of state government accountability as subject to arbitrary stops and starts; it lacks a guiding principle that students can use to reason to the solution of new problems. See Jeffries (1998). Instead, the law has a set of guiding principles, often in tension, that result in a mixed collection of decisions, some affirming accountability, some championing immunity. The decisions lack consistency, and can seem quite frustrating, but they may reflect an attempt to balance the values of respect for state dignity, protection of the state fisc, and the enforcement of federal law.

Subsequent cases in the *Ex Parte Young* line reveal the tension between immunity and accountability. In *Edelman v. Jordan* (1974), for example, a group of welfare recipients had successfully challenged delays in the state's administration of a federal welfare benefit program as violative of applicable federal law and regulations. The lower federal court had ordered the state administrators to provide relatively speedy processing of claims. The court had also ordered equitable restitution of the benefit amounts that the members of the class would have received had their claims been more promptly handled. On review, the Court upheld the power of the lower courts to decree future compliance with federal law, but concluded that the equitable restitution order exceeded the court's power under the Eleventh Amendment. Such relief would expend itself on the state treasury, not the private assets of state officials, and it would operate retrospectively, much like a damages award.

In suggesting a distinction between prospective and retrospective relief, the Court introduced a new wrinkle into the administration of its *Ex parte Young* fiction. On the one hand, the recognition of some sort of restriction on a doctrine of equitable restitution seems essential to preserve the integrity and coherence of the *Hans* rule. Otherwise, a federal court might order state officials to pay money and thereby accomplish what *Hans* had sought to prevent. On the other hand, the Court has struggled to justify and administer its prospective-retrospective distinction. Structural injunctions of the kind that lower court entered in an effort to desegregate the public schools can occasion the expenditures of large sums of money from state coffers; yet such awards fall on the permissibly prospective side of the line. See *Milliken v. Bradley* (1977). In the aftermath of *Edelman*, moreover, the Court recognized the power of the lower court to order notice relief that would inform class members of their right to pursue state remedies to collect an award of past-due benefits. See *Quern v. Jordan* (1979). Finally, the Court has allowed an award of attorney's fees as sanction ancillary to a grant of injunctive relief, at least where the defendants acted in bad faith. See *Hutto v. Finney* (1978).

The Court added another wrinkle in *Pennhurst State School & Hospital v. Halderman* (1984). There, the plaintiffs had sued state officials in federal court, seeking relief from a range of alleged constitutional and statutory violations. In addition, the plaintiffs sought relief on the basis of state law, invoking the district court's supplemental jurisdiction. Ultimately, the district court granted relief on state law grounds, in part to avoid the determination of constitutional issues. But the Court ruled that such an order violated the state's immunity from suit. While the Court acknowledged that the order would qualify as prospective relief within the meaning of *Edelman*, it concluded that the *Ex parte Young* fiction did not extend to injunctive relief based upon state law. As to such claims, there was no need to ensure the enforcement of federal law and no justification for overriding the state's immunity. In effect, the Court balanced the two interests and concluded that the state interest in immunity predominated, apparently on the ground that the state courts themselves ought to bear responsibility for determining how vigorously to enforce state law against state actors.

The Court flirted with the possibility of extending this balancing approach to at least some claims based upon federal law. In *Idaho v. Coeur d'Alene Tribe* (1997), the Court refused to permit the federal courts to entertain an *Ex parte Young* action in which the tribe sought an injunction directing the state of Idaho to respect its ownership of certain submerged lands within the state. In a plurality opinion, Justice Kennedy argued that the doctrine of *Ex parte Young* should be viewed as a discretionary tool for the enforcement of federal rights, one whose applicability would depend on a variety of consideration in any particular case. Although the other Justices rejected Kennedy's discretionary view, Justice O'Connor's controlling opinion for the majority offered an equally unsatisfying rationale by emphasizing the state's sovereign interests in submerged land. Later, the Court seemingly abandoned Justice Kennedy's move to make the doctrine discretionary. See *Verizon Maryland v. Public Service Comm'n* (2002).

7.4.4 *Seminole Tribe* and the Abrogation of Eleventh Amendment Immunity

Hans and its progeny established a principle of state immunity that applied to cases arising under federal law. But the Court had no occasion to consider whether the case would have turned out differently had Congress provided an explicit right of action that expressly allowed individuals to sue the states in federal court. (Recall that Justice Iredell in *Chisholm* had emphasized the absence of any federal legislation authorizing suits against the states.) Such express rights of action, missing in *Hans*, became increasingly common in the latter half of the twentieth century as Congress exercised broader authority over the national economy. In addition, Congress frequently included the states within the regulatory ambit of federal civil rights laws that imposed broad duties on many institutions to refrain from discrimination on the basis of race, sex, and disability. Such statutes, often adopted pursuant to Congress's powers under the Commerce Clause and Section 5 of the Fourteenth Amendment, raised questions both about the scope of Congress's power to regulate the states as states and about the power of the federal courts to entertain such suits under the Eleventh Amendment.

A word about terminology: Congress regulates "the states as states" when it establishes a set of federal rights and obligations and expressly includes the states as such within the regulatory scheme. For example, in the Fair Labor Standards Act, Congress established a forty-hour work week, and required employers to pay extra for overtime.   In the 1960s, Congress brought the states under the Act, expressly extending federal protections to employees of enterprises run by state governments.   To the extent that they employed individuals within the industries covered by the Act, states were obliged to honor the forty-hour work week and pay extra for overtime.   States questioned both Congress's power to place new regulatory obligations on the states, and the federal courts' power, under the Eleventh Amendment, to exercise jurisdiction over claims against the states to enforce those rights.

As part of the (old) new federalism jurisprudence of the 1970s, the Burger Court struck down the extension of the Fair Labor Standards Act, concluding that it exceeded Congress's power.   In *National League of Cities v. Usery* (1976), the Court drew a distinction between the regulation of private actors, and the regulation of the "states as states."   In an effort to protect the separate existence of the states in the federal system, the Court held that the Commerce Clause and the Tenth Amendment foreclosed regulation that reached traditional government functions.   After struggling for a time to define the scope of this protection, the Court backed down in *Garcia v. San Antonio Metropolitan Transit Authority* (1985).   In *Garcia*, a narrowly divided Court overruled *Usery*, concluding that it would leave the issue to the political process. Congress could regulate the states as states, and the states could seek protection through what were referred to as the political safeguards of federalism.   States were said to be well represented in Congress, and capable of using their political clout to obtain an exemption from regulation.

Garcia empowered Congress to apply commercial regulations to the states.   But that raised the second-order question of how individuals were to enforce their rights.   They might sue in federal court, seeking both declaratory and injunctive relief and back pay. While the *Ex parte Young* exception would seemingly permit a suit for prospective relief, *Hans* and *Edelman* would raise doubts about the power of the federal courts to hear the damages claim.   But many observers argued that the damages suit might proceed notwithstanding *Hans*; perhaps Congress had the power to "abrogate" the states' immunity from suit by enacting legislation that clearly authorized the exercise of jurisdiction over an action for damages or a suit against the state itself.   The political safeguards of federalism, some argued, could be trusted to protect the states from suit in federal court, just as they could protect the states from regulation. See Nowak (1975).   Again, note the difference in terminology: *Garcia* overruled an immunity from regulation under *Usery*, and now some called for a power in Congress to abrogate the states's sovereign immunity from suit under *Hans* and the Eleventh Amendment.

Although the Court initially agreed with the abrogation argument in *Pennsylvania v. Union Gas Co.* (1989), it changed course a short time later. In *Seminole Tribe v. Florida* (1996), the Court ruled that Congress lacked the power under the Commerce Clause to adopt laws abrogating the states' immunity from suit. The case arose from a law, adopted under the Indian Commerce Clause, that created a structure by which Native American tribes could bargain with the state to establish sites for tribal casinos. The law provided for the tribes to sue the state to compel its participation in the bargaining process. The Seminole Tribe of Florida brought such a suit, naming both the state of Florida itself as a defendant and the state's governor. The Court refused to permit either claim, rejecting both the abrogation argument (as to the state) and the argument that an officer suit could proceed (against the governor) under *Ex parte Young.*

In the course of its opinion, the Court established a framework for the analysis of abrogation issues, although it may have raised more questions than it answered. First, the Court reaffirmed its clear statement rule, a requirement that Congress "unequivocally" express its intent to subject the states to suit. Presumably, this clear statement rule helps to activate the political safeguards of federalism by making the consequences for state sovereignty evident to members of Congress and state lobbyists alike. Second, the Court concluded that, although the intent to abrogate was clear, Congress lacked the constitutional power to do so under the Commerce Clause. Third, the Court reaffirmed an earlier decision, *Fitzpatrick v. Bitzer* (1976), which had upheld the power of Congress to abrogate state sovereign immunity to enforce the Fourteenth Amendment. In *Fitzpatrick*, the Court had upheld a provision of Title VII that subjected states to monetary liability for workplace discrimination on the basis of sex.

The Court's abrogation decision raises a range of difficulties, both conceptual and practical. At the conceptual level, the Court was required to explain how the legislative power under the Fourteenth Amendment could support an abrogation authority that other constitutional provisions could not. The Court responded with a temporal argument; the Eleventh Amendment came after the Commerce Clause, and thus restricted Congress's regulatory authority under that provision whereas the Fourteenth Amendment came after the Eleventh and qualified its restrictions. Such talk of varying congressional authority takes us further and further away from the text of the Eleventh Amendment, which leaves the legislative power altogether intact, and restricts only the judicial power in cases brought by two disfavored plaintiffs. The dissent placed a good deal of emphasis on the text and history of the Amendment, adopting a version of the diversity explanation. But the Court dismissed this effort as a theory "cobbled together from law review articles."

At the practical level, the Court's decision raises the issue of how an individual can enforce restrictions on state conduct that, at least in theory, Congress still has the power to adopt under *Garcia*. *Seminole Tribe* itself ruled out the possibility of a suit brought against the state in federal court. What about other avenues of enforcement? In a significant extension of its decision, the Court ruled in part III of its opinion that Seminole Tribe could not enforce the duty to negotiate by bringing suit against the governor under *Ex parte Young*. Its rationale for that ruling remains obscure and controversial. In brief, the Court noted that Congress retains control over the enforcement of the rights it creates. Here, Congress apparently meant to authorize enforcement actions against the government as an entity, and the Court concluded that the congressional preference impliedly displaced the *Ex parte Young* remedy on the facts of this case. One might view this aspect of the opinion as somewhat contrived; the federal government had argued (in its brief in support of the tribe) that the obvious availability of *Ex parte Young* relief made it unnecessary for the Court to reach the abrogation issue.

Whatever its rationale, the *Ex parte Young* ruling has generated controversy. It seems quite implausible to ascribe to Congress a desire to rely on suit against the state as the sole method of enforcement, especially after the Court had invalidated that form of litigation in federal court. Congress more plausibly would have preferred officer suit enforcement as a second-best alternative. Moreover, as critics of the opinion noted, section 1983 provided an independent foundation for the suit against state officials, one that authorizes the enforcement of federal constitutional and statutory rights. See Meltzer (1996); Jackson (1997). The Court declined to discuss section 1983 as a possible vehicle for the claim against the state official. Although the Court claimed that its decision left individuals with an adequate array of enforcement tools, the Court's one-two punch raised serious doubts about the ability of individuals to enforce congressionally created rights.

Many turned to state court. If Congress had the power to fashion rights against the states, and if the Eleventh Amendment foreclosed the enforcement of such rights in federal courts, then perhaps individuals could pursue their claims in state court, relying either on the states' own waivers of sovereign immunity or on the obligation of the states to make a forum available for the enforcement of federal rights. (As noted in Section 10.2.2, States cannot refuse to hear federal claims if they open their doors to analogous state law claims.) Litigants filing suit in state court could point to a fairly impressive collection of cases in which the Court appeared to assume that state courts were open for the enforcement of federal rights, even where the Eleventh Amendment would bar suit in federal court. See *Hilton v. South Carolina Public Railways Comm'n* (1991). Under long-standing decisional law, moreover, the Supreme Court exercised appellate jurisdiction over state court decisions, even where the same cases would lie beyond the power of the district courts under the Eleventh Amendment. See *Cohens v. Virginia* (1821). Some viewed the Eleventh Amendment as a forum-allocation principle, calling for the initial determination of state-party suits in state courts followed by review in the Supreme Court. See Jackson (1988); Pfander (1998).

The Court rejected the state court option in *Alden v. Maine* (1999). There, a group of state workers brought suit for back pay under the Fair Labor Standards Act. When their federal action was dismissed on the basis of *Seminole Tribe*, the employees re-filed in state court. The Supreme Court of Maine rejected the suit, concluding that the state was free to claim the same immunity from suit in state court that the Court had previously made available in federal court. The case thus presented a fundamental question about the nature of the *Seminole Tribe* immunity: was it an immunity from federal jurisdiction that left the employees' federal right to damages intact and available for enforcement in another forum, or was it an immunity from liability that effectively deprived Congress and the affected employees of any way to secure the enforcement of the wage claim? See Vazquez (1997).

Dividing along now-familiar lines in a 5–4 decision, the *Alden* Court concluded in effect that the *Seminole Tribe* immunity barred liability and thus foreclosed suit in state court. In the first section of its opinion, the Court labored to show that the issue remained open for decision, distinguishing by brute force many of the precedents that leaned in the other direction. In the second part, the Court returned to the history and structure of government accountability, emphasizing the absence of any assured opportunity to litigate money claims against the states in state courts at the time of the framing. As the Court explained, it was extremely unlikely that the framers meant to empower Congress to impose an obligation on state courts to hear federal claims. The Court's statement may have been true, but it missed the point. The framers had responded to the absence of assured state court remedies by empowering the federal courts to hear state-party claims. Federal authority was preserved under the Eleventh Amendment, and later impaired by judicial interpretation in *Hans*. Having discarded the original understanding of the Eleventh Amendment, the majority's interest in the historical understanding appears quite selective.

Note too the changing nature of the work being done by state sovereignty. At the time of the framing, state sovereign immunity had the practical effect of precluding individuals from pursuing their claims in state courts, requiring instead that they file a petition with the legislature. Sovereign immunity thus operated to establish a rule of legislative primacy, requiring the legislature to create a judicial mode of determination. By the time of *Alden*, virtually all the states had abandoned the legislative mode in favor of judicial determination; Maine, for example, authorized individual suits against the state on wage claims. Application of the rule of sovereign immunity in *Alden* does not operate to protect legislative primacy in handling claims; it effectively bars Congress from creating an enforceable liability against the state. Ironically, the state employees were ultimately forced to seek relief by petition to the Maine legislature, a mode that they pursued successfully.

After *Alden v. Maine*, the Court's evolving government accountability doctrine bears some resemblance to its discarded *Usery* decision. Individuals simply cannot enforce a federal action for damages against the states, in state or federal court, so long as Congress created the right of action in the exercise of its commerce authority. To be sure, Congress retains its power to regulate the states as states following *Garcia*. Subsequent decisions make clear that Congress can continue to impose statutory obligations on the states as such. See *Reno v. Condon* (2000). Moreover, state obligations to respect federal law remain intact, and subject to enforcement through actions for declaratory and injunctive relief. Indeed, the Court has seemingly restored the *Ex parte Young* remedy that it had undermined in *Seminole Tribe*, concluding in *Verizon Maryland v. Public Service Comm'n* (2002) that individuals can enforce federal statutory obligations through suit brought against state officials. The Court has seemingly achieved a balance, permitting injunctive relief to secure individual rights but invalidating legislation that would threaten the state's treasury (by allowing an award of damages) or the state's dignity (by permitting individuals to name a state as a party). Its conclusion can claim precious little support in the Eleventh Amendment, but perhaps no less support than the Court had found in the Tenth Amendment for the result in *Usery*. To some extent, then, these cases vindicate then-Justice Rehnquist's prediction, dissenting in *Garcia*, that *Usery* would again command a majority of the Court. In fact, the *Alden* Court based its decision less on the Eleventh Amendment than on the fundamental commitment to state sovereignty that it discovered in the Tenth Amendment.

Conceptualizing the *Seminole Tribe/Alden* immunity as a limit on congressional power, rather than as a jurisdictional rule, tends to suggest that the whole business belongs in a book on constitutional law, rather than in one on federal jurisdiction. It also helps to explain the Court's determined efforts to prevent Congress from circumventing its new state sovereign immunity. *Alden* rules out suits in state court, and also includes dicta that apparently seeks to ward off other forms of litigation. Some have argued that individuals might step into the shoes of the federal government, bringing suit on behalf of the United States to enforce their rights against the states. See Caminker (1999); Siegel (1999). Under a long-standing exception, the Eleventh Amendment immunity does not apply to federal government suits on the theory that the states surrendered this immunity in the "plan of the convention." (Note that the Fair Labor Standards Act, and some other federal statutes, expressly authorize the federal government to bring enforcement actions, including, presumably, actions against the states.) Recognizing delegation as a potential threat, the *Alden* Court distinguished permissible suits by executive branch officials of the federal government who exercise political responsibility in the name of the United States from suits brought by private persons pursuant to a delegation of the government's authority.

More recently, the Court concluded that the states surrendered their immunity from suit in bankruptcy in the plan of the convention. See *Central Virginia Community College v. Katz* (2006). The decision builds in part on the Court's earlier conclusion that certain in rem proceedings in bankruptcy could go forward against the states without implicating their sovereign immunity. See *Tennessee Student Assistance Corp. v. Hood* (2004). But the decision's significance lies in its conclusion that constitutional provisions other than the Fourteenth Amendment may qualify the states' immunity from suit. The *Katz* Court concluded that it had been too hasty in *Seminole Tribe* in assuming that the power to fashion uniform rules of bankruptcy, like other Article I powers, would not support the abrogation of state sovereign immunity. On further reflection (a process that apparently led Justice O'Connor to abandon the five-Justice immunity majority), the Court concluded that states were fully subject to suits in bankruptcy, including suits by the bankruptcy trustee to avoid preferences and recover money from state entities. Though not strictly an abrogation decision, the *Katz* approach certainly enables Congress to fashion uniform bankruptcy rules that include the possibility of suits against the states. Instead of a congressional abrogation of immunity, however, the decision portrays the states as having no immunity to assert as a defense in the bankruptcy context.

7.4.5 Abrogation of State Sovereign Immunity Under the Fourteenth Amendment

Although it broke ranks in the bankruptcy context, the Court has attempted to ward off the legislative circumvention of its rule by narrowly interpreting the scope of Congress's abrogation power under the Fourteenth Amendment. Analysis of abrogation under the Fourteenth Amendment begins with the Court's decision in *City of Boerne v. Flores* (1997), which struck down the Religious Freedom Restoration Act on the ground that it exceeded congressional power to remedy violations of the Fourteenth Amendment. As the Court viewed the legislation, Congress had attempted to rewrite the constitutional test for assessing alleged violations of the religion clauses of the First Amendment and thus exceeded congressional power. Proper enforcement legislation must accept the Court's definition of constitutional rights, and adopt remedial measures that satisfy a "congruence" and "proportionality" test. The remedy must target an identified violation of constitutional rights, congruence, and adopt measures well tailored to remedy the problem at hand, proportionality.

The Court has considered a wide range of abrogation statutes since *Seminole Tribe* and *Boerne*, invalidating them almost without exception. The pattern was early set in *Florida Prepaid Expense Board v. College Savings Bank* (1999). The action for patent infringement had been brought under the Patent Remedy Act, a statute that satisfied the clear statement test for abrogation of state immunity. In considering the legality of the abrogation, the Court first ruled that the statute was invalid under Article I of the Constitution. Although Congress has power to regulate intellectual property, and although the power differs from the commerce power at issue in *Seminole Tribe* and *Alden*, it was nonetheless a power that pre-dated and was qualified by the ratification of the Eleventh Amendment.

The Court next considered if the abrogation would pass muster under the Fourteenth Amendment. Although the Court acknowledged that the patent laws created a species of property, and that the property in question was entitled to the protection of the due process clause of the Fourteenth Amendment, the Court found that Congress had failed to make a record that would support an abrogation of state immunity. In the Court's view, a simple patent infringement would not give rise to a constitutional violation, and trigger congressional remedial powers. Only where the states committed infringements and failed to provide the sort of remedy necessary to satisfy the demands of procedural due process would a violation arise. Congress had failed to document any pattern of infringements or any pattern of failed state remediation and could not justify the provision of a remedy under the congruence and proportionality test. Viewing the statute as a regulation of commerce, the Court vigorously resisted circumvention of its no-abrogation rule through a switch to Fourteenth Amendment analysis.

Following the approach taken in *Florida Prepaid*, the Court has invalidated federal abrogation statutes with monotonous regularity. In *Kimel v. Florida Board of Regents* (2000), the Court considered a statute that allowed suit against both private and public employers for violation of the federal ban on age discrimination. Although Congress had power to regulate the private sector under the Commerce Clause and to extend the regulations to the states under *Garcia*, the Court invalidated the abrogation of state immunity. The Court first noted that age discrimination did not itself violate the Constitution, and could not support remedial legislation. The Court also considered and rejected the claim that the legislative record of state discrimination against the aged justified remedial legislation under section 5.

The Court adopted much the same approach in *University of Alabama v. Garrett* (2001), invalidating provisions of the Americans with Disabilities Act (ADA) that authorized disabled individuals to sue states for workplace discrimination. As in *Kimel*, the federal statute established comprehensive federal prohibitions against discrimination, applicable to private and public employers alike. In considering the abrogation of state immunity, the Court noted that it had previously found that the disabled do not constitute a suspect class for purposes of triggering heightened scrutiny under the Fourteenth Amendment's equal protection clause. Abrogation thus required a showing that states had followed a pattern of engaging in discrimination against the disabled so irrational and pervasive as to justify remedial legislation. Again, the Court concluded that the showing had not been made.

If the Court's desire to protect its *Seminole Tribe/Alden* framework helps to explain its restrictive view of congressional power under the Fourteenth Amendment, so too does it explain the decision to abandon the doctrine of constructive consent to suit. Constructive consent appeared in *Parden v. Terminal Railway* (1964), a case involving the application of the Federal Employers Liability Act to a state-owned railroad in Alabama. The *Parden* Court reasoned its way to constructive consent by noting that the federal law had established conditions for the operation of railroads. When Alabama knowingly entered the field by acquiring a railroad, it was said to have impliedly consented to the regulatory conditions in place at the time, which included the right of injured employees to bring suit against the railroad for personal injuries. Subsequent decisions had chipped away at the *Parden* conclusion, and the Court formally overruled the doctrine in *College Savings Bank v. Florida Prepaid Expense Board* (1999). In *College Savings Bank*, the Court rejected constructive waiver as inconsistent with the no-abrogation rule of *Seminole Tribe*.

Some departure from this unbroken string of decisions came in *Tennessee v. Lane* (2004), *Nevada Dep't of Human Resources v. Hibbs* (2003), and *United States v. Georgia* (2006). All three cases found that the plaintiff had put forward a claim with some basis in the Fourteenth Amendment. In *Lane*, the plaintiff sought damages for a violation of Title II of the federal Americans with Disabilities Act (ADA), arguing that the state had denied him access to a place of public accommodation. The facts cried out for a remedy; Lane had to drag himself up two flights of stairs at the courthouse because the state had failed to install an elevator. The Court found that he had stated a claim for a violation of his right of access to court (rooted in the First and Fourteenth Amendments). It accordingly concluded that the ADA had properly abrogated state immunity, at least insofar as it applied to constitutional claims for denial of access to court.

The same approach informed the decision to allow a suit under the ADA by a disabled individual who alleged that he had been imprisoned by the state of Georgia in conditions that violated his rights under the Fourteenth Amendment. See *United States v. Georgia* (2006). Here again, the complaint alleged serious mistreatment of the prisoner, and the Court simply reiterated its conclusion that state conduct in violation of the Fourteenth Amendment may justify an abrogation of sovereign immunity and an award of damages against the state.

In *Hibbs*, the plaintiff sued his former employer, seeking damages for the state's failure to accommodate his request for family leave under the federal Family and Medical Leave Act. The Court permitted the action for damages to proceed, emphasizing that the Act sought to combat gender stereotypes in the workplace by making family leave available to all without regard to their sex. By linking family leave to the Fourteenth Amendment's prohibition of discrimination on the basis of sex, the Court identified a constitutional predicate for the abrogation of immunity that was missing in *Kimel, Garrett,* and *Florida Prepaid.* Although the legislation outlawed more conduct by the states than would the constitutional assurance of equal protection, the Court regarded the affirmative grant of family leave to women and men alike as a prophylactic provision that would help to ward off state action based upon improper stereotypes.

Lane and *Hibbs* suggest the possibility that some statutes abrogating state immunity, though potentially vulnerable to a *Florida Prepaid* analysis, might nonetheless withstand scrutiny. If the plaintiff can show, as in *Lane*, that the state's conduct violates the Constitution, a statute that provides for an award of damages would presumably pass muster (even if the statute might also apply to a number of situations in which no constitutional violation was apparent). Similarly, if the plaintiff can identify a constitutional foundation, as in *Hibbs*, then legislation that goes beyond the enforcement of the specific constitutional right may withstand scrutiny. This prospect troubled Justice Scalia, whose dissenting opinion in *Lane* complained about the particularity of such an approach and argued instead for an across-the-board approach to the legality of the abrogation. Justice Scalia also criticized the congruence and proportionality test as opening the door to judicial balancing, and urged the Court to confine that approach to congressional attempts to deal with racial discrimination.

The future of the Court's restrictive view of Congress's power to abrogate state sovereign immunity remains much in doubt. Four Justices have announced ongoing opposition to *Seminole Tribe* and *Alden*. Other Justices have occasionally joined with them to create a majority to uphold particular laws. In addition to *Lane* and *Hibbs*, the Court concluded that state sovereign immunity does not apply to claims within the federal courts' in rem jurisdiction over an estate in bankruptcy, see *Tennessee Student Assistance Corp. v. Hood* (2004), or to suits against the states to avoid and recover certain preference items in bankruptcy. See *Central Virginia Community College v. Katz* (2006).

Such occasional departures may threaten the coherence of the *Seminole Tribe/Alden* framework, and may eventually persuade the Court to reconsider those decisions. When the *Garcia* Court overruled *Usery*, it did so in part because it had failed to apply the *Usery* rule consistently. Similar inconsistency in the application of *Seminole Tribe* may persuade the Court that the task of balancing interests in state autonomy and federal accountability should be left to Congress. Much will depend on how the changing membership of the Court views the doctrine of state sovereign immunity.

7.4.6   Sovereign Immunity for Arms of the State

Although the Court ruled in *Hans v. Louisiana* (1890) that states enjoyed an Eleventh Amendment immunity from suit, it also concluded that a county government did not share the state's immunity. See *Lincoln County v. Luning* (1890). The Court has adhered to this view ever since, steadfastly refusing to permit local governmental bodies to claim a sovereign immunity from suit in federal court. Some view the distinction as consistent with nineteenth century authorities, which treated municipal corporations as analogous to private corporations for purposes of their being subject to suit in a common name. See Fletcher (1983). Others question the distinction, noting that local government bodies typically act pursuant to organic statutes adopted by the state, and qualify as state actors for purposes of the Fourteenth Amendment. However poorly theorized, it appears that the distinction between state and local governments has become firmly embedded in the law of government accountability.

In contrast to local governments, the Court has long treated statewide agencies as arms of the state for purposes of the Eleventh Amendment. See *Edelman v. Jordan* (1974). Thus, state welfare agencies, state police departments, state correctional facilities, and state universities all may invoke the state's Eleventh Amendment immunity from suit in federal court. One can understand the cases to some degree by noting the extent of the state's financial responsibility for any judgments rendered against these agencies. Where such ultimate financial responsibility does not exist, the Court may decline to make sovereign immunity available to a state agency. See *Hess v. Port Authority Trans–Hudson Corp.* (1994).

7.5   State Official Action and Section 1983

As with the federal government, the law of state government accountability relies heavily on suits brought against officials of the state. The Court's *Ex parte Young* (1908) jurisprudence developed after the Court ruled out suits against the states in *Hans v. Louisiana* (1890). In addition, Congress has provided for suit against state officials:

> Every person who, under color of any statute, ordinance, regulation, custom, or usage, of any State or Territory, subjects, or causes to be subjected, any citizen of the United States or other person within the jurisdiction thereof to the deprivation of any rights, privileges, or immunities secured by the Constitution and laws, shall be liable to the party injured in an action at law, suit in equity, or other proper proceeding for redress.

42 U.S.C. § 1983. The statute provides for damages and injunctive relief against state and local officials and plays a central role in assuring state government accountability. It reaches both constitutional and statutory violations of federal law, and applies to all constitutional violations (unlike the *Bivens* doctrine, for example, which applies only to select constitutional violations by federal officials).

Section 1983's place at the center of state government accountability dates from the Warren Court decision in *Monroe v. Pape* (1961). In a case that bears some resemblance to *Bivens*, officials of the Chicago police department broke into the Monroe home without a warrant, searched the premises, and eventually arrested Mr. Monroe on "open" charges. Although he was questioned about a murder, he was not taken before a magistrate or allowed to telephone a lawyer. Eventually, he was released without any charges being filed. He filed suit under section 1983, arguing that his constitutional rights had been violated by police officials acting under color of state and local authority. The police officers defended against federal liability on the ground that the actions alleged in the complaint were unlawful under state law. As a result, they argued that the actions should not be regarded as actions under color of state law within the meaning of section 1983.

The officers' defense, if accepted, would have made state law the primary tool for remedying unlawful action on the part of the police, and other state and local officials. So long as state law barred the practice at issue, the officials could be seen as engaging in unauthorized actions that were not properly attributable to the state for purposes of the "color of state law" analysis under section 1983. (Note the resemblance between the officers' argument and the authority-stripping rationale that underlies the *Ex parte Young* decision.) Section 1983 and the constitutional provisions to which it gives effect would lie in reserve, applying only where state officials had complied with state law but had allegedly violated federal law. Thus, the case ultimately turned on whether the state courts were to be entrusted with the initial determination of these claims, or whether the federal courts were to provide an independent remedy for state official misconduct.

The Court resolved this issue largely by reference to legislative history. For the majority, the history of section 1983 revealed a desire on the part of Congress to provide a freestanding federal remedy. Concerned with the depredations of the Ku Klux Klan, drafters of the bill had come to distrust state courts and feared that remedies theoretically available to certain citizens of the southern states were not available in fact. This history persuaded the *Monroe* Court that the federal remedy should not depend on the formal availability of state remedies. In dissent, Justice Frankfurter argued that the legislative history pointed toward a more deferential result, one in which the federal remedy came into play only where redress was barred in state court due to some custom or usage of non-enforcement. Justice Frankfurter's approach could have required the federal courts to conduct a threshold inquiry into the adequacy of state remedies as a condition of hearing the claim. The majority, by contrast, allows the plaintiff to assess the two legal systems at the time of forum selection, and to choose state or federal court depending on the relative adequacy of state and federal remedies.

Monroe has come to stand for the proposition that section 1983 litigants need not exhaust their state remedies, and has contributed to some growth in the number of section 1983 filings in federal court. Other factors contributing to the growth of filings include the expansion of the number of constitutional and statutory rights to which the provision applies and the passage in 1976 of a provision that authorizes the payment of attorney's fees to prevailing parties in section 1983 litigation. The question of how to assess this growing caseload remains disputed, however. Congress has assumed that growing caseloads reflect an increase in frivolous litigation, and justify some reduction in the scope of the federal remedy. The Prison Litigation Reform Act (1996) imposes important limits on section 1983 claims by individuals held in state (and federal) prisons. In doing so, Congress reinforced a view of prison litigation that had taken hold at the Supreme Court some years earlier.

7.5.1   Section 1983 and the Fourteenth Amendment

Although *Monroe v. Pape* remains good law, the Court has since narrowed the scope of the Fourteenth Amendment and thereby narrowed the effective range of remedies under Section 1983. Early decisions chipped away at the reach of the constitutional provisions often relied upon in prison litigation. In *Parratt v. Taylor* (1981), a Nebraska prisoner brought suit in federal court under section 1983, seeking to recover the value of a hobby kit that prison officials had lost or misplaced through negligence. After rehearsing the elements of a section 1983 claim, the Court focused on the prisoner's constitutional claim for deprivation of property without due process of law. Although the Court noted that its procedural due process cases had sometimes required the state to provide a pre-deprivation hearing before a final deprivation of property, it concluded that these cases were inapplicable to actions by state officials that were "random and unauthorized." As to such conduct, the state lacks meaningful control and can provide process only after the initial deprivation occurs. Here, the Court noted the availability of state tort remedies for property losses. Although those remedies would not necessarily provide the plaintiff with all of the relief available under section 1983, they did offer full compensation for loss and the Court held that nothing more was required to satisfy the Constitution.

Parratt illustrates the way in which an expansive federal remedy for constitutional violations (under section 1983) may result in a contraction of the constitutional rights available to plaintiffs. The *Monroe* Court had interpreted section 1983 to reach official conduct that, from the perspective of the government, might appear random and unauthorized. That decision confronted the Court with the prospect that virtually any negligent state deprivation of property, including an automobile accident caused by a state official, could lead to constitutional tort litigation as a deprivation of property without due process. To forestall that possibility, the Court consigned claims for procedural due process violations to the state courts, at least where the state post-deprivation remedy was adequate and the state action at issue was random and unauthorized, rather than adopted pursuant to some state policy.

The Court cut back further on the scope of the constitutional right to procedural due process in another prison case. In *Daniels v. Williams* (1986), the prisoner sued for personal injuries he sustained when he tripped over a pillow that a guard had negligently left on the staircase. Without reaching any question as to the adequacy of the state remedy, the Court found that the Fourteenth Amendment did not apply. Interpreting the Fourteenth Amendment's requirement of a "deprivation" of property, the Court concluded that merely negligent conduct on the part of state officials could not give rise to a constitutional claim. Overruling a portion of *Parratt v. Taylor* on this point, the *Daniels* Court concluded that only where state officials intentionally deprived the prisoner of property would they implicate the plaintiff's right to procedural due process.

A final significant case in the *Parratt* line, *Zinermon v. Burch* (1990), narrowed the potential scope of the doctrine. The plaintiff brought suit alleging a deprivation of liberty without due process, claiming that he lacked the capacity to admit himself voluntarily to a mental facility and should have been processed under the procedures for involuntary commitment. Although the Court held that the *Parratt* doctrine applies to deprivations of liberty, it restricted the doctrine in other respects. For one thing, the Court noted that claimed violations of the bill of rights and of the substantive due process component of the Fourteenth Amendment were complete when the deprivation occurred. As to such claims, the availability of adequate post-deprivation remedies was irrelevant to the plaintiff's ability to state a claim. Turning to the application of the *Parratt* doctrine to the particular case, the Court found that the deprivation (improper commitment) was not random and unauthorized. State officials could have anticipated the deprivation, and could have taken pre-deprivation steps to reduce its likelihood.

7.5.2 Section 1983 Liability of State and Local Governments

Section 1983 creates a liability that runs against every "person" who commits a violation of federal constitutional and statutory rights under color of state law. But the Court has been quite selective in defining which government bodies qualify as persons for purposes of liability. On the one hand, it has concluded that the states themselves, and state agencies, do not qualify as persons within the meaning of section 1983. See *Will v. Michigan Dep't of State Police* (1989). This decision complements the state's immunity from suit in federal court under the Eleventh Amendment, and serves to preclude the state courts from being obliged to entertain section 1983 claims against the states themselves. On the other hand, the Court has found that local governments are proper defendants in section 1983 litigation. Its opinions reveal a deep disagreement about the basis of government liability.

In its first decision on the issue, the Court concluded that the City of Chicago did not qualify as a person within the meaning of the statute. See *Monroe v. Pape* (1961). But the Court overruled that decision some years later, concluding that local governments were subject to liability under section 1983. See *Monell v. Dep't of Social Services* (1978). The *Monell* Court reached that conclusion after a detailed review of the legislative history persuaded it that municipal corporations were viewed as persons as a matter of general legal usage at the time of the statute's adoption. But even as it confirmed municipal liability for section 1983 purposes, the Court observed that the local government did not bear respondeat superior liability for the unlawful actions of its employees. Only where the plaintiff could show that the action in question "implements or executes" an official policy, ordinance, or regulation adopted by the government body's officers was the government to be held responsible.

Much section 1983 litigation against county and city governmental bodies now turns on the extent to which the challenged action represents an official policy of the government in question. Plaintiffs cannot recover on a theory of respondeat superior simply by showing a violation of the constitution or laws by an employee of the local government. Rather, the plaintiff must show that the government body somehow instituted, embraced, or officially tolerated the policy that led to the tortious conduct. That inquiry, in turn, has proven quite difficult. Counties may bear liability when they adopt a policy or custom that violates the Constitution. But the task of identifying local government policy can lead to fairly intricate inquiries into government rulebooks and lines of official authority within the government. The Court treats state law as controlling in defining who makes policy for the local government. See *City of St. Louis v. Praprotnik* (1988). But the local government may also bear liability when its conduct results from the absence of any policy. Thus, a failure to train city police officers to deal with the situations they face on the job may lead to liability when the failure reveals a deliberate indifference to the rights of persons with whom the police will come into contact. See *City of Canton v. Harris* (1989).

At the same time that the Court has developed these limitations on the liability of local governments, it has refused to extend the benefit of qualified immunity to such government bodies. See *Owen v. City of Independence* (1980). This conclusion contrasts with the Court's view of the liability of natural persons; the Court has long accorded individual defendants a qualified immunity from liability so long as they act in good faith or, more recently, refrain from conduct that violates clearly established federal rights. See *Harlow v. Fitzgerald* (1982). Local governments can face a relatively strict form of liability when they happen to adopt a policy that the courts later judge to have violated federal law. At the same time, local governments may escape liability altogether when the absence of a policy leaves officers to exercise discretion in carrying out their duties.

Rules that govern indemnification of individual defendants further complicate the interaction of these rules of government liability. Although not universal, indemnification programs have grown quite common at the state level and among the larger and better financed local governments. Such an indemnity policy may result in the state or local government (or its insurance carrier) paying the full amount of any damages awarded to the plaintiff in a section 1983 case, even though the nominal defendant in such a suit was an employee of the governmental body, rather than the body itself. A local government may thus avoid direct liability under section 1983 only to face an obligation to provide indemnity for any award made against its employees. A state government that enjoys a fairly firm immunity both from suit under section 1983 and from federal litigation under the Eleventh Amendment may nonetheless incur liability through its duty to indemnify its employees.

The treatment of indemnification agreements highlights the formalism that often characterizes the Court's handling of government accountability issues. The Court has generally declined to treat indemnification agreements as relevant to its assessment of the proper scope of government accountability. As noted below, the existence of indemnification arrangements does not appear to have influenced the Court's analysis of the qualified immunity question. Moreover, the Court has refused to treat the presence of an indemnity agreement as triggering the applicability of Eleventh Amendment immunity. Thus, when the plaintiff names a state official in his or her personal capacity, the existence of an indemnification policy that requires the state to bear the ultimate financial responsibility for any award of damages does not transform the suit into one against the state for Eleventh Amendment purposes.

In contrast, if the complaint happens to name a state officer in her official (not personal) capacity, the Court will treat the action as seeking an award of damages against the state, and will block the suit on Eleventh Amendment grounds. See *Will v. Michigan Dep't of State Police* (1989). At the same time, when the suit names an official in her official capacity and seeks prospective relief, the defendant will qualify as a person for section 1983 purposes, so as to effectuate the *Ex parte Young* exception to the Eleventh Amendment. The party-of-record rule of *Hans* and *Ex parte Young* places significant weight on the manner in which the plaintiff identifies the defendant in the complaint, and informs the Court's definition of persons under section 1983.

7.5.3   Section 1983 and Other Federal Statutes

Although the Court held that section 1983 provides a right of action with which individuals can enforce rights under other federal statutes, recent decisions have cut back sharply on the availability of such claims. The story begins with *Maine v. Thiboutot* (1980), in which the Court held that the reference to "laws" in section 1983 encompassed a federal welfare statute that Congress had adopted in the exercise of its spending powers. The Court's decision enabled welfare claimants to enforce federal restrictions on the way the state administered the welfare program (as in *Edelman v. Jordan*), and to do so in an action brought in state court. In effect, then, the Court interpreted section 1983 as providing an all-purpose right of action for use in enforcing other federal rights that Congress has established in legislation that applies to state governments. In doing so, the Court rejected both the argument that section 1983 applies only to rights aimed at securing equal protection under the Fourteenth Amendment and the argument that rights created under the Spending Clause are to be enforced only through a cut-off of funds, rather than coercive relief.

The Court has since retreated from the broadest implications of the *Maine v. Thiboutot* decision. In one line of cases, the Court has taken a restrictive view of what constitutes a federal statutory right for purposes of enforcement against the states under section 1983. In *Gonzaga University v. Doe* (2002), the Court considered an action brought to enforce a right to privacy in educational records that Congress had created under the Family Educational Rights and Privacy Act. The Court concluded that the statute in question, enacted under the Spending Clause, did not create a right that was enforceable in private litigation. Instead, the Court noted the availability of a funds cut-off, and noted the many ways in which the Act appeared to speak in terms of institutional practice rather than individual rights. The Court also drew upon its restrictive approach to the recognition of implied rights of action in deciding whether a right existed for purposes of enforcement against the states under section 1983. Although the Court stopped short of saying that Congress lacks power to create privately enforceable rights under its spending power, such a federal statute will trigger private enforcement against state officials under section 1983 only by including a fairly clear statement of its intent to establish rights in individuals.

Even statutes that include language creating rights in individuals may not be enforceable under section 1983 if the statute provides some fairly specific remedial provisions. In *Middlesex County Sewerage Auth. v. National Sea Clammers Ass'n* (1981), the plaintiff brought suit against state actors under section 1983, seeking relief for the discharge of sewage in violation of federal pollution statutes. Although the statutes included language that created individual rights, and authorized citizens suits against polluters for injunctive relief, the Court found that the rights were not enforceable through section 1983. As the Court saw matters, the statutes at issue had included comprehensive enforcement mechanisms that impliedly displaced supplemental enforcement through section 1983.

7.6 Official Immunity

As was the case in the nineteenth century with successful common law trespass claims, successful litigants under section 1983 obtain a judgment for damages that imposes personal or individual liability on the defendant. Successful *Bivens* claimants obtain similar judgments, imposing personal liability on federal defendants. Personal liability threatens the public official with fairly serious financial consequences; plaintiffs may enforce their judgments by seizing a personal bank account, say, or a private home. To be sure, the government may choose to indemnify the officer from any such liability. But not all state and local governments have adopted indemnity policies for their employees, and not all official misconduct falls within the scope of the policies that have been adopted.

At first blush, the prospect of personal liability for conduct undertaken on behalf of the government appears quite difficult to justify. Consider what would happen in the private sector. Under the doctrine of respondeat superior, firms bear responsibility for the torts of their employees and firms purchase insurance to spread the risk of financial loss. Rarely would an injured victim seek to impose personal liability on an employee (even though such liability might in theory be available). But in the public sector, the doctrine of sovereign immunity precludes the imposition of respondeat superior liability on government entities. (Recall that individual officers do not ordinarily bear liability for the government's contracts.) Section 1983 bars respondeat superior liability for local governments that lack Eleventh Amendment immunity. With no firm or governmental entity to sue, the victims of government wrongdoing bring suit against officers out of necessity. Personal liability thus substitutes for respondeat superior liability, providing victims with an opportunity to secure redress for an invasion of their rights.

The legislative branch of government can lessen the perceived problems with personal liability in two ways. First, it can provide the official with indemnification, either by adopting a private bill (as the federal government did throughout much of the nineteenth century) or by establishing a formal indemnification program for government employees. Today, the federal government and many state and local governments have indemnity programs (perhaps backed by insurance policies); as a consequence, federal government officials rarely face personal liability for tortious conduct. Apart from indemnity programs, the government can simply substitute itself as a defendant for the official by adopting a statute that creates a liability running against the government as an entity. Such statutes would constitute a waiver of sovereign immunity and would enable suit to proceed against the government itself. Many state legislatures have adopted such statutes in the tort field, as has the federal government in the Federal Tort Claims Act.

The law's reliance on a regime of personal official liability makes more sense when viewed in the context of sovereign immunity and the inability of the courts to fashion a liability running against the government. Judicial insistence on fairly strict official liability assures a degree of compensation for injured parties and encourages the legislature either to waive the government's immunity from suit or to provide full indemnification. Such considerations doubtless informed the Court's decision in *Little v. Barreme* (1804) (discussed in section 7.2.3 above), which imposed liability despite the fact that a naval officer apparently acted in good faith in carrying out the (unlawful) seizure of a vessel. Official liability operates as a second-best solution. It permits the plaintiff to recover damages where the law provides no alternative remedy, and it places the legislature in control of deciding how to address any resulting unfairness to the individual official.

Despite the arguments for legislative primacy, the Supreme Court has developed a fairly intricate doctrine of official immunity as a matter of federal common law. Beginning in the middle of the twentieth century, and developing quickly, the doctrine of official immunity protects government officials from liability unless their actions violate clearly established legal rules of which a reasonable person would have known. See *Harlow v. Fitzgerald* (1982). Apart from this qualified immunity for executive branch officials, the Court has clarified that more absolute forms of official immunity apply to prosecutors, judges and legislators. This section surveys the development of these doctrines of qualified and absolute official immunity.

7.6.1 Qualified Immunity for Executive Branch Employees

Most executive branch employees enjoy qualified immunity from suit. The Court has explained its decision to provide such an immunity as reflecting a balance of competing interests. On the one hand, an action for damages against the responsible official may provide victims of an official abuse of power with the only realistic chance to vindicate their constitutional rights. On the other hand, too strict a regime of official liability may distract officers by embroiling them in time-consuming litigation, may make public-spirited citizens reluctant to accept public employment, and may "dampen the ardor of all but the most resolute ... in the unflinching discharge of their duties." *Harlow v. Fitzgerald* (1982).

One can question each of these pro-immunity premises. Most governments provide attorneys to help defend any official charged with a constitutional tort. Except in complex cases or cases of serious misconduct, litigation may not unduly distract officers from their daily responsibilities. Similarly, the willingness of talented individuals to accept government employment may reflect a variety of considerations other than the rules of qualified immunity; individuals concerned with placing their own assets at risk will presumably demand some assurance of indemnification. Finally, the "ardor" of public servants in the discharge of their duties may reflect liability rules, along with a range of other considerations. The desire for advancement within a particular agency, and the desire to enhance one's reputation in the larger employment market, may provide ample incentives for ardor and zeal. Finally, the influence of these factors may depend on the culture of the particular agency and the degree to which agency heads reinforce a culture of ardor and zeal.

Despite the likelihood that official conduct will depend on a variety of factors, including the availability of indemnity policies, the Court has established an across-the-board standard for qualified immunity. It formulated the standard in *Harlow v. Fitzgerarld* (1982), and expressly designed the standard to apply as a general rule to govern suits seeking to impose liability on executive branch employees. Thus, the Court noted in passing that the same standard would apply both to state officers, sued under section 1983, and federal officers sued on a *Bivens* claim.

Moreover, the Court took pains to establish an objective test, thereby eliminating the subjective inquiry into good faith that had previously informed its analysis. In *Harlow*, then, the Court held that executive branch officials performing discretionary functions "generally are shielded from liability for civil damages insofar as their conduct does not violate clearly established statutory or constitutional rights of which a reasonable person would have known." The test enables a lower court to grant some form of summary judgment to the defendant official based upon an inquiry into the state of the law. Previous cases considered whether the defendant was acting in good faith at the time and such inquiries prove notoriously difficult to conduct at early stages of the litigation process.

The facts of *Harlow* itself illustrate the difficulty. The plaintiff, a whistleblower in the Nixon administration, contended that the defendants had conspired to cause his discharge in violation of his first amendment rights. Liability might well turn on the defendants' state of mind when they participated in the decision to discharge the plaintiff. Assuming that the plaintiff could allege and prove that the defendants played a role in his discharge, and did so with knowledge of the plaintiff's activities, allegations of bad faith and retaliation would certainly survive a motion to dismiss and might survive a summary judgment motion. By shifting to an objective standard that focused on the law governing the first amendment rights of whistleblowers, the Court provided the defendants with a way out of the litigation on a threshold motion.

The *Harlow* decision has yielded some uncertainty as the lower courts have struggled to define clearly established law. For one thing, the courts have disagreed about what sources to rely upon in searching for a clearly established legal standard. Some have demanded precedents from the Supreme Court; others have considered circuit authority in the relevant geographic circuit as establishing clear law. The Supreme Court resolved this issue in *Hope v. Pelzer* (2002), concluding that officials at the state prison had violated the Eighth Amendment by handcuffing prisoners to a hitching post in the summer sun for an extended seven hour period without providing bathroom or water breaks. Not only did the Court find that the Constitution prohibited the use of the hitching post as a form of discipline, it concluded that the rule was clearly established (thereby placing the officer on notice that liability could ensue). In making its decision, the Court relied upon two decisions of the Eleventh Circuit as well as Department of Justice guidelines. The absence of Supreme Court decisional law did not foreclose the finding, nor did the presence of a modest number of unpublished district court decisions that pointed in the other direction.

Hope v. Pelzer highlights the importance of determining the appropriate level of generality at which the court should operate in attempting to define clearly established law. Without a Supreme Court decision in a similar case, litigants and lower courts must reason by analogy in deciding whether the Constitution clearly prohibits the conduct. In considering clarity for qualified immunity purposes, one might focus on the general language of the Eighth Amendment's prohibition of cruel and unusual punishment. As a highly general matter, one might say that the provision provides prison guards with notice that cruel conduct violates the Constitution. Or, courts might demand a high level of specificity, insisting upon decisions that address the specific conduct of the prison guards. Such a level of specificity could result in fairly fact-bound determinations, and a resulting expansion in the scope of qualified immunity. The Court obviously enjoys a great deal of discretion in choosing a level of generality; it can stress continuity with past decisions or it can treat each case as an independent event. While the Court did not address the question in terms of the level of generality, *Hope v. Pelzer* did steer a middle course between the general and the particular.

A second problem after *Harlow* was the resulting stultification of the law. Lower courts, seeking to avoid constitutional issues where possible, often refused to address the question of whether the executive officer had violated a constitutional right; they would skip that issue if they concluded that the right would not be considered clearly established under the *Harlow* standard. Consider, for example, the facts in *Wilson v. Layne* (1999). Police officers brought a media crew along to witness and photograph the execution of an arrest warrant in a private home in Maryland. The homeowner sued under the Fourth Amendment, seeking damages. The Fourth Circuit upheld the claim of qualified immunity ruling that the relevant decisional law at the circuit or Supreme Court level failed to establish clearly that media ride-alongs violated the Constitution. The lower court's decisional process has the advantage of resolving the case on a point of law, but it failed to say whether the Fourth Amendment bars media from a private home.

For a time, the Supreme Court attempted to deal with the problem of stultification by imposing a fairly strict decisional process on the lower courts. In passing on an issue of qualified immunity, the lower court was required first to address the constitutional question, and only if the court finds that the Constitution prohibits the conduct in question may the court proceed to consider whether the right has been established with the clarity necessary to satisfy *Harlow*. See *Saucier v. Katz* (2001). In *Wilson v. Layne*, the Court followed this approach, first finding that the presence of the media in the home violated the Fourth Amendment, and then granting qualified immunity after finding that the rule was not clearly established for *Harlow* purposes. Such a decisional process has the advantage of facilitating the elaboration of legal rules, and avoids the stagnation that might result if lower courts consistently declined to pass on the constitutional issue.

There were drawbacks, however. For starters, the *Saucier* rule obliged lower courts to reach difficult constitutional questions that they might have avoided by pointing to the absence of clearly established law. In addition, the *Saucier* decision rule introduced some awkwardness into the process of appellate review. Suppose that, in a case like *Wilson v. Layne*, the circuit court ruled that media ride-alongs violated the Constitution. Suppose further that the circuit court found that the rule was not clearly enough established to warrant an award of damages. Obviously, the victim could appeal; the circuit decision upheld the defense of qualified immunity. But could the government official appeal? The official (or her government employer) might disagree with the circuit court's interpretation of the Constitution. But because the circuit court upheld the immunity defense on other grounds, the government official might lack standing to seek review in the Supreme Court.

Both of these practical concerns informed the Court's decision to abandon *Saucier*'s rigid order-of-decision rule. In *Pearson v. Callahan* (2009), the plaintiff filed suit seeking damages for an allegedly unconstitutional entry into his home. An undercover police informant had gained access to the plaintiff's home for the purpose of making a drug purchase, but the police officers who later arrived to make the arrest were not similarly welcome. They defended their entry on a "consent-once-removed" theory, arguing that the invitation to the undercover agent extended to them. The Tenth Circuit rejected the consent theory and the officers' claim that the law was sufficiently unsettled to give rise to qualified immunity. On review, the Supreme Court overturned *Saucier*, ruling that the lower courts have discretion to tailor the order of decision as they see fit. Turning to qualified immunity, the Court did not actually decide the consent issue under the Fourth Amendment, thus underscoring its conclusion that *Saucier* no longer controlled. But the Court did find that there was no clearly established rule against reliance on consent once-removed and on that basis upheld the immunity defense.

In the context in which the *Pearson* Court acted, some relaxation of the strict *Saucier* rule may make sense. After all, both state and federal courts have ample opportunities to rule on Fourth Amendment issues in connection with motions to block the introduction of evidence in criminal proceedings. But in a variety of other settings, the action for damages provides the sole basis with which to address constitutional issues. Consider, for example, a post-release suit for damages brought by an individual detained at Guantanamo Bay who wishes to challenge his treatment at the hands of detention officials. Motions to suppress evidence and applications for habeas relief do not offer a vehicle for mounting a constitutional challenge to government conduct. One can argue that the *Saucier* order-of-decision continues to make sense in such settings where constitutional law might otherwise go undeveloped. See Jeffries (2009).

7.6.2 Absolute Immunity for Legislators, Judges, and the President

In the Anglo–American model of government accountability litigation, most claims for damages and injunctive relief proceed against the officials charged with the execution of the laws. Litigants who wish to challenge a law's constitutionality, as in *Ex parte Young*, normally sue the state official charged with enforcement, rather than the members of the legislature that voted to enact the bill into law or the judges that have enforced the law. In the United States, the Supreme Court has formalized this preference for suits against executive branch officials by establishing a doctrine of absolute immunity for those acting in a legislative and judicial capacity. Unlike the qualified immunity for executive officers (which applies only to suits for damages), the absolute immunity may extend to suits for both damages and injunctive relief. As with other rules of government accountability, rules of absolute immunity often consider the availability of alternative remedies and the capacity in which particular officials acted.

The absolute immunity of legislators finds some support in the Constitution. Article I, section 6 provides a privilege from arrest for members of the House and Senate and further states that they shall not be questioned "in any place" for "any Speech or Debate in either House." Interpreting the Speech and Debate clause in *Kilbourn v. Thompson* (1880), the Court found that federal legislators were immune from a claim for damages brought by an individual who was imprisoned for contempt of Congress. (At one time, legislative assemblies claimed a power to imprison for contempt, and Congress once maintained a prison in the basement. Today, contempt of Congress would normally be dealt with through the judiciary.) Since *Kilbourn*, the legislative immunity has expanded to include all legislative acts through which members of Congress participate in the consideration and passage of proposed legislation. The immunity has been extended to members of Congress and to their aides as well. See *Gravel v. United States* (1972). Despite the absence of explicit constitutional support, similar absolute immunities have been extended to the members of state and local legislative assemblies, including members of a city council. See *Tenney v. Brandhove* (1951) (state legislature); *Bogan v. Scott–Harris* (1998) (city council).

The Court has justified absolute immunity both by pointing to Parliamentary tradition in England and by emphasizing the functional importance of immunity in encouraging members of assemblies to conduct their business without fear of personal liability. As with executive branch officials, the Court has expressed concern with the distractions of lawsuits and with the risk that liability might deter part-time citizen legislators from participating in the process. But one can question whether these considerations justify an absolute immunity, an immunity by definition that operates even where the legislative official acted in bad faith and in disregard of clearly established constitutional rights. So far, the Court has done little to explain why, aside from history and tradition, legislative branch officials need the greater measure of protection that absolute immunity confers.

Officials involved with the judicial process enjoy absolute immunity as well. This absolute immunity applies to the work of prosecutors, *Imbler v. Pachtman* (1976), as well as to that of judges. See *Stump v. Sparkman* (1978). As with legislative immunity, the common law had recognized an absolute immunity for both prosecutors and judges (at least judges of a court of record). The Court has emphasized this common law tradition in extending absolute immunity to officers of the courts. Prosecutors, according to the Court, might be frequent targets of litigation by criminal defendants who wish to vent their frustration after a failed proceeding. Judges, too, might be the common targets of disappointed litigants. In addition, though this has not been a factor that the Court has invariably emphasized in justifying absolute immunity, judicial processes generally afford the litigant an opportunity to vindicate her rights in the context of the judicial proceeding itself. The opportunity to ask a jury to reject the prosecutor's charges or to ask an appellate court to overturn the biased decisions of a trial judge may provide an important remedy that lessens the need for a suit against the particular judicial official.

In deciding whether any particular official enjoys an absolute or qualified immunity, the Court has adopted a functional test. Rather than looking at the title of the office, courts must consider the nature or function of the job the official was performing. See *Butz v. Economou* (1978). This means that individuals may lose their absolute immunity if they were not acting in their capacity as legislators, prosecutors, or judicial officials. Consider *Burns v. Reed* (1991). There, the Court held that a prosecutor enjoyed absolute immunity for actions taken in submitting evidence to a court in support of a search warrant (a prosecutorial function), but lacked such immunity when advising the police that they could question a suspect (a police function). Similarly, the Court denied absolute immunity to a judge sued for discrimination on the basis of sex in the discharge of a court employee. See *Forrester v. White* (1988). The Court viewed the judge's management of employment relations as work performed in an administrative or executive capacity, rather than in a judicial capacity.

The Court's characterization of certain judicial acts as administrative reflects the fact that judicial immunity traditionally extends only to acts taken within the scope of the judge's jurisdiction. In defining this limitation, however, the Court has taken quite a broad view of what constitutes a judicial act for immunity purposes. In *Stump v. Sparkman* (1978), an Indiana state judge approved a parental application for the sterilization of their fifteen-year old daughter. The proceeding was never docketed in court, and no guardian was appointed to represent the child's interests. When the child reached adulthood and could not conceive, she sued the judge for damages. Despite the absence of any authority in state law that could support the judge's actions, the Supreme Court upheld absolute immunity. Granting petitions in chambers was a function normally performed by judges and the child's parents had appealed to the judge's judicial discretion in submitting the case for decision.

By upholding absolute immunity in *Stump*, the Court created a situation in which the victim of the judge's decision lacked any remedy for judicial misconduct. Having failed to docket the case, appoint a guardian, and make a record of his decision, the judge frustrated any possibility of appellate review. One can argue that appellate review lies at the heart of judicial immunity at common law. Judges of a court of record enjoyed absolute immunity at common law; their decisions were subject to as-of-right review on a writ of error. But the writ of error was not available to review the decisions of courts not of record, and the judges of such courts did not enjoy immunity. To the contrary, inferior tribunals and justices of the peace were often subject to suit at common law if they took action in excess of their authority or jurisdiction. The very purpose of such proceedings against the judge was to test the court's authority and to secure some review of the court's decision. When a judge acts as in *Stump* in a way that frustrates the very possibility of appellate review, the claim of absolute immunity becomes quite difficult to justify.

One final government official, the President of the United States, enjoys absolute immunity for actions taken within the outer perimeter of his or her official duties in office. See *Nixon v. Fitzgerald* (1982). In contrast, the Court has extended state governors only a qualified immunity from suit. See *Scheuer v. Rhodes* (1974). The Court justified the presidential immunity with familiar (if unproven) claims about the visibility of the presidency and the likelihood of distracting litigation if such were permitted. The President's immunity, though absolute, does not extend to actions taken before the individual took office. Thus, President Clinton's conduct before his inauguration was not entitled to absolute immunity, or even to a stay that would protect him from the distractions of ongoing litigation until he left office. See *Clinton v. Jones* (1997). Nor does the president's immunity necessarily prevent courts from entering specific orders that name the president.

Thus, the Court has held that federal courts may issue a subpoena to the president, see *United States v. Nixon* (1974), and has left open the possibility that an injunction may be entered against the president to compel the performance of a ministerial act. See *Mississippi v. Johnson* (1866).

7.7 Government Accountability: Conclusion

The Court's government accountability decisions reveal some distrust of the legislative branch of government. In its Eleventh Amendment decisions, the Court has repeatedly struck down federal statutes that express a congressional judgment that the effective enforcement of the rights in question requires both injunctive relief, and a damages remedy that runs against the state itself. The Court has justified these decisions in part on the common law immunity of governmental bodies, as reflected in the debate over the meaning of the Eleventh Amendment. Similarly, in its qualified immunity decisions, the Court has declined to maintain the rigorous system of common law liability for government officials that was seen in the nineteenth century as the necessary counterweight to sovereign immunity. By fashioning judge-made rules of immunity, the Court has frustrated the claims of victims and taken away the incentives that might have encouraged broader legislative adoption of statutory waivers of immunity and more effective indemnity programs.

The Court's approach raises profound questions about the effectiveness of the resulting body of rules, and about the ability of the federal courts to secure rough and ready compliance with federal law. Some scholars have argued that the system works pretty well. It facilitates injunctive and declaratory relief, and permits the recovery of damages in circumstances involving intentional or clearly illegal misconduct on the part state and local government employees. On this view, the existence of indemnity programs means, as a practical matter, that the state pays for most constitutional torts despite its formal immunity from suit under the Eleventh Amendment. See Jeffries (1998). Yet the effectiveness of the officer suit as a substitute for the liability of the government itself might well be doubted. It's not at all clear that the liability that welfare recipients sought to impose in *Edelman v. Jordan* or the back pay that the employees sought to collect in *Alden v. Maine* could be recovered through a suit brought against the officers in their personal capacity. Sovereign immunity inevitably means that the state will escape liability for some otherwise valid money claims and that may leave victims without a remedy and governments without an adequate incentive to comply with the law.

On the other hand, the recognition of immunity may help to facilitate changes in the law. If the Court established a rigid requirement of full compensation for past constitutional violations, it may grow wary of overruling any of its past decisions. The Court's decision in *Brown v. Board of Education* (1954), overturned *Plessy v. Ferguson* (1896), and made state government policies of racial segregation unconstitutional. Suits for damages to remedy the losses associated with the maintenance of segregation would have produced a huge potential liability. See Jeffries (1999). Better to concentrate the states' resources on building the schools and hiring the teachers required to comply with the dictates of *Brown* in the future than to focus state and local resources on the payment of damages to past victims of segregation. One can see the combination of immunity and accountability as easing constitutional transitions and expressing a preference for the claims of future generations.

Chapter Eight

HABEAS CORPUS AND GOVERNMENT ACCOUNTABILITY

8.1 Introduction

As a test of the legality of present detention, the writ of habeas corpus has offered both an enduring and supple procedure for the protection of individual liberty. The "great writ of freedom" today performs its liberty-protecting function on behalf of a variety of different prisoners. State prisoners file petitions for habeas corpus to seek federal post-conviction review of state criminal proceedings. An elaborate body of law has grown up around these petitions for post-conviction review, as Congress and the Court seek to balance the goal of relatively error-free criminal justice with the practical need for finality. Immigrants rely on habeas corpus to challenge the legal basis for their exclusion or deportation. Enemy combatants captured in the global war on terror invoke habeas corpus in challenging their confinement at Guantanamo Bay, Cuba and elsewhere. In all these settings, habeas corpus requires the official jailer or custodian to justify detention in accordance with law.

This chapter examines the writ of habeas corpus, focusing initially on the writ's history in securing judicial review of executive detention. The historical inquiry helps to give meaning to the Constitution's Suspension Clause, which prohibits suspension of the privilege of the writ of habeas corpus except in defined circumstances. After analyzing federal detention, this chapter examines developments in the use of habeas to review state criminal convictions. The jurisdictional framework for such review dates from Reconstruction, and the practice picked up considerable steam during the latter half of the twentieth century. The chapter concludes with a discussion of restrictions that Congress has placed on the writ's availability.

8.2 The Historic Function of Habeas Corpus

As with other tools of government accountability, the United States borrowed the writ of habeas corpus from English common law. The writ earned its fame during the constitutional struggles of the seventeenth century, as a check on the Crown's practice of imprisonment by executive fiat. Parliament beefed up the common law writ in the Habeas Corpus Act of 1640, providing that habeas would issue to test the legality of royal fiat imprisonment. Further reforms in Habeas Corpus Act of 1679 addressed procedural flaws that the practice of the last century had revealed. Thus, Parliament took specific steps to ensure that judges were available to grant the writ (even at times when the courts were formally closed), that officers of the Crown did not transport petitioners beyond the seas to evade the reach of the writ, that the courts resolved the issues quickly, and that the executive could not recommit individuals after their release on habeas. See Sharpe (1989).

Habeas corpus operated both to oversee and to ensure access to the criminal justice system. An individual could not be held without being charged with a crime. Once an individual was charged, the writ of habeas corpus would issue to bring the individual before a magistrate for a determination of the existence of cause to hold the individual for trial. (Today, habeas no longer performs this function; the arraignment has become a standard feature of criminal procedure and has been codified in most jurisdictions.) If the court judged the evidence insufficient, or found that the individual was not properly charged with the crime, the court would grant the writ and the accused would go free. Apart from arraignment, habeas corpus would issue to protect the defendant's right to post bail and obtain release from custody pending trial. Finally, if the defendant were languishing, habeas would issue to enforce her right to a speedy and public trial. Many of these procedural protections (due process, bail, speedy trial) were later enshrined in the Constitution's bill of rights, and habeas was central to their enforcement. Criminal defendants often had no right to appeal from their conviction; the absence of appeal made habeas the primary tool for ensuring due process of law.

Recognizing the presumptive availability of habeas corpus, Parliament enacted statutes "suspending" the writ of habeas corpus during periods of public insecurity. Following an invasion by foreign troops or a local rebellion or act of sabotage, the Crown would round up and imprison the usual suspects. But under the law governing habeas corpus, the writ would issue to free a prisoner, unless the prosecutor could make out a chargeable criminal case against the defendant and persuade the court to decline to admit the prisoner to bail. The Crown would accordingly approach Parliament to secure a suspension of the writ. George II obtained suspensions of the writ in connection with an "invasion by a French Power" in 1743, and a "wicked and unnatural rebellion" in Scotland in 1745. George III secured a more famous suspension in 1777, to deal with a "rebellion and war" in certain of his plantations and colonies in America. In all such cases, the act of suspension authorized the detention of persons imprisoned on suspicion of treason, denied them admission to bail, and remained in effect until a specified date some five or six months in the future. By suspending the writ, Parliament prevented any release of prisoners for a time, after which habeas once again became available and the Crown would again face the choice of either charging the defendants with crimes or releasing them from custody.

Habeas corpus was among the writs that the common law courts of the colonies and the early American states routinely issued in connection with criminal proceedings (and other forms of detention). All thirteen states authorized their superior courts to issue writs of habeas corpus. See Duker (1980). Habeas was also the only writ that the Constitution secures against improper suspension. The Suspension Clause appears in Article I, section 9 and provides that the privilege of the writ of habeas corpus shall not be suspended unless, "when in Cases of Rebellion or Invasion the public Safety may require it." The debates leading to the inclusion of the provision do not appear especially contentious; members of the founding generation took the availability of the writ for granted and barred Congress from adopting a suspension act except in the situations identified.

8.2.1 Habeas Corpus in the Antebellum Period

In the Judiciary Act of 1789, Congress provided for the issuance of writs of habeas corpus. Section 14 reads as follows:

> [A]ll the before-mentioned courts of the United States shall have power to issue writs of scire facias, habeas corpus, and all other writs not specially provided for by statute, which may be necessary for the exercise of their respective jurisdictions, and agreeable to the principles and usages of law. And that either of the justices of the supreme court, as well as judges of the district courts, shall have power to grant writs of habeas corpus for the purpose of an inquiry into the cause of commitment.— Provided, That writs of habeas corpus shall in no case extend to prisoners in gaol, unless where they are in custody, under or by colour of the authority of the United States.

The statute thus contains three references to habeas, a general grant of power to issue writs of habeas corpus, a more specific grant of authority to issue habeas for the purpose of an inquiry into the cause of commitment that extends to federal judges, and a proviso that limits habeas to situations involving prisoners in custody of the federal government.

Although other readings have been suggested, one can best interpret these three provisions as conferring freestanding authority on all federal courts to issue the writ of habeas corpus to inquire into the legality of detention. See Pfander (2000). The second reference broadens that power to include judges of the district courts and justices of the Supreme Court to ensure that the writ would be available during recess or vacation just as in England under the Habeas Corpus Act of 1679. (Note that the Judiciary Act created circuit courts but did not staff them with circuit judges; instead, the justices staffed the circuit courts with the assistance of the district judges.) This provision for the exercise of a freestanding habeas power contrasts with the "all other writs" provision, which made such writs available only where necessary in aid of a jurisdiction otherwise conferred. State prisoners were apparently excluded from federal court by the proviso, and left to pursue state court remedies.

In *Ex parte Bollman* (1807), section 14 and the habeas power received a definitive early interpretation. Two individuals, Bollman and Swartout, had been arrested and charged with complicity in Aaron Burr's Western machinations. Despite the issuance of habeas by territorial judges in New Orleans, the US government brought the two to Washington, D.C. for trial on treason charges. After a lower court in the District refused the writ, the petitioners sought relief from the Supreme Court. Meanwhile, President Jefferson asked Congress for a law suspending the writ of habeas corpus, but Congress refused. Before the Supreme Court (which was then held in the basement of the capitol building and was packed with members of Congress), the first question was one of jurisdiction to issue the writ, and then the Court inquired into the sufficiency of the evidence against the two defendants. Ultimately, the Court reaffirmed its jurisdiction and concluded that the evidence required to sustain the charges was lacking. The two defendants, who were present in the Court on a writ of habeas corpus, were discharged by the Court's order.

The Court's decision in *Bollman* contributes three important ideas to our understanding of habeas. First, the Court treated its power to issue habeas as a creature of statute, thus fueling an ongoing debate about whether Congress may refrain from conferring habeas authority on the federal courts. Second, the Court suggested that the Constitution's Suspension Clause may influence the question; Congress had acted under the "immediate influence" of that Clause in enacting section 14 and may have been constitutionally obliged to do so. (Of course, the federal courts may not have been in a position to enforce Congress's constitutional duty to make habeas available had Congress chosen to ignore it.) Third, the Court found that the proceeding to review commitment for trial was, on the facts of the case, appropriately appellate because it involved a review of the commitment and habeas decisions of the lower court in Washington, D.C. On this basis, the Court distinguished *Marbury* (and its prohibition against congressional expansion of the Court's original jurisdiction) and found that it had power to hear the claim on the merits.

Celebrated instances of the exercise of habeas authority continued through the antebellum period, often corresponding to periods of national insecurity. During the waning weeks of the War of 1812, General Andrew Jackson imposed martial law in the city of New Orleans and jailed individuals who violated a military curfew. One federal judge who ordered release of a prisoner on habeas was promptly deported by the military. He later brought suit successfully against Old Hickory, and obtained a substantial award of damages. (Congress later indemnified Jackson for the amount of the verdict.) More dramatically, President Abraham Lincoln took unilateral action suspending the writ of habeas corpus in the opening weeks of the Civil War. He authorized officers of the Union military to imprison southern sympathizers and agitators who were disrupting the war effort in Baltimore, and along the military line.

The legality of Lincoln's suspension of the writ came to a head in *Ex parte Merryman* (1861). Merryman was arrested on suspicion of Southern sympathies and of drilling members of the Maryland militia to join the Southern cause. After Merryman's imprisonment, Chief Justice Roger Taney, author of the Court's *Dred Scott* decision, issued a writ of habeas corpus from his chambers in Baltimore. (Note that section 14 empowered Taney to grant the writ in his capacity as a single justice of the Supreme Court.) Although the marshal served the writ on the fort where Merryman was held, military officers refused to deliver Merryman into court, citing Lincoln's suspension of the writ. Taney wrote a detailed opinion explaining that the Constitution assigned the power to suspend to the legislative branch, not to the president acting alone. Taney had the better of the constitutional issue, but Merryman stayed in prison. Eventually, after two years of military arrests and imprisonment on an impressive scale, Congress ratified Lincoln's suspension of the writ in a carefully worded statute that also gave the president power to suspend the writ in future cases until the hostilities ended.

Clashes between the judicial authority and the military occurred with surprising frequency in the North throughout the Civil War. (We know less about the interplay between military government and judicial authority in the South.) In *Ex parte Vallandigham* (1863), the Court declined to intervene in the case of a Southern sympathizer who was imprisoned on orders of General McClellan and eventually sent across the border to the South. Like those of Chief Justice Taney, writs of habeas corpus issued by judges of the lower federal court in Washington, D.C. were essentially ignored. Congress dealt with that troublesome court by simply reconstituting the tribunal and appointing a collection of new judges sympathetic to the Northern cause. See Bloch & Ginsburg (2000). After President Lincoln's assassination, the federal government refused to bring the accused conspirators before a jury but tried them as illegal combatants before a military commission.

After the hostilities ended, the Court sought to re-claim a measure of judicial authority. *Ex parte Milligan* (1866) arose from an application for habeas corpus on behalf of a Southern sympathizer in Indiana who had been subjected to trial before a military commission. The Court acknowledged that the judicial power had been eroded to a considerable degree during the Civil War, but nonetheless portrayed the right to trial by jury as a fundamental right of citizens. According to the Court, trial of citizens by military tribunal was unlawful so long as the "courts are open and their process unobstructed." Such had been the case in Indiana throughout the war, rendering trial by commission unlawful. Concurring justices based their decision on the absence of congressional authority to convene such tribunals.

8.2.2 Habeas Jurisdiction and Procedure

At common law, litigants needed a writ to commence an action. For many common law proceedings, such as actions for trespass or breach of contract, writs were available as a matter of course. Once the writ issued and was served, the case got underway and the defendant was compelled to answer on pain of default. In a habeas proceeding, petitioners did not get their writs as a matter of course, they had to ask for them. Habeas proceedings began with a petition or application (perhaps with an accompanying affidavit). Often submitted on an ex parte basis, these motion papers would set out the details of the petitioner's imprisonment along with an argument that the custody was unlawful. If the court agreed, it would issue the writ, directing the custodian or jailer on pain of contempt to bring the petitioner into court along with a "return" or reply to the writ that explained on what basis the jailer justified the confinement. (Habeas corpus literally means to "have the body" of the petitioner brought before the court.) On the day of the petitioner's production, the court (as in *Ex parte Bollman*) would decide the legality of custody on the basis of the facts set out in the jailer's reply and the legal arguments of the parties.

Early practice on petitions for habeas corpus resembled modern day proceedings for a preliminary injunction. The process was summary; no jury was impaneled to resolve factual issues. If successful, the proceeding resulted in a judicial decree directing specific action on the part of an officer of the government, whether production of the petitioner in court or release of the prisoner from custody. Enforcement of these orders was secured through the threat of contempt; a jailer who failed to reply to the writ or honor an order of release was subject to arrest and imprisonment. To issue a writ of habeas corpus at common law was not necessarily to free the petitioner, but simply to require the petitioner's production in court for a determination of the custody's legality.

The simple fact of territorially restricted judicial power, coupled with the obligation of the custodian to produce the petitioner in court, gave rise to the "district of confinement" rule. Under the rule, the federal courts entertain habeas petitions only by those actually detained within the territorial boundaries of the district. This jurisdictional limit derives from language in the 1867 law empowering federal courts and judges to issue the writ only "within their respective jurisdictions." Congress included this language to prevent compelled production of prisoners outside their district of confinement and the Court has occasionally applied the rule. For example, in *Ahrens v. Clark* (1948), the Court ruled that the district court for the District of Columbia could not entertain a habeas petition on behalf of petitioners held at Ellis Island, New York. Even though the Attorney General of the United States was in the District, and subject to the court's authority, the Court held that the action was to proceed against the immediate custodian, in the district of confinement.

Practice has changed considerably since the territorial restriction was attached to the habeas power. Perhaps most importantly, the tradition of in-court production has ended. Instead of a writ of habeas corpus, requiring production of the petitioner, federal courts that find merit in a petition will issue an order requiring the government to justify the detention in a written submission. Neither the prisoner nor the jailer appears in court anymore (unless the court orders live testimony on the circumstances surrounding the detention, an exceedingly rare event). The proceeding results in a determination on the basis of the pleadings, affidavits, and legal arguments and if successful, the petitioner will gain release from custody. Today, a court may issue a writ of habeas corpus at the end of the proceeding to effect the release of the prisoner, rather than at the outset to gain jurisdiction over the jailer.

Changing practice has produced some relaxation of the district of confinement rule. In *Braden v. Judicial Circuit Court of Kentucky* (1973), the Court allowed a federal district court in Kentucky to hear a habeas petition, even though the petitioner himself was confined in a state prison in Alabama. The Court noted that the case concerned the legality of a extradition request by Kentucky, and it made good sense to allow the action to proceed in the district court there. Instead of inflexibly requiring litigation in the district

of confinement, then, the Court authorized litigation in other
districts so long as the district court could obtain jurisdiction over
the custodian. In cases involving overseas detention, moreover, the
Court has permitted the district court for the District of Columbia
to entertain a habeas proceeding, despite the fact that the immediate custodian is not present within the District. See *Burns v.
Wilson* (1953); *Toth v. Quarles* (1955). In such cases, the action
typically proceeds not against the immediate custodian but against
a high administrative official with ultimate responsibility for the
detention, such as the secretary of defense.

While *Burns* and *Toth* control overseas detention, the Court
revived the district of confinement rule for domestic cases. *Rumsfeld v. Padilla* (2004), began when Padilla was arrested in Chicago,
and taken to New York for processing on federal criminal charges.
Once there, the Defense Department made a finding that he was an
enemy combatant and transferred him out of the criminal justice
system and into military custody in South Carolina. He challenged
his custody successfully in litigation that began in the district court
of New York where he had a lawyer; jurisdiction over the Secretary
of Defense was based on New York's long-arm statute. But the
Court ruled that the district of confinement rule barred the New
York district court from entertaining a challenge to custody in
South Carolina. Although it distinguished the overseas cases, and
preserved the possibility of litigation of them in the District of
Columbia, it found that in cases involving domestic custody, the
immediate custodian and district of confinement rules still apply.

It seems odd that a rule adopted in the nineteenth century to
prevent the inconvenience of distant travel would continue to fix
the venue of habeas litigation long after the practice of in-court
production and territorial restrictions on process had ended. To be
sure, some habeas litigation might proceed most conveniently in the
district of confinement; habeas has sometimes been used to contest
unlawful conditions of confinement. But in cases such as *Padilla*,
the litigation challenges the power of high government officials at
the Pentagon and White House to designate illegal combatants and
the district of confinement may be a less convenient forum for such
litigation. Rather than the inflexibility of the district of confinement rule, the Court might have done better to recognize a range of
venues in which litigation could proceed. District courts could then
address issues of convenience more effectively through a change of
venue under 28 U.S.C. § 1404.

8.3 Habeas Review of Federal Detention and the Sus-
pension Clause

As the survey of antebellum practice reveals, the writ of habeas
corpus has played an important (if somewhat variably effective) role

in facilitating the judicial oversight of federal government detention. It continues to play that role today. Federal habeas corpus provides a possible remedy anytime an individual wishes to challenge present confinement as a violation of federal law. It has thus provided the remedial vehicle for an impressive body of law that cuts across a wide range of federal government activity. When the federal government wrongly enlists or drafts an individual into the armed services, habeas provides a possible remedy. When immigration authorities detain an immigrant at the border, or threaten an alien with deportation, habeas may require legal justification. Even where an individual has been convicted of a federal crime, habeas might conceivably issue to challenge some aspect of the conviction or sentence.

In many cases today, however, Congress has provided individuals in federal custody with more particularized remedies that push the habeas remedy into the background. In 1948, for example, Congress enacted 28 U.S.C. § 2255 to provide individuals with an opportunity to secure review of their federal criminal convictions by motion, instead of by petition for habeas corpus. Congress did so in part to simplify practice and in part to assign litigation of petitions for post-conviction review to the district courts that imposed the sentence (rather than the overworked federal courts in the districts where the prisons were located). During the 1990s, Congress reworked the rules that govern review of immigration matters and in many cases switched from review in the district courts by petition for habeas to review in the appellate courts. In both instances, displacement of habeas corpus was challenged as raising questions about the scope of Congress's power to suspend the privilege of the writ under Article I of the Constitution.

In considering such challenges, the Court has accepted new procedures so long as they preserve the essence of habeas review, but it has resisted federal statutes that go too far in curtailing access to federal court. The contrast between *United States v. Hayman* (1952) and *INS v. St. Cyr* (2001) illustrates the Court's approach. In *Hayman*, the Court considered the constitutionality of section 2255 as a substitute for post-conviction review of federal convictions by petition for habeas corpus. The Court found no constitutional problem. Practice under section 2255, which was designed as the Court noted to facilitate rather than to frustrate judicial review, preserved an individual's right to challenge the legality of a federal conviction. While the statute switched the form and forum of the challenge, and did away with the routine production of the petitioner in court, these changes were not seen as altering the essential elements of the habeas remedy. In all events, the right of a petitioner to file a habeas petition remained intact under section 2241 and available for use in a case where the restrictions in section 2255 bore too heavily on the individual's right to petition for review.

The Court took a less accommodating approach to the reform of immigration review in *INS v. St. Cyr.* There, the Court faced a challenge to a federal statute that had generally shifted review of immigration proceedings to the federal appellate courts, and had proposed to restrict access to habeas review in district court. St. Cyr himself had been convicted of a drug trafficking offense that triggered provisions of the law that made him presumptively subject to deportation and that foreclosed judicial review. St. Cyr argued that such a restriction on review would violate the Suspension Clause and the Court agreed. Instead of invalidating the law, however, the Court used the canon of constitutional avoidance in interpreting the statute to preserve the possibility of habeas review by petition to the district court. In the course of its opinion, the Court helped to frame the habeas issues that would arise from the detentions at Guantanamo Bay.

Building on past decisions, the *St. Cyr* Court found that the Suspension Clause served at a minimum to protect the common law function of the writ as it had existed in 1789. As of that date, habeas corpus operated to facilitate judicial review of executive detention, and extended to pure questions of law as well as to questions of the custodian's jurisdiction. The Court accordingly concluded that any legislation proposing to restrict habeas review within this historical core would present a serious question under the Suspension Clause. In order to avoid that question, the Court construed the immigration law as leaving the habeas power intact for purposes of enforcing St. Cyr's demand for discretionary review of the deportation decision. The Court viewed the Suspension Clause not as conferring power on the federal courts to issue the writ, but as limiting the power of Congress to cut back on the scope of habeas, at least where the remedial options were judged insufficient. So long as the general habeas statute remains on the books, such a strategy of narrowly interpreting restrictions on judicial review will suffice to ensure access to the writ.

8.3.1 Habeas Review and Enemy Combatants

Following the attacks of September 11, 2001, the federal government under President George W. Bush re-imagined its approach to two elements of its war on terrorism. First, the government proposed simply to detain "enemy combatants," holding them in prison-like facilities at Guantanamo Bay for the duration of the hostilities somewhat in the same way that the United States has held prisoners of war during past conflicts. Many but not all of these detainees were taken prisoner during fighting to oust the Taliban from Afghanistan. The government contended that the

Guantanamo detainees were not prisoners of war within the meaning of the Geneva conventions, and were not entitled to the protections that such status would confer. The government took this position in part to avoid the restrictions that the Geneva conventions would impose on its ability to interrogate the prisoners.

Apart from detaining prisoners as enemy combatants at Guantanamo Bay, the government proposed to try certain individuals for acts of terrorism. But the government sought to hold these trials before tribunals other than the Article III courts that had heard such cases in the past. By choosing to characterize terrorism as unlawful combat subject to punishment before military commissions, the Bush administration sought to address a number of concerns. First, under the terms of the military commission order, defendants would enjoy neither the right to remain silent nor the right to counsel during custodial interrogation that would make such a right effective. The government could continue to interrogate the detainees, and use any statements they made in the course of the proceedings. Second, the military order authorized the admission of hearsay evidence, thus allowing the commission to base a conviction on out-of-court statements and documentary evidence. Perhaps most importantly, the military order provided for review only through the military chain of command and expressly foreclosed review of military commission judgments in the constitutional courts by writ of habeas corpus or otherwise.

The government defended the legality of such tribunals by pointing to two decisions that had upheld the use of military commissions in the past. In *Ex parte Quirin* (1942), the Court upheld the use of commissions to try Nazi saboteurs captured in civilian clothes after they landed on the Atlantic coast during World War II. Yet *Quirin* had reaffirmed the availability of habeas review. In addition, the government relied on the ambiguous terms of the Supreme Court's decision in *Johnson v. Eisentrager* (1950). There, the Court found that German nationals, in the custody of the United States military after the end of World War II, had no right to habeas corpus relief in the federal courts. In denying relief, the Court mentioned a number of factors: the location of the prison in Germany, the German nationality of the petitioners, the fact that the acts of illegal combat had occurred in China and had led to convictions there before a military commission, the absence of any affiliating connections to the United States, and the deference owed to the military in the detention of convicted unlawful combatants. By analogy, the government argued that individuals detained at Guantanamo Bay were aliens with no affiliating connections to the United States and no right to pursue habeas corpus relief.

In a series of decisions culminating in *Boumediene v. Bush* (2008), the Court has consistently rejected the government's attempt to avoid judicial review of detention at Guantanamo Bay. The pattern of governmental setbacks began with the Court's decision in *Rasul v. Bush* (2004) that the aliens detained at Guantanamo Bay could seek review of their detention by filing habeas petitions with the federal district court in the District of Columbia. *Rasul* and its companion cases answered two questions: they clarified that the Authorization of the Use of Military Force (AUMF) was broad enough to authorize the military to detain combatants captured in Afghanistan and Iraq and it held that the jurisdiction of the federal district courts extended to the detention at Guantanamo Bay, thus rejecting the government's claim that the prison facility's location outside the territory of the United States placed it beyond judicial scrutiny.

The prospect of judicial review triggered two changes in detention policy at Guantanamo Bay. First, the government instituted internal review of its detention decisions by military tribunals called Combatant Status Review Tribunals, or CSRTs. Second, well after the *Rasul* decision, Congress adopted the Detainee Treatment Act of 2005 (DTA), amending the federal habeas statute to declare that no court or judge was to exercise jurisdiction over habeas petitions by aliens at Guantanamo Bay. Instead, the DTA provided for review of detainee challenges to their detention before the United States Court of Appeals for the District of Columbia Circuit (DC Circuit) for those individuals whom a CSRT has found to be subject to detention as an enemy combatant. For those convicted before a military commission as unlawful enemy combatants, the DTA also provided for review in the DC Circuit. On the basis of this legislation, the government sought the dismissal of all pending habeas petitions. In response to the argument that the elimination of habeas jurisdiction would violate the constitutional prohibition against suspension of the writ, the government took the view that the DTA provided a constitutionally adequate substitute for the habeas review that the Court had recognized in *Rasul*.

One of the cases affected by the curtailment of habeas was a petition by Salim Hamdan to challenge the legality of the military commission system of punishment. Accused of being Osama Bin Laden's driver and bodyguard in Afghanistan at the time of the US invasion, Hamdan had been charged with acts of unlawful combat and placed in line for trial. His petition argued that such a trial violated international law and the Geneva conventions (on the theory that the commission was not properly constituted and the charges did not state a claim of unlawful combat) as well as the Constitution and laws of the United States. The DC Circuit had rejected Hamdan's claims in 2005, and the Supreme Court granted certiorari before the DTA was adopted in December of that year. One of the questions the Court faced, then, was how to evaluate a statute that could have been interpreted as foreclosing all habeas authority and, with it, curtailing the Court's jurisdiction to review the DC Circuit decision.

On its face, the DTA contained a fairly sweeping restriction on the habeas authority of the federal courts. In addition, a separate provision proclaimed that the statute was in general to take effect on the statute's date of enactment. Muddying the waters slightly, one final provision proclaimed that certain aspects of the statute were to apply to claims pending on the date of enactment. Some legislative history supported the argument that at least some members of Congress viewed the exception as preserving jurisdiction over some pending challenges. In a replay of *Ex parte McCardle* (1868), the government promptly moved to dismiss the action from the Court's appellate docket on the basis that the statute created a lawful exception to the Court's appellate jurisdiction. The Court concluded that its appellate jurisdiction remained intact. It explained that ordinary principles would "suffice" to rebut the government's argument, at least as to pending claims. Thus, the Court did not rule out the use of avoidance or resistance norms in a different setting.

After maintaining its appellate jurisdiction, the Court reached the merits and invalidated the government's proposed use of military commissions to try Hamdan. While much was said in the course of a lengthy opinion, one can summarize the Court's conclusion as a finding that the commissions in question had not been properly authorized by an act of Congress. The applicable body of federal military law declared that the creation of courts-martial jurisdiction was not to be construed as depriving military commissions of jurisdiction "in respect of offenders or offenses that by statute or the law of war may be tried by such commissions." As the Court understood matters, the Uniform Code of Military Justice allowed the use of military commissions only where consistent both with the UCMJ and the law of war. Among the procedural provisions that particularly concerned the Court were those allowing the admission of hearsay evidence and qualifying the ability of the accused and his counsel to confront witnesses and evidence used against him. Justice Kennedy emphasized the importance of the role of Congress in his separate opinion; if Congress, "after due consideration, deems it appropriate to change the controlling statutes, in conformance with the Constitution and other laws, it has the power and prerogative to do so."

Congress exercised this prerogative in 2006, enacting the Military Commission Act (MCA). The MCA provides independent statutory authorization for the use of military commissions, thereby sidestepping the problem of compliance with the UCMJ. The new law also declared the Geneva conventions inapplicable, thus providing a statutory response to the Court's decision in *Hamdan*. In addition to restating and expanding the DTA's restrictions on habeas jurisdiction, the MCA included a rather sweeping declaration that the law was to "apply to all cases, without exception, pending on or after the date of the enactment of this Act" that relate to detention of aliens since September 11, 2001. Gone was any suggestion that some habeas petitions might stay in the federal courts as well as any suggestion that the restriction on jurisdiction was limited to those detained at Guantanamo Bay.

The MCA thus rather pointedly raised the issue that Justice Kennedy had identified in *Hamdan*: the extent to which Congress, in providing for military commissions, had acted in compliance with the Constitution. Writing for a five-Justice majority in *Boumediene*, Kennedy provided the answer: Congress had violated the constitutional guarantee of assured access to the privilege of the writ of habeas corpus; the MCA's restrictions amounted to a de facto suspension of the writ. The opinion contained three significant parts. In the first, Justice Kennedy examined the history of the writ, concluding, as in *Rasul*, that the detainees enjoyed the "privilege" of the writ of habeas corpus to challenge the legality of their detention. In the second, Kennedy adopted what he characterized as a functional approach to the evaluation of the extra-territorial application of the right to invoke the privilege of habeas corpus. Under this approach, aliens detained at Guantanamo Bay were said to enjoy access to the writ. Finally, Kennedy considered whether the MCA provided an adequate substitute for the judicial review available via habeas. After describing the scope of review available through habeas, and contrasting the more constricted review available through the MCA, Kennedy invalidated the MCA provisions dealing with habeas.

Likely to be much discussed both for its understanding of the scope of the constitutional habeas guarantee and for its analysis of extra-territorial constitutionalism, the *Boumediene* decision also includes a collection of interesting reflections on the role of habeas in securing judicial review. See Neuman (2009); Fallon (2010); Neuman (2010). For starters, Kennedy suggested that the constitutional core of habeas would, at a minimum, ensure review of legal issues and enable the habeas court to order release if it were to conclude that detention was unlawful. Kennedy also noted, though, that the scope of review was somewhat malleable and depended on the circumstances. Thus, in cases involving pre-trial and executive detention, habeas courts historically displayed a greater willingness to inquire into the facts than in cases where the habeas petitioner had received the benefit of a full and fair adjudication of the legality of confinement before a court of competent jurisdiction.

8.3.2　Post-*Boumediene* Developments

The Obama administration promised to close Guantanamo Bay by January 2010, but did not meet that self-imposed deadline. As a result, the habeas petitions revived in *Boumediene* have long since arrived in the District of Columbia, confronting the district court with the messy task of passing on the legality of the government's justifications for continuing to detain prisoners at Guantanamo Bay. The most striking feature of the post-*Boumediene* decisions has been the extent to which the government has been unable to defend continuing detention. As of March 2010, the district court had passed on some 44 habeas petitions, granting relief in 33 cases. To be sure, 17 of the successful habeas petitioners were ethnic Uighurs, a Chinese minority, for whom the case for detention was dubious from the outset. The Uighurs have now for the most part been transferred to other countries (rather than being returned to China, where they feared persecution, or being released into the Uighur community in the United States). Setting the Uighurs to one side, the government has still lost more cases (16) than it has won (11).

Beneath the surface of these results, one finds some disagreement about what standards should apply to detainees' claims. First, judges disagree about the scope of the government's detention authority. In light of the Court's decision in *Hamdi* upholding the government's power to detain as a traditional incident of war, the detention authority extends least controversially to those captured in battles with the forces identified in the AUMF: the Taliban and al Qaeda. But the war on terror potentially extends well beyond the battlefield, to al Qaeda operatives in other countries and in the United States. The Obama administration has continued to argue that its detention authority extends to supporters of al Qaeda. Here, the judges diverge. Most allow detention only of members of al Qaeda, but acknowledge the fuzzy line between support and membership, and allow detention of those whose support for al Qaeda makes them functional members of the group. Yet judges disagree about how much support is enough to constitute membership and what an individual can do, later, to disavow functional membership and escape continued detention.

Judges also disagree about how permanent detention can be and what sorts of evidence can be introduced in support. Hearsay abounds in these proceedings, and includes both the documents created at the time of initial custody and those created by CSRTs set up after the *Hamdi* decision. Judges have approached the problem by emphasizing the importance of reliability instead of

excluding such evidence altogether. Depending on how demanding
the standard proves to be, it will doubtless influence the amount of
record-keeping required at the time of initial custody and may
increase the burden on military officers to continue to defend the
legality of detention.

Most controversial, of course, has been the evidentiary treatment of involuntary statements secured through harsh methods of
interrogation. Here a degree of agreement has emerged. The
district judges all agree that *Miranda*-style warning requirements
and the right to counsel do not apply. But they disagree on how
coercive the interrogation must be to render the statements involuntary and subject to exclusion. In addition, the judges differ on
how to treat statements made in the course of previous interrogations, including interrogations that occurred in circumstances that
could be extremely coercive. Some view the earlier interrogation as
tainting subsequent inquiries, at least by interrogation teams with
knowledge of the subject's prior statements. Such taint rulings
may have implications for the manner in which the United States
conducts interrogations of subjects handed over from other countries. Inevitably, judges also differ on how to resolve factual
disagreements about the degree of coercion involved.

One important question, perhaps destined for Supreme Court
review, concerns the future viability of *Boumediene*-style review on
behalf of individuals detained at sites other than Guantanamo Bay.
The Court itself has ruled that habeas extends to US citizens
detained by the US military in Iraq, although it concluded on
reaching the merits that there was no right to relief. See *Munaf v.
Geren* (2008). The government has long detained individuals at the
Bagram Airfield Military Base in Afghanistan, some of whom were
captured in Afghanistan and others of whom were captured in
other countries and transferred to Bagram for Guantanamo Bay-
style detention. The DC Circuit ruled that habeas does not extend
to aliens detained at Bagram, even those who were captured outside
of Afghanistan. See *Al Maqaleh v. Gates* (D.C. Cir. 2010). Critical
to the court's decision was its view that the entire nation of
Afghanistan remains an active theater of war.

The future of military commission trials for illegal combatants
also remains in question. By the end of 2010, the government had
tried a handful of individuals before military commissions. See
Silliman (2009). The Obama Administration indicated that there
were plans to bring at least some high-value detainees to trial
before the federal district courts. (High-value detainees include
those, like the alleged September 11 mastermind Khalid Sheikh
Mohammed, who were kept at CIA black sites until 2006 when they
were transferred to Guantanamo Bay.) Indeed, at least one detainee, Ahmed Ghailani, was tried and convicted before the New York

federal district court on charges relating to the 1998 bombings of US embassies in Kenya and Tanzania. Yet both the proposed transfer of detainees and the proposed trial of high-value detainees ran into political difficulties. As a result, the Obama administration secured new legislation, the Military Commission Act of 2009. As of the end of 2010, the Administration continued to debate how best to handle high-value detainees; trials before military commissions remained a distinct possibility.

8.4   Habeas Review of State Criminal Convictions

Federal judicial power to conduct habeas review of state detention began in 1867. At the height of Reconstruction, Congress authorized the federal courts to grants writs of habeas corpus "within their respective jurisdictions" in all cases of restraint in violation of the Constitution, laws, and treaties of the United States. The story of how this provision evolved to encompass state post-conviction review has been told again and again, often with a view towards criticizing or defending the Court's expansion of the federal habeas power in *Brown v. Allen* (1953). Compare Bator (1963) with Peller (1982). But the federal judicial role in overseeing state criminal proceedings was no new thing in 1953. Section 25 of the Judiciary Act of 1789 authorized the Supreme Court to hear state criminal cases on appeal whenever the state court rejected a defense grounded in the federal Constitution and laws. For much of the nineteenth century, individuals who faced state criminal prosecution were entitled to federal judicial review of rejected federal defenses. Congress ended this entitlement by giving the Court discretionary control over its own appellate docket; *Brown v. Allen* restores the entitlement by empowering the *lower* federal courts to review state criminal convictions through the writ of habeas corpus.

State post-conviction review started slowly, then grew apace. Early decisions granted habeas relief only in circumstances where the trial at the state court level had been so fundamentally unfair as to deprive the defendant of due process. See *Moore v. Dempsey* (1923). Two factors led to a more expansive reliance on the writ. First, the Court's decision in *Brown v. Allen* (1953) introduced an era of federal habeas re-litigation under which issues that had been fully and fairly considered in the state system were nonetheless subject to further review in a federal habeas proceeding. Second, throughout the 1960s, the Warren Court extended a host of criminal procedural protections to state defendants. In combination, *Brown's* rule of habeas re-litigation and the expansive recognition of constitutional rights increased the number and complexity of federal habeas claims. State post-conviction habeas petitions in the federal courts numbered only 560 in 1950 but rose to some 9000 by

1970, and involved a growing percentage of the individuals in state custody. See H & W (2009). Habeas filings have continued to grow in absolute terms, but have not kept pace with the growth of state prison populations.

The story since the 1970s has been one of judicial and legislative retrenchment, driven in part by the sheer number of petitions, in part by a perception that state criminal procedure has improved, and in part by the costs associated with the issuance of relief. This section will trace the early development of the writ and the series of doctrines that now curtail its availability. Elaborate procedural rules create pitfalls and complexity for habeas petitioners, many of whom file pro se petitions. Complex escape hatches open for the claims of individuals who can make a showing of actual innocence. In the end, the world of post-conviction review has come to resemble Grant Gilmore's vision of hell, where there's nothing but law and due process is rigorously observed.

The complexity of habeas litigation may have increased in the early years of the 21st century, following a series of highly publicized exonerations of individuals on death row. A famous series of cases in Illinois led the state's Republican governor, George Ryan, to clear the state's death row as his term in office drew to a close in 2002. DNA exonerations in other well publicized cases have led to calls for a moratorium on the death penalty and have cast doubt on the workings of the criminal justice system. A study of the fifteen-year period from 1989 to 2003 revealed that some 340 individuals were exonerated of the crimes for which they had been convicted; at least 144 of those were cleared by DNA evidence. See Gross, et al. (2005).

Such developments may influence attitudes of those in both the political and judicial branches as to the importance of preserving the core features of habeas review. Congress responded to the DNA exonerations in part with the passage of the Innocence Protection Act of 2004, which takes a few modest steps in the direction of helping to ensure the availability of DNA testing at the state level. At the Supreme Court, the exonerations may subtly influence the attitude of the Justices to the work at hand. The Court has taken more habeas cases in recent years and habeas petitioners have occasionally succeeded. These decisions all turn on their own factual and legal contexts, of course, and do not explicitly reflect the influence of exonerations. Yet the record of exonerations may have slowed the trend towards further restrictions on the rights of habeas petitioners.

8.4.1 State Post–Conviction Review: *Brown v. Allen*

The Court's decision in *Brown v. Allen* (1953) establishes the foundation for modern use of habeas corpus as a mode of federal post-conviction review of constitutional errors in state criminal proceedings. In *Brown*, the Court simply held that an individual who had presented a claim of constitutional error to the state courts was free to re-litigate that claim in a federal habeas corpus proceeding. Doctrines of finality, such as those of claim and issue preclusion, were not seen as a barrier to federal judicial re-consideration of constitutional claims. Although the Court hemmed in this right of federal habeas re-litigation by requiring habeas petitioners to exhaust state court remedies and by encouraging the federal courts to pay respectful attention to the factual findings and legal conclusions of the state court, federal courts were to make an independent judgment and were free to disregard the state court resolution.

Criticism of the *Brown* regime of habeas re-litigation began immediately, and focused on the importance of deference to state criminal justice. But one cannot evaluate the call for deference without understanding the setting of the *Brown* decision. In *Brown* itself, and in two companion cases that were consolidated for joint consideration, African–American defendants had been convicted in North Carolina courts of interracial rape or murder and sentenced to death. (Several years later, the Court barred the imposition of the death penalty for rape of an adult woman in *Coker v. Georgia* (1977).) All three petitioners contended that the state had systematically excluded African–Americans from their grand or petit juries. The decision came down in February 1953, a few short months before the Court was to order re-argument in the school desegregation cases that would become known to the world as *Brown v. Board of Education* (1954). *Brown v. Allen* thus deserves to be seen as part of the Court's broader project to eliminate racially discriminatory practices in the Jim Crow South. The role it envisions for the lower federal courts bears a striking resemblance to that which those same courts were to play in overseeing the desegregation of the public schools.

The decisions came in a context, moreover, that underscored the Court's inability to conduct effective direct review of state criminal convictions. In two of the cases, the state prisoner had sought Supreme Court review by petition for a writ of certiorari. In both cases, certiorari had been denied and the state prisoner later filed a petition for habeas corpus in the federal district court. In reviewing the district court's habeas decisions, the Fourth Circuit had ruled in effect that the Court's earlier denial of certiorari operated as a rejection of the prisoner's constitutional claims and should be regarded as a bar to further litigation by way of habeas corpus. In a separate opinion by Justice Frankfurter, the Court rejected the Fourth Circuit view. Denials of certiorari were not to be regarded as decisions on the merits, and not to be treated as preclusive of further review by way of habeas corpus.

Although he did not say so explicitly, Frankfurter can be understood as shifting responsibility for correcting errors in state criminal proceedings from the Supreme Court to the lower federal courts, and as doing so through the expansion of habeas corpus. Subsequent developments lend some support to such an appellate-review characterization of habeas re-litigation. Recall that the Supreme Court will give effect to state court procedural defaults if they constitute an adequate and independent state ground for denial of appellate jurisdiction over federal constitutional claims. (Chapter 3 discusses the Supreme Court's appellate jurisdiction.) A state prisoner who wishes to challenge racial discrimination in jury selection must present the constitutional claim to the state court in accordance with the state procedures that apply to such claims. If the state court treats the claim as procedurally default-ed, and declines to reach the constitutional issue, the Supreme Court may decline review so long as the default was both adequate and independent. Much the same rules apply to constitutional claims in the habeas context. Thus, in a companion case to *Brown v. Allen*, the Court ruled that a procedural default (if adequate and independent) barred the federal habeas court from reaching the merits of the petitioner's racial discrimination claim (just as it would have presumably barred direct appellate review). See *Daniels v. Allen* (1953).

8.4.2 Restrictions on the Scope of Review: *Stone v. Powell*

By the 1970s, the concern with ensuring fair criminal practices in state court had given way to a growing concern with the costs of federal habeas review. Professor Bator's critique of habeas as a tool of state post-conviction review argued that the writ should serve as a mechanism for ensuring that the state courts provide generally fair procedures, not for providing claim by claim review of erroneous state rulings. See Bator (1963). Judge Friendly echoed these concerns, criticizing habeas re-litigation on a number of grounds: too few habeas petitions had merit to warrant the judicial resources devoted to them, the few meritorious petitions imposed high costs on the states by making it difficult for prosecutors to obtain a second conviction, and too little attention was paid to the petitioner's guilt or innocence in the decision to grant habeas relief. See Friendly (1970).

This catalog of costs played a central role in the Court's decision to narrow the scope of habeas review in *Stone v. Powell* (1976). There, the state prisoner had been convicted in California state court of a murder committed in the course of a liquor store robbery. A crucial piece of evidence—the gun used in the crime—had been found in Powell's possession during a police stop. Powell challenged the admission of the gun under the Fourth Amendment. The state courts rejected Powell's claim, but the lower federal court granted habeas relief. Powell would go free unless the state could obtain a second conviction without introducing the murder weapon.

The Supreme Court reversed, ruling that Powell's claim for the suppression of tainted evidence under the Fourth Amendment was not cognizable through federal habeas corpus review. In justifying its conclusion, the Court weighed the costs and benefits of habeas review. On the cost side of the ledger, suppression of the murder weapon presented real difficulties for a second trial. The crime had occurred in 1968. The case reached the Supreme Court in 1976, and any second trial would occur at least eight years after the fact. Lacking physical evidence to tie Powell to the murder, prosecutors would have been forced to depend on eye-witness testimony. But such testimony may have presented problems: Powell's appearance may have changed and the memories of witnesses to the crime may have faded. In any event, the police may have relied on the availability of the murder weapon at the first trial, and failed to develop other evidence of Powell's guilt. Now, with the weapon unavailable, it might be too late to collect corroborating evidence and testimony.

On the benefit side, the Court acknowledged that suppression of the evidence following habeas review might produce some modest additional deterrence of police misconduct. But the Court doubted that such deterrence would have much impact on police behavior. After all, the Court had focused on only those cases where the state courts had afforded the petitioner a "full and fair" opportunity to present the Fourth Amendment claim. In most cases, state trial and appellate courts would suppress the evidence and provide any needed deterrence; the marginal deterrence provided by a suppression decision at the habeas stage would not likely alter the constable's calculus. Moreover, relief at the habeas stage and the required second trial would add little to the fundamental justness of the petitioner's incarceration. The Court noted that most convicted defendants who raise Fourth Amendment claims are guilty of the underlying offense. While the Court did not make guilt or innocence an explicit part of the habeas inquiry, it did provide a conceptual foundation for foreclosing habeas review over a range of criminal procedure rules that seek to shape police conduct or have little impact on the fairness of the trial.

Remarkably, however, the *Stone v. Powell* decision has had little generative influence on the range of issues cognizable in habeas. In *Rose v. Mitchell* (1979), the Court declined to extend the *Stone* rule to claims of racial discrimination in the selection of the grand jury. The Court could have attempted to treat discrimination removed from the events at trial as unrelated to the guilt or innocence determination, but chose instead to distinguish *Stone*. Similarly, in *Withrow v. Williams* (1993), the Court declined to extend *Stone* to claims seeking to suppress out-of-court statements obtained in violation of *Miranda v. Arizona* (1966). According to the Court, *Miranda* claims relate to the admissibility of evidence at trial that could affect the guilt or innocence calculus and thus operate to safeguard a fundamental trial right. So far, then, only Fourth Amendment claims have been placed categorically beyond the scope of habeas review, and only where the state has provided a full and fair opportunity for their consideration.

8.4.3 Restrictions on the Scope of Review: *Teague v. Lane*

Stone v. Powell introduced the notion that the review of constitutional claims might differ, depending on whether the claim was being heard on direct review or on collateral review through federal habeas corpus. *Teague v. Lane* (1989), a decision nominally about the retroactive application of new rules of constitutional law, introduced an important new distinction between direct review and habeas review. In practice, *Teague* establishes an across-the-board restriction on federal habeas review, limiting relief to situations in which the state courts have failed to apply established rules of constitutional law. *Teague's* limits on habeas review, coming after *Stone v. Powell*, help to explain why the Court has not seen fit to extend the *Stone* decision.

Analysis of *Teague* begins with an understanding of the problem of retroactivity that gave rise to the decision, a problem that was particularly acute during the era of the Warren Court. Consider the Court's decision in *Miranda v. Arizona* (1966), announcing a new set of warnings that police must give to suspects before conducting a custodial interrogation. If the Court were to apply the *Miranda* rule retroactively, it could have had a disruptive influence. Not only could defendants raise *Miranda* claims at trials, and on appeal from their convictions, but state prisoners whose convictions had been obtained on the basis of custodial statements might seek habeas corpus relief. Full retroactive application of the rule was judged to have too high a cost; the Court accordingly concluded that the *Miranda* rule should apply prospectively. It would thus apply only to those criminal trials that took place after the *Miranda* decision came down. See *Johnson v. New Jersey* (1966).

Justice Harlan and others criticized this regime of prospectivity. *Miranda* stated a new rule of law but Harlan would have started from the premise that the Court must apply its *Miranda* rule to at least one party, Miranda himself. (A purely prospective opinion, one that did not apply even to Miranda, could constitute a prohibited advisory opinion.) Given that Miranda was to gain the benefit of the new rule, Harlan believed that all persons similarly situated should be treated the same way. For Harlan, that meant all individuals whose criminal proceedings were still pending on direct review at the time of the *Miranda* decision. See *Desist v. United States* (1969); *Mackey v. United States* (1971). This included those involved in criminal proceedings that had begun at the state trial level, as well as those whose cases had reached the state appellate courts and were awaiting direct review in the Supreme Court itself. Harlan recognized that these defendants might not fairly claim the benefit of the newly minted *Miranda* warnings; their interrogations had occurred long before the *Miranda* decision came down. But they were no less deserving than Miranda himself.

While Harlan would have extended the benefit of new rules to all defendants like Miranda whose claims were pending on direct review, he distinguished those who were pursuing claims for habeas relief. Habeas review was an extraordinary remedy, not a substitute for direct review. It should serve not to correct errors that had occurred at trial but more generally to ensure that state trial and appellate courts conduct their proceedings in accordance with "established constitutional standards." New rules should not apply to habeas proceedings, but the legality of prior convictions should be measured in accordance with the standards that were in place at that earlier time. Harlan recognized two exceptions: one for conduct that had been newly immunized from punishment (such as interracial marriage after the decision in *Loving v. Virginia* (1967)) and one for newly recognized procedural rights that could be regarded as "implicit in the concept of ordered liberty." Habeas petitioners can claim the benefit of new rules that fall into either one of these two exceptional categories.

It took some time, but Harlan's framework eventually became the law of the land. The Court took the first step in *Griffith v. Kentucky* (1987), ruling that new rules of constitutional law apply to all cases on direct review. The next step came in *Teague v. Lane* (1989). There, the Court ruled that new rules of constitutional law do not apply for the benefit of those seeking review by habeas corpus. The decision had two logical consequences. First, it meant that habeas petitioners could not argue for the application to their case of new rules that had been announced after their conviction became final on direct review. Second, it meant that habeas review would secure only the rights that were clearly established at the time their convictions became final; claims to enforce less well established rights would be regarded as seeking the application or development of a new rule and that sort of argument would now be unavailing on collateral review.

Teague nicely illustrates the habeas implications of the adoption of Harlan's framework. Teague claimed that the prosecutor had violated the equal protection clause by using peremptory challenges in a racially exclusionary way, and sought relief on two theories. First, he argued that the equal protection clause as interpreted in *Batson v. Kentucky* (1986) barred the use of unexplained peremptory challenges. Second, he claimed that the Sixth Amendment included a fair cross-section requirement, applicable to the petit jury, that also blocked discriminatory use of peremptory challenges. After setting out the Harlan framework, the Court rejected both claims. As to the *Batson* claim, the Court had previously ruled that *Batson* established a new rule of constitutional law applicable only to those in the direct review pipeline. *Batson* had come down in 1986, well after Teague's conviction had become final on direct review through the denial of his petition for certiorari in 1983. Teague could not rely on *Batson* for relief.

The Court's treatment of Teague's second claim illustrates a further implication of its approach to habeas review. Viewing retroactivity as a threshold issue in habeas proceedings, the Court examined the nature of Teague's fair cross-section claim. The Court's previous decisions had rejected a fair cross-section requirement, and had refused to require proportional representation on a petit jury. The Court thus concluded that the petitioner's second claim, if adopted, would establish a new rule of constitutional law. But under Harlan's framework, such new rules do not apply to habeas petitioners. The Court accordingly declined to reach the merits of the claim, reasoning that the rule, even if adopted, would not apply to Teague.

The *Teague* Court also retained, and tightened, the two exceptions that Harlan had identified. As for the first exception, the Court noted that neither the *Batson* rule nor the proposed fair cross-section rule would place primary conduct beyond the power of the state to criminalize. Both were procedural rules, aimed at improving the fairness of criminal proceedings. As for the second exception, the Court found that the new procedural rules were not sufficiently "fundamental" to require retroactive application to habeas claims. New procedural rules would reach this threshold of fundamentality only when the Court found that their absence would "seriously diminish" the likelihood of an accurate conviction. The Court candidly acknowledged its view that cases in the second category would be exceedingly rare; few basic norms of due process had yet to emerge.

Teague's impact on habeas review depends to some extent on what constitutes a new rule of constitutional law. Old rules of constitutional law, in place at the time the petitioner's conviction became final on direct review, are fully applicable to habeas petitioners; new rules announced after the date of finality are not. The Court addressed this distinction between the old and the new in *Butler v. McKellar* (1990). Under the decision in *Edwards v. Arizona* (1981), police conducting a custodial interrogation must stop after the suspect requests counsel; they cannot initiate further questioning until the attorney arrives. In a later decision, *Arizona v. Roberson* (1988), the Court ruled that this obligation to refrain from renewed questioning applies even where the police initiate questioning about a different crime. Butler's situation was similar to that in *Roberson*, but his conviction had become final on direct review in 1982 (after *Edwards*, but before *Roberson*). Thus, Butler was entitled to the benefit of the *Edwards* decision, but not to any new rules that the Court announced in *Roberson*. Was *Roberson* new or was it simply a logical extension or elaboration of the old rule that the Court had previously announced in *Edwards* (or in *Miranda*)?

In a divided decision, the Court ruled that *Roberson* had announced a new rule to govern custodial interrogation that was unavailable to Butler. The Court acknowledged that the *Roberson* Court had regarded its decision as controlled by the prior decision in *Edwards*. But instead of treating that statement in *Roberson* as decisive, the Court adopted the vantage point of a reasonable jurist on a lower court. Such a jurist would not necessarily have seen *Edwards* as compelling the result in *Roberson*, but could have distinguished the two cases on the basis that the interrogation about a new crime altered the *Miranda* calculus. Indeed, the fact that certain lower courts (and the author of the majority opinion in *Butler*) had refused to anticipate the decision in *Roberson* was evidence that *Edwards* did not ineluctably lead to that result. The new rule principle was meant to validate good faith interpretations of existing precedents by state courts, even if (as in *Roberson*) they turn out to have been erroneous. This expansive definition of new law depends upon a legislative model of the Court's own process in which the Court announces new rules by votes taken in conference, rather than a common law model in which law develops from case to case through the application of established principles to new situations. See Meyer (1994).

The *Teague* rule has implications both for the manner in which the Court administers its docket and for the way in which lower federal courts consider habeas petitions. As for the Court's docket, *Teague* makes it quite difficult for the Court to elaborate principles of criminal procedure by granting review of habeas cases. The expansive definition of new law in *Butler* means that many proposed extensions of existing procedural rights, unless plainly entailed in a prior decision, would simply not apply to habeas petitioners. As a consequence, the extension of rules of criminal procedure must come through the Court's exercise of direct review of state criminal convictions (or of federal convictions). Moreover, the Court will ordinarily hold related cases on its direct review docket until it has decided an issue. Otherwise, denial of certiorari might end the process of direct review prematurely and deny the defendant access to the new rule in question. Thus, if the Court grants review in a case like *Batson*, it will normally hold all the petitions for direct review that raise similar claims until it decides the *Batson* case. Then it will grant certiorari in the held cases, vacate the decision below, and remand for further proceedings. The use of holds, coupled with GVR practice, keeps the petitioners' conviction from becoming final on direct review through an untimely certiorari denial, and maintains the distinction between direct and collateral review.

Teague also changes the way in which lower federal courts review habeas claims. Rather than applying their own best conception of the law to determine the claim, lower federal courts sitting in habeas must apply the law that was clearly established as of the date the petitioner's conviction became final through denial of certiorari. Such clearly established law will include Supreme Court rules on the books as of that date, as well as those agreed-upon extensions that had gained relatively wide acceptance in the state and lower federal courts. If, however, the lower courts have divided on an issue, or if the state court could in good faith decline to extend a Supreme Court decision, then habeas relief will be unavailable. *Teague* thus accomplishes something similar to *Stone v. Powell's* distinction between direct and habeas review, but does so on a much broader basis. Rather than foreclosing federal habeas review of a particular constitutional issue that have been fully and fairly litigated in the state courts, as in *Stone*, the *Teague* rule forecloses review of all constitutional errors, except where the state court has failed to apply existing law correctly. Small errors and close calls provide no basis for relief.

While *Teague* re-orients the process of *federal* post-conviction review, it may not have quite so dramatic an impact on *state* post-conviction review. The issue arose in Minnesota, where a state petition for post-conviction relief sought to rely on an interpretation of the Confrontation Clause that the Supreme Court had announced in 2004 and had characterized as "new" for *Teague* purposes in 2007. While the "newness" of the rule would block a federal court from providing habeas relief, there was some uncertainty as to whether state courts were similarly constrained. In

Danforth v. Minnesota (2008), the Supreme Court ruled that states were not bound by *Teague* to deny relief on novel claims; instead, they were free to develop their own body of post-conviction remedial law. Justice Stevens, a consistent proponent of the power of state courts to over-protect federal rights free from corrective federal oversight, wrote the majority opinion. Justice Stevens characterized *Teague* as having arisen to address the availability of remedies. Chief Justice Roberts dissented, arguing that *Teague* and its progeny created rules of federal constitutional law from which the states were forbidden to depart.

8.4.4 Exhaustion and Custody

Apart from its decision to restrict the scope of habeas review in *Teague v. Lane*, the Court has adopted certain procedural rules that frame the manner in which habeas petitioners must present their claims to federal court. Under one important and long-standing rule that seeks to ensure respect for state judicial processes, habeas petitioners must exhaust available remedies in state court before filing their federal habeas petition. See *Rose v. Lundy* (1982). The exhaustion rule means that habeas petitioners must first seek review of their federal constitutional claims by pursuing direct appellate review of those claims in the state courts. If they learn of new claims—claims that they did not present to the state courts on direct review—habeas petitioners must present them to the state courts in the form of an application for state post-conviction review if the state makes such an avenue of relief available. The exhaustion rule requires petitioners to pursue available state remedies on the theory that state courts should be given an opportunity to correct any errors, and federal review should come as a last resort.

Like all procedural rules in habeas, the exhaustion rule has produced a flowering of detailed procedural corollaries. First, the Court has ruled that to satisfy the exhaustion rule, the petitioner must clearly identify the federal nature of the claim. It was not enough simply to object to the admission of certain evidence at trial as a "miscarriage of justice"; the petitioner must label the claim as a federal due process claim. See *Duncan v. Henry* (1995). Second, the Court has required the dismissal of "mixed" habeas petitions— those that include both exhausted and unexhausted claims. See *Rose v. Lundy* (1982). Following the dismissal of such mixed petitions, habeas petitioners can either abandon their unexhausted claims or return to state court to exhaust them by pursuing an available remedy. Third, the rule of exhaustion applies even where the state court would likely view the claim as foreclosed under rules of procedural default. In effect, habeas petitioners must attempt to overcome the procedural default by presenting the claim to the state courts along with their argument that the court should reach the merits.

The exhaustion rule has been tempered somewhat to forgive a habeas petitioner's failure to exhaust if the state fails to make a corrective procedure available or if, as a practical matter, the state procedure offers no realistic prospect of relief. For example, the Court has ruled that a habeas petitioner need not present a claim to the state courts when the state supreme court had recently rejected the same claim. See *Lynce v. Mathis* (1997). But the habeas petitioner must exhaust state remedies, even where the prospect of securing review and reversal can seem quite remote. Thus, the Court has ruled that a habeas petitioner must exhaust federal claims by presenting them to the state supreme court, even where that court exercises discretion in deciding whether to review decisions of an intermediate appellate court. See *O'Sullivan v. Boerckel* (1999). (By contrast, the Court has ruled that the exhaustion doctrine does not require a habeas petitioner to seek discretionary direct review in the Supreme Court.) As *O'Sullivan* reveals, strict application of the exhaustion rule can burden state courts with relatively pro-forma assertion of federal claims that serve little purpose other than the preservation of the claims for future review by way of federal habeas.

In addition to imposing an exhaustion rule, habeas law has long restricted the right to petition to those in actual custody. At one time, the custody requirement applied with relative severity, but the Court eased the requirement somewhat to expand the scope of habeas review. Thus, the Court ruled that an individual was in custody for habeas purposes even if he had been released from prison on parole; the Court reasoned that the individual still faced restraints on freedom and the possibility of re-imprisonment. See *Jones v. Cunningham* (1963). Similarly, an individual awaiting the completion of judicial review who remained free on his own recognizance was in custody for purposes of a habeas challenge. See *Hensley v. Municipal Court* (1973). But the Court continues to require some present threat of future incarceration on the basis of the conviction under review to satisfy the custody requirement. Accordingly, an individual who has fully served his sentence and has been unconditionally discharged from the penal system cannot pursue a habeas claim; even though he may face civil disabilities incident to his conviction, custody has ended. See *Maleng v. Cook* (1989).

Exhaustion combines with the custody requirement to limit federal habeas review to individuals who have been convicted of relatively serious offenses and who face relatively lengthy prison terms. Most habeas petitioners must litigate through the state system once, and perhaps twice, before filing a federal habeas petition. Many would-be habeas petitioners will have completed their sentences for relatively minor offenses before exhausting their state remedies. The absence of present custody following their discharge from prison or jail will bar any federal habeas challenge.

8.4.5 Procedural Defaults Under *Wainwright v. Sykes*

Apart from the exhaustion and custody rules, the Court has required habeas petitioners to comply with state procedural rules in presenting and preserving constitutional issues for further review. Thus, in a companion case to *Brown v. Allen*, the Court held that the petitioner's failure to comply with a state procedural rule barred federal habeas review of the petitioner's constitutional claims. See *Daniels v. Allen* (1953). State procedural defaults occur with striking regularity, either because counsel failed to spot an issue, failed to take appropriate steps to present the issue, or failed to preserve the issue by pursuing appellate review. For example, many states require counsel to make a contemporaneous objection in order to challenge the admission of certain evidence; a lawyer's failure to do so may bar consideration of the claim. Similarly, state laws impose filing deadlines for notices of appeal; counsel's failure to file a timely notice may be viewed as barring review of the claims. State courts may agree to forgive harmless procedural errors, but if they decide to forfeit the defendant's claim in state court, such a forfeiture will often block habeas review.

The Court's decision in *Wainwright v. Sykes* (1977) provides the starting point for assessing procedural defaults. There, the habeas petitioner had apparently killed a companion during the course of a drunken argument. When the police arrived, the defendant admitted to the crime, and did so again after receiving *Miranda* warnings. At trial, the defendant's statement was admitted without objection, perhaps as a result of trial counsel's strategic decision to rely on drunkenness as a form of diminished capacity to lessen the defendant's culpability. Following the defendant's conviction of third-degree murder, and unsuccessful appeal, he sought to overturn his conviction on the ground that he had not understood his *Miranda* warning. He exhausted this claim by presenting it for the first time in a state court post-conviction proceeding, which held that he had defaulted the claim by failing to raise the issue at trial or on appeal. Next, he sought federal habeas review of the involuntariness claim, but the Court treated the default as a bar to review. In the course of its opinion, the Court deliberately narrowed federal habeas review of procedurally defaulted claims by adopting a "cause and prejudice" standard.

The "cause and prejudice" standard was driven by a desire on the part of the Court to make the trial of the case the main event, and by a particular view of the origins of procedural defaults. As the Court saw matters, trial counsel make strategic decisions about how best to mount a successful defense, and defendants can fairly be charged with the consequences of those strategic choices. Thus, trial counsel in *Sykes* may not have raised the *Miranda* claim because the statement was not inconsistent with a diminished capacity defense that had apparently succeeded in persuading the jury to convict only of third-degree murder. Sykes was seen as sandbagging; he had taken his best shot at trial and now sought to challenge his conviction on the basis of issues that trial counsel had declined to present. If procedural defaults were routinely forgiven on habeas, sandbagging would undermine the centrality of the trial. Indeed, the willingness of federal courts to consider defaulted issues would tend to encourage the state courts to forgive defaults and consider the merits, further eroding the state's interest in the enforcement of its procedural rules and detracting from the importance of the trial.

The dissenting judges offered quite a different account of the origin of procedural defaults. Rather than strategic decisions made by competent counsel, the dissent viewed most defaults as the product of the negligence of overworked and inadequately prepared public defenders. The state bore ultimate responsibility for these defaults; the Sixth Amendment requires the state to provide indigent defendants with good legal representation and the financial support necessary to mount a successful defense. Thus, as the dissent saw matters, all procedural defaults were ultimately chargeable to the state, rather than to the defendant, and should be forgiven on habeas so long as the defendant did not himself make a deliberate decision to bypass the assertion of a particular claim. The dissent drew its "deliberate bypass" standard from the language of an earlier decision, *Fay v. Noia* (1963), in which the Court had permitted a habeas challenge despite the failure of the petitioner to file a timely appeal from his state court conviction. The *Fay* standard, if applied to errors at trial, would result in widespread forgiveness of defaults. Correcting constitutional errors was more important, in the dissent's view, than the state's interest in an airtight system of procedural defaults.

The dissent rightly observed that many procedural defaults result from the negligence or inadvertence of overworked trial counsel, but the issuance of habeas relief will not necessarily improve matters. Rather than committing resources to federal habeas re-litigation of these issues, several years after the fact, a more rational system would devote resources to improving the quality of trial counsel. Habeas relief comes too late to induce state, city, and county governments to increase spending on the public defender function, and it may not address the root of the problem. Some defendants (those serving short sentences) will have already left custody before corrective habeas can issue. Moreover, many of the most serious defaults by overworked public defenders come not through trial errors but through the failure to investigate cases adequately. Defendants who lack the financial resources to hire their own lawyers and mount their own investigation must accept proffered guilty plea agreements. Ineffective assistance of counsel may have occurred, but the defendant's guilty plea will often block any collateral attack.

However persuasive the Court's decision to charge defendants with the mistakes of their lawyers, the sheer press of business in the state criminal courts makes some sort of federal deference to state procedural errors inevitable (just as it forces the system to accept plea bargaining). The *Sykes* Court's cause-and-prejudice standard now governs federal review of procedural defaults that occur at both the trial and appellate stages of state court proceedings. See *Coleman v. Thompson* (1991). Subsequent cases have helped to flesh out the meaning of cause and prejudice, terms that the *Sykes* Court had left largely undefined. As for cause, the Court has required a showing that some "objective factor external to the defense impeded counsel's efforts to comply with the state's procedural rule." *Murray v. Carrier* (1986). So long as counsel's performance meets the standard for effective assistance of counsel under *Strickland v. Washington* (1984), the risk of attorney error will fall on the defendant. *Strickland*, in turn, requires a showing that counsel's representation fell below an objective standard of reasonableness and that there is a reasonable probability that, but for the unprofessional errors, the result in the proceeding would have been different. A single procedural error or mere inadvertence in failing to raise an issue will not meet the *Strickland* standard; instead, courts must evaluate counsel's performance in the trial as a whole in determining whether counsel was ineffective.

Apart from ineffective assistance of counsel, only a modest collection of external impediments have been recognized as establishing cause to excuse a procedural default. In one early case, the Court accepted that the sheer novelty of a legal contention could constitute cause for the failure of counsel to have raised an issue at trial. See *Reed v. Ross* (1984). But the Court's subsequent decision in *Teague v. Lane* (1989) drained the decision of much of its significance by foreclosing habeas review of novel claims altogether. In addition, the Court has treated some forms of official misconduct as providing cause to excuse a procedural default. In *Amadeo v. Zant* (1988), for example, the Court found cause to excuse the failure of the habeas petitioner to raise at trial a claim that the prosecutor had excluded blacks and women from a Georgia jury pool. The prosecutor had concealed its discriminatory practice by fixing the number of minority jurors at a level designed to avoid scrutiny, and this deliberate concealment operated as an external impediment. See also *Strickler v. Green* (1999) (prosecutor failed to disclose exculpatory information).

In addition to cause, petitioners must show prejudice to overcome a procedural default. To establish prejudice, the petitioner must show that the default worked to "his actual and substantial disadvantage, infecting his entire trial with error of constitutional dimensions." *United States v. Frady* (1982). In many cases, a showing of ineffective assistance of counsel will satisfy this standard; after all, the ineffective assistance standard requires a showing that the result in the proceeding would have been different, an inquiry with which the prejudice test overlaps. In other instances of external impediment, the requisite showing of prejudice may prove more elusive. In *Strickler v. Green*, for example, the Court found (as part of its inquiry into the merits of the constitutional claim) that wrongfully withheld exculpatory evidence would not have influenced the conviction or sentence.

When the petitioner cannot show cause and prejudice, the Court has recognized a narrow exception for claims of actual innocence. In *Murray v. Carrier* (1986), the Court expressed a willingness to forgive a procedural default "in an extraordinary case, where a constitutional violation has probably resulted in the conviction of one who is actually innocent." So far, however, the prospect of review on behalf of the actually innocent has proven more theoretical than real. A review of lower court decisions (albeit one conducted before DNA exonerations became more common) reports that in only a handful have the courts granted relief on the basis of actual innocence, and no Supreme Court decision had yet done so. See Steiker (1993). Application of the actual innocence exception to claims omitted from a death penalty proceeding has grown quite refined. See *Sawyer v. Whitley* (1992) (attempted showing of innocence failed to disprove the aggravating factors that made the defendant eligible for the death penalty); *Schlup v. Delo* (1995) (petitioner sought to show innocence of the underlying offense; Court applied less stringent standard than in *Sawyer*). Note that in all these cases, the showing of actual innocence operates as a key that opens the door to consideration of a constitutional claim that counsel failed to raise earlier in the proceeding. The assertion of a freestanding claim of innocence, unconnected to a defaulted constitutional claim, presents a different question.

The Supreme Court in *House v. Bell* (2006) explored the difference between these so-called "gateway" claims of innocence and freestanding innocence claims. There, the habeas petitioner sought to raise procedurally defaulted claims of ineffective assistance of counsel and a failure by the prosecutor to disclose exculpatory evidence. In attempting to show his innocence as a gateway to the consideration of these defaulted issues, House offered physical and other forms of evidence that the victim had been killed not by House but by her own husband. Applying the *Schlup* standard, the Court concluded that the evidence was sufficient, though barely, to establish that it is "more likely than not" that no reasonable juror would have convicted. On that basis, the Court remanded for further consideration of the defaulted issues. In addition to his gateway claim, House put forward a freestanding claim of innocence under *Herrera v. Collins* (1993). Such a claim argues that the criminal punishment of an innocent person would violate the Constitution (even in the absence of any constitutional errors at trial). Without deciding whether such a claim was viable, the Court found that House had not made a sufficiently persuasive showing of innocence to justify relief. Despite this rejection of the *Herrera* claim, however, the Court's finding of gateway innocence puts some pressure on the lower courts to afford House relief.

Together, the exhaustion and procedural default rules mean that many state prisoners will have litigated through the state judicial system twice, once on direct review and once on collateral attack, before filing a federal habeas petition. Note that the state prisoner does not have to re-exhaust any federal claim. Assertion of a federal claim on direct review will suffice, and the federal habeas petitioner need not re-submit (or re-exhaust) the claim in the context of any state collateral proceeding. But if the lawyer procedurally defaulted any constitutional claims on direct review, the habeas petitioner may attempt to revive those claims by making a showing of cause and prejudice, perhaps by arguing that counsel was constitutionally ineffective. Under the exhaustion rule, such claims, not yet presented on direct review, must first be submitted to the state courts through a state post-conviction review proceeding (if available). Thus, state post-conviction review will often feature an ineffective assistance claim as well as one or more constitutional issues that were defaulted on direct review; ineffective assistance provides both an independent basis for relief and the key to the assertion of other procedurally defaulted constitutional claims. Assuming the state court denies the ineffective assistance claim, and upholds the procedural defaults, the habeas petitioner can pursue all these claims in federal court. Federal habeas petitions often combine several constitutional claims that were exhausted on direct review, and several additional claims that were exhausted on state collateral review, along with a claim of ineffective assistance.

The Court has recognized the importance of post-conviction review in evaluating the effectiveness of trial counsel. In *Massaro v. United States* (2003), a case involving a federal prisoner who sought collateral review of a claim that his lawyer at trial was ineffective, the Court rejected a lower court decision that would have shifted from collateral to direct review of such claims. (As noted in section 8.3.1 above, federal prisoners seek collateral review of their federal convictions not by habeas petition but by motion under section 2255 before the same district court that heard their criminal proceeding at trial.) The Second Circuit had ruled that the petitioner was required to present his claim of ineffective assistance on direct appellate review, at least in cases where the petitioner's lawyer on appeal was different from his trial counsel and the trial record revealed evidence of ineffective assistance. In refusing to adopt this direct review model for ineffective assistance claims, the Court emphasized a variety of concerns including the need to go outside the trial record to develop evidence of ineffectiveness and the difficulties that the lawyer would face in attempting to make the ineffective assistance claim in the limited time available on direct review.

8.5   The AEDPA and Habeas Re–Litigation

In 1996, Congress adopted a major new statute, codifying and extending judge-made restrictions on state prisoner access to federal post-conviction review. The Antiterrorism and Effective Death Penalty Act (AEDPA) divides habeas proceedings into two separate chapters: chapter 153 generally governs habeas petitions by state and federal prisoners and chapter 154 provides special rules for state prisoners on death row. The next few sections will focus on the most important provisions of chapter 153. (This book does not cover chapter 154; its rules rarely apply because few states have succeeded in satisfying the competent-counsel requirements necessary to bring the provisions into play. Interested readers may refer to the treatment of chapter 154 in more specialized treatises. See Hertz & Liebman (2001).)

Determining the meaning and application of the AEDPA can be a bit tricky. To begin with, the Court has ruled that the chapter 153 provisions of the AEDPA apply only to habeas petitions filed after the effective date of the Act (April 24, 1996). See *Lindh v. Murphy* (1997). Of course, with each passing year, fewer pre-AEDPA petitions remain alive in the federal system. Moreover, the AEDPA does not codify every element of habeas practice, but in many instances assumes the applicability of pre-existing law. For example, the AEDPA does not set forth rules of procedural default, leaving in place the cause-and-prejudice standard of *Wainwright v. Sykes*. Courts rely on pre-AEDPA law both to give meaning to the new provisions and to fill gaps in the statute.

8.5.1   AEDPA and the Scope of Review

The AEDPA includes a new provision that specifies the standard of review for the grant of habeas relief on behalf of state prisoners. Section 2254(d) provides as follows:

> An application for a writ of habeas corpus on behalf of a person in custody pursuant to the judgment of a State court shall not be granted with respect to any claim that was adjudicated on the merits in State court proceedings unless the adjudication of the claim—
>
> (1) resulted in a decision that was contrary to, or involved an unreasonable application of, clearly established Federal law, as determined by the Supreme Court of the United States; or
>
> (2) resulted in a decision that was based on an unreasonable determination of the facts in light of the evidence presented in the State court proceeding.

Section 2254(d)(1) provides the standard for reviewing a claim that the state courts misapplied controlling law, and thus implements a version of the clear law standard that the Court had already applied in *Teague v. Lane* (1989). Subsection (d)(2) sets forth the standard for reviewing the state court's factual determinations, again calling for a measure of deference to state court findings.

While subsection (d)(1) obviously drew its inspiration from *Teague*, the provision goes beyond that decision in a number of respects. First, in determining what constitutes "clearly established" federal law, subsection (d)(1) looks only to the law as determined by the Court itself. Lower federal court decisions do not count for the purpose of defining clearly established law. Second, section 2254(d)(1) does not include *Teague's* two exceptions for substantive conduct immunized from criminality and fundamental guarantees of procedural fairness (although other provisions seek to address these issues). Third, the statute limits habeas relief to situations in which the state courts reached a decision that was contrary to or involved an unreasonable application of such clearly established law. Like *Butler v. McKellar*, then, the new statute apparently validates reasonable state court interpretations of Supreme Court decisional law, even if those interpretations turn out to have been in error.

That indeed was the lesson of the Court's analysis of subsection (d)(1) in *Terry Williams v. Taylor* (2000). At issue was the Virginia Supreme Court's application of the Court's standard for ineffective assistance of counsel. The Court found that its decision in *Strickland* stated the applicable legal standard, and that the Virginia court had unreasonably applied that standard. Accordingly, the Court reversed a Fourth Circuit decision, which had upheld the state decision. In addition, the Court rejected the Fourth Circuit standard for determining the degree of deference due to state court interpretations. The Fourth Circuit's approach was to validate the state determination unless "reasonable jurists would all agree" that the decision was unreasonable. The controlling opinion of Justice O'Connor rejected this focus on subjective reasonableness, which would ascribe weight to any division of lower court opinion however unreasonable, and favored instead an objective standard.

In addition to imposing a *Teague*-like limit on the habeas standard of review for state court errors of law, the AEDPA imposes restrictions on the ability of federal habeas courts to second-guess state court factual determinations. Section 2254(d)(2), above, requires deference to reasonable state court factual findings. The Court wrestled with the implications of this deference requirement in *Miller–El v. Dretke* (2005). The petitioner raised a *Batson* claim, arguing that the prosecution had failed to provide a raceneutral justification for striking blacks from the jury. The state court rejected the claim, finding the justification completely credible. The Court reviewed the factual basis for this determination in some detail, and concluded that the prosecutor's differential treatment of prospective black and white jurors belied any claim of race neutrality. In doing so, the Court considered material that had not been made part of the record at the state trial, but had been included in the federal habeas record. The dissent argued that this consideration of outside evidence was inconsistent with the requirement that the reasonableness of the state finding be resolved "in light of the evidence presented" in state court.

8.5.2 AEDPA: Limitations Periods, Exhaustion and Amended Petitions

In addition to recasting the standard of review for legal and factual claims, the AEDPA for the first time imposes a period of limitations for the filing of habeas claims and codifies the exhaustion rule. The limitations period appears in section 2244(d)(1) and requires habeas petitioners in state custody to file their petitions within one year of the completion of direct review of their state court conviction. The statute recognizes a modest collection of exceptions to this one-year provision: it permits tolling of the one-year period during the time a petitioner spends pursuing state court post-conviction remedies (as required by the exhaustion rule); it gives the petitioner a one-year period in which to file if the Supreme Court makes a new constitutional right retroactively available on habeas to the state prisoner; and it permits a filing within one-year of the date on which the petitioner, with diligence, could have discovered the factual predicate of a new claim. This exception for newly discovered evidence may, for example, operate to allow DNA claims, but only where the petitioner had no reason to pursue a DNA test earlier in the proceeding.

One can question the need for this new limitation period. Congress appears to have taken the idea from a report by a commission headed by then retired Justice Lewis Powell. The Powell Commission had recommended a limitation period to encourage timely filing of habeas claims in death penalty cases. The idea of a required filing was to counter the tactics of some death penalty lawyers who would wait until the execution was scheduled to file a federal habeas petition. But the Powell Commission had not recommended the extension of a limitations period to non-death penalty petitions. Unlike those on death row, habeas petitioners who face a prison term have no incentive to delay their filings until the last second. To the contrary, one would expect them to file quickly to obtain release from present custody.

As applied outside the death penalty context, therefore, the new one-year limitation period operates primarily to threaten state prisoners with a forfeiture of claims. Such forfeitures can present questions of fairness, especially when applied to prisoners who lack counsel in the post-conviction process or lack the mental acuity to represent themselves effectively. Lack of counsel can present a serious problem. To be sure, many states with a death penalty provide capital defendants with counsel in the state post-conviction review process. Moreover, in death penalty cases, Congress pays for counsel in federal habeas proceedings. But the Court has yet to extend the constitutional right to counsel to the process of post-conviction review. As a result, most state prisoners in non-death cases represent themselves in collateral proceedings, perhaps with the assistance of jailhouse lawyers.

Issues of fairness arise from the interaction of the new limitation period and other procedural rules. Consider the rule of *Rose v. Lundy* (1982), which requires the dismissal of habeas petitions with exhausted and unexhausted claims. At the time of the *Rose* decision, dismissal would force the habeas petitioner either to return to state court to exhaust the unexhausted claims, or to drop those claims from the federal petition and proceed with the fully exhausted claims. Today, a dismissal under *Rose v. Lundy* could present more serious problems; the one-year limitation period does not include a tolling provision for the time spent litigating in federal court. A petitioner who initially satisfied the one-year period might suffer a *Rose* dismissal after the one-year period runs, and could face a time bar to re-submission of the federal claims. Some courts addressed the problem by agreeing to stay the federal claims, pending exhaustion of the unexhausted claims, and then revive the federal petition. The Court approved this solution in *Rhines v. Weber* (2005), so long as the habeas petitioner has good cause for having failed to exhaust, has a potentially meritorious claim, and has not engaged in dilatory litigation tactics.

The time bar may also present problems when a habeas petitioner seeks to amend the petition to add a new claim after the passage of the one-year period. Under Rule 15 of the Federal Rules of Civil Procedure, a new claim added to an existing complaint ordinarily relates back to the filing date of the complaint for purposes of complying with the limitations period, so long as the new claim arises from the same transaction or occurrence as the original claims. Application of the transaction or occurrence test in the habeas context would permit broad relation back of amended petitions; new claims would presumably seek to challenge the same state conviction. But despite the fact that the Federal Rules generally apply to habeas proceedings, the Supreme Court refused to apply the civil rules' conception of relation back to habeas claims. See *Mayle v. Felix* (2005). Instead of defining the transaction as the conviction itself, the Court treated the specific cluster of facts surrounding the legal claim as the relevant transaction or occurrence. As a result, the petitioner's Confrontation Clause claim, which was based upon the admission of another witness's videotaped statement, was said to involve a transaction or occurrence different from the petitioner's challenge under the Fifth Amendment to the introduction of his own confession. Accordingly, the Court found that the Fifth Amendment claim would not relate back to the filing date of the Confrontation Clause claim for purposes of satisfying the limitations period.

In *Holland v. Florida* (2010), the Court continued to wrestle with the application of timeliness rules to habeas petitioners. There, the petitioner in a capital habeas case asked the federal court to toll the limitations period on equitable grounds not specified in section 2244(d). In particular, the petitioner argued that his attorney had been grossly negligent in failing to file his federal habeas petition, thereby providing a basis for relief from the time limitation. In agreeing with the petitioner that equitable tolling should be available in rare cases involving extreme or unusual facts, the Court had to sidestep two potential barriers. First, it had to characterize the time period in question as non-jurisdictional (and therefore subject to equitable tolling). Second, it faced the fact that the text of the limitations provision includes a variety of exceptions that provide petitioners with relief from the one-year period. The dissent emphasized these textual exceptions in arguing against the recognition of an additional exception for equitable considerations.

8.5.3   AEDPA and Successive Petitions

The AEDPA also codifies and extends the Court's own restrictive approach to the submission of successive habeas petitions. At common law, habeas petitioners were free to pursue their claims successively; denial of their claim by one court did not bar an application to a second court. Thus, in *Ex parte Bollman* (1807), the petitioners filed successive petitions, one in New Orleans, a second after they were transported to the District of Columbia, and third with the Supreme Court. But in the state post-conviction context, the Court now regards the practice as an abuse of the writ and requires the petitioner to offer special justifications for a successive petition. Thus, in *McCleskey v. Zant* (1991), the Court ruled that the claims in a second or successive habeas petition should be dismissed unless the petitioner can justify the omission of those claims from his first habeas petition under the cause-and-prejudice standard of *Wainwright v. Sykes*. Values of finality and efficiency were seen as requiring habeas petitioners to include all of their claims in their first (and only) federal habeas petition.

The AEDPA extends this restriction on successive petitions. New section 2244(b)(1) requires dismissal of any claim that had been presented in a prior habeas petition. As for claims in a second or successive petition that had not been previously presented, section 2244(b)(2) requires dismissal unless the claim "relies on a new rule of constitutional law, made retroactive to cases on collateral review by the Supreme Court, that was previously unavailable." Alternatively, the AEDPA permits the federal court to reach a new claim in a successive petition if the factual predicate could not have been discovered previously, and the facts would establish by clear and convincing evidence that no reasonable factfinder would have found the petitioner guilty of the underlying offense. See 28 U.S.C. § 2244(b)(2)(B). This imposes a standard for relief from procedural defaults that occur in the submission of a first habeas petition more demanding than the cause-and-prejudice standard of *McCleskey* and *Sykes*.

The AEDPA also creates a fairly elaborate gate-keeping mechanism. Rather than filing a second or successive petition with the district court, alleging facts that bring the petition within a statutory exception, petitioners must first seek leave to file from the federal circuit court of appeals. See section 2244(b)(3). A three-judge panel of the appellate court must rule within 30 days, and the petitioner can pursue the claim only if that panel grants authorization. The statute apparently attempted to make the three-judge decision final; it declared that the decision shall not be subject to a petition for a rehearing or a petition for certiorari. The reference to certiorari apparently sought to foreclose review by the Supreme Court.

In a decision notable for the speed with which it was rendered, the Supreme Court rejected the claim that this statutory restriction operated to curtail its powers of review. In *Felker v. Turpin* (1996), a death row petitioner had unsuccessfully sought leave to file a successive petition only days after the AEDPA took effect. Following denial of the motion by the court of appeals, the petitioner sought review in the Supreme Court. The state argued against review, invoking the statutory bar. The Court issued a stay of execution, ordered briefing on the extent of its authority, and eventually issued a decision upholding its authority to conduct review. On the merits, the Court found no error in the denial of Felker's motion to file a successive habeas petition.

The Court's rationale was rather intricate. Although the Court found that the AEDPA had restricted its certiorari jurisdiction, the statute did not restrict the Court's authority to exercise appellate review through an original application for a writ of habeas corpus. (Such "original" writs actually invoke the Court's appellate jurisdiction, so long as they seek the functional equivalent of appellate review within the meaning of *Marbury v. Madison* (1803) and *Ex parte Bollman* (1807) See Section 8.2.1.) The Court's conclusion was driven in part by precedent (*Ex parte Yerger* (1868) had reached a similar conclusion) and in part by its desire to avoid the constitutional question that might arise if the statute were interpreted as totally foreclosing its appellate jurisdiction. (Chapter 10 explores this aspect of the decision in greater detail.) But while it upheld its jurisdiction to entertain applications for the original writ, the Court made clear that it would grant such applications only in the rarest of cases. In most cases, the courts of appeal exercise final authority over leave to file successive petitions.

A word about the timing of the decision. The Court ordered expedited briefing on the jurisdictional issue, and rendered its decision in late June, less than two months after granting review in early May. Few decisions had gone more quickly from initial application to a decision on the merits. In acting quickly, the Court not only cleared the way for Felker's execution, but also avoided the likely bottleneck in all executions that would have occurred had the decision been held over for decision the next year. After granting review of Felker's challenge to the restriction on appellate review, the Court could not well have denied a stay for other death row habeas petitioners in the same situation. Had it held over the decision until next term, the Court would have effectively imposed a moratorium on the death penalty throughout the nation. Depending on one's attitude toward the death penalty, its decision to act quickly might be seen either as an unseemly rush to judgment or as a commendable attempt to avoid technical barriers to the administration of state justice.

8.6   State Post–Conviction Review and the Role of Congress

With the adoption of the AEDPA, a Congress concerned with expansive federal review of state convictions cut back significantly on the scope federal habeas corpus. But these restrictions on the ambit of the writ do not necessarily violate the Suspension Clause. To be sure, the Court has clearly indicated that, at a minimum, the Suspension Clause protects the core function of the writ as it existed in 1789. See *Boumediene v. Bush* (2008); *INS v. St. Cyr* (2001). But the Judiciary Act of 1789 did not authorize federal courts to entertain petitions for writs of habeas corpus on behalf of state prisoners. State prisoners did not gain access to the federal writ until Congress expanded federal habeas in 1867. The Court recited this history in *Felker v. Turpin* (1996), downplaying any possibility that the restriction on successive petitions could pose a suspension problem under the Constitution. In the end, the *Felker* Court assumed that the Constitution protects habeas corpus in its more modern guise as a tool of state post-conviction review. But even with that assumption, the Court found that the restrictions on successive petitions were well within the evolutionary tradition that characterized the ebb and flow of habeas protection.

Scholars have argued that other provisions of the Constitution may have operated to entrench state post-conviction review against congressional restriction. The Fourteenth Amendment prohibits states from abridging the "privileges and immunities" of citizens of the United States. This constitutional restriction took effect in 1868, shortly after Congress expanded federal habeas authority to reach state prisoners. Perhaps the "privilege" of the writ of habeas corpus was among those that the Fourteenth Amendment protects against state abridgement. See Steiker (1994). But the claim that the Fourteenth Amendment entrenches federal habeas for state prisoners has been subjected to two telling criticisms: it fails to explain how the Fourteenth Amendment operates to restrict the power of Congress (rather than that of the states) and it fails to take account of the relatively broad power Congress apparently enjoys over the jurisdiction of the lower federal courts under the Madisonian compromise. See H & W (2009).

If it cannot be based on the core function of the writ, circa 1789, or on the ratification of the Fourteenth Amendment, circa 1868, the right of state prisoners to federal habeas review may be based on traditional power of the federal courts to review state criminal convictions (and other state court judgments) on direct review. Under section 25 of the Judiciary Act of 1789, individuals convicted of a crime in state court had an absolute right to appellate review of their rejected federal defenses by the Supreme

Court. Review as of right gave way to discretionary review in the early years of the twentieth century, after Congress had already been expanded the habeas power of the district courts. To the extent one views federal appellate oversight of state courts as constitutionally compelled (a possibility that chapter 10 explores), one might argue that the Constitution obliges Congress to empower the federal courts to exercise the necessary jurisdiction. If the Court can no longer perform the role, perhaps Congress owes a constitutional obligation to provide the lower federal courts with the necessary authority to do so. See Amar (1985); Eisenberg (1974).

Chapter Nine

JUDICIAL RESTRAINT, ABSTENTION, AND COORDINATION

9.1 Introduction

The law of federal jurisdiction includes a number of doctrines that allocate the initial determination of specific disputes between state and federal courts. The well-pleaded complaint rule, hardly compelled by statutory language, narrows federal power by consigning many federal defenses to state court. The *Ex parte Young* doctrine works in somewhat the opposite way, expanding access to federal court by allowing those with what were once regarded as federal defenses to assert them as affirmative claims against state officials. Access to federal habeas corpus for state prisoners has expanded and contracted in accordance with the Court's (often unspoken) perception of the fairness and effectiveness of the state criminal justice system. All of these doctrines channel litigation to state or federal court in light of the Court's perception of the importance of the federal interests at stake and the need for an original federal docket.

In addition to the channeling of litigation performed by these jurisdictional rules, the Court has fashioned rules of abstention and coordination that require the federal district courts to defer to the states in the determination of certain federal claims. Some of these rules of abstention have their origins in federal statutes, such as the Anti–Injunction Act, 28 U.S.C. § 2283. Others originate in "our federalism," the slogan that animates the decision in *Younger v. Harris* (1971) and the doctrine of equitable restraint to which it gave voice. This chapter examines these doctrines of judicial restraint, abstention, and coordination. It begins by providing an overview of our system of overlapping litigation, which assumes that the parties may more or less freely file parallel proceedings in state and federal courts. It next examines the tools that have arisen for coordinating such overlapping litigation, including the use of anti-suit injunctions. Then, it turns to the statutory and judge-made restrictions on the use of anti-suit injunctions and other tools with which the Court coordinates the adjudication of federal constitutional claims.

275

9.2 The Presumptive Propriety of Overlapping Litigation

In general, our judicial system assumes that the parties may file overlapping and duplicative litigation in the state and federal courts, an assumption well illustrated in *Kline v. Burke Construction Co.* (1922). The litigation began when the Burke Company brought suit for breach of contract in federal court on the basis of diversity of citizenship. Kline defended and counterclaimed in federal court, and also brought the same contract dispute before an Arkansas state court. After the federal court declared a mistrial, Burke (the federal plaintiff) sought a federal injunction against any further prosecution of the state proceeding. Although the federal court granted the requested injunction to protect Burke's right to a federal forum, the Supreme Court reversed. The Court acknowledged that the first court to obtain jurisdiction over a "res" that confers *in rem* jurisdiction may enjoin litigation over the same property elsewhere. But the Court refused to extend the rule of first-court primacy to *in personam* proceedings. Most suits for damages and injunctive relief fall on the *in personam* side of the Court's line.

One can question the *Kline* Court's benign view of overlapping or parallel litigation. While litigation in the state court did not threaten the federal court's ability to enter a judgment binding on the parties, the state court's own entry of judgment would bar any further federal litigation under the doctrine of claim preclusion. As a practical matter, then, the continued prosecution of the state proceeding did pose a threat to the federal court's ability to resolve the dispute, even if it did not threaten the federal court's jurisdiction. Moreover, the Court's approach tends to encourage the commencement of overlapping and duplicative proceedings. Rather than treating the first-filed action as presumptively entitled to proceed to judgment, the Court foreclosed the issuance of injunctive relief that would have blocked the duplicative state proceeding. It thus enables the parties to engage in what may prove to have been wasteful litigation. Instead of a race to the courthouse, the Court has created a race to judgment: the doctrine of claim preclusion will require deference to the first action that produces a final judgment on the merits.

In the European Union, a different approach prevails, one that tends to discourage overlapping litigation. Under the *lis pendens* rule, the first court to obtain jurisdiction over a dispute involving the same parties and subject matter may proceed to judgment. (Such a rule, if applicable in the United States, would have required the state court to defer to the federal proceeding in *Kline v. Burke Construction*, even though the action sought an *in personam* judgment.) In Europe, in short, the parties race to the courthouse, rather than to judgment, with results that may seem no more satisfactory. For example, in Europe, the *lis pendens* rule does not allow consideration of which court might most conveniently or appropriately hear the action. Nor does the rule take account of the possibility that one party might bring suit in the courts of a member state, like Italy, with a reputation for lengthy delays in litigation. *Lis pendens* can lock litigation into an inappropriate forum and greatly reward well-advised litigants for filing the first action. (On the other hand, the European Union reduces the threat of such behavior in certain kinds of litigation by limiting the range of appropriate forums in which firms can pursue such claims.) If the first-mover advantages are significant, *lis pendens* may encourage parties in the midst of negotiations to break off discussions and head to court.

9.2.1   Tools for Coordinating Overlapping Litigation

Although it has rejected *lis pendens*, the United States has developed a number of tools that help to coordinate overlapping litigation. The provisions of 28 U.S.C. § 1404 authorize the transfer of a civil action from one federal district court to another for the convenience of the parties. In the federal courts, therefore, motions to transfer can help to address the problems associated with the initiation of litigation in an inconvenient forum. In addition, the doctrine of *forum non conveniens* (FNC) confers discretion on both state and federal courts to dismiss an action that has been filed in an inconvenient forum. See *Piper Aircraft Co. v. Reyno* (1981). As in *Piper* itself, the case for granting such motions to dismiss in the federal courts has been viewed as strongest when foreign nationals who have suffered personal injuries overseas bring suit against U.S. firms in the courts of the United States, rather than instituting claims in their local courts. Many of the individuals who brought suit against Union Carbide in the United States following the deadly release of toxic gases at Bhopal, India in 1984 were subject to FNC dismissals.

Transfer and dismissal may shift a single piece of litigation from one court to another, but the doctrines do little to address the need for consolidation of overlapping claims. Modern mass tort litigation often produces hundreds or thousands of personal injury claims, many of which share common questions of fact and law. But the common law tradition of tolerance for overlapping litigation does little to address the need for coordinated treatment. Enter the Judicial Panel on Multidistrict Litigation, a court comprised of federal judges that rules on motions to transfer claims for consolidated pre-trial treatment whenever the claims share a common question of fact. See 28 U.S.C. § 1407. The JPML, as it is known, has become increasingly active in the last generation, transferring mass tort and other complex proceedings to a single district court (the multidistrict litigation or MDL court) for consolidated handling. After transfer, the MDL will oversee the discovery process and prepare the cases for trial or settlement. Except where federal law otherwise provides, the MDL must transfer the cases back to their court of origin for trial, if the parties fail to settle their case. See *Lexecon v. Milberg Weiss* (1997).

Despite its success in coordinating complex multi-district litigation, the JPML procedure suffers from a significant drawback: it applies only to cases pending in the federal district courts and does not reach state court litigation. The JPML could not address the *Kline v. Burke Construction* situation; the two cases were filed in state and federal court. More generally, the ability of plaintiffs to fashion their state court claims in ways that defeat removal on the basis of either diversity or federal question jurisdiction often lessens the effectiveness of the JPML as a coordination device. For example, the JPML approved the creation of an MDL court (in the Eastern District of Pennsylvania) to hear asbestos personal injury claims and the court has been effective in closing many federal cases through settlement. But some members of the plaintiffs' bar shifted litigation of such claims to the state courts, partly in an effort to avoid transfer to the MDL. So long as the claims arise under state law, and plaintiffs can defeat diversity, the claims will stay in state court and the JPML will lack authority to order their consolidated treatment.

Overlapping class action litigation presents a particular challenge for the federal system. Imagine a nationwide class action pending before the federal district court in Pennsylvania, seeking damages for defective design of GM pick-up trucks. Although such an action might in theory bind the whole group of GM consumers, such preclusion does not come into play until the parties either settle the case, or the court resolves the case on the merits and enters judgment. In the meantime, the presumption in favor of overlapping litigation enables other members of the plaintiff class to institute virtually the identical class action in other courts around the country. With a nationwide group of consumers to serve as plaintiffs, the plaintiffs' class action bar can almost always find a local plaintiff willing to represent the class in any preferred court.

The presumptive propriety of overlapping litigation has afforded the plaintiff's bar a broad choice of forums in which to pursue class action claims. It has also enabled them to re-litigate their class claims in state court, following denial of a class certification motion in federal court. (Class certification decisions, though often central to the resolution of the case, do not involve a decision on the merits to which claim or issue preclusive effect normally attaches, especially if the certification standards differ in state and federal court as they often do.) Moreover, the availability of alternate forums that comes with such overlapping litigation enables the defendant to conduct what has become known as a reverse-auction, one in which the lawyers for the plaintiff class bid against one another to settle the case at the lowest possible figure. Some embarrassing class action settlements have been blamed on the reverse auctions that result in part from the absence of effective coordination. See, e.g., *Kamilewicz v. Bank of Boston* (7th Cir. 1996) (refusing to permit collateral attack on judgment that required plaintiffs to pay more in attorneys' fees than they had recovered in damages).

Courts tried to introduce a measure of coordination into the class action world by pushing for tools with which to remove actions from state to federal court. One strategy was to deploy the All Writs Act, 28 U.S.C. § 1651, as a mechanism for removing duplicative class actions that presented the same issues as a pending federal proceeding. Once removal was accomplished, the district courts would transfer or consolidate the actions for joint proceedings. But the Supreme Court has now decisively rejected the All Writs Act as an all-purpose source of removal jurisdiction, ruling that state class actions must stay in state court unless they would be subject to removal under the usual rules of federal jurisdiction. See *Syngenta Crop Protection, Inc. v. Henson* (2002). Only where the federal court renders a judgment on the merits that resolves the class action may the federal courts enjoin or otherwise attempt to coordinate state proceedings. The simple grant or denial of class certification has not been regarded as preclusive, and does not bring into play the federal arsenal of coordination tools.

Congress can address these coordination difficulties by shifting the litigation into federal court for consolidated treatment under section 1407. Twice, it has done so in the past few years. In 2002, Congress adopted the Multi-party, Multi-forum Trial Jurisdiction Act, which confers jurisdiction on the federal courts to hear mass injury cases arising from a single disaster (such as a plane crash) that claims 75 lives. See 28 U.S.C. §§ 1369, 1441(e), 1697. In 2005, Congress enacted the Class Action Fairness Act, which authorizes the assertion of federal jurisdiction over any nationwide and many regional class actions, so long as the aggregate value of all the claims exceeds $5,000,000. See 28 U.S.C. §§ 1332(d), 1453, 1711–15. Both statutes rely upon minimal diversity as the mechanism for shifting the litigation from state to federal court, and both assume that the pre-trial consolidation procedures of section 1407 will come into play following removal of such actions to federal court. The combined operation of the consolidation regime of section 1407 and the expansive definition of subject matter jurisdiction on the basis of minimal diversity represents a partial rejection of the model of duplicative litigation reflected in *Kline v. Burke Construction*. But note that the *Kline* presumption continues to control absent federal jurisdiction that triggers consolidated treatment of related or over-lapping claims.

9.3   The Anti–Injunction Act: Federal Injunctions to Stay State Proceedings

As *Kline* suggests, anti-suit injunctions can perform a coordination role by permitting one court to insist that others defer to its proceedings. But as *Kline* also indicates, the Anti–Injunction Act (AIA) imposes important restrictions on a federal court's power to issue injunctions to stay proceedings in state court. The AIA provides as follows:

> A court of the United States may not grant an injunction to stay proceedings in a State court except as expressly authorized by Act of Congress, or where necessary in aid of its jurisdiction, or to protect or effectuate its judgments.

28 U.S.C. § 2283. First adopted in 1793, the Act represents the most important of several statutes that restrict the equitable power of federal courts in relation to state court proceedings. But as its wording reveals, the AIA does not erect an absolute barrier to the issuance of anti-suit injunctions.

The AIA comes into play when one of the parties asks a federal court to issue an injunction restraining the prosecution of a state court proceeding. Note that the injunction, if granted, would enjoin one party (typically the federal defendant) from continuing to prosecute the state court action. Anti-suit injunctions do not bind the judge of the state proceeding; state judges do not become formal parties to the federal litigation and do not become subject to the equitable power of the federal court. (Recall that the state judge's absolute judicial immunity, discussed in chapter 7, will prevent the initiation of actions in federal court naming the judge as a party in many situations.) Despite the fact that an anti-suit injunction does not bind the state judge directly, it does represent a major intrusion into the autonomy that state judges (and parties) normally enjoy in managing their docket (and in prosecuting over-lapping actions). As a consequence, both the AIA and the Supreme Court have treated anti-suit injunctions as exceptional.

Anti-suit injunctions do not arise solely in the context of overlapping state and federal litigation. It's at least conceivable that one federal judge might issue an anti-suit injunction to restrain proceedings in another federal court, although the existence of alternative forms of coordination (transfer and consolidation) make such a prospect somewhat remote. Similarly, state court judges occasionally grant anti-suit injunctions to stay proceedings in other state courts. (Dueling anti-suit injunctions at the state level, like other equitable decrees, present difficult questions under the Full, Faith and Credit Clause. See *Baker v. General Motors Corp.* (1998).) Finally, state courts have sometimes granted anti-suit injunctions to stay federal proceedings. Despite the absence of any statutory restrictions, the Supreme Court has taken a narrow view of the power of state courts to grant such injunctions. Thus, in *Donovan v. City of Dallas* (1964), the Court overturned a state court decision that had enjoined the prosecution of a federal action as barred by the preclusive effect of a prior state judgment. The Court based its decision on what it described as "the old and well established judicially declared rule" that state courts lack the power to restrain a federal *in personam* proceeding. *Donovan* suggests that state courts may enjoin federal proceedings to protect their jurisdiction in an *in rem* action.

Parties may seek anti-suit injunctions in private litigation, such as the dispute over contract enforcement in *Kline v. Burke Construction*, and in public law litigation as well. For example, civil rights supporters mounted a series of freedom rides to desegregate bus transportation in the South in the early 1960s. The freedom riders were prosecuted in state court on various charges; some brought suit in federal court to restrain the prosecutions as a violation of their constitutional rights. Applications for injunctive relief against pending state criminal proceedings present a difficult conflict of values. On the one hand, the federal plaintiff may have a right under the Constitution and *Ex parte Young* to freedom from enforcement of unconstitutional state laws; on the other hand, such injunctions may interfere with a pending state proceeding or block the initiation of a proceeding to enforce state criminal laws. This conflict between the state's interest in the enforcement of state criminal law and the federal interest in preventing an unconstitutional prosecution accounts for much of the tension that underlies the doctrine of equitable restraint.

Whether the litigation seeks to enforce public or private rights, parties who wish to obtain an injunction against a pending state court proceeding must bring their application within one of the AIA's three statutory exceptions. See *Atlantic Coast Line R. v. Brotherhood of Locomotive Engineers* (1970). The next few sections consider the exceptions in turn.

9.3.1   Injunctions Expressly Authorized by Statute

The first exception to the AIA permits injunctions where expressly authorized by statute, recognizing that Congress may maintain a general policy against anti-suit injunctions, and still create specific exceptions. A variety of federal statutes grant the necessary authority. In bankruptcy, for example, the filing of a petition initiates an automatic stay of state court proceedings against the debtor. See Brubaker (2000). Under the federal interpleader statute, district courts have been given express authority to restrain all claimants "from instituting or prosecuting any proceeding in State or United States court" affecting the subject of the interpleader action. 28 U.S.C. § 2361. Similar language in the federal habeas statute authorizes a judge of the United States to "stay any proceeding against the person detained in any State court . . . for any matter involved" in the habeas corpus proceeding. 28 U.S.C. § 2251. The bankruptcy and interpleader exceptions reflect a desire for federal coordination, and also share something in common with the traditional exception for *in rem* litigation. Both proceedings seek to protect interests in property by creating an orderly process of litigation before a single court.

In addition to these fairly explicit examples of statutory authority, the Court has interpreted section 1983 as providing express authority for the issuance of anti-suit injunctions. In *Mitchum v. Foster* (1972), the Court admitted that the text of section 1983 did not in explicit terms authorize the issuance of anti-suit injunctions. But that gap in the statute was not seen as fatal. After reviewing the other statutes that had been treated as expressly authorizing the issuance of anti-suit injunctions, the Court found that explicit language in the text was not essential. It was enough if an Act of Congress, clearly creating a federal right or remedy enforceable in a federal court of equity, could be given its intended scope only by a stay of a state court proceeding. In the end, the Court found that the desire of Congress in adopting section 1983 to effect a "vast transformation" in prevailing concepts of federalism was enough to confer the needed authority.

However poorly grounded in statutory text, the decision has enormous practical significance for public law litigation. It means that parties (like the freedom riders) may pursue federal injunctive relief against a pending state court criminal prosecution on the ground that the prosecution violates federal constitutional rights. Such authority goes beyond *Ex parte Young*, which allowed an injunction *before* any state criminal proceeding had begun (and did so in part because the state criminal law imposed such severe penalties as to justify a pre-enforcement test of its legality). Of course, the authority recognized in *Mitchum v. Foster* is not unlimited; the federal plaintiff must still make a case for injunctive relief, and that requires a showing of likely success on the merits of the constitutional claim, and irreparable harm if relief were denied. Moreover, the federal plaintiff must also thread the increasingly elaborate procedural needles created by the doctrine of equitable restraint. In the end, *Mitchum* makes sense not as a broad grant of injunctive authority, but as a formal statement of judicial authority that had already been carefully regulated by the judge-made doctrine of judicial restraint in *Younger v. Harris* (1971), one year before.

9.3.2 Injunctions Necessary in Aid of Jurisdiction

Two examples illustrate the use of anti-suit injunctions in aid of the federal court's jurisdiction. First, the long-standing *in rem* exception recognizes that a district court may issue an anti-suit injunction where it first obtains judicial control over property that provides the basis for its jurisdiction. (A leading casebook reports that this exception has been consistently reaffirmed in dicta but has never been applied in a Supreme Court decision that upholds an injunction issued on this basis. See H & W (2009).) Second, the federal removal statute declares that the state court should proceed no further with an action, following its removal from state to federal court. See 28 U.S.C. § 1446(d). A district court may accordingly grant an injunction to stay further proceedings if the state court refuses to comply with this statutory dictate. See *Mitchum v. Foster* (1972) (citing *French v. Hay* (1874)). In both instances, the federal court can be seen as acting to protect its own jurisdiction.

9.3.3 Injunctions to Effectuate Judgments

The exception for effectuation of judgments enables the district courts to enjoin state court re-litigation of issues that have been previously settled by a federal judgment. The Supreme Court had rejected such a re-litigation exception in *Toucey v. New York Life Ins. Co.* (1941). But the reviser's note that accompanied the 1948 version of the Anti–Injunction Act expressly rejected *Toucey* and restored the law as understood prior to that decision. As matters now stand, federal courts can enforce the doctrines of claim and issue preclusion by enjoining proceedings in state court that would run afoul of those doctrines. Note again that a federal court with the authority to grant an injunction is not obligated to do so; rather, the party seeking the injunction must explain why the state court proceedings should be regarded as vexatious or abusive and why the assertion of a re-litigation defense in state court would not adequately protect the interests of the federal plaintiff.

While district courts may issue injunctions to bar re-litigation, any injunction should extend no more broadly than the preclusive scope of the prior federal judgment. The Court's decision in *Chick Kam Choo v. Exxon Corp.* (1988) nicely illustrates the importance of narrow tailoring. There, plaintiff brought suit for wrongful death that had occurred in Singapore. Applying choice-of-law analysis, the federal district court concluded that Singapore law, not Texas law, controlled the issue of liability. Further, the district court applied the doctrine of forum non conveniens and dismissed the action, viewing the Singapore courts as a more convenient forum. Plaintiff chose instead to re-file the action in Texas state courts. The defendant went back to federal court to obtain an injunction against the Texas state proceeding.

Although the lower federal court granted the requested injunction, the Court reversed in part. One part of the injunction was fine; the federal court had ruled that Singapore law should control, and that determination barred the state court from applying a different body of law (Texas law) in a subsequent proceeding between the same parties. But the injunction was overbroad to the extent that it foreclosed the litigation in the Texas state courts on grounds of forum non conveniens. So long as the Texas courts respected the previous choice-of-law ruling, they were free to decide whether their own state doctrine of FNC required dismissal in favor of a Singapore forum. In other words, the state was not bound by federal FNC standards and could not be compelled to honor those standards through an anti-suit injunction.

9.4   Other Statutory Limits on Federal Equitable Proceedings

Congress has adopted other statutes aimed at restricting the exercise of the equity authority conferred on the federal district courts in *Ex parte Young* (1908). One innovation was to require the creation of a three-judge court to hear actions seeking to enjoin the actions of state officials. Although such three-judge courts became relatively common in the middle of the last century, legislation in the 1970s cut back on their scope. A second innovation, the Johnson Act of 1934, barred the federal courts from issuing an injunction directed at state and local regulation of public utilities, at least so long as the state courts afford a plain, speedy, and efficient remedy. See 28 U.S.C. § 1342. A third statute, the Tax Injunction Act, imposes similar limitations on federal jurisdiction to enjoin the assessment, levy, or collection of state and local taxes, so long as the state courts provide a plain, speedy, and efficient remedy. See 28 U.S.C. § 1341. Much of the litigation under these statutes focuses on the adequacy of the state court remedy.

The Court recently narrowed the scope of the Tax Injunction Act as a limitation on federal judicial power. In *Hibbs v. Winn* (2004), the Court considered an action to enjoin an Arizona tax credit program as a violation of the Establishment Clause. The state had argued that the Tax Injunction Act broadly foreclosed any federal judicial involvement in enjoining the operation of the state tax system. The Supreme Court disagreed. Focusing on the language of the Act, and its similarity to another statute that restricts the role of injunctive relief in disputes over the collection of federal taxes, the Court found that the Act was limited to disputes between a taxpayer and the state or local government over the amount and payment of that taxpayer's own taxes. The goal of the Act was to bar pre-enforcement litigation, and force taxpayers to pay first and litigate later. The third-party challenge to Arizona's tax-credit scheme on Establishment Clause grounds did not have any direct implications for the plaintiff's own tax liability; it was the benefit conferred on others to which the plaintiff objected. The Court was unwilling to consign all such challenges to the state courts.

The passage of time may have influenced the Court's approach. At the time of the Tax Injunction Act's enactment in 1937, Congress was primarily concerned with protecting the states' power to collect taxes from firms and individuals by foreclosing anticipatory constitutional challenges in federal court. The use of state tax credits to undermine federal constitutional values did not become an issue until the civil rights era of the 1960s, when the Court affirmed the invalidation of tax benefits for private schools that practiced racial discrimination. The approval of federal Establishment Clause challenges to state tax and expenditure programs came later, with the Court's recognition of third-party taxpayer standing in *Flast v. Cohen* (1968). In effect, the *Hibbs* Court concluded that the Act did not speak to the issues raised by Establishment Clause litigation many years later.

9.5 Judge–Made Doctrines of Restraint, Exhaustion, and the Parity Debate

In addition to statutory limits on the equitable powers of federal courts, the Court has fashioned a number of abstention doctrines that operate to protect the role of the state courts in specific areas. The next several sections summarize these judge-made abstention doctrines, examining *Pullman* abstention, equitable restraint, and *Burford* abstention. The chapter concludes with a discussion of the *Rooker–Feldman* and *Heck–Preiser* doctrines.

Debate over the legitimacy of these doctrines often features a discussion of the separation of powers and the role of the federal courts in defining their own jurisdiction. In cases to which the abstention doctrines apply, the district courts enjoy a formal grant of statutory jurisdiction over the dispute in question. Application of the doctrine requires the district court to abstain from deciding a case properly before the court, often in deference to a proceeding in state court. The abstention doctrines thus represent a departure from the traditional view that the parties may freely prosecute overlapping or parallel litigation and have a right to invoke the jurisdiction of the federal courts in appropriate cases. Scholars have questioned the legitimacy of abstention doctrines, arguing that the federal courts should defer to legislative definitions of their jurisdiction and lack power to impose new restrictions on access to the federal courts. See Redish (1991).

A leading defense of the abstention doctrines emphasizes the federal courts' traditional exercise of discretion in deciding which cases to hear. See Shapiro (1985). This defense identifies a range of jurisdictional doctrines that include an element of judicial discretion: the Court's original jurisdiction, supplemental jurisdiction, federal question jurisdiction over state claims with federal ingredients, the justiciability doctrines (standing, ripeness, and mootness) and various doctrines of equitable restraint. The judicial department's ability to protect its role in the constitutional order may depend on maintaining a degree of control over jurisdiction. More subtly, the federal courts may be in a better position institutionally to work out the details of their jurisdictional grants if they can take into account a range of considerations that may vary from case to case. A rigidly rule-based approach to jurisdictional issues could deny the system the benefit of these more fine-grained decisions.

Issues of state-federal judicial parity also inform the debate over the abstention doctrines. The parity debate centers on the question of the comparative effectiveness of state and federal courts in the recognition and enforcement of federal rights. In a celebrated early article, one scholar argued that parity was a myth, and the federal courts were much more effective in enforcing federal rights than their state counterparts. See Neuborne (1977). Among the reasons listed: federal judges enjoy independence from the political pressures that often impinge on the decisions of elected state judges; federal judicial positions are better paid and more prestigious, and thus attract a more technically proficient set of lawyers; federal judges act as employees of the federal government and develop a broader view of the nation's interests simply by virtue of having joined the federal workforce; and federal judges enjoy greater institutional support and have more time to spend on complex questions.

Some scholars have attempted to shed light on the parity debate through the use of statistical methods. In one early effort, two scholars examined state and federal judicial decisions, comparing outcomes to determine if the two systems differed in terms of their comparative willingness to enforce federal rights. See Solimine & Walker (1983). But it can be quite difficult to account and control for all of the factors that may influence specific outcomes. For example, differences in the factual and legal strength of the claims would presumably influence judicial decisions. See Chemerinsky (1988). In addition, the subtle influence of political ideology on the decision-making process may complicate statistical measures of state-federal parity. The research of political scientists reveals the unsurprising truth that political attitudes influence the way judges resolve some close legal questions. See Ruger, Kim, Martin & Quinn (2004). Some observed differences in state and federal outcomes may derive from differences in political affiliation rather than from differences in the willingness of state and federal judges to enforce federal rights.

9.5.1 Pullman Abstention

Named after the leading case, *Railroad Commission of Texas v. Pullman Co.* (1941), the *Pullman* abstention doctrine seeks to avoid the necessity of federal judicial resolution of difficult or controversial constitutional issues. It does so by requiring the prior submission of certain potentially controlling and unsettled issues of state law to state court for resolution. Controversial since its inception, the doctrine requires a federal court with jurisdiction to stay its hand during the course of potentially lengthy and burdensome state court proceedings. While the doctrine permits the federal plaintiff to return to federal court if the state court denies relief, the federal system may have lost its ability to provide a timely or effective remedy. Critics argue that the goals of preventing undue friction and preserving the state court's ability to avoid constitutional issues through the interpretation of state law do not justify the resulting burden on federal rights.

In evaluating these criticisms, one should first understand the mechanics of *Pullman* abstention and the rationale for the Court's approach. The litigation began when the Texas Railroad Commission entered an order requiring all trains with sleeping cars to employ a Pullman conductor. The order restricted the employment of the all-black Pullman porter work force in favor of the all-white conductors, and raised the labor costs of the firms. The Pullman Company and the affected railroads attacked the order as exceeding the Commission's authority under state law and as a violation of the Due Process, Equal Protection, and Commerce Clauses of the Constitution. The porters intervened as plaintiffs to join the challenge, and the conductors made common cause with the defendant Commission. For background on these dynamics, see Resnik (1994). A three-judge federal district court granted an injunction, barring enforcement of the order as having exceeded the Commission's authority under state law.

On direct appeal, the Supreme Court reversed and remanded with directions that the district court abstain from deciding the case until proceedings were had in the state court to determine the

Commission's authority to issue the order in question. (Decisions of three-judge district courts are not usually subject to review by the circuit court of appeals but go directly to the Court for review as of right.) The abstention decision was influenced by the following considerations: (1) the parties had identified an unsettled question of state law; (2) the resolution of that unsettled question could obviate the need to decide a constitutional issue, thereby eliminating a potential source of federal-state friction; (3) the law of Texas afforded "an easy and ample means" for resolving the issue; (4) the constitutional issue to be avoided was substantial and touched a sensitive issue of social policy. In other words, if the state court were to invalidate the Commission's order, the federal court would have no occasion to decide a difficult and potentially divisive constitutional issue.

To understand the way the doctrine works, consider the related requirements that the district court identify an unsettled question of state law that has the potential to moot the federal issue. In *Pullman*, the state court could moot the federal issues by ruling that the Railroad Commission lacked statutory power to enter the contested order. Such a ruling would invalidate the order on state law grounds, and obviate the federal question. Not every state law issue will qualify for *Pullman* abstention; the issue must offer the promise of avoidance or obviation of the federal question. Moreover, the state law issue must meet the *Pullman* test as "unsettled." The evident purpose of the requirement of an unsettled question is to emphasize the role of the state courts in offering definitive interpretations of new or ambiguous state laws. Once the state law issue becomes settled through state court interpretation, the federal courts may freely apply those settled readings and the justification for *Pullman* abstention disappears. The doctrine confronts the state court with the possibility of constitutional invalidation, and encourages the court to interpret state law with that possibility in mind. *Pullman* abstention applies to unsettled issues of both state statutory and constitutional law.

Avoidance could have been achieved at the federal court level, without an abstention requirement. In *Pullman* itself, the three-judge court had invalidated the order on state law grounds. As the Court acknowledged, the two district court judges on the three-judge panel were both from Texas and presumably quite knowledgeable about the content of that state's law. If constitutional avoidance were the Court's only goal, a simple affirmance of the district court's interpretation of state law would have sufficed. (Indeed, an earlier decision, *Siler v. Louisville & N. R. Co.* (1909) had advised district courts to rely on state law grounds where possible.) But writing three years after the *Erie* decision, the *Pullman* Court recognized that a district court decision could not settle the meaning of state law in quite the same way as a state court determination. The federal court could decide the issue for purposes of a single case. But so long as claim or issue preclusion did not apply to the federal decision, state courts would be free to disagree with the three-judge panel's interpretation of state law in future cases. Only a state court decision could resolve the matter once and for all.

Subsequent changes in the law of state sovereign immunity may reduce the likelihood of *Pullman* abstention. In *Pennhurst State School & Hosp. v. Halderman* (1984), as discussed in chapter 7, the Court ruled that the Eleventh Amendment bars the district courts from entertaining an *Ex parte Young* proceeding to enjoin state action as a violation of state law. *Pennhurst* means that the district courts no longer have authority to reach and decide the state law question, at least so long as the defendant officer works for an arm of the state that enjoys Eleventh Amendment immunity. As a consequence, plaintiffs who wish to challenge the constitutionality of state practices through an *Ex parte Young* action no longer have reason to include state law challenges in their complaint. Unless the plaintiff has initiated a state court challenge to the practice (splitting the cause of action into state and federal claims as required by *Pennhurst*), the federal court may have no way of knowing of the existence of a state law predicate for *Pullman* abstention. As a practical matter, the burden will often fall on defendants to identify the unsettled state law questions that could justify abstention.

Critics often point to delay as an argument against *Pullman* abstention. *Pullman* requires the plaintiff to institute a state court proceeding, perhaps at the trial court level, and litigate through the state system to obtain a definitive ruling on a question of state law. One can fairly ask whether such a process affords the plaintiff the required "easy and ample means" to secure an interpretation of state law. Some federal courts have retained jurisdiction following *Pullman* abstention either to afford interim relief or to intervene in the event of lengthy delays. Moreover, the Supreme Court has expressed a fairly strong preference for reliance on state certification procedures. The vast majority of states have adopted rules that permit a federal court to certify questions of state law to the state's highest court for determination. See H & W (2009) (reporting that 45 states have adopted such procedures). Such certification procedures enable the parties to obtain a definitive ruling on state law issues directly from the state's high court, instead of beginning at the lowest level of the state judicial system. Viewing the process as less time consuming and burdensome, the Court has embraced certification as a supplement to and to some extent a replacement for the old *Pullman* requirement of a new filing in state court. See *Arizonans for Official English v. Arizona* (1997).

With the mechanics understood, one can fairly debate the central premises of the Court's decision, namely that abstention will reduce state-federal friction and that the federal courts may legitimately deploy the doctrine to avoid constitutional issues. As for friction, the *Pullman* abstention doctrine does not eliminate the prospect of constitutional invalidation; that prospect remains if the state court upholds the practice and the parties return to federal court. At that stage of the proceeding, federal invalidation may actually produce more friction than a decision taken at an earlier stage of the proceedings, before the state court had announced its ruling. Even at the earlier stage of the proceeding, moreover, the doctrine can produce a measure of friction; a decision to grant *Pullman* abstention puts some pressure on the state courts to invalidate the state practice at issue. Indeed, as a procedural matter, the Court has ruled that the parties must inform the state court about the issues raised in the federal proceeding and about the possibility that a particular state law ruling will obviate a constitutional challenge. See *Government & Civic Employees, CIO v. Windsor* (1957). The Court explained that state courts can take adequate account of the avoidance possibility in interpreting state law only when informed of the constitutional challenge.

As for the legitimacy of the Court's avoidance strategies, opinions vary. (Chapter 2 considered avoidance issues in the course of discussing the mootness doctrine and the decision in *DeFunis v. Odegard*.) In *Pullman*, the Court refused to consider the constitutionality of racial segregation, an issue that it confronted later in *Brown v. Board of Education* (1954) in the context of public school education. With the benefit of hindsight, the Court appears to have simply delayed its decision to prohibit racial segregation by thirteen years without any obvious justification. To be sure, and as the Court noted, racial segregation constituted a sensitive issue of public policy. But the very importance of the issue would seem to demand a resolution, rather than an elaborate avoidance game designed to prevent a decision on the merits.

But scholars have defended the propriety of avoidance tactics, especially in the context of decisions such as *Brown*. See Bickel (1962). Justice Frankfurter (author of the *Pullman* decision) had worked very hard to avoid the *Brown* issue, waiting for the unanimity that would help to ensure acceptance of the Court's decree and improve prospects for compliance in the South. Had the Court rushed in, Frankfurter feared that the doctrine of *Plessy v. Ferguson* would have been reaffirmed and made more difficult to overturn. Alternatively, Frankfurter feared that a divided Court would lend support to intransigent Southern opinion, which would doubtless decry the invalidation of Jim Crow as a judicial usurpation. Either way, the better part of discretion seemed to counsel delay and avoidance, and Frankfurter's opinion in *Pullman* can be seen as part of a long-term strategy to put off the resolution of the racial segregation question. Supporting scholars, including Professor Bickel, have endorsed Frankfurter's approach, noting that the arrival of Earl Warren to replace a reluctant Chief Justice Vinson, helped to secure the needed unanimity in *Brown*.

While *Brown* may appear to have vindicated the avoidance strategy in *Pullman* (and other cases), Frankfurter may have exaggerated the likelihood that the Justices would have actually voted to reaffirm *Plessy*. Perhaps Frankfurter's desire to avoid the issue reflected his own ambivalence, as well as the doubts of his brethren. He may have shared Justice Jackson's misgivings about the Court's ability to write a persuasive decision to overturn segregation, and shared Jackson's sense that the task should be left to Congress. Moreover, Frankfurter advocated the "all deliberate speed" formula that appeared in *Brown II* (1955), a formula that perfectly expressed Frankfurter's instinct for avoidance of any direct confrontation. But just as delaying the *Brown* decision may have simply left racial minorities outside the protection of the laws, so did the "deliberate speed" formula invite the South to take its own bittersweet time to come into compliance. With a remedial formula that promised no immediate enforcement, the Court's desire to dodge a direct confrontation may have invited stronger oppositional conduct. See Pfander (2006).

Even if one regards the story of *Brown's* timing as a success, one can question the Court's decision in *Pullman* to authorize avoidance at the district court level in other cases involving "substantial" and "sensitive" questions of constitutional policy. In the last century or so, the Court has decided few constitutional questions that approach *Brown* in terms of significance. Perhaps a handful of cases come close: those involving the right to terminate a pregnancy, the right to die, the right of same-sex couples to cohabit and marry, the right to freedom from so-called reverse discrimination and rights of conscious in relation to religious observation. But *Pullman* abstention has been applied more broadly, not just to epoch-making constitutional issues, but to any constitutional question that the Court regards as difficult. As a consequence, the Court has approved abstention in actions challenging state regulatory practices under the Commerce and Due Process Clauses (as in *Pullman*) and in actions to challenge state laws restricting the speech and association rights of members of the Communist party. While the Court has held that federal statutory challenges to state action do not qualify for *Pullman* abstention, see *Propper v. Clark*

(1949), the Court has imposed few limits on the kinds of federal constitutional issues that may trigger abstention.

Procedural niceties complicate *Pullman* abstention. As we have seen, the plaintiff owes an obligation to inform the state court of the existence of a pending federal constitutional challenge. State courts sometimes respond by choosing to decide both the state law and federal questions, thereby raising doubts about the ability of the plaintiff to return to federal court for a resolution of the federal issue. (Of course, if the plaintiff chooses to submit the federal issue to the state court, she will be bound by claim preclusion if she does, and cannot return to federal court.) To avoid a preclusive state court decision of the federal constitutional claim, the Court has ruled that the plaintiff need only clarify that she has raised the federal issue in state court only for the purpose of facilitating determination of the state law matter. See *England v. Louisiana State Bd. of Medical Examiners* (1964). Many plaintiffs will formally "reserve" the constitutional issue for federal determination to avoid any misunderstanding. One additional reason to prefer the certification procedure is that it enables the federal court to frame the issue for decision rather precisely, and lessens the likelihood of a broader state court ruling.

In a different setting, the division of state and federal claims as required by *Pennhurst* may complicate a party's ability to perfect an *England* reservation. In *San Remo Hotel v. San Francisco* (2005), the plaintiff initiated parallel state and federal proceedings to challenge a city ordinance that required a substantial payment to convert a hotel from residential to tourist usage. The federal court abstained under *Pullman*, and the plaintiff duly attempted to reserve its federal constitutional claims on returning to state court. Despite the formal reservation, the Court viewed the state constitutional claims as functionally identical to the federal constitutional claims. In effect, then, the plaintiff was deemed to have submitted the issue to the state court for decision and could not avoid claim preclusive effect of the ruling by making an *England* reservation.

9.5.2 *Burford* Abstention

The Court has occasionally ruled that federal courts should defer to complex state administrative schemes, especially when the state courts actively participate in the development of state regulatory policy. The leading case, *Burford v. Sun Oil Co.* (1943), arose from a dispute over the regulation of Texas oil production. A state agency had awarded drilling rights to a nearby competitor of Sun Oil. Instead of seeking review in the state courts, Sun Oil brought a claim to enjoin enforcement of the order based on both diversity and federal question jurisdiction. The Court ruled that the district court should abstain from hearing the case, in deference to the role of the state courts in reviewing the agency's oil and gas regulations. As the Court saw matters, the need to protect the state's interest in the preservation of a unitary system of regulation required the federal courts to stay out of the process of administrative review.

Burford abstention differs from *Pullman* abstention in two important respects. First, in *Pullman*, the point of abstention was to avoid a federal constitutional issue by inviting state court resolution of an unsettled issue of state law. *Burford* does not seek to avoid the decision of any particular question, but simply to shift responsibility for the decision to the state court. Second, *Pullman* abstention may lead to a return to federal court, depending on how the state court resolves the state law issue. In *Burford* abstention, by contrast, the decision to abstain essentially ends the federal judicial role and places the whole case before the state court for ultimate resolution there. Justice Frankfurter may have had these differences in mind when he dissented in *Burford*. Whatever the strength of the federal issues, Frankfurter did not understand how the Court could authorize the district court to decline the exercise of jurisdiction that it clearly enjoyed under the diversity statute.

Burford abstention has not produced a very impressive collection of offspring. In only one subsequent case, *Alabama Pub. Serv. Comm'n v. Southern Railway* (1951), has the Court concluded that *Burford* abstention was required. There, the Court emphasized its view that the regulation of intrastate railroad commerce was a matter of primary concern to the state. In other cases, by contrast, the Court has rejected *Burford* abstention. Thus, in *McNeese v. Board of Education* (1963), the Court found no basis for abstention to a state procedure for the resolution of issues arising in connection with efforts to desegregate public schools. According to the Court, the state law issue was not bound up in a complex web of state administrative law. Moreover, the Court viewed federal jurisdiction as important in securing the federal constitutional rights of those pushing for desegregation.

Perhaps this emphasis on the constitutional rights at issue helps to explain the rise, and fall, of *Burford* abstention. *Burford* came along sometime after the Court had backed away from its use of substantive due process to oversee the fairness of state administrative regulations. As a result, both *Burford* abstention cases presented constitutional issues that had much less salience for the FDR and Truman Courts of the 1940s and 1950s than for the Court that had decided *Ex parte Young* (1908) and *Lochner v. New York* (1905). Meanwhile, *McNeese* reveals that, as to constitutional issues that had gained new importance in the wake of the *Brown* decision, the plaintiff's right of access to federal court for the determination of substantial issues of federal law remained fully intact. If *Burford* let the air out of *Ex parte Young* for certain kinds of due process claimants, *McNeese* preserves the doctrine for use in enforcing civil rights.

Pennhurst may also help to explain why *Burford* has produced relatively few abstention decisions. By foreclosing federal courts from entertaining state law challenges to state administrative action, *Pennhurst* accomplishes through the expansive interpretation of the Eleventh Amendment part of what *Burford* had set out to achieve. *Pennhurst* bars federal courts from hearing suits to enjoin state administrative action on the basis of state law. Today, for example, *Pennhurst* would bar the federal courts from hearing the state law issues on which the *Burford* and *Southern Railway* Courts ordered abstention. To be sure, *Burford* went further, foreclosing review of certain federal constitutional claims as well. But as Justice Frankfurter observed, those claims may have lacked the substantiality needed to warrant federal jurisdiction.

9.5.3   Equitable Restraint

Ex parte Young transformed federal constitutional defenses asserted in state court criminal proceedings into affirmative claims brought in federal court to restrain the enforcement of state criminal laws. Recall further that in *Ex parte Young*, the railroad's shareholders instituted their action *before* any state court proceeding had gotten under way. Had there been a pending state criminal proceeding, the federal court may well have declined jurisdiction, invoking a long-standing rule that federal courts of equity were not to enjoin pending criminal proceedings. This doctrine of equitable restraint was formalized and extended to the sphere of federal-state relations in *Younger v. Harris* (1971).

The case began when four plaintiffs (John Harris, Jim Dan, Diane Hirsch, and Farrell Broslawsky) brought suit to restrain the enforcement of California's criminal syndicalism statute. They argued that, by making it a crime to advocate the violent overthrow of the capitalist system, the statute was vague and overbroad in violation of their free speech rights under the First Amendment. Harris had been indicted by the prosecutor and a case was pending against him in state court; Dan and Hirsch were members of the Progressive Labor Party, who alleged that their political activities were chilled; Broslawsky wanted to teach the doctrines of Karl Marx in class and feared prosecution. A three-judge district court convened to hear the claims, and granted an injunction restraining further prosecution of the pending proceeding against Harris and shielding the others from future prosecution.

On review, the Court reversed the grant of injunctive relief, partly on standing grounds. Three of the plaintiffs, Dan, Hirsch, and Broslawsky, were said to lack standing to pursue their claims.

While the Court acknowledged that the case as to those three might be different if they were threatened with prosecution for their activities, apparently no such threats had been made. Instead, the Court viewed the three plaintiffs as having only claimed that the prosecution of Harris made them "feel inhibited." Fears of prosecution that the Court viewed as imaginary or speculative were said to be insufficient to bring into play the equitable jurisdiction of the federal courts. As to Harris, the Court found that standing was present; his indictment and prosecution produced an acute, live controversy with the state's attorney.

Though he had standing, Harris's action ran afoul of the Court's doctrine of equitable restraint. Under the doctrine, federal courts of equity should ordinarily refrain from granting injunctions to stay pending state criminal proceedings. The Court traced the doctrine in part to the history of federal equity jurisprudence and in part to the value of federal respect for the rightful independence of state judicial systems, a value that the Court described as "Our Federalism." After this paean to history and tradition, the Court set about to distinguish the various cases on which the three-judge district court had based its decision to grant relief. Chief among them was *Dombroski v. Pfister* (1965), in which the Court had allowed an injunction against the enforcement of state criminal laws on behalf of the members of the Southern Conference Educational Fund, a group that sought to foster civil rights for African–Americans in the South. Louisiana officials viewed the SCEF as a Communist front or subversive organization and conducted raids on its offices under the authority of Louisiana law. The *Dombroski* Court granted relief in a decision that seemed to invite federal courts to enjoin state criminal proceedings that threaten speech and associational rights.

The *Younger* Court paused, and stepped back from the transformative implications of the *Dombroski* decision. In most cases, the *Younger* Court reasoned, individuals in the position of Mr. Harris can raise their federal constitutional claims as defenses to a state criminal proceeding. Such defensive assertions will adequately vindicate federal rights, especially when coupled with the possibility of further review in the Court itself. The existence of a pending state criminal proceeding affords the state defendant an assured forum in which to litigate. Moreover, a rule that enabled state court defendants routinely to secure federal injunctive relief against state prosecutions could flood the federal courts with anti-suit litigation, and undermine the traditional authority of the states to operate their own criminal justice systems. By 1971, the Court had greatly expanded the range of criminal procedure protections available to state defendants. If every Fourth Amendment motion to suppress were to justify a federal suit to enjoin state prosecution, the consequences would be dramatic indeed.

The *Younger* Court also feared a loss of state court primacy in the interpretation of state law, an *Erie-type* concern that mirrors the worry expressed by the *Pullman* Court. Facial challenges to state laws in federal court lead to federal judicial interpretation and application of state laws, often in a somewhat abstract setting. If successful, such challenges may deprive state courts of their traditional power to interpret, apply, and narrow state law to avoid constitutional problems. While injunctive relief may help to remove the chilling effect of overly broad state statutes, federal equity may provide only a partial solution. After all, the state law remains on the books, and may provide the basis for a prosecution if others violate the law or if the federal court lifts the injunction. Unless the federal courts were to grant extremely broad and durable injunctions—an option the Court refused to embrace—only the state courts can provide a definitive narrowing interpretation of the statute that can shield prospective defendants from criminal liability. *Younger* aims in part to preserve the state court's ability to do the necessary winnowing and narrowing.

The Court's own habeas corpus jurisprudence may have influenced the decision as well. As we saw in chapter 8, the decision in *Brown v. Allen* (1953) established federal habeas review of federal constitutional issues that had been previously decided in state court. Rules of exhaustion also require state prisoners to present their claims to the state courts in the first instance. Habeas was designed to ensure the primacy of the state courts in the administration of state criminal law, subject to federal judicial review of constitutional defenses. Having put in place a structure that preserved the state courts, but also ensured federal review upon the conclusion of state criminal process, the *Younger* Court may have understandably worried about expanding the scope of federal judicial review at the front end of the process. In any case, the Court treated *Dombroski* as a narrow exception to the general rule of restraint, an exception driven by evidence of harassment on the part of state officials and related questions about the adequacy of state criminal process to vindicate the plaintiffs' rights.

Yet one can question whether the remedies available to people in the position of the *Younger* plaintiffs were truly adequate. With the prosecution of Harris, the state's attorney signaled that the criminal syndicalism statute was not a moribund relic of an earlier day but a possible source of current criminal enforcement. Individuals may contemplate speech that they genuinely believe to enjoy first amendment protection, but may also recognize that it may exceed constitutional protections and subject them to state criminal sanctions. It may not suffice to tell such plaintiffs that they can obtain a judicial determination of their first amendment rights by the simple expedient of violating the law. Many plaintiffs wish to speak and protest within the boundaries of the law, and need to know the rules in order to conform their conduct to the law. Otherwise, the threat of criminal sanctions may foreclose protected speech as individuals draw back from the brink. (First amendment overbreadth doctrine addresses these problems. See Monaghan (1981); Fallon (1991).)

Other modes of federal judicial review, such as declaratory judgments and habeas corpus, will not solve the problem of how to define in advance the scope of federal free speech rights. Although the federal courts may entertain actions for a declaratory judgment in cases of actual controversy, the Court ruled in a companion case to *Younger v. Harris* that the doctrine of equitable restraint applies to such proceedings as well. See *Samuels v. Mackell* (1971). Thus, parties in the position of Mr. Harris who face a pending state criminal proceeding may not secure a declaration of their rights in federal court, at least absent some exceptional circumstances. Nor can the other Harris plaintiffs (Dan, Hirsch, and Broslawski) obtain declaratory relief. The same lack of standing that forecloses their suit for injunctive relief will also preclude the federal court from issuing a declaratory judgment. Nor will habeas corpus provide an effective basis for federal judicial involvement. At the time of the indictment, the state court defendant may not yet be in custody; in any case, the exhaustion rule will prevent a resort to habeas until after the state defendant has raised constitutional defenses in the course of state judicial proceedings. By the time state criminal proceedings end and the prisoner exhausts avenues of direct appellate review, release from custody may prevent the habeas challenge (at least where the sentence was of a relatively short duration).

Federal plaintiffs who seek a definitive federal ruling on their constitutional claims may attempt to bring their claims within one of the three exceptions recognized in *Younger v. Harris*: (i) bad faith or harassment, (ii) patent and flagrant unconstitutionality, and (iii) other extraordinary circumstances. These exceptions apparently derive from the elements that guide the issuance of injunctive relief. Under established law, injunctive relief typically requires a showing that the party will likely succeed on the merits and will suffer irreparable harm if the requested relief be denied, and that the balance of public and private interests favors the issuance of relief. The equity tradition invites the court to weigh the strength of the plaintiff's claim on the merits, and the existence of alternative remedies that could obviate the need for any injunctive relief.

Younger's exception for bad faith or harassment finds support in the willingness of equity courts to consider the availability of alternative remedies. Recall the *Younger* Court's decision to distinguish *Dombrowski* as a case involving elements of bad faith and harassment. One feature of the bad faith in that case was the prosecutor's use of a pattern of threats and prosecutions to chill first amendment activity with no expectation of obtaining a valid state court conviction. A practice of initiating and dropping state prosecutions could deprive the state court defendants of an opportunity to secure needed relief through the assertion of a valid constitutional defense. In a case where the prosecutor repeatedly dropped the charges, the state court criminal proceeding would no longer provide an acceptable remedy and equitable relief may become appropriate.

Younger's exception for patent or flagrant unconstitutionality may also reflect the equity tradition of considering likely success on the merits as a factor in granting relief. Thus, the *Younger* Court acknowledged that a state law might so clearly violate the federal constitution in all its possible applications as to make injunctive relief appropriate. Such an exception has a certain intuitive appeal; if the state statute suffers from obvious and widespread constitutional flaws, it makes little sense to require the defendant to undergo the burden of a state criminal prosecution to vindicate his federal rights.

One can nonetheless question the breadth of the "patent unconstitutionality" exception. The statute involved in *Younger* itself was pretty clearly unconstitutional, but the *Younger* Court did not apply the exception. The Court's reluctance may have reflected its general perception that state courts can be trusted to decide constitutional issues correctly, especially those in which the constitutional flaws are obvious. The Court may have also considered the fact that states provide remedies for patently unconstitutional indictments; in *Younger*, the state defendant asked the trial court to dismiss the indictment and then asked a superior court to issue a writ of prohibition to block the prosecution. The availability of state remedies for patently unconstitutional statutes may have been viewed as lessening the need for federal intervention. In light of the range of considerations, it may make sense to envision patent unconstitutionality less as a categorical exception, than as a factor informing the exercise of equitable discretion.

9.5.4 Equitable Restraint and Pre–Enforcement Review

By its terms, the *Younger* decision requires deference to *pending* state criminal proceedings, and does not address situations in which the federal plaintiff institutes an action in federal court *before* the commencement of state criminal proceedings. Although the *Younger* Court dismissed the pre-enforcement claims of Dan,

Hirsch, and Broslawski, it did so on the basis of standing, not on the basis of equitable restraint. Since *Younger* came down, the Court has approved of the use of declaratory and injunctive relief in the pre-enforcement context. See *Steffel v. Thompson* (1974); *Doran v. Salem Inn* (1975). But it has also expanded the notion of a pending state proceeding to include proceedings instituted *after* the federal action was filed, see *Hicks v. Miranda* (1975), and to include some civil proceedings as well.

The leading case on pre-enforcement review, *Steffel v. Thompson*, established the proposition that the federal court has the power to entertain an action for a declaratory judgment brought by a plaintiff who faces the threat of an unconstitutional state criminal prosecution. The first hurdle to overcome, after *Younger v. Harris*, was to establish the sort of concrete dispute that would satisfy the standing requirement. Steffel wanted to distribute handbills at a mall, expressing his opposition to the war in Vietnam. The mall considered Steffel a trespasser and called the police. The police threatened to arrest Steffel and a colleague if they continued to distribute handbills. Steffel stopped; his colleague continued and was placed under arrest. Steffel brought an action claiming that he still wished to distribute handbills and asking for a declaratory judgment to the effect that he could do so free from arrest and prosecution.

The Court agreed that Steffel had standing to pursue his claim and was entitled to declaratory relief notwithstanding the doctrine of equitable restraint. As for standing, the Court regarded the combination of threatened arrest and the arrest of a colleague as sufficient to show that Steffel faced no mere abstract threat to his first amendment rights. His dispute with the local prosecutor met the *Younger* test of concreteness and immediacy. As for the availability of declaratory relief, the Court emphasized the absence of a pending state prosecution and the inability of Steffel to obtain a determination of his legal rights except through pre-enforcement review. The Court stressed the history of the Declaratory Judgment Act, and the desire of Congress to facilitate pre-enforcement determinations of legal rights.

The Court extended the availability of pre-enforcement review to include preliminary injunctions against prosecution pending the completion of the federal litigation. The leading case began when the village of North Hempstead, New York adopted an ordinance banning topless dancing. Three bars in the town had featured such dancing in the past, and wished to continue to do so. They filed a federal action seeking injunctive relief on the ground that the ordinance violated the first amendment. One (M & L) resumed topless dancing just after the federal complaint was filed, and was quickly prosecuted in state court. Two others (Salem and Tim–

Rob) chose to comply with the ordinance and refrain from topless dancing. In *Doran v. Salem Inn* (1975), the Supreme Court upheld preliminary injunctive relief as to the compliant bars, but rejected relief for M & L as to which there was a pending state criminal proceeding. Together, *Steffel* and *Doran* make clear that the district court may issue declaratory and injunctive relief in the pre-enforcement setting.

The Court nonetheless established an important limitation on the availability of pre-enforcement review in *Hicks v. Miranda* (1975). Police raided a theater to prevent the public display of the movie "Deep Throat." The prosecutor instituted a civil proceeding to shut down the theatre and a criminal proceeding against the employees who had screened the movie on the night of the raid. The theatre's owner, not yet a defendant in state criminal proceedings, brought an action in federal court, seeking an injunction against any prosecution. Some months later, in the midst of briefing on the plaintiff's application for a preliminary injunction, the state prosecutor expanded the state criminal proceeding by adding the owner as an additional defendant. The district court proceeded with the federal action, and eventually granted an injunction against the state prosecution. On review, the Court concluded that the doctrine of equitable restraint required the district court to stay its hand once a proceeding had gotten underway in state court in which the owner could assert a federal defense of his right to screen the movie.

In extending the doctrine of equitable restraint to a pending state criminal proceeding filed after the federal action, the Court rejected a first-to-file rule. Instead, the Court emphasized the fact that the federal proceeding, though first filed, had not yet reached the point of "proceedings of substance on the merits." Although the Court did not define this new construct, it suggested that simply filing a federal complaint and answer, perhaps coupled with a motion for a temporary restraining order (TRO), would not sufficiently draw the merits of the case into dispute to prevent an after-filed state prosecution from triggering a duty of equitable restraint. On the other hand, a district court's resolution of motions for preliminary injunctive relief or for summary judgment, both of which necessarily entail some consideration of the merits, would presumably qualify as proceedings of substance on the merits. The test apparently reflects a desire to protect federal jurisdiction if, but only if, the federal district court has invested some substantial judge-time in the resolution of the case. If the case remains at a preliminary stage, dismissal in favor of an after-filed but pending state prosecution represents no particular affront to federal authority.

One can question the Court's approach on a variety of levels. To begin with, the *Hicks* Court seemingly allows the state prosecutor to evade the jurisdiction of a federal district court by the simple expedient of initiating a criminal prosecution to which the doctrine of equitable restraint will apply. In doing so, the *Hicks* decision may appear to reward the tactics of a prosecutor who failed to move quickly to institute a criminal proceeding, and only later recognized the advantages of securing a state judicial determination. Granted that, as in all cases of parallel litigation, the parties are *both* jousting for forum-shopping advantages, the *Hicks* rule may appear to reward the party that (as the dissent noted caustically) started late and lost the race to the courthouse. Apart from fairness concerns, the Court left the trigger somewhat ill-defined, failing to specify precisely what it meant by "proceedings of substance" on the merits.

Yet the *Hicks* rule does not establish an absolute right on the part of the state prosecutor to evade federal jurisdiction through the institution of a state criminal proceeding. The federal plaintiff who succeeds in the race to the courthouse may be able to retain the federal forum. If the federal plaintiff obtains a TRO, the district court can prevent the prosecutor from filing the sort of proceeding to which the doctrine of equitable restraint would apply. Of course, a TRO remains in effect only for a short period of time but it may lead to the issuance of preliminary injunctive relief. The grant of a preliminary injunction would tie the prosecutor's hands and prevent the institution of proceedings; even if such a motion were denied, it may constitute proceedings of substance that would prevent a subsequent prosecution from triggering equitable restraint. In cases of clearly unconstitutional threatened prosecution, therefore, the district court retains some power to provide relief to the federal plaintiff. While the playing field might tilt in the prosecutor's favor, the federal plaintiff can still seek and obtain federal judicial relief.

Hicks also preserves the opportunity to obtain federal judicial relief for parties who refrain from violations of a state law pending a resolution of their federal challenge. Recall that two of the bars that wished to challenge the topless dancing ordinance in *Doran* had complied with the ordinance after filing their federal complaint. So long as they continued to refrain from topless dancing displays, the local prosecutor could not institute a state criminal proceeding against them and the federal court would have no occasion to defer to state proceedings. Some observers argue that such cases present a fairly strong argument for pre-enforcement review in federal court; the two bars were attempting to clarify the legality of their conduct before they took action. See Friedman (2004); Fallon (1991). By contrast, in *Hicks*, the theatre's owner had previously displayed the movie and those displays were the subject of pending state criminal and civil abatement proceedings. With ample opportunities to test the constitutional issue, the owner in *Hicks* had a less compelling claim on a federal docket.

In evaluating the Court's success in managing overlapping jurisdiction, one should also consider the impact on the state courts' traditional role in the interpretation and application of new state laws. The extent of the preserved state court role may turn in part on the extent to which the federal plaintiff pursues claims by way of class action and on the application of the doctrines of claim and issue preclusion. *Steffel* and *Doran* authorize the issuance of declaratory and injunctive relief against prosecutions under state laws that violate the Constitution. If successful, such proceedings may lead to permanent injunctions against prosecution that prevent the institution of any proceeding in state court. (Such pre-enforcement challenges to state laws regulating the right to an abortion have become fairly common.) If the action brought in federal court proceeds as a class action, a federal injunction might foreclose prosecution under state law in a range of circumstances. Limits on prosecution, in turn, may deprive the state courts of a role in applying and perhaps narrowing the state law. Such a restricted state judicial role may implicate *Pullman*, and its preference for the avoidance of federal constitutional questions through state court application of state law.

But not all federal proceedings under *Steffel* and *Doran* will prevent the state courts from considering arguments about the application of state law. In both cases, the plaintiffs did not seek to pursue a class action. In both, the prosecutor had commenced state criminal proceedings against other parties (Steffel's colleague and the bar M&L) for violations of the laws in question. Such proceedings allow the state courts to interpret state law and consider constitutional defenses. In doing so, state courts will not necessarily follow the precedents of the lower federal courts; that obligation applies most clearly to the decisional law of the Supreme Court. Moreover, the doctrine of claim and issue preclusion would not ordinarily bar such state prosecutions. Even if the federal court ruled in favor of the federal plaintiffs on the first amendment issue, that ruling would not be given issue preclusive effect if the prosecutor instituted proceedings against a different party. As a general matter, the doctrine of non-mutual collateral estoppel does not apply to pure issues of law and rarely applies to governmental parties. See generally Buck & Rienzi (2002). So unless the federal court certifies a class action that includes every potential target of prosecution, the prosecutor's ability to pursue claims in state court against other defendants will often remain intact.

The prosecutor's right to proceed in state court may also apply to the federal plaintiff in certain circumstances. Consider, for example, what might happen after the district court granted a preliminary injunction in the *Doran* case and the bars began to offer topless dancing. If that injunction were later vacated (either at trial or on appeal), it would not necessarily prevent a subsequent state court prosecution for topless dancing displays that occurred while it remained in effect. If the injunction or declaratory judgment remains intact, however, then the federal plaintiff would presumably enjoy protection from subsequent prosecution. In *Steffel*, a concurring opinion by then Justice Rehnquist expressed doubt on that point, portraying the declaratory judgment that the Court approved as leaving the prosecutor free to pursue state criminal proceedings against Mr. Steffel himself. But Justice Rehnquist's view was rejected by another separate opinion, which cogently argued that a declaratory judgment that failed to bind the prosecutor in subsequent state court litigation with Mr. Steffel on the same question would violate the ban on advisory opinions. In general, as discussed in chapter 2, preclusive effect applies to declaratory judgments.

The Supreme Court has extended the doctrine of equitable restraint to require federal judicial deference not only to state criminal proceedings but to some pending state civil proceedings. The cases do not all point in one direction. In the first such case, the state initiated a civil proceeding to abate the showing of allegedly obscene films. See *Huffman v. Pursue, Ltd.* (1975). The target of the state abatement proceeding brought a federal action to enjoin prosecution under state law. The Court ruled that the doctrine of equitable restraint applied, at least where the abatement proceeding was in aid of and closely related to a criminal statute. Later cases extended the doctrine to civil proceedings instituted by the state to collect welfare payments allegedly obtained by fraud, even though the connection to criminal enforcement was less obvious. See *Trainor v. Hernandez* (1977). Still later cases extended the doctrine to actions in which the state itself did not appear as a party in the state court proceedings. See *Juidice v. Vail* (1977); *Pennzoil Co. v. Texaco, Inc.* (1987). It was enough, the Court concluded, that the federal proceeding would interfere with an important state interest. In *Juidice*, the federal action challenged the state's system of civil contempt; in *Pennzoil*, the federal action sought to enjoin the application of the state's appellate bond requirement. Both federal actions thus sought to challenge the constitutionality of state procedures that could have been challenged during the pendency of the state proceeding.

The Court may have narrowed the requirement of deference somewhat in *New Orleans Public Service, Inc. v. City of New*

Orleans (1989). In *NOPSI*, the City of New Orleans refused to grant a requested rate increase to cover the costs of building a nuclear reactor. In addition to challenging the rate denial order in state court, NOPSI turned to federal court with an argument that the City's authority to deny the increase had been preempted by federal law. The City responded by bringing suit in state court, seeking a declaratory judgment of the legality of its rate order. The two state court proceedings were consolidated, and the City argued that the federal court should exercise equitable restraint. Not so, the Court ruled. In general, the Court took the position that NOPSI was free to mount a judicial challenge to completed rate-making in either state or federal court. Having chosen the federal forum (and expressed a willingness to forgo the state court challenge), NOPSI was entitled to proceed. The City's suit for declaratory relief was not the sort of pending state proceeding to which the doctrine of equitable restraint applied, but was simply an overlapping state court proceeding that was governed by the doctrine of *Kline v. Burke Construction Co.* (1922).

9.5.5 The Domestic Relations and Probate "Exceptions"

At the time of the framing of Article III, the Anglo–American legal tradition recognized four broad categories of judicial power: cases at law, cases in equity, cases before the admiralty court, and cases before the ecclesiastical courts. Ecclesiastical matters included a wide range of family law issues, including divorce and child custody, as well as matters relating to the probate of decedents' estates. Article III pointedly omits any reference to such matters; it confers jurisdiction over cases in law, equity and admiralty but makes no mention of ecclesiastical matters. Courts and litigants more or less naturally assumed, therefore, that such matters had been left to the state courts. Nineteenth century decisional law confirmed this supposition. A series of Supreme Court decisions expressed the view that the federal courts lacked power to entertain suits to obtain a divorce or to secure child support or custody, or to issue letters of administration in connection with the probate of an estate. See *Barber v. Barber* (1858) (divorce and alimony); *In re Burrus* (1890) (child custody); *Hook v. Payne* (1871) (decedent's estate).

The constitutional foundation for the recognition of these exceptions to federal judicial power was subjected to telling criticism in *Spindel v. Spindel* (EDNY 1968). There, in the context of a dispute over alimony, Judge Weinstein traced the origins of English practice and demonstrated that the courts of equity often handled matrimonial matters. Moreover, Judge Weinstein noted that only the subject matter grants in Article III (cases arising under the constitution, laws and treaties of the United States, and cases of admiralty and maritime jurisdiction) specifically refer to cases at law, equity, and admiralty. The party-alignment grants of jurisdiction—including the diversity grant—require only a "controversy" between identified parties; there is no requirement that the "controversy" fit within the law, equity and admiralty categories. As a consequence, Judge Weinstein questioned the basis for the domestic relations and (by implication) probate exceptions, particularly in matters in which the parties invoked the diversity or party-alignment jurisdiction of the federal courts.

Despite the critique, the Court has indicated that the domestic relations and probate exceptions continue to apply, albeit in a somewhat narrowed form. The leading case, *Ankenbrandt v. Richards* (1992), began as an action by Ms. Ankenbrandt for money damages against her former husband and his new girlfriend. The complaint alleged that the two defendants had physically and sexually abused the plaintiff's children, and jurisdiction was based on diversity of citizenship. The lower federal courts had applied the domestic relations exception and dismissed on the ground that the action raised issues relating to child custody. The Court reversed, deliberately narrowing the scope of the exception. As the Court explained, the domestic relations exception applied only to actions that seek an order of divorce, or an order establishing child custody, alimony, or the amount of any child support. Although the state courts must handle such matters, the federal courts remain free to enforce the obligations thereby created in appropriate proceedings instituted on the basis of diversity jurisdiction. So while the federal courts may not award child support, they may entertain an action to collect such support if they have jurisdiction. Because the plaintiff in *Ankenbrandt* did not seek a divorce decree, or a custody or support award, it was an easy case for concluding that the domestic relations exception did not apply.

Apart from defining the exception in narrow terms, the *Ankenbrandt* Court chose to treat the domestic relations exception as a creature of the diversity statute, and not as a constitutional limit on federal judicial power. In a somewhat forced review of the relevant history, the Court first noted that it had sometimes reviewed on appeal decisions from the territorial courts that granted a divorce; these decisions were treated as establishing the existence of judicial power in a constitutional sense. Next, the Court reviewed the cases in which it had applied the domestic relations exception, noting that it had done so chiefly in the context of diversity proceedings. Then came the payoff: the Court presumed that when Congress re-enacted the diversity statute as part of its 1948 re-codification, it did so with full knowledge of the domestic relations exception and thus incorporated the exception into the statute. For the Court, then, the domestic relations exception applies primarily and perhaps solely to actions brought in federal court on the basis of diversity.

This was too much for Justice Blackmun, whose concurrence pointed out the many ways in which the diversity account of the domestic relations exception did violence both to the nineteenth century cases and to the likely assumptions of the 1948 codification. But Justice Blackmun did not dissent; he too thought the case was properly brought in federal court and agreed that the domestic relations exception was limited to the modest collection of matters that the majority had identified. Justice Blackmun would have implemented the exception by way of abstention; he viewed the domestic relations exceptions as an example of *Burford* abstention, under which the district courts refrain from deciding matters that implicate a complex state administrative scheme. Such an abstention model would have left the statutory power of the district courts otherwise intact and available for use in appropriate cases.

One might well wonder why the Court's majority spent so much energy re-conceptualizing the domestic relations exception as a restriction only on the district court's diversity jurisdiction. The answer may lie in the Court's recognition of the importance of ensuring that the judicial power remain co-extensive with the legislative power. When the domestic relations exception first arose, Congress would have had little reason to regulate matters of domestic relations; most observers would have regarded such matters as reserved to the states. Today, by contrast, with the expansion of the commerce and treaty powers, Congress often regulates matters that touch upon domestic relations. For example, Congress has imposed a federal statutory obligation on the states to respect the child custody determinations of the first court with jurisdiction to rule on the matter. See 28 U.S.C. § 1738A. Furthermore, Congress has implemented the Hague convention on child abduction by requiring courts in the United States to honor the custody decrees of courts in other countries. See 42 U.S.C. §§ 11601–11610. Perhaps the *Ankenbrandt* Court foresaw that Congress might one day legislate on matters within the domestic relations exception. By tying the exception to the diversity statute, the Court ensured that the district courts could exercise original federal question jurisdiction over any federal claims that arose from such legislation.

Like the domestic relations exception, the probate exception does not apply to all disputes that implicate decedents' estates, but only to the formal commencement of probate proceedings and the administration of estates. Consider *Markham v. Allen* (1946). There, the will of a decedent was admitted to probate in California state court. The heirs challenged the right of certain German nationals to take under the will. A federal officer, appointed to serve as Alien Property Custodian during the war with Germany, brought suit in federal court against the executor of the estate under the precursor to 28 U.S.C. § 1345 (which confers jurisdiction over a suit by a federal officer), and obtained a decree confirming the right of the German legatees. The Court upheld the district court's jurisdiction against a challenge based upon the probate exception. Even though the federal decree determined the most significant issue in the probate proceeding, federal courts had long been permitted to hear suits by and against the executors of estates in the exercise of their diversity jurisdiction, so long as the federal courts refrained from the formal act of admitting a will to probate or administering an estate. While state courts retain the power to administer the estate, in doing so they must give effect to *in personam* federal judgments between parties to a will contest.

One can see the advantage of limiting the domestic relations exception reflected in the Court's handling of *Abbott v. Abbott* (2010). Following the separation of a couple living in Chile, the local courts awarded custody to the mother and a *ne exeat* right entitling the father to be notified and given an opportunity to consent prior to the child's departure from the country. Ignoring the prior consent right, the mother left with the child and settled in Texas. The father brought suit in Texas federal court, seeking recognition of his *ne exeat* right under the Hague convention on child abduction and its federal implementing legislation. Ultimately, the Supreme Court ruled in favor of the father, concluding that his rights under Chilean law were custody rights protected by the convention. To be sure, one might argue that the domestic relations exception was inapplicable to the claims in *Abbott*, which sought not to establish custody but to enforce custody orders entered elsewhere. But the recognition of the Chilean custody order could potentially interfere with the custody decisions of the Texas state courts. In the end, the lower federal courts were not obliged to draw fine distinctions. Because the case arose under federal law and implicated the federal treaty, it was obvious that the Court's reformulated domestic relations exception did not apply.

The probate exception found its way into the tabloids following its invocation in a high-profile estate contest between two individuals with claims on the estate of J. Howard Marshall. One claimant, Vickie Marshall (also known as Anna Nicole Smith), was married to J. Howard at the time of his death. The second, E. Pierce Marshall, was J. Howard's son by a previous marriage. Much of the probate litigation unfolded in Texas, resulting in judgments in favor of Pierce. Vickie filed a personal bankruptcy proceeding in California and instituted a claim against Pierce for tortious interference with her expected inheritance. While she succeeded at the district court level, the Ninth Circuit invalidated her sizable judgment on the ground that the probate exception deprived the bankruptcy court of jurisdiction. In *Marshall v. Marshall* (2006), the Supreme Court reversed, concluding that the bankruptcy proceeding did not involve the admission of a will to probate and did not come within the scope of the probate exception. On remand, the Ninth Circuit ruled that the prior adjudication in Texas barred the tortious interference claim under the doctrine of claim preclusion. As this book went to press, the *Marshall* litigation had made its second trip to the Supreme Court, this time to clarify when a federal judgment becomes effective for claim preclusion purposes. Meanwhile, the death of the two leading antagonists (Vickie and Pierce) has done little to moderate the intensity of the battle.

9.5.6   The *Rooker–Feldman* Doctrine

Though not formally a matter of abstention, the *Rooker–Feldman* doctrine operates as a restriction on the exercise of original jurisdiction by the lower federal courts. Named after the two leading cases, *Rooker v. Fidelity Trust Co.* (1923) and *District of Columbia Court of Appeals v. Feldman* (1983), the doctrine essentially bars the federal district courts from entertaining an action that seeks the functional equivalent of appellate review of a state court decision. Based on the statutory assignment of appellate jurisdiction to the Supreme Court in what is now 28 U.S.C. § 1257, the doctrine does not operate as a matter of constitutional compulsion. Rather, it simply derives from the fact that Congress has chosen to assign the appellate jurisdiction to the Supreme Court and has deprived the lower federal courts of that role. Notably, the doctrine does not bar lower federal courts from conducting collateral review of state criminal convictions by way of federal habeas corpus; even though such review may resemble appellate review, it rests on an independent grant of statutory authority.

Many have raised questions about the need for such a doctrine, pointing out that it often duplicates the results that would obtain under the doctrine of claim preclusion. Consider *Rooker* itself. There, the plaintiff brought suit in federal court to nullify a prior state court judgment involving the same parties, contending that the earlier judgment violated the federal Constitution as an impairment of the obligation of contract. The federal action was seemingly subject to dismissal on claim preclusion grounds; the contract impairment claim could have been presented to the state court in the first proceeding, either at the outset or in a motion to reconsider the state court judgment. Instead of relying on the claim preclusive effect of the state court judgment, however, the Court concluded that the federal trial court lacked appellate jurisdiction to review the state judgment.

The Court adopted much the same approach, several years later in *Feldman*. There, disappointed applicants for admission to the DC bar brought suit in federal district court, asserting two claims. The first claim was that the DC Court of Appeals (a creature of federal statute that serves in some respects as an analog to a state supreme court) had violated the Constitution in denying a waiver of its rule requiring graduation from an ABA-accredited law school. The second claim was that the bar-admission requirement itself violated the Constitution. On review of the federal court's dismissal for want of jurisdiction, the Court affirmed in part. It first ruled that the DC Court had acted judicially (not legislatively or administratively) in denying a waiver of its bar admission rules. Accordingly, review of the DC Court's decision was available under section 1257, and could not be had by way of collateral attack in federal district court. (If, by contrast, the Court had found the DC Court had acted in a non-judicial capacity in making its waiver ruling, a constitutional challenge to that decision would have been proper in a lower federal court.) As to the second claim, the Court concluded that the federal district court retained jurisdiction, apparently on the ground that it had not been previously resolved by the DC Court and was not "inextricably intertwined" with that decision. A vigorous dissent argued against a jurisdictional holding, and urged reliance instead on the doctrine of claim preclusion.

A series of decisions threatened to transform the *Rooker–Feldman* doctrine from a restriction on collateral attacks on completed state proceedings and into an all-purpose tool with which to coordinate overlapping state and federal litigation. One source of the expansion was procedural. By placing the doctrine on jurisdictional grounds, the Court invited the federal courts to dismiss federal actions on their own motion, and to do so for the first time at the federal appellate level. By contrast, the parties must raise claim preclusion defenses affirmatively; the federal courts do not typically raise such issues on their own motion. A second source of the expansion derived from the apparent desire of the lower federal courts to impose some restrictions on parallel state and federal court proceedings. As discussed in section 9.2.1, parties have traditionally been permitted to mount parallel proceedings in state and federal court; the first judgment will be given claim preclusive effect. Applying *Rooker–Feldman,* some lower courts refused to permit an assertion of federal jurisdiction in the parallel litigation context on the ground that any state judgment would eventually bring the doctrine into play. Finally, and most curiously, some lower federal courts applied the doctrine to bar a claim by a litigant

who was not a party to the prior state court litigation. See
Lemonds v. St. Louis County (8th Cir. 2000).

It now appears that such decisions will have a short shelf life.
In *Exxon Mobil Corp. v. Saudi Basic Industries Corp.* (2005), the
Court defined a narrow scope for the *Rooker–Feldman* doctrine,
confining its operation to the circumstances of the two leading
cases. In those cases, the state court had rendered a final judgment before the federal action had been commenced. In the *Exxon
Mobil* case, by contrast, the federal proceeding had begun while the
state court action remained pending and only later did the state
court enter a judgment. In such a situation, the Court ruled, the
doctrine of claim preclusion was to supply the exclusive tool of
coordination. The Court therefore unanimously reversed a lower
federal court decision that had applied the *Rooker–Feldman* doctrine in dismissing the federal action for want of jurisdiction. The
tone, if not the holding of the decision, casts grave doubt on any
extension of the doctrine to cases involving non-parties to the state
litigation.

9.5.7 Coordinating Federal Remedies: Habeas and Section 1983

Federal remedies for state prisoners overlap to some extent.
Prisoners can bring suit under 42 U.S.C. § 1983 and *Ex parte
Young* to challenge unconstitutional conditions of confinement and
petitions for habeas corpus under 28 U.S.C. § 2254 seeking release
from custody. Despite areas of overlap, the remedies differ in
important respects. Section 1983 has been interpreted to permit
the plaintiff to pursue claims without first exhausting state judicial
remedies. See *Patsy v. Board of Regents* (1982); *Monroe v. Pape*
(1961). This no-exhaustion rule for section 1983 claimants contrasts with the requirement of exhaustion that applies to habeas
petitioners. Moreover, the section 1983 remedy includes a provision for the award of attorney's fees, making it a more attractive
vehicle for a challenge to state confinement. These and other
restrictions on the availability of habeas relief have led, perhaps
inevitably, to efforts on the part of litigants to test the boundary
between section 1983 and habeas relief.

In a first cut at the problem of coordination, the Court proffered a distinction between habeas claims that challenge the "fact
or duration" of confinement and section 1983 claims that seek
other forms of relief, such as damages. In *Preiser v. Rodriguez*
(1973), the prisoner sought to challenge the state's denial of good
time credits, credits that if granted would have resulted in the
prisoner's release from prison. The prisoner framed the action as
one under section 1983, and did not first exhaust state remedies.
The majority held that the action must be characterized as a

petition for habeas corpus because it challenged the duration of confinement. Accordingly, the exhaustion rule applied, and required dismissal of the plaintiff's action. In dicta, the Court suggested that section 1983 claims remained available for litigants who sought relief, such as damages, that did not contest the legality of confinement.

The *Preiser* dicta was discarded in *Heck v. Humphrey* (1994) and the ambit of habeas exclusivity was expanded. In *Heck*, the plaintiff brought suit under section 1983 for damages, alleging that various prosecutors and police officials had engaged in an unlawful investigation and had destroyed evidence all as part of a plan to secure his conviction for the murder of his wife. He carefully refrained from seeking any relief other than damages, apparently relying on the *Preiser* dicta. At the same time, Heck filed a series of unsuccessful federal habeas petitions, seeking to challenge his conviction and secure release from custody. Drawing an analogy to the common law tort of malicious prosecution, which required the prior termination of a criminal proceeding in the plaintiff's favor, the Court held that the section 1983 claim was simply unavailable. Before bringing a section 1983 claim to challenge actions that would render a conviction or imprisonment unlawful, the prisoner must first secure the invalidation of his conviction through other established means. These means were said to include direct appellate review within the state court system, an executive order expunging the conviction, and federal habeas corpus review. So long as the section 1983 claim would "imply the invalidity" of the plaintiff's conviction or sentence, the plaintiff must first secure its invalidation through some other mode.

The *Heck* Court's emphasis on the need for proceedings that imply the invalidity of a conviction led to some uncertainty as to the date on which the limitation period accrues on suits brought under section 1983. In *Wallace v. Kato* (2007), the Court attempted to dispel the uncertainty. In a suit analogous to one for false imprisonment, Wallace sought damages for having been wrongfully subject to criminal process in state court. Wallace argued that his claim did not accrue for limitations purposes until the state court charges were dropped. The Court disagreed, finding that the claims accrued on the date Wallace was subjected to imprisonment without lawful process. In response to Wallace's invocation of *Heck*, the Court observed that the plaintiff might simply file his section 1983 action within the limitations period and allow it to be stayed pending further proceedings in state court. Once those proceedings succeed in invalidating or implying the invalidity of state process, the plaintiff can revive the timely filed action for damages.

The Court has since extended *Heck's* doctrine of habeas prima-cy to certain kinds of prison disciplinary proceedings. In *Edwards v. Balisok* (1997), the plaintiff brought suit under section 1983 to challenge the loss of good time credits imposed as a disciplinary sanction for violation of prison rules. The Court concluded that the prisoner's due process challenge would imply the invalidity of the disciplinary order. Such an implication would affect the legali-ty or duration of the prisoner's confinement, and brought into play the *Heck* doctrine. Accordingly, the Court concluded that section 1983 was unavailable and the prisoner must rely upon federal (or state) habeas or other methods of challenging the disciplinary decision. Note that disciplinary sanctions unrelated to the length of the prison term would not apparently implicate the *Edwards* rule.

The limits of the *Heck* doctrine were underscored in *Wilkinson v. Dotson* (2005). There, the prisoners brought suit under section 1983 to compel the state to furnish them with a new or speedier parole hearing, contending that their prior hearing had been taint-ed by the retroactive application to them of new, harsher parole guidelines. The state argued that a successful claim could result in a release from confinement, thereby implicating the *Heck* doctrine of habeas primacy. But the Court disagreed. The *Heck* doctrine was concerned only with claims that seek to invalidate the duration of confinement, either directly by compelling release or indirectly by a judicial determination that implies the unlawfulness of state custody. Here, by contrast, the prisoners sought neither release from custody nor a judgment that would imply the invalidity of their convictions or sentences. At most, they sought a new or earlier parole determination untainted by the imposition of alleged-ly unlawful standards.

As this book went to press, the Court was struggling to define the line between habeas and section 1983 in the fraught world of DNA testing. In *Skinner v. Switzer* (2011), the plaintiff brought suit under section 1983, asking the federal district court to order DNA testing that had allegedly been wrongly denied by the Texas state court. The Court had previously rejected a petitioner's argu-ment that substantive due process conferred a freestanding right to DNA testing. See *District Attorney's Office v. Osborne* (2009). Skinner argued that his right rested not on substantive due process but a state DNA testing statute that gave rise to a liberty interest protected by procedural due process; the Texas state courts were said to have arbitrarily denied his application for DNA testing. The Court's decision of the case will require it to resolve the tension between the "necessarily implies the invalidity" language of *Heck* and the suggestion in *Wilkinson v. Dotson* that issues not directly related to the length of incarceration do not fall within the

Heck principle as necessarily controlled by habeas restrictions. The Court might dodge the issue on *Rooker–Feldman* grounds, pointing to the prior state court criminal proceedings as a bar to section 1983 relitigation.

9.5.8 Conclusion

The Court's various abstention doctrines reflect an attempt to coordinate the respective roles of the state and federal courts as courts of first instance for the determination of federal claims. The exercise of this coordinating function doubtless reflects the Court's own view of the salience of the constitutional rights at stake and the degree to which the state courts can be relied upon to effectuate them. The Court's decisions in *Ex parte Young* (1908) and *Brown v. Allen* (1953) both reflect profound distrust of the state courts as a forum for the effective vindication of federal constitutional rights, and both adopt an expansive view of federal jurisdiction. Since those decisions were issued, the Court's view of the importance of the underlying constitutional rights and its assessment of state court performance have clearly changed. By the 1940s, the Court no longer saw substantive due process as an important check on state regulation; the *Burford* abstention doctrine signals a jurisdictional retreat as well. By the 1980s, the Court viewed its work in reforming state court criminal procedure as essentially complete, as the decision in *Teague v. Lane* reveals. The *Heck–Preiser* doctrine seeks to ensure that litigants cannot evade the Court's many restrictions on habeas review by packaging their claims under other jurisdictional statutes.

Changes in the salience of constitutional claims may produce new allocations of jurisdiction in the future. One can predict, for example, that if the Court were to retreat further from the strict enforcement of abortion rights, its conception of when such disputes become ripe for federal adjudication may change as well. Similarly, if taking claims grow in constitutional salience, the Court may well ease access to federal courts for determination of such claims. In short, the Court's changing view of the importance of particular constitutional rights inevitably leads to changes in jurisdictional assumptions. That inevitable connection helps to explain the controversy that surrounds the exercise of congressional control over federal jurisdiction, the subject of the next chapter.

Chapter Ten

CONGRESSIONAL CONTROL OF STATE AND FEDERAL JURISDICTION

10.1 Introduction

As we saw in Chapter 1, the Madisonian Compromise empowers but does not require Congress to create inferior federal courts. The Compromise means that the creation of full-fledged Article III courts with life-tenured judges, though an available option, may not be the only avenue available to a Congress that has decided to provide for the adjudication of federal rights. Congress might instead rely upon the state courts, perhaps by simply establishing a federal right for the state courts to enforce in the exercise of their general jurisdiction. State courts have long exercised jurisdiction over federal rights of action. Alternatively, Congress might constitute a non-Article III tribunal, such as a legislative court or administrative agency, to hear the federal claim at issue. Such tribunals date from the early days of the Republic, and belie (in practice if not in theory) any claim that all courts of Congress's own creation must meet the standards of Article III.

With these three options generally available to Congress, the Court has faced the task of defining the limits of congressional discretion. Article III courts play a distinctive role in the federal scheme of government, operating as a check on the political branches of government and an institutional guarantor of individual rights. Many regard the combination of life tenure and salary protection as making Article III judges particularly well suited to the task of constitutional interpretation and enforcement. State courts, by contrast, typically employ judges who lack Article III protections; such judges may find it more difficult to uphold politically unpopular individual rights. Similarly, the judges of legislative courts and administrative agencies enjoy civil service protections but lack the distinctive qualities that Article III judges share. While the judges of such non-Article III courts may gain something in terms of expertise (by facing similar problems over time), they may also lose a measure of independence by developing cozy relations with repeat litigants and the political branches of government that control their dockets and budgets.

This chapter explores the rules that govern Congress's ability to rely upon and control the jurisdiction of these three available tribunals. It begins with a discussion of congressional control of state court jurisdiction, and then considers Congress's power to create non-Article III tribunals. Finally, the chapter assesses congressional control over the jurisdiction of the federal courts. The last section considers the much-debated issue of Congress's power to strip the federal courts of jurisdiction. After a period of relative quiet, jurisdiction-stripping questions arose with renewed frequency and intensity in the early years of the twenty-first century as some members of Congress have grown increasingly hostile to the exercise of judicial review.

10.2   Congressional Control of State Court Jurisdiction and the Presumption of Concurrent Jurisdiction

Two questions arise in discussions of the power of Congress to control the jurisdiction of the state courts. One question centers on the power of the state courts to entertain federal rights of action. In general, the Court has answered this question with a presumption that state courts may exercise concurrent jurisdiction over all federal rights of action, unless Congress otherwise provides. See *Tafflin v. Levitt* (1990); *Claflin v. Houseman* (1876). A second question centers on the power of Congress to compel the state courts to hear federal claims. Here, the Court has found that state courts owe a duty to entertain federal claims under the Supremacy Clause and must tender a valid excuse if they would refuse to do so. This section explores these two aspects of the state courts' role in our federal judicial system.

The modern presumption of concurrent state court jurisdiction derives from Alexander Hamilton's analysis in *Federalist No. 82*. Hamilton explained that the Constitution generally assumed that the states would retain all of their powers except those that had been expressly ceded to the federal government. (Thus, for example, the federal government's power to collect taxes would not displace the states' taxing authority.) While Article III authorized the exercise of federal judicial power, Hamilton did not read the provision as a delegation of exclusive power. State courts would retain their authority to entertain pre-existing claims, including claims arising under common law that Article III defined as controversies between citizens of different states. Even as to newly created federal claims, such as claims to enforce the Constitution and laws of the United States, Hamilton foresaw a regime of concurrent state jurisdiction. While such federal claims could not be said to fall within the state courts' pre-existing authority, and while Congress could foreclose state adjudication by conferring exclusive federal jurisdiction, Hamilton nonetheless viewed the state courts as competent to hear them.

Congress and the Court have both subscribed to Hamilton's understanding. The Judiciary Act of 1789 left the state courts in charge of many cases arising under federal law, subject to review of any rejected federal claims by the Supreme Court. In addition, the Act assumed that many disputes between diverse parties would begin in state court, subject to removal to the federal courts in certain situations. A modest collection of federal causes were placed within the exclusive jurisdiction of the federal courts, including certain federal criminal proceedings, certain causes of admiralty and maritime jurisdiction, suits against foreign envoys, and certain state-party cases. When the Court has considered the competence of the state courts, it has drawn on this tradition in presuming them capable of hearing newly created federal rights of action unless Congress explicitly or by clear implication forecloses state jurisdiction.

The Court's decision in *Tafflin v. Levitt* (1990) nicely illustrates the presumption of state court concurrent jurisdiction. In *Tafflin*, the Court confronted the question whether state courts may hear civil claims for damages under the federal RICO statute. RICO creates a federal right of action for treble damages on behalf of those that suffer injuries in their business or property as a result of a pattern of racketeering activity. (Although RICO certainly authorizes litigation against the mafia, it also sweeps in predicate offenses such as mail and wire fraud that more legitimate businesses may sometimes commit.) The treble damages provision had led to a division in authority, with some courts taking the position that state courts were foreclosed from entertaining claims for penalties under federal law. But the Court rejected that view, and upheld the concurrent jurisdiction of the state courts.

In deciding the case, the Court began by restating the presumption of state court concurrency. Congress could rebut that presumption either by express language in the statute, by an "unmistakable implication from legislative history, or by a clear incompatibility between state-court jurisdiction and federal interests." Because there was no express language, the Court considered other evidence of federal exclusivity. But the arguments drawn from the legislative history and the claims of clear incompatibility failed to persuade. Even though RICO incorporated federal criminal law as predicate offenses, and even though federal courts enjoy exclusive jurisdiction over federal criminal prosecutions, the interpretation of federal criminal law necessitated by state court adjudication of RICO claims did not establish clear incompatibility from the Court's vantage point. State courts often apply and interpret federal law, subject to review in the Supreme Court, and their role in hearing civil RICO proceedings posed no greater threat to the goal of federal uniformity than that in hearing other federal claims.

A significant, though unspoken, factor in the Court's decision may have been its recognition that the jurisdictional statutes ordinarily provide defendants with a right to remove any federal right of action over which the state courts exercise concurrent jurisdiction. As noted in chapter 5, the general removal statute, 28 U.S.C. § 1441, authorizes federal district courts to assert removal jurisdiction over state court proceedings whenever the plaintiff's complaint presents claims that come within the original jurisdiction of the federal courts. Civil RICO claims plainly fit that description. The Court's confidence in the ability of the state courts to handle complex civil RICO claims may have stemmed in part from its recognition that such cases would stay in state court only if they have been brought there initially by the plaintiff and left there by the failure or refusal of the defendant to remove. Where both parties express confidence in state adjudication, the Court might sensibly refrain from displacing state power.

Like the presumption of concurrency, removal jurisdiction has been around for some time. The Judiciary Act of 1789 provided for the removal of actions from state to federal court and removal has been a part of state-federal judicial relations ever since. But removal does not fully explain the rise of the presumption of concurrent jurisdiction. In *Claflin v. Houseman* (1876), a leading case for the presumption of concurrency that draws extensively on Hamilton's comments in *Federalist No. 82*, the Court upheld the jurisdiction of the state courts to hear federal claims in bankruptcy. It did so, moreover, as to a claim that arose before Congress had given the district courts general authority to exercise removal jurisdiction over federal question claims. But although the defendant may have lacked an assured right to remove, the Court would have provided an assured federal appellate docket for review of any state court decision that rejected federal claims of right. With ample power to correct erroneous state court interpretations of federal law, the Court may have concluded that the state court's exercise of concurrent jurisdiction posed little threat to rights based on federal law. The consistent theme connecting *Claflin* and *Tafflin* (aside from the poetic similarity of the case names) is less a right of removal than a right of access to federal court, either by removal or appeal.

If assured access to federal court helps to explain the Court's willingness to entrust state courts with federal claims, it raises serious questions about the wisdom of a curious line of cases. The federal appellate courts have concluded with virtual unanimity that the state courts enjoy *exclusive* jurisdiction over federal actions to

enforce the provisions of the Telephone Consumer Protection Act
(TCPA), 47 U.S.C. § 277. The conclusion seems odd in view of the
fact that the statute creates a federal right of action, allowing
individuals to sue for damages and injunctive relief (including a
stipulated award of at least $500) when any person sends unwanted
facsimile messages in violation of the law. Ordinarily, state and
federal courts would enjoy concurrent jurisdiction over such claims,
and the claims would be subject to removal from state to federal
court in the absence of some provision expressly barring removal or
otherwise conferring exclusive jurisdiction on the state courts.
Despite this usual assumption, six federal circuits have concluded
that the states enjoy exclusive jurisdiction over the claims, pointing
to language in the statute declaring that the state courts "may"
hear such claims.

The judicial creation of a regime of state exclusivity seems
problematic from a variety of perspectives. First, state exclusivity
appears at odds with the ordinary assumption that federal courts
may exercise jurisdiction over all federal question claims in the
exercise of general arising-under jurisdiction. Second, state exclusivity appears to violate the presumption of concurrency articulated
in *Tafflin* and *Claflin*. The statute neither clearly states nor
necessarily implies that state courts are to have exclusive jurisdiction over TCPA claims. Third, the finding of exclusivity seems
inconsistent with the considerations that gave rise to the presumption of concurrency in the first place. State exclusivity forecloses
access to federal district court on removal, and does so in a context
in which as-of-right review in the Supreme Court is no longer
possible,* as it was when *Claflin* was decided. Access to federal
court under a regime of state exclusivity thus depends on the
Court's willingness to allow discretionary review of state court
decisions. For these reasons, and others having to do with the
specific language of the statute, the Seventh Circuit recently rejected the claim of state exclusivity. See *Brill v. Countrywide Home
Loans, Inc.* (7th Cir. 2005).

10.2.1 State Concurrent Jurisdiction and *Tarble's Case*

The Court announced an important exception to the rule of
concurrent state court jurisdiction in *Tarble's Case* (1871). There,
a father brought a petition for habeas corpus in state court to
contest the legality of his son's enlistment in the United States
army. He named the army's recruitment officer as custodian and
respondent. The Wisconsin state supreme court affirmed the decision of the lower tribunal to grant relief, concluding that the boy
was a minor and his father had not consented to the enlistment.
On review, the Supreme Court reversed. It found that the federal
courts enjoyed exclusive jurisdiction over petitions for habeas relief

directed at federal officers. Thus, quite in contrast to the presumption of concurrency that the Court was to announce a few years later in *Claflin v. Houseman* (1876), the Court in *Tarble's Case* found that state courts lacked jurisdiction to hear challenges to federal custody through habeas corpus.

The rationale of *Tarble's Case* seems quite difficult to square with the approach of later cases. The language of the federal habeas statute does not confer exclusive jurisdiction on the federal courts to entertain habeas petitions directed at federal officers. To the contrary, it simply confers authority on the federal courts and judges and says nothing about the possibility that state courts might also entertain such claims. Moreover, for much of the nineteenth century, state courts had assumed that they enjoyed authority to hear habeas petitions involving federal custody. Examples of the exercise of state habeas authority recur throughout the period leading up to the Civil War. See Warren (1930). One might suppose that this practice and the absence of any statutory language to the contrary would have brought the presumption of state court concurrent jurisdiction into play.

In rejecting state court concurrency, the Court offered two rationales. The first was based on its view of the independent relationship between the state and federal government. Quite in contrast to Hamilton's perception of the two systems as parts of one whole, the Court treated the state and federal systems as separate sovereigns operating within a single territorial space with little power to control the actions of the other government. Citing *Ableman v. Booth* (1858), the Court explained that the state of Wisconsin had no more power over the federal official in Wisconsin than it would have had over a state official operating in Michigan (into which Wisconsin could not issue judicial process). This separate spheres ideology was among the fatalities of the Civil War, although it survived in judicial opinions for a time. See *Puerto Rico v. Branstad* (1987).

The second argument, based on the threat that state court jurisdiction posed to the success of federal military objectives, has greater modern resonance. The Court reminded the nation that the Civil War underscored both the need for decisive action to furnish troops in time of conflict and the willingness of some to disrupt those efforts by any means available. Habeas proceedings were summary, and they ordered specific performance of the obligation to release the individual from custody. While the federal government might eventually contest the award of habeas relief through the state court system and to the Supreme Court for review, such litigation could take years. In the meantime, the ability of the government to raise an army might be compromised.

The perceived ineffectiveness of Supreme Court review thus helps to explain the decision in *Tarble's Case*. Note that, unlike the situation in *Tafflin v. Levitt*, the defendant federal officers in *Tarble's Case* could not remove the state court habeas corpus proceeding to a federal tribunal. (Today, federal officers may remove state court civil and criminal actions that challenge their official conduct. See 28 U.S.C. § 1442, 1442a. Federal officer removal provisions originated in the nineteenth century to protect officers involved in the collection of customs and taxes, but they were not extended to military officers until the twentieth century.) Relief from an erroneous state court decision could be had only on review of a final state court decision in the Supreme Court. In effect, the Court appears to have concluded that the exercise of state habeas authority was inherently inconsistent with federal interests, a conclusion that may bring the case within the "clear incompatibility" prong of the *Tafflin v. Levitt* test. Still, it's hard to deny the force of Chief Justice Chase's dissenting opinion, which argued that federal jurisdictional law at the time assumed that state court errors were to be corrected case by case on appeal rather than prevented through a wholesale denial of state power to proceed.

Tarble's Case also finds some support in antebellum decisions that denied state courts the power to issue writs of mandamus to federal officers. See *McClung v. Silliman* (1821). Mandamus practice at the time operated in the same way as that for habeas corpus; the proceeding began with a motion or petition. If the court viewed the petition as well grounded, it would issue a writ asking the respondent official to explain her failure to take action apparently required by law. If the officer failed to provide proper justification, the court would issue a summary (non-jury trial) determination, and order the official to perform the disputed action. The summary nature of the proceeding, coupled with the specific nature of the relief granted, makes mandamus similar to habeas in terms of its tendency to place control of official action in the hands of judicial officers. (Recall that Jeffersonians criticized the issuance of an initial writ of mandamus in *Marbury v. Madison* on the theory that the courts had no business controlling the action of executive branch officials.) Although the rationale for the Court's decision in *McClung* seems somewhat obscure today, it may have rested on the perception that judicial officers of the state government should not control the executive officials of the federal government.

Scholars have made much of the inability of state courts to hear habeas claims in the wake of *Tarble's Case*. Some contend that the decision operates to counter the force of the Madisonian Compromise; perhaps Congress owes a constitutional duty to furnish lower federal courts for claims that the state courts lack the power to hear. See Redish & Woods (1975). Others have argued that *Tarble's Case* illustrates a view shared by many of the Constitution's framers that Article III obligates Congress to furnish lower federal courts to hear some matters (suits in admiralty, and criminal proceedings) that were viewed as inherently or exclusively federal. See Collins (2005); Collins (1995). While much of the antebellum history seems to confirm the existence of congressional discretion, Professor Collins raises important questions about the degree to which the Madisonian Compromise actually informed the early implementation of Article III. Still, the scholarly consensus continues to view Congress as retaining some choice in the matter, and under such a view, the decision in *Tarble's Case* can best be seen as resting on statutory or federal common law grounds that Congress can freely re-visit, rather than on constitutional grounds that would altogether foreclose state judicial involvement.

Tarble's Case also raises questions about the scope of state authority to hear other sorts of claims against federal officers. On the one hand, the Court has ruled out such forms of specific relief as habeas corpus and mandamus. On the other hand, the Court has approved the exercise of state court jurisdiction over suits against federal officers for damages. See H & W (2009). An action for damages may threaten the officer with personal liability, and may distract the officer from the performance of her duties, but the action does not control the official's conduct in quite the same way as do habeas and mandamus decrees. An award of damages leaves the official free to act, and free to appeal from the award to the Supreme Court. Moreover, such suits will almost invariably trigger a right to removal under the federal officer's removal statute, 28 U.S.C. § 1442 (at least so long as the officer tenders a federal immunity defense sufficient to satisfy the jurisdictional requirements of *Mesa v. California*, discussed in chapter 5).

What remains unsettled is the scope of the state courts' authority to entertain an action for injunctive relief against federal officials. To be sure, the specific quality of the relief sought makes an action for injunctive relief more closely resemble mandamus and habeas proceedings than actions for damages; injunctions propose to control the action of the official defendant. Yet many scholars nonetheless believe that the state courts possess injunctive authority. See Arnold (1964). The weakness of the rationale of *Tarble's Case* and the continuing significance of the Madisonian Compromise drive this conclusion. After all, if Congress were free to deny federal courts to power to grant injunctions under the Compromise, and state courts were also foreclosed from entertaining such actions, Congress might place a federal program entirely beyond the power of the state and federal courts to review. The perceived constitutional importance of ensuring a forum for the determination of constitutional claims against the federal government explains the scholarly presumption in favor of the availability of state court injunctive authority. On the other hand, the continuing vitality of *Tarble's Case* may lead to closer scrutiny of legislation proposing to restrict the habeas power of the federal courts. See *Boumediene v. Bush* (2008)

10.2.2 State Court Duty to Entertain Federal Claims

The Court has not only held that state courts may entertain federal claims (under the presumption of concurrency), it has also held that state courts owe an obligation to hear federal claims in certain circumstances. In the leading case, *Testa v. Katt* (1947), the plaintiff brought suit in state court in Rhode Island, seeking to enforce a federal law that imposed penalties on those who violated a war-time measure that restricted price increases. The state supreme court ruled that the state courts were not available to hear such claims, and two considerations seemed to support its conclusion. First, Congress can freely create inferior federal courts under Article III, and can rely upon such courts to hear federal claims if the state courts prove unwilling to do so or display hostility to the enforcement of federal rights. Second, a long line of cases had expressed the view that state courts may sometimes close their doors to enforcement of penalty claims created under the laws of another state.

Despite the arguments for recognizing the right of state courts to close their doors to the enforcement of federal actions, the Supreme Court reversed. But in justifying the obligation of the state courts to hear federal claims, the Court created some ambiguity. For much of its opinion, the Court focused on the Supremacy Clause and the duty of state courts to enforce the Constitution, laws, and treaties of the United States, notwithstanding anything to the contrary in state law. According to the Court, the Clause required the state courts to treat the laws of the United States as laws of the state, rather than treating them as laws of a foreign government. The Court thus concluded that the policy judgment about the enforcement of the federal claim was one for Congress to make and for the state courts simply to accept as supreme federal law. The Court's view of the state and federal judicial systems as closely intertwined stands in contrast to the portrait of independence drawn in *Tarble's Case*.

In the second part of the opinion, however, the Court appeared to qualify this strong statement of the nature of the state court's obligation. The Court noted that the courts of Rhode Island often hear analogous claims under state law to recover a penalty. It thus appeared to the Court that Rhode Island had discriminated against the federal penalty claim by refusing to hear the claim despite the existence of jurisdiction ample to the task. The co-existence of the supremacy and discrimination components of the opinion has created some uncertainty as to whether the state owes an absolute obligation to entertain federal claims, or a more qualified obligation to refrain from discriminating against federal claims. Some earlier cases had recognized that states can dismiss federal claims so long as they offer a neutral or valid excuse for doing so. Typically, such valid excuses originate in state procedural rules that apply across the board to state and federal claims.

Subsequent developments do not resolve the ambiguity in the *Testa* decision. On the one hand, the Court has ruled that state courts may not apply a notice of claim provision to bar a federal claim under section 1983. See *Felder v. Casey* (1988). State law required plaintiffs to file notice of claims against the government and its officers within 120 days of the alleged injury. Even though the state applied this rule on a non-discriminatory basis to claims based upon both state and federal law, the Court invalidated the notice rule. (By way of comparison, the Federal Tort Claims Act requires the plaintiff to provide notice of a claim for damages to the relevant federal agency within two years of the accrual of the claim.) *Felder* thus suggests an obligation on the part of the states to afford federal claims a reasonably hospitable reception, even in the absence of discrimination. On the other hand, the Court has upheld some state court rules that, applied on a non-discriminatory basis, require dismissal of a federal claim. See *Missouri ex rel. Southern Ry. v. Mayfield* (1950) (upholding right of state court to apply non-discriminatory doctrine of forum non conveniens to dismiss a claim arising under federal law).

Ambiguity remains at the level of constitutional theory as well. Rehnquist Court decisions establish the principle that Congress may not commandeer the institutions of state government. The anti-commandeering principle first appeared in *New York v. United States* (1992), a state challenge to the constitutionality of a federal statute that purported to require the states to enact laws to provide for the disposal of low-level radioactive nuclear waste. While the Court upheld the power of Congress to induce the states to enact legislation through the threat of federal preemption and the use of conditional spending programs, the Court invalidated a naked duty to legislate as inconsistent with the sovereignty of state governments in the federal system. A few years later, the Court extended the anti-commandeering principle to state executive branch officials. See *Printz v. United States* (1997). Together *NY v. US* and *Printz* establish that Congress cannot obligate state legislatures to enact provisions into state law and cannot obligate state executive branch officials to administer federal regulatory programs. In effect, the decisions require Congress to secure the states' cooperation through means other than naked command.

On their face, the anti-commandeering decisions in *NY v. US* and *Printz* would seem to cast doubt on the *Testa* principle, which appears in its strongest form to empower Congress to commandeer the state courts as agents for the enforcement of federal law. But both the *NY v. US* and *Printz* decisions were careful to distinguish *Testa*. Unlike state legislatures and executive branch officials, state courts were seen by the Constitution as natural instruments for the enforcement of federal rights. The Supremacy Clause assumes that federal issues will arise in the course of state court litigation, and imposes an obligation on state judges to enforce federal law. Moreover, the Madisonian Compromise assumes that Congress can implement the judicial power of the United States by relying upon the state courts to hear federal claims in the first instance, subject to an appeal to the Supreme Court. Both structural assumptions help to distinguish the commandeering of state courts approved in *Testa* from the prohibited commandeering of the other branches of state government.

One might also justify the commandeering of state courts that the Court approved in *Testa* on wholly practical grounds. The price control scheme anticipated that consumers might bring a good many claims of relatively modest size to impose sanctions on those who charged more than the fixed war-time price. State courts provide a relatively convenient and inexpensive forum for the assertion of such claims. From the perspective of a representative citizen and taxpayer, who pays taxes to support both the cost of state and federal courts, it may well make sense to allow the federal government to rely upon existing and relatively inexpensive state judicial systems, as an alternative to the creation of new and more expensive federal courthouses and judgeships. Such a taxpayer might prefer a regime that permits federal reliance on state courts to one that requires the federal government to create its own courts.

Yet one must recognize that a ban on commandeering would not foreclose the cost-effective reliance on state courts. Even where Congress cannot commandeer the states, it can offer grants to encourage state cooperation. The anti-commandeering rule serves to ensure that the federal government will pay a portion of the costs associated with reliance on state institutions, and thus serves to protect against the possibility that Congress will shift enforcement costs to the states in an effort to balance its own budget. *Testa* thus seems anomalous in permitting Congress to rely on the state court system without any corresponding obligation to pay some portion of the costs thereby imposed.

Alden v. Maine (1999) represents a final challenge to the development of a coherent theory of state court duty under *Testa v. Katt*. *Alden* held that Congress may not create a federal right of action running against the state as a state and impose an obligation on the state courts to hear the claim. As discussed in chapter 7, the Court had previously ruled that Congress lacked the power to abrogate the states' sovereign immunity from suit in legislation enacted under the Commerce Clause. See *Seminole Tribe v. Florida* (1996). *Alden* extended the no-abrogation rule to suits brought in state court. In the course of its decision, the *Alden* Court faced a *Testa* problem. The state of Maine had authorized the state's courts to hear wage claims against state employers that were functionally identical to the federal wage and hour claims that the plaintiffs asserted in the *Alden* case. It thus appeared that Maine was discriminating against the federal right of action within the meaning of *Testa*. Nonetheless, the Court upheld the state's immunity from suit, although its effort to distinguish *Testa* was particularly undistinguished. Essentially, the Court concluded that the state was entitled to discriminate against the federal claim in order to ensure the effectiveness of its *Seminole Tribe*-based immunity from suit on specified federal causes of action. *Alden* makes the immunity one from liability at the suit of an individual rather than an immunity from individual suit in federal court. Cf. Vazquez (1997).

One can understand *Testa* and *Alden* as insisting that the same duties and immunities apply with equal force in the litigation of federal law claims in state and federal courts. This preference for state-federal remedial consistency appears to have informed the Court's approach to a New York state law purporting to immunize state prison officials from personal liability. New York did two things: it immunized its prison officials and authorized suits to proceed instead against the state before the state's court of claims. (Congress made a similar switch, immunizing most federal officers from tort liability and transferring the liability to the federal government in the Westfall Act.) In *Haywood v. Drown* (2009), the Supreme Court evaluated New York's approach under the *Testa* standard. The action began in state court as a suit against state prison officials under section 1983. The officials moved to dismiss, citing the state immunity law and the availability of alternative relief. The state's high court upheld the state law, viewing it as a non-discriminatory rule that deprived state courts of jurisdiction over all claims against state prison officials, including claims based on both state and federal law.

On review, the Court reversed. Although the Court recognized that the states can refuse to exercise jurisdiction because of a neutral rule governing the administration of justice, the New York rule did not qualify as neutral. Instead, the New York rule was portrayed as inconsistent with the congressional view that all persons who commit constitutional torts should be subject to liability as defined by federal law. The New York court of claims lacked the authority to award injunctive relief, attorney's fees, and punitive damages—all familiar incidents of section 1983 litigation. As a result, the Court found that the New York law was less a neutral rule of jurisdiction than an attempt to nullify federal law in pursuit of a local policy preference. In the course of its opinion, the Court observed that the absence of discrimination between state and federal claims cannot alone save a state law from invalidation under *Testa*. But the Court stopped short of reaching the question whether Congress can compel a state court to provide a forum; instead, the Court observed that New York state courts of general jurisdiction routinely entertain section 1983 suits against state officials outside the prison context and thus had jurisdiction sufficient to hear prison claims as well.

In a dissenting opinion clearly meant to break new ground, Justice Clarence Thomas questioned the *Testa* doctrine and the notion that the Supremacy Clause should be read to oblige state courts to hear federal claims. Justice Thomas's fundamental insight was that a state court can dismiss an action for want of subject matter jurisdiction without deciding or undermining the merits of the federal claim. The party who suffers such a dismissal can simply re-file in another forum that has jurisdiction over the cause. Nothing in the Constitution, according to Justice Thomas, authorized Congress to assume the existence of a state forum or to rely on state courts without their consent. Rather, the question of how to allocate jurisdiction among state courts was a matter for the states alone to decide. One might question this view of jurisdiction by noting that the New York law not only deprived state courts of jurisdiction but switched the identity of the defendant, thereby conferring an immunity on state officials not warranted by federal law. But in Justice Thomas's defense, the federal courts remain available for 1983 suits against state officials.

Recent scholarship suggests a second, more basic reason to question Justice Thomas's view of congressional power and state duty. Article I of the Constitution provides that Congress has the power to "constitute tribunals inferior to the Supreme Court." One can sensibly read this language as giving Congress a choice of lower courts. It might ordain and establish lower federal courts within the meaning of Article III. Or it might appoint the state courts as federal "tribunals" for the adjudication of federal causes under Article I. Such a reading makes sense in light of the Madisonian compromise and it would give effect to the textual distinction between the tribunals in Article I and the courts described in Article III. Congress could appoint or "constitute" the state courts as tribunals without being required to give the judges of those courts life tenure and salary protection; such requirements apply as a textual matter only to the judges of Article III courts. Perhaps, then, Article I provides Congress with authority to rely on state courts for the adjudication of federal claims by appointing them or constituting them as inferior tribunals. No less a figure than Alexander Hamilton appeared to contemplate such appointments: *Federalist No. 81* observes that to assign causes of a federal nature to the state courts would be tantamount to constituting those courts inferior tribunals within the meaning of Article I. See Pfander (2009); Pfander (2007). (Section 10.5 discusses state court inferiority as greater length.)

Despite these lingering questions about their consistency with other doctrines of constitutional federalism, the *Testa* and *Haywood* decisions provide an important foundation for the state courts' obligation to entertain federal claims. Absent contrary statement by Congress or a valid excuse, the states will be viewed as an appropriate forum for the adjudication of federal claims. This means not only that the states may hear most federal claims, but also that in most cases, they have an affirmative duty to make a forum available.

10.3 Legislative Courts and Article I Tribunals

Congress has not only relied upon state courts to hear federal claims in the first instance, it has also created tribunals outside of Article III to hear certain kinds of proceedings. These legislative courts and Article I tribunals date from the early years of the Republic, and include such familiar bodies as courts-martial, territorial courts, and administrative agencies. Such courts and tribunals often employ judges that lack the tenure-in-office and salary protections that Article III confers on the judges of constitutional courts. The absence of Article III protections has raised textual and structural doubts as to whether these tribunals can properly hear cases and controversies within the judicial power of the United States. Article III declares in no uncertain terms that the judicial power shall be vested in one supreme court, and in such inferior courts as Congress may ordain and establish. The associated salary and tenure in office guarantees were meant to ensure the independence of the Article III judiciary in relation to both the legislative and executive branch of government. Congressional creation of legislative courts with judges who lack tenure in office and salary protections seemingly violates both the literal text of Article III and the functional goal of judicial independence.

If legislative courts and Article I tribunals occupy an anomalous place in the Article III judiciary, their position appears too well established as an institutional matter to yield to arguments based upon text and structure. Congress has established Article I tribunals to hear a wide range of matters that seemingly implicate the judicial power of the United States, and the Court has generally upheld the constitutionality of these bodies. Thus, in *American Insurance Co. v. 356 Bales of Cotton (Canter)* (1828), the Court upheld the power of the Florida territorial court to exercise jurisdiction over an admiralty proceeding. The opinion was not one of Chief Justice Marshall's stronger efforts. He appears to have treated the absence of life-tenured judges as foreclosing territorial courts from "receiving" the judicial power of the United States under Article III. But he did not regard the absence of Article III judges as fatal to the court's operation. Rather than a constitutional court under Article III, the territorial courts of Florida were created as "legislative courts" in exercise of Congress's sovereign power to regulate the territories of the United States. Although legislative courts were incapable of acting as Article III courts, they could nonetheless exercise jurisdiction over admiralty proceedings. To this day, when Congress organizes territories, it may exercise discretion in deciding whether to create a legislative court, or a full-fledged Article III court. Sometimes, as in the District of Columbia, Congress has furnished both institutions.

Other examples of Article I tribunals abound. Beginning in 1855, Congress created a specialized court of claims to hear suits against the federal government. Although the court employed life-tenured judges, the Supreme Court ruled that the court could not exercise the judicial power of the United States because its judgments were subject to legislative review. (On the importance of finality to the exercise of judicial power under Article III, see chapter 2.) Although the Court of Claims briefly achieved Article III status during the 20th century, see *Glidden Co. v. Zdanok* (1962), Congress later re-established the tribunal under Article I as the United States Court of Federal Claims with non-life tenured judges. Congressional use of courts-martial extends even further back into the nation's history, dating from the 1770s when Congress first put the Continental Army into the field against the British. Courts-martial employ members of the military as judges, rather than life-tenured judges in civil courts. While the Court has long permitted Article III courts to review the work of courts-martial, see *Schlesinger v. Councilman* (1975); *Dynes v. Hoover* (1857); *Wise v. Withers* (1806), it has never suggested that courts-martial themselves must be constituted in accordance with the requirements of Article III.

Today, Article I tribunals make their most ubiquitous appearance in the form of administrative agencies. The growth of the administrative state began during the latter half of the nineteenth century, with the creation of the Interstate Commerce Commission. The pace of growth picked up considerably during the New Deal, and now administrative agencies perform a wide range of lawmaking and adjudicative functions. Indeed, a single agency—the Social Security Administration—employs more judges (administrative law judges who hear disability and other benefit claims) than does the entire federal judiciary. Typically, administrative law judges do not enjoy life tenure, although they do serve for a term of years and enjoy civil service-style protections against discharge without cause. While the Court has imposed important limits on the degree to which Congress can insulate such agencies from Article III review, see *Crowell v. Benson* (1932), it has not foreclosed reliance on agency adjudication as an initial matter.

10.3.1 Assessing the Constitutionality of Article I Tribunals

If Article I tribunals have multiplied to the point of no return, it nonetheless remains true that the Court has established certain limitations on the extent to which Congress may substitute such tribunals for Article III courts. Three cases seem central to an understanding of current law: *Crowell v. Benson* (1932); *Northern Pipeline Construction Co. v. Marathon Pipe Line Co.* (1982); and *Commodities Futures Trading Comm'n v. Schor* (1986). This section explores these cases in turn, then examines the theories that have emerged in the academic literature.

Adjudication in the modern administrative state owes much to the foundational decision in *Crowell v. Benson* (1932), which came down at the dawn of the New Deal. In *Crowell*, an injured worker sought compensation under the Longshoremen's and Harbor Workers' Compensation Act (LHWCA) by filing a claim against his employer, Benson. When the commissioner, Crowell, ruled in favor of the worker, Benson went to district court seeking to enjoin the enforcement of the award. Benson argued that the LHWCA violated both the due process clause of the Constitution (by re-working the judge-made rules that had previously governed liability for injury to workers in maritime commerce) and Article III of the Constitution (by assigning a matter within the admiralty and maritime jurisdiction of the federal courts to an Article I tribunal). The district court concluded, based on its own independent review of the facts, that worker was not an employee of Benson within the meaning of the Act, and granted the requested injunction. On review, the Court affirmed.

While the Court thus upheld a lower court decision that invalidated an agency determination, much in the Court's decision actually supported the ability of Congress to make use of agency adjudication. As an initial matter, the Court acknowledged that the dispute between private parties over the compensation to be paid to a worker in maritime commerce fell squarely within the judicial power of the United States and was a proper subject for Article III adjudication. But the Court held that Article III permitted Congress to rely on an agency to develop a factual record and propose a disposition based upon the applicable law. As the Court noted, Article III courts resolve legal issues themselves, but may rely on adjuncts (like juries) to find the facts. Agencies might play a similar fact-finding role as adjuncts to federal courts without threatening to undermine judicial independence. Nonetheless, the Court ruled that federal courts must retain certain chores for themselves: they must determine the law independently of the agency and they must determine for themselves the facts necessary to resolve constitutional and jurisdictional issues. Because the LHWCA's definition of a statutory employer was seen as a jurisdictional issue, the Court concluded that the district court had been correct to make its own factual findings on that point and to intervene on Benson's behalf.

Progressives found the *Crowell* decision too confining, and questioned the Court's reliance on Article III as a limitation on congressional power. In a lengthy dissent, Justice Brandeis gave enduring voice to these concerns, which he shared with then Professor Felix Frankfurter. Brandeis noted that the state courts lacked life-tenured judges but were nonetheless viewed as competent to entertain claims within the judicial power of the United States. For Brandeis, this state court competence indicated that Article III played no independent role as a limit on Congress's ability to assign matters to non-Article III tribunals for determination in the first instance. Rather, for Brandeis, the relevant constitutional limits were supplied by the due process clause. Like state courts, Article I tribunals need only provide fair procedures and impartial adjudicators; if they did so, then the Constitution imposed no further restriction on Congress's authority except in a narrow and unexplained category of cases in which due process was said to demand judicial process. Brandeis may have meant to include federal criminal proceedings in this category.

The state court option explored in Brandeis's dissent invites some consideration of the comparative independence of state courts and federal agencies. Although Brandeis viewed agencies as comparable to state courts, state courts may offer a relatively more independent forum, at least on the issues that matter for agency adjudication. For one thing, federal agencies receive their annual budget allocation from Congress and agency heads may face some pressure to conform their internal processes to the suggestions of their legislative overseers. For another, the executive branch may exercise a degree of agency oversight and control, by making political appointments to positions of leadership within the agency. Budget and appointment considerations will not likely determine the identity of agency judges, but the mood within the agency may very well reflect shifting political developments. State courts, by contrast, receive their operating budget and their marching orders from the state legislatures. They seem relatively immune to changes in the political environment in Washington, D.C. As a result, congressional reliance on state courts may present fewer Article III concerns than reliance on federal agencies.

The political context in which Congress turns to agencies may also influence their relative independence and determine the degree to which they threaten Article III values of judicial independence. The compensation scheme at issue in *Crowell* may have reflected a measure of congressional dissatisfaction with the Court's handling of maritime personal injuries. Similarly, the decision of Congress in 1935 to assign the determination of unfair labor practices to the National Labor Relations Board (NLRB) doubtless reflected a perception that the federal courts were hostile to the right of employees to bargain collectively for improvements in wages, hours, and working conditions. While Congress may turn to agencies to gain needed expertise, distrust of the federal judiciary may have also influenced its choice of agency structure. Viewed from the perspective of the Court, then, reliance on federal agencies might seem to pose a threat to judicial independence as Congress substitutes quiescent or compliant agencies for the vigilance of federal courts. Depending on one's perspective, new agencies may offer a new vision and needed expertise or merely serve as the lackeys of a temporary majority in Congress. This agency-as-lackey problem provided the subtext of the debate between the majority and dissent in *Crowell*.

Crowell helps to explain the role federal courts play in reviewing the work of adjudicative agencies such as the NLRB. As noted, Congress created the NLRB to hear unfair labor practice complaints. Following a hearing, the NLRB issues a proposed order based upon its factual and legal conclusions. If the parties disagree with the proposed disposition, they may petition for review in a federal appellate court. On review, the appellate courts are to redetermine issues of law on a de novo basis, and to review findings of fact to ensure that they have the support of substantial evidence in the record as a whole. The order of the appellate court, enforcing the proposed disposition of the agency, becomes a judgment enforceable in accordance with its terms against the assets of the respondent (typically an employer or union). Thus, although many parties will treat the NLRB's order as practically final (especially if they cannot find grounds for a successful challenge), the order operates as a preliminary step toward the issuance of a federal judgment.

Many organic statutes that create federal agencies follow the NLRB model in assigning responsibility for judicial review under *Crowell* to the federal appellate courts. Although it seems odd to place the responsibility for entry of judgment in an appellate court, appellate review makes a certain amount of structural sense in light of the agency's role in developing the factual record and the *Crowell* requirement that the federal courts conduct de novo review of legal issues. Federal appellate courts typically take the factual record of the lower court as a given, and review for errors of law. Assignment of the task of review to the appellate courts does, however, tend to slight the federal judicial role in conducting de novo review of jurisdictional and constitutional facts; appellate courts are not particularly well suited to develop their own factual records (or to take action to enforce their own judgments). Perhaps in part as a result, these elements of judicial review have grown less important over time (especially in the more mature agencies, where the constitutional and jurisdictional boundaries have become well settled).

Benefit agencies, like the Social Security Administration, present slightly different issues from an Article III perspective. Rather than an adjudication of claims between private parties (as in *Crowell* and the NLRB example), a benefit agency acts on behalf of the United States in distributing government benefits to individuals who qualify under the terms of the statute. Litigation may ensue, but it pits the individual against the federal government following an administrative denial of a claim. Under the public rights doctrine, Congress may have somewhat greater leeway in assigning the determination of public benefit issues to an Article I tribunal for final resolution. Recall that in *Hayburn's Case* (1792), the Justices of the Supreme Court took the position as circuit judges that Congress could not assign benefit determinations to the federal judiciary so long as Congress retained control over the decision to fund the payment of benefits. (Chapter 2 discusses *Hayburn's Case*, and the doctrine of finality.) Under this doctrine of finality, Congress turned to Article I tribunals to hear certain kinds of benefit claims against the government. So long as Congress retained control of payment, the federal courts were obliged to refrain from reviewing benefit determinations. Today, however, most benefit agencies enjoy statutory authority to make final decisions as to the payment of benefits, thereby clearing the way for routine payment and for judicial review. The Social Security Administration enjoys such authority, and review follows in the federal district courts for those who wish to challenge a denial of benefits.

One hears echoes of *Crowell* in *Northern Pipeline*, the Court's next important decision on the meaning of Article III. *Northern Pipeline* raised questions about the constitutionality of an expansion of the role of bankruptcy courts. Before the adoption of the Bankruptcy Reform Act of 1978, bankruptcy judges or commissioners performed certain administrative tasks but exercised a relatively limited summary jurisdiction over allowance claims brought by creditors against the bankrupt estate. Actions by the bankrupt estate against third-party debtors were viewed as plenary proceedings and were traditionally heard before Article III courts, with a right to trial by jury. The 1978 legislation transferred these plenary matters from Article III courts to bankruptcy courts, but did not establish the bankruptcy courts as Article III bodies with life-tenured judges. *Northern Pipeline* presented a challenge to the constitutionality of the assignment of judicial power over a state law contract claim to an Article I tribunal.

The Court responded by invalidating the 1978 legislation insofar as it assigned traditional Article III disputes to the bankruptcy courts for determination. In an opinion for a plurality, Justice Brennan acknowledged that many forms of legislative courts had been approved in the past, including courts-martial, territorial courts, courts to hear claims involving public rights, and administrative agencies. The matter before the bankruptcy court was none of these. It was a traditional judicial dispute between private parties that did not involve the United States as a party and could not be considered as a matter involving public rights. Nor had the bankruptcy court been structured as an adjunct to Article III courts. Rather, the bankruptcy court enjoyed many of the features one associates with a freestanding tribunal: the right to take evidence, punish for contempt, and enter judgments. Although the plurality noted that the decisions of the bankruptcy courts were subject to review in Article III courts, the presence of appellate review did not resolve the plurality's concern about the power of the bankruptcy court to make initial determinations of matters within the judicial power. In the end, the plurality's desire to protect judicial independence led it to adopt a kind of thus-far-and-no-further approach, accepting past Article I tribunals but invalidating further expansions.

The dissent offered a telling criticism of the plurality's approach, pointing out the absence of any coherent theory of judicial power that could explain the acceptance of previous Article I tribunals and invalidation of the bankruptcy court. Justice White, author of the dissenting opinion, observed that past decisions had upheld Article I tribunals to hear virtually every sort of federal dispute. Rather than the drawing of formalistic lines, the dissent proposed a functional approach under which the Court would balance the threat to judicial independence posed by the assignment of judicial power to a non-Article III tribunal against the values that Congress apparently sought to obtain through the use of Article I courts. Ultimately, the Court would retain the final word. For the dissent, the crucial considerations included the presence of appellate review, the absence of any design on Congress's part to expand its power at the expense of the judiciary, and the need for flexibility in dealing with the ranks of bankruptcy judges. All these factors weighed in favor of approving the bankruptcy courts as an acceptable expedient.

Later decisions apparently adopt such a balancing approach. *CFTC v. Schor* (1986) arose from a dispute between a commodities broker (Conti) and a dissatisfied customer (Schor). Alleging that Conti had administered his brokerage account in violation of the Commodities Exchange Act, Schor brought an action to recoup his losses before the Commodities Futures Trading Commission. The CFTC had power under the Act to entertain the federal recoupment claim and Conti's counterclaim for the amounts Schor owed under their brokerage agreement. The two claims bore a close connection; if Schor did not succeed in invalidating Conti's trades, then Schor would owe the money as a matter of state contract law. When the CFTC ruled against him on both claims, Schor challenged the CFTC's authority under Article III to hear Conti's state law counterclaim. Applying *Northern Pipeline*, the federal appellate court agreed that the agency could not hear the state law claim.

Reversing, the Supreme Court identified two key concerns that animated its Article III decisions. One focus of its decisions was to preserve the role of the federal judiciary in a government of separated powers. A second concern was to preserve the right of individuals to an adjudication before an independent judiciary. The Court found that Schor had waived his individual right to an Article III determination, both by instituting an action before the CFTC and by pushing for the dismissal of a diversity action that Conti had brought against him in federal court. That left the institutional interest of the federal courts in preserving their role in the federal government (a concern Schor could not waive). As for that interest, the Court found no impermissible intrusion into the province of the judiciary. Among the factors the Court weighed was the fact that the CFTC had been structured somewhat like the agency in *Crowell*, with power only to enter an initial disposition that would become final upon review in the federal district court. The Court thus found no attempt on the part of Congress to threaten the separation of powers; indeed, the Court found that Congress had acted understandably to provide an inexpensive and expeditious forum for the adjudication of reparations and related claims. Viewing any threat to judicial independence as minimal, the Court upheld the agency's authority.

With its retreat from the categorical rigidity of *Northern Pipeline, CFTC v. Schor* signals the advent of a balancing methodology that may tend to validate new Article I tribunals. A variety of factors will be included in the balance. First, the Court will apparently continue to uphold previously approved categories of legislative courts (territorial courts, courts martial, agency adjuncts and the like). Second, the Court will consider the individual's interest in an independent federal forum and the threat posed to the judiciary's institutional role. Third, the Court will evaluate the degree to which the case involves the adjudication or public or private rights. Public rights cases might appear to fall into an exception to Article III, but that's not a conclusion that the Court has reached, at least in cases involving benefit agencies with the power to render final judgments. Once Congress invests the agency with final authority (and refrains from retaining its budgetary oversight of awards to individual claimants), it has eliminated any barrier to federal judicial involvement. Fourth, the Court may consider the degree to which the tribunal has to power to issue judgments and other court-like decrees (of the kind that led to the invalidation of the bankruptcy courts in *Northern Pipeline*). Finally, the Court will consider the degree to which the work of Article I tribunal remains subject to the oversight of the Article III courts.

One can test the significance of these factors by considering the Court's puzzling decision in *Thomas v. Union Carbide Agricultural Prods. Co.* (1985). A federal statute required companies like Dow and Union Carbide to provide the EPA with research data on the safety and environmental impact of chemicals they proposed to register for sale as pesticides and fungicides. It further provided that "follow-on" or me-too registrants could rely on the previously submitted research data to support their registration of similar chemicals. To address the free-rider problem, the statute entitled the first registrants to recover a share of their expenses from the follow-on registrants. To resolve the inevitable disputes that would arise from this compensation scheme, the statute created a system of binding arbitration. Any resulting arbitral award was subject only to limited judicial review for "fraud, misrepresentation, or other misconduct." The absence of consent, the presence of private rights, and the absence of searching appellate review all appear to imply the invalidity of the scheme.

Yet the Court upheld the arbitration program. A variety of factors appear to have informed the Court's decision. First, the Court characterized the rights in question as federal rights, thus distinguishing the state law claims that were involved in *Northern Pipeline*. Second, the Court regarded the federal rights as part of a complex regulatory scheme. The concurring opinion of Justice Brennan picked up this point, treating the compensation scheme as having created a species of quasi-public rights. Justice Brennan's formulation may have meant to refer to the fact that the compensation system was designed to forestall the assertion of claims that the United States had taken the property of first registrants through compelled disclosure of trade secret information. Third, a factor that may deserve more attention, the statutory scheme did not authorize the judicial enforcement of the arbitration award against the assets of either the first or follow-on registrants. Rather, the statute directs the agency to deny the benefits of registration as a way to compel compliance with awards. Because the arbitration does not produce a court-like judgment, one can better understand the Court's willingness to accept the limited scope of Article III review.

Scholars have criticized the Court's Article III jurisprudence and have proposed a variety of alternative approaches. On one view, the Court should return to Article III literalism, and take a relatively restrictive view of attempts by Congress to empower Article I tribunals to handle disputes within the judicial power of the United States. See Redish (1983). On another view, the Court should accord Congress broad authority to rely upon Article I tribunals in the first instance, so long as it preserves relatively searching appellate review in Article III courts. See Fallon (1988); Saphire & Solimine (1988). The appellate review theory would validate the bankruptcy courts in *Northern Pipeline*, and would allow Congress to rely more widely on magistrate judges, so long as it preserved appellate review in the federal district courts. Cf. *United States v. Raddatz* (1980) (upholding reliance on magistrate judges, but doing so on the basis that magistrates served either with the parties consent or with oversight sufficient to bring them within the adjunct theory of *Crowell*); *Peretz v. United States* (1991) (finding that consent validated magistrate's oversight of jury selection in felony jury trial).

One alternative theory would emphasize the textual distinction between Article I "tribunals" and Article III "courts." Although Article III vests the judicial power in Article III courts and requires them to employ life tenured judges, it does not impose similar obligation on the judges who serve in Article I tribunals. Perhaps the textual distinction between tribunals and courts can be read as authorizing Congress to fashion Article I tribunals to hear certain kinds of claims. Article I also requires that such tribunals remain "inferior to the Supreme Court." One might read this requirement of inferiority as obligating Congress to ensure that Article I tribunals remain subject to the oversight and control of the Article III judiciary. While the required inferiority would not necessarily require strict appellate review in every case, it would require oversight sufficient to ensure that Article I tribunals stay within their jurisdictional boundaries and give effect to supreme federal law as articulated by the Supreme Court. See Pfander (2004).

10.4   Congressional Control of the Jurisdiction of the Federal Courts

The next several sections explore prominent arguments about the extent of Congress's power to regulate the jurisdiction of the federal courts. On the one hand, the exercise of such regulatory power seems quite uncontroversial. Congress has power under the Necessary and Proper Clause to fashion laws to carry into effect all powers vested in the judicial department, as well as power under Article III itself to ordain and establish lower federal courts. Since the Judiciary Act of 1789, Congress has exercised these powers to decide upon the structure of the federal courts and to define their jurisdiction. On the other hand, the Constitution establishes a federal judiciary and requires at a minimum that it consist of one Supreme Court. The Court's role as the head of the judicial branch includes a power to invalidate local and national laws that violate the Constitution. When Congress disagrees with constitutional rulings, it may retaliate by proposing to strip federal courts of jurisdiction. Such jurisdictional restrictions might serve both to express congressional disapproval and to deny the federal courts the power to entertain specific constitutional claims. For example, over the past generation, Congress has considered jurisdictional restrictions that would deny the federal courts any authority to hear cases that implicate school busing, school prayer, abortion, gay marriage, the pledge of allegiance, and other hot button issues.

Attitudes vary about the implications and constitutionality of such legislation. Some regard jurisdiction-stripping legislation as aimed at securing a constitutional amendment through the passage of ordinary legislation. If the jurisdictional restriction curtails the power of the federal courts only, then state courts may continue to hear the claims and can do so free from the threat that their decisions will be overturned on appeal. In a world without federal judicial oversight, many predict that some state courts would reject the Court's precedent and develop their own constitutional doctrine. If that were to happen, then proponents of the jurisdictional restriction would have obtained a change in constitutional law by ordinary legislation (rather than going through the more cumbersome process of obtaining a constitutional amendment). Others doubt that jurisdictional restrictions would produce a change in law. After all, the Court's precedents remain on the books, and state courts might continue to regard themselves as bound to apply existing doctrine in future cases. From this vantage point, jurisdictional restrictions may appear somewhat self-defeating inasmuch as they foreclose the federal courts from reconsidering prior decisions.

Jurisdiction-stripping activity in Congress appears to have picked up on either side of the turn of the twenty-first century. Apart from considering a series of jurisdiction-stripping proposals to deal with gay marriage and the pledge of allegiance, Congress has actually adopted a number of jurisdictional restrictions. For example, the Prison Litigation Reform Act restricted the remedial authority of the federal courts in litigation involving conditions of prison confinement. The AEDPA cut back on the scope of the federal courts' authority to entertain habeas petitions, and immigration reform legislation sought to curtail the availability of judicial review for those under deportation orders. The Graham-Levin amendment became law in late 2005 as part of the Detainee Treatment Act (DTA), restricting the authority of the federal courts to entertain habeas petitions and other actions to review the confinement of enemy combatants at Guantanamo Bay, Cuba. (Section 10.5.3 examines some of the issues raised by the DTA.)

The threat posed by jurisdiction-stripping legislation depends in part on the scope of the jurisdictional restriction. While the DTA restricts the jurisdiction of the federal courts only, the government might contend that decisions such as *Tarble's Case* also prohibit state courts from hearing habeas petitions on behalf of federal detainees. If *Tarble's Case* were viewed as controlling, then a restriction nominally addressed to federal power could operate to foreclose all judicial review. The expected absence of state court review might put pressure on the federal courts to recognize review under some alternative jurisdictional provision. In general, the Court has struggled to avoid the conclusion that Congress has acted to foreclose all judicial review. See, e.g., *INS v. St. Cyr* (2001).

A sophisticated understanding of the jurisdiction-stripping debate requires some familiarity with the leading academic arguments. There have simply been too few Supreme Court precedents to enable the student to make a confident doctrinal prediction about the outcome of a challenge to jurisdiction-stripping legislation. This section focuses on prominent academic accounts of the scope of congressional power, identifying leading cases where relevant. It concludes with an account of supremacy and inferiority that may help to tie together the many themes of the current debate.

10.4.1 The Orthodox Account

The text of Article III provides a relatively straightforward basis on which to conclude that Congress has broad power over the jurisdiction of the federal courts. Article III, section 1, clause 1 vests the "judicial power" in one supreme Court, and in such inferior courts as Congress may from time to time ordain and establish. Conventional wisdom holds that this provision requires the establishment and preservation of a single Supreme Court to preside over the interpretation and enforcement of federal law. At the same time, Article III empowers Congress to establish inferior federal courts "from time to time" but does not require Congress to do so. Instead, in keeping with the terms of the Madisonian Compromise,[1] Congress may decline to create lower federal courts and rely instead on the state courts as courts of first instance for the adjudication of federal claims.

Many commentators view the Madisonian Compromise and its provision for congressional control over the establishment of the inferior federal courts as giving Congress plenary control over the jurisdiction of those courts. On this "orthodox" view, Congress may establish lower federal courts and provide them with jurisdiction over the matters listed in Article III, section 2, clause 1, or it may refrain from doing so. Moreover, the orthodox view holds that Congress may amend the jurisdictional grants, by withholding jurisdiction from some lower courts and shifting it to others. Finally, orthodoxy holds that Congress may simply disestablish the courts in question, and return to a pre-constitutional world of reliance upon state courts. In 1802, the Jeffersonian Congress repealed a controversial judiciary law that had created federal circuit courts as freestanding courts with their own judges and a general grant of federal-question jurisdiction; in the process, the Jeffersonians turned sitting judges out of office and returned many federal question cases to the state courts. Although judges today would presumably keep their jobs or their paychecks, the Jeffersonian precedent underscores the scope of congressional control over the existence and jurisdiction of inferior federal courts.

The scope of congressional control over the jurisdiction of the Supreme Court poses different Article III issues. Article III itself provides for the existence of the Court, and does not leave the matter within the discretion of Congress. Moreover, Article III, section 2, clause 2 vests the Supreme Court with original and appellate jurisdiction in a specified collection of cases. Thus, in ambassador cases, and those involving the states as parties, Article III confers original jurisdiction on the Court. In all the other cases,

---

1. The original draft of the Virginia Plan of the Constitution provided for the establishment of both supreme and inferior federal courts. Some delegates to the Convention preferred reliance on state courts, rather than inferior federal courts, and successfully pressed to eliminate the provision for the establishment of inferior courts. After mandatory lower federal courts fell, Madison pushed for a provision that would empower but not require Congress to establish lower federal courts. For an overview, see Collins (1995) Prakash (1993); Liebman & Ryan (1998).

Article III confers appellate jurisdiction on the Court. These constitutional grants of jurisdiction have long influenced thinking about the scope of congressional control over the Supreme Court's docket. Most observers, for example, regard the Court's original jurisdiction as mandatory and self-executing, meaning that it does not depend on enabling legislation from Congress to set it in motion, and is not subject to congressional expansion or diminution.

The text presents a more complex question as it concerns the Court's appellate jurisdiction. While Article III confers appellate jurisdiction in "all the other cases," it also qualifies the grant of jurisdiction by subjecting the Court's appellate jurisdiction to such "Exceptions and Regulations" as the Congress shall make. Many observers read this Exceptions and Regulations Clause as conferring broad power on Congress to regulate the Court's appellate jurisdiction, and to deny the Court authority over a specified collection of cases. As supporters of the orthodox position note, the Exceptions and Regulations Clause empowers Congress to fashion exceptions without specifying any limits on the Exceptions power. So while Congress has no power to disestablish the Supreme Court, and while it cannot alter the Court's original jurisdiction, the Exceptions Clause creates a substantial textual predicate for the exercise of congressional power over the Court's appellate jurisdiction.

Here, then, lies the textual foundation of the orthodox account of congressional power over the jurisdiction of the federal courts. Orthodoxy holds that Congress has complete control over the jurisdiction of the inferior federal courts, and essentially unrestricted power over the Court's appellate jurisdiction. A long list of distinguished observers, including such figures as William Van Alstyne, Gerald Gunther, Herbert Wechsler, and Marty Redish have aligned themselves with the orthodox view of relatively unlimited congressional power. See Gunther (1984); Redish (1982); Van Alstyne (1973); Wechsler (1965). Many of these observers also share the view that Congress should, as a matter of policy, refrain from adopting politically motivated jurisdiction stripping legislation, and they celebrate the fact that Congress has moved cautiously in this area.

10.4.2 Challenges to Orthodoxy: Mandatory Jurisdiction

Two theorists have suggested important limits on the power of Congress to strip the jurisdiction of the federal courts. Professor Robert Clinton contends that Congress must vest the federal courts with jurisdiction over the entire list of matters on the jurisdictional "menu" of Article III, section 2. See Clinton (1984); Clinton

(1986). Professor Clinton bases this argument on the text of Article III itself, which provides that the judicial power "shall be vested" in the federal courts, and "shall extend" to the entire list of cases and controversies identified in Article III. Reading these terms as mandatory, Clinton argues that Congress has a duty to ensure that federal courts may exercise jurisdiction over all of the matters on the menu. Clinton's argument draws support from the comments of Justice Joseph Story, whose well-known opinion in *Martin v. Hunter's Lessee* (1816) contended that Article III made it obligatory on Congress to vest federal courts with all of the heads of federal jurisdiction.

Professor Akhil Amar refined Clinton's argument, distinguishing between Article III's provision for mandatory jurisdiction over "cases" and permissive jurisdiction over "controversies." See Amar (1985); Amar (1990). On Amar's reading, the mandate of Article III applies only to the federal question and admiralty "cases" that the provision describes as such and that the Framers of the Constitution regarded as central to the work of the federal judiciary. As to "controversies," such as disputes between diverse citizens, Amar reads Article III to permit grants of federal jurisdiction but not to compel such grants. Amar attaches a good deal of significance both to the mandatory terms of Article III, and to its selective usage of the term "all" to distinguish between "cases" and "controversies."

Although Clinton and Amar muster a good deal of historical support for their claims that Article III mandates the exercise of federal jurisdiction, at least in some cases, their positions do not seem to have attracted broad support within the academy. Professor Daniel Meltzer has offered a detailed critique of Amar's account, showing in many particulars just how widely the two-tier theory departs from the understanding of the Congress that first implemented Article III. See Meltzer (1990). Two scholars have taken aim at Amar's reading of the text, urging that the statement in Article III that the judicial power "shall extend" to specified cases and controversies operates to define the maximum extent of federal power, and does not mandate that power shall extend so far. See Harrison (1997); Velasco (1997). But see Pushaw (1997). Two others have offered a detailed reconstruction of the debates that shaped Article III, arguing that the judicial article leaves Congress with control over the extent of federal jurisdiction. See Liebman & Ryan (1998). In a careful review of the textual case for mandatory jurisdiction, Judge William Fletcher has taken aim at Amar's reliance on the selective use of the word "all" in Article III. See Fletcher (2010). Fletcher shows that the word was more likely meant to describe the "cases" (those arising under the Constitution, laws, and treaties of the United States and those of admiralty and maritime jurisdiction) that Congress could assign to the exclusive jurisdiction of the federal courts. On this view, the all-cases formulation does not mandate the vesting of federal jurisdiction but simply confers power to exclude state courts from the adjudication of federal matters by assigning them to federal courts alone. By contrast, Article III does not extend the judicial power to all "controversies"; on Fletcher's view, the omission of all signifies that Congress could not exclude the state courts from exercising concurrent jurisdiction over such matters (many of which were understood to turn on state common law). On the whole, the orthodox view of Article III appears to have survived the revisionist work of Clinton and Amar.

Others have suggested alternative accounts of the way Article III limits the power of Congress. Perhaps the best known, and most successful account focuses on the unique role that the Supreme Court plays as the head of the judicial department. Beginning with Henry Hart, many scholars have been troubled by the notion that Congress might curtail the "essential role" of the Court by fashioning exceptions and regulations to its appellate jurisdiction. See Hart (1953).

On this account, which remains fairly open-ended, Congress may have power to regulate appellate jurisdiction, but such restrictions may not go so far as to impair the Court's essential function. The most complete statement of the essential function thesis appears in the work of Professor Ratner, who argues that Congress may not impede the Court's role in ensuring the uniform and effective enforcement of federal law. See Ratner (1960). Such an approach, by emphasizing the need for uniformity, would apparently ensure Supreme Court review in all matters as to which the lower courts (state and federal) developed differences of opinion as to the meaning of federal law.

Note that these various theories propose a variety of different limits on the scope of congressional power. Some consider the judicial power as a whole, and suggest that either the lower federal courts or the Supreme Court must hear federal question claims. See Amar (1985). Others, like Ratner, focus on the jurisdiction of the Supreme Court (and seemingly assume that Congress may exercise broad control over the lower federal courts). By common agreement, jurisdiction strips that limit the power of both the inferior federal courts and the Supreme Court present a graver threat to the preservation of an independent Article III judiciary. Some, indeed, have gone so far as to suggest that zoning constitutional claims out of the Article III courts would tend to burden the enforcement of the rights at issue and would violate the Constitution on that basis. See Tribe (1981). But such an argument depends heavily on the claim that litigation of federal claims in the

state courts represents an unconstitutional burden on their enforcement, a claim hard to square with the Madisonian Compromise and its assumption that the state courts may play a role as
equal partners in the adjudication of federal claims. See H & W
(2009).

10.4.3 Limits on Congressional Power External to Arti-cle III

Apart from claims that Article III itself does so, many scholars
agree that other constitutional constraints may limit the power of
Congress. For example, scholars broadly agree that Congress may
not single out a disfavored group, such as African–Americans or
women, and deny them access to federal court. Such jurisdictional
strips would violate the Equal Protection component of the Fifth
Amendment. Similarly, the Due Process Clause may limit Congress's power to foreclose all judicial consideration of constitutional
claims. Decisions such as that in *Webster v. Doe* (1988) appear to
proceed on the assumption that preclusion of judicial review would
present a due process issue, at least where the claimant raised
colorable constitutional claims. See also *Battaglia v. General Motors Corp.* (2d Cir. 1948). But *Webster* may not provide strong
support for an attack on legislation that preserves the state courts
as a forum for the determination of constitutional challenges. Due
process may require a court, but many would view state courts as
filling the bill. Thus, many scholars have concluded that the
ultimate check on the power of Congress to deny judicial review lies
in the willingness of state courts to hear claims, and enforce federal
law, after Congress has acted to close the federal courts. See Hart
(1953).

Other provisions of the Constitution may act as external restraints, including the Constitution's prohibition of suspension of
the privilege of the writ of habeas corpus. In *INS v. St. Cyr* (2001),
Congress apparently restricted the scope of judicial review for
aliens who faced deportation after admission to the United States
as permanent residents. The Court agreed that legislation had
restricted appellate review, but took the position that the elimination of review of present detention by way of habeas corpus would
present serious constitutional questions under the suspension
clause. It accordingly concluded that Congress had not acted with
the clarity necessary to effect a restriction on habeas review.
(Perhaps due to the influence of *Tarble's Case*, the state court
option did not arise as a possible alternative source of judicial
review.)

In addition, some have argued that the Necessary and Proper
Clause may impose limits on the scope of congressional power. See
Engdahl (1999). The Clause empowers Congress to make laws for

the judicial department, but only laws that help "carry into execution" the powers that have been vested in the judicial "department" in Article III. Rather than a power to undermine the judiciary's role as a co-ordinate department of government, the Necessary and Proper Clause seemingly imposes a duty of good stewardship on Congress in the development of judicial legislation. While Congress may help carry the judicial power into execution, it may not on this account pass legislation designed to frustrate the work of a co-ordinate department.

Questions may arise as to the nature of the state courts' duty to follow federal law in the wake of jurisdiction-stripping legislation, and external restraints may prove relevant here as well. Some bills in Congress have proceeded on the assumption that at least some state courts would reconsider the Supreme Court's decisional law as to matters covered by a jurisdictional restriction. They would accordingly free the states from the duty to follow the decisional law of the federal courts, presumably targeting such decisions as those addressing prayer in the schools and the public display of the Ten Commandments. But state courts may be unwilling to heed such an apparent invitation to disobey Supreme Court decisional law. The Supremacy Clause explicitly directs state courts to give effect to federal law, notwithstanding anything to the contrary in state law. As Professor Herbert Wechsler noted, such an obligation coupled with the general rules of hierarchical precedent may well require state courts to follow Supreme Court decisions as the supreme law of the land. See Wechsler (1965). If it were taken seriously, an obligation on the part of state courts to give effect to aging precedents, coupled with an absence of appellate jurisdiction in the Supreme Court, may have the perverse effect of freezing old decisions in place and depriving the Court itself of the power to revisit them. To avoid such a result, Professor Caminker has argued that, following the adoption of jurisdiction-stripping legislation, inferior courts may reconsider aging precedents in deciding whether to adhere to past statements of constitutional law. See Caminker (1994). See also Pfander (2007).

To summarize, many scholars have suggested one or more bases on which the Supreme Court might resist the baldest forms of jurisdiction stripping. The Court itself has shown some willingness to embrace these resistance norms, and has invoked the doctrine of constitutional doubt as the predicate for the creative narrowing of threatening legislation. See Young (2000). Yet the orthodox account of congressional power may survive revisionist challenges especially those that rely upon limits internal to Article III itself. Orthodoxy provides the framework within which Congress has acted in considering recent jurisdiction-stripping legislation.

10.4.4   Control of the Jurisdiction of the Lower Federal Courts

History demonstrates that Congress enjoys broad control over the jurisdiction of the lower federal courts. When Congress first established the lower federal courts in 1789, it did not confer the full range of federal jurisdiction on them. Many federal question claims were left to originate in the state courts, subject to review in the Supreme Court. Indeed, lower federal courts did not receive a lasting grant of general federal question jurisdiction until 1875. The Court's decisions confirm the lessons of history. In *Sheldon v. Sill* (1850), the Court considered a challenge to legislation that required the existence of diversity jurisdiction to be based on the citizenship of the initial owners of a promissory note rather than on the citizenship of one to whom the note was later assigned. In the course of upholding this ban on an assignment to create jurisdiction, the Court rejected the idea that the lower federal courts had been given jurisdiction in Article III. Rather, as creatures of statute, the lower courts "can have no jurisdiction but such as the statute confers."

As noted above, scholars have occasionally questioned this thesis of broad congressional control. Professor Collins has collected evidence from the antebellum period and from the drafting of the Judiciary Act of 1789 that offers some support for the claim that some members of the founding generation regarded certain matters as exclusively subject to federal adjudication. See Collins (2005); Collins (1995). Such exclusivity, in cases involving admiralty jurisdiction, federal criminal proceedings, or federal detention (as in *Tarble's Case*) might necessitate the creation of lower federal courts. A more modern argument for lower federal courts emphasizes the changing nature of the Court's appellate capacity. Although the antebellum Court offered litigants assured appellate review of any decision by state courts rejecting a federal claim of right, the Court can no longer play this role. Perhaps Congress owes an obligation to provide lower federal courts as an alternative to the Court's now inadequate appellate docket. See Eisenberg (1974).

10.4.5   Control of the Supreme Court's Appellate Jurisdiction

The Court receives its appellate jurisdiction directly from Article III in all cases not assigned to its original docket. Convention holds that the Court's authority is less dependent on Congress than that of the lower federal courts. Nonetheless, the appellate jurisdiction clause of Article III includes an important qualification, providing the Court with jurisdiction with such exceptions and under such regulations as the Congress shall make. Congress has always assumed that it enjoys the authority to specify the Court's appellate jurisdiction and has, since 1789, done so by statute. The Court has generally given effect to these provisions, treating the affirmative grants of jurisdiction as implying the creation of exceptions and regulations in the areas not granted. See *Wiscart v. D'Auchy* (1796); *Durousseau v. United States* (1810). Yet it always remains open to the Court to ignore restrictions or limitations, as it did in *Durousseau,* and fall back on its constitutional grant of appellate jurisdiction.

The Court has not directly faced questions concerning the constitutionality of a broad-gauged restriction on its appellate jurisdiction. Rather, its strategy has been to read statutory restrictions narrowly, and to reaffirm the existence alternative sources of appellate jurisdiction. For example, in *Ex parte McCardle* (1868), the Court had docketed a substantial appeal in a habeas case that challenged the constitutionality of military reconstruction in the South. While the appeal was pending, Congress adopted legislation curtailing the Court's appellate jurisdiction in cases involving the issuance of the writ of habeas corpus. In response, the Court dismissed the appeal for want of jurisdiction. The Court mentioned in passing that counsel had assumed that the statute would have foreclosed the whole appellate power of the Court in cases involving habeas corpus. But this was wrong; the Court noted in dicta that it had statutory authority to exercise appellate jurisdiction through the "original" writ of habeas corpus. In a subsequent case, the Court confirmed this dicta, granting the "original" writ to provide the functional equivalent of appellate review. See *Ex parte Yerger* (1868).

The Court deployed a similar avoidance strategy in the more recent case of *Felker v. Turpin* (1996). There, Congress had restricted the Court's authority to review a federal appellate court's denial of a state prisoner's motion for leave to file a second or successive habeas petition. The petitioner argued that the statute represented an unconstitutional restriction on the Court's appellate jurisdiction; the Court dodged this question by emphasizing the continuing availability of appellate jurisdiction through the original writ. Both in *Yerger* and in *Felker*, the Court took a narrow view of the scope of the statutory restriction on its appellate jurisdiction. In *Felker*, the Court noted that such a narrow reading was informed by its desire to avoid the serious constitutional question that would arise if Congress adopted legislation that repealed all appellate authority. While the Court did not identify the precise source of this constitutional restriction, a concurring opinion observed that appellate jurisdiction stripping could interfere with the Court's constitutional "supremacy." For an elaboration of this suggestion, see Pfander (2000).

Shortly after *McCardle*, the Court invalidated a statutory restriction on its appellate jurisdiction, but the rationale of the decision has puzzled scholars ever since. In *United States v. Klein* (1871), a southerner brought suit before the Court of Claims to recover the value of property that the Union army had taken during the Civil War. The statute provided that only loyal southerners could bring such claims, but the Court's prior decisions had treated those who had received a presidential pardon as loyal within the meaning of federal law. The statute responded to those decisions, and to Klein's success in litigation before the Court of Claims, by directing all courts to treat the receipt of a presidential pardon as conclusive evidence of disloyalty, and to dismiss for want of jurisdiction. On review, the Court invalidated the statute, and affirmed the award in Klein's favor. At a minimum, the case stands for the proposition that Congress cannot simply denominate legislation as jurisdictional and avoid constitutional scrutiny.

What else can one make of the opinion? By requiring dismissal on jurisdictional grounds, the legislation would have overturned the result in a decided case. There was an element of retroactivity to the legislation; it could be seen as exercising the functional equivalent of legislative review of judicial decisions in violation of the principle of judicial finality. In addition, the legislation could be seen as interfering with the president's pardon authority. Finally, one might question the legislation as effecting a taking of property from those in the position of Klein. But the Court did not emphasize these considerations so much as its conclusion that Congress lacked power to prescribe a rule of decision for application to a pending case. One should be careful, however, not to exaggerate the significance of that statement. Congress has the power to change rules of decision, and courts often apply new rules to cases pending at the time the legislation takes effect. So long as the decision has not become final on appeal (and the *Klein* case had not), congressional authority over the rule of decision remains intact. See *Robertson v. Seattle Audobon Society* (1992).

10.4.6 Denial of All Jurisdiction, State and Federal

When Congress acts more broadly to foreclose all judicial jurisdiction, including that of both the state and federal courts, its action may present both Article III and due process concerns. In *Battaglia v. General Motors Corp.* (2d Cir. 1948), the federal appellate court invoked due process principles in raising doubts about Congress's power to foreclose all judicial review of legislation that threatened a taking of life, liberty or property. On the merits, however, the court found that no such legislative invasion had occurred. Similarly, in *Webster v. Doe* (1988), the Court expressed the view that denial of all judicial review of a constitutional claim would present a serious constitutional question. It thus concluded that a statute conferring broad discretion over employment decisions on the director of the Central Intelligence Agency did not bar a former employee from challenging his discharge in federal district court on constitutional grounds. (The state court option could well have been foreclosed either by the same grant of discretion or by the prospect of removal from state to federal court.)

Federal sovereign immunity operates to foreclose all jurisdiction in cases to which it applies. (State courts may not hear suits against the federal government without explicit statutory authorization, and cannot generally entertain suits against federal officers for mandamus and habeas relief.) But the doctrine applies only to suits brought against the government itself. So long as the suit names a federal government officer, the doctrine of federal immunity does not necessarily come into play. As we saw in chapter 7, the federal courts relied extensively on officer suits to ensure government accountability during the antebellum period. Such suits provided remedies for erroneous tax and customs collection as well as for government trespasses and other invasions of property rights. Perhaps the major gap in the regime of judicial enforcement occurred in connection with suits against the government for breach of contract. But Congress transferred responsibility for such matters to the Court of Claims in 1855, and has maintained a provision for the judicial determination of contract and other money claims ever since.

Jurists often conclude that the doctrine of federal sovereign immunity implies that Congress can place some matters beyond the jurisdiction of the federal courts. (On this view, sovereign immunity would act not as an external restraint on Congress's power to restrict federal jurisdiction, but as an external empowerment.) A good illustration appears in the dissenting opinion of Judge Robert Bork in *Bartlett v. Bowen* (D.C. Cir. 1987). There, plaintiffs sought to recover medicare benefits that were withheld on the basis of a rule that differentiated between end-of-life care provided by Christian scientists and other providers. Despite the plaintiffs' contention that the benefit schedule discriminated against rights to free exercise of religion, Judge Bork would not have reached the question. He regarded the claim as foreclosed by the language of a statute foreclosing judicial review of benefits claim worth less than $1000. On Judge Bork's view, Congress had simply reserved its sovereign immunity as to claims below the threshold and this retention of authority foreclosed the assertion of jurisdiction over any constitutional challenge plaintiffs might mount.

Judge Bork's approach drew a well-reasoned response from the majority, which upheld the district court's jurisdiction to reach the claim. The majority cited the presumption in favor of judicial review of administrative action and the due process principle that constitutional claims must be heard before an independent judicial body. Together, these principles argued in favor of federal judicial oversight as essentially the only judicial review game in town. (State courts generally have no power to review federal administrative action, particular in suits brought against a federal agency or the United States.) The majority rejected the notion that sovereign immunity could trump these principles. After all, Congress could not (consistent with notions of equal protection embedded in the Fifth Amendment's due process clause) create a benefit scheme that excluded individuals on the basis of race or sex. Nor should it be permitted to avoid judicial review of constitutional challenges to such a scheme on the basis that it has chosen to retain its sovereign immunity with respect to claims on behalf of anyone excluded from the program.

One might generalize from the conclusion that the doctrine of sovereign immunity should not be regarded as a trump that blocks the assertion of jurisdiction over constitutional claims. Jurisdictional legislation, though certainly permissible, can be seen as an instance of ordinary legislation that cannot operate to foreclose the vindication of constitutional rights. Where Congress adopts jurisdictional legislation with the purpose to deny or burden the exercise of constitutional rights, the Court might view the legislation as infirm on that ground alone. Of course, the trick lies in discerning congressional purpose, a task that some scholars regard the federal courts as competent to perform. See Fallon (2010).

10.5 Toward a Unitary Theory of Supreme Judicial Oversight and Control

It may be possible to develop a theory of Supreme Court oversight and control that fits tolerably well with the text, structure and history of Article III. The account proposed here emphasizes three features of Article III: its provision for a single Supreme Court, its requirement that any federal courts that Congress ordains and establishes shall be inferior to the Supreme Court, and the related Article I requirement that any tribunals that Congress constitutes as such must remain "inferior to" the Supreme Court. These provisions recognize that Congress has a certain amount of freedom to assign matters to state courts, Article I tribunals, and Article III courts for initial and possibly final determination. What Congress may not do is to place these inferior bodies beyond the supervision and control of the Supreme Court. On the account developed here, the Court must remain in a supreme-inferior relationship to all courts that handle matters within the judicial power of the United States. This means not only that inferior courts and tribunals must give effect to the Court's precedents, but also that

Congress must respect the Court's power to supervise the administration of justice in those courts and tribunals through use of the supervisory writs. See Pfander (2009)

Two themes animate this theory of judicial supremacy. First is the notion that the Supreme Court, by virtue of its supremacy, must have the power to oversee and control the work of inferior courts. This linkage between supremacy and judicial oversight and control was a well-established feature of Anglo-American jurisprudence at the time of the framing. As early as 1700, the Chief Justice of King's Bench had deployed a presumption in favor of judicial review in order to sustain that court's power to issue writs of certiorari to review the work of inferior tribunals. See *Groenvelt v. Burwell* (1700). As the English judge explained, the work of every inferior court of record was subject to review in King's Bench to see that they keep themselves within the limits of their jurisdiction. William Blackstone echoed this conclusion later in the eighteenth century by specifically linking the supremacy of King's Bench with its authority to issue the supervisory writs to inferior tribunals. These writs included the common law or supervisory writs of habeas corpus, mandamus, certiorari, and prohibition, among others. All of these writs made their way to the colonies and were regarded as inherent features of the common law jurisdiction of state supreme courts. See Pfander (2000).

A second feature of the theory of supremacy derives from the constitutional requirement that all courts that Congress constitutes as inferior federal tribunals must remain inferior to the Supreme Court. This requirement of inferiority operates in tandem with the Court's supremacy to require Congress to refrain from placing any judicial body beyond the oversight of a hierarchical Article III judicial department. Inferiority means that all inferior tribunals must answer to the federal judiciary and ultimately to the Supreme Court, both as to the law they apply and as to the manner in which they conduct their proceedings. Judicial independence within a system of separated powers implies that Congress lacks power to set up a new set of courts and make them immune to the oversight and control of the one Supreme Court.

One advantage of the theory's emphasis on supremacy and inferiority lies in its ability to accommodate important institutional features of the Article III judicial establishment. The history of the framing and early implementation of Article III features widespread reliance both on inferior federal courts and state courts to hear federal claims. Moreover, Congress did not provide for as-of-right appellate review of all these judicial decisions in every case. Rather, in keeping with its power to fashion exceptions and regulations to the Court's appellate jurisdiction, Congress created a series of exceptions such that state and lower federal courts exercised final authority over many federal disputes when the amount in controversy was relatively modest. The governing idea was to offer a relatively inexpensive form of justice in cases of modest value so that the parties would not have to invoke the Court's appellate jurisdiction in every case.

Crucial to the ability to economize on the cost of delivering federal justice was an obligation on the part of inferior tribunals to give effect to the legal interpretations announced by the Supreme Court. Supreme Court review was essential to give voice to a single, uniform body of federal law that would apply in inferior courts and tribunals around the country. But review was not essential in every case so long as inferior bodies gave effect to the precedents of their judicial superior. The difference between appellate jurisdiction and supervisory power takes on significance here. Appellate jurisdiction at the time of the framing entailed review as a matter of right, perhaps through the common law writ of error, or the civil law appeal. By contrast, the supervisory writs did not apply as a matter of right; instead, like habeas corpus and mandamus, they issued upon petition and good cause shown. Even in the absence of a formal grant of appellate jurisdiction, supreme courts might issue supervisory writs to inferior courts and tribunals to keep them within the boundaries of their jurisdiction and to compel them to administer justice in accordance with law.

The distinction between appellate jurisdiction as a matter of right and supervisory power in the exercise of discretion helps to explain how the Court's supremacy could co-exist with broad power in Congress to fashion exceptions and regulations to the Court's appellate jurisdiction. The distinction also maps onto important distinctions that Congress drew in the language of the Judiciary Act of 1789. In section 13 of the Act, Congress referred to the Court's appellate jurisdiction from the circuit courts and courts of the several states and then conferred "power" on the Court to issue writs of prohibition to the district courts and writs of mandamus "in cases warranted by the principles and usages of law, to any courts appointed, or persons holding office, under the authority of the United States." This broad grant of mandamus authority applied without qualification to the federal district and circuit courts that Congress had "established" in the Act, and to any courts "appointed" under the authority of the United States. One can read the grant of mandamus as purposefully designed to extend to all federal tribunals, including any that Congress might later appoint to hear federal cases in subsequent legislation.

Today, the Court's jurisdictional statutes have switched from the as-of-right appellate jurisdiction of the early years to discretionary review by way of certiorari. In other words, Congress has taken full advantage of its power to fashion exceptions and regulations to the Court's appellate jurisdiction under Article III. Further restrictions on the Court's authority to hear claims coming from the dockets of the state and lower federal courts could violate the requirement that the Court remain in a relationship of supremacy to all inferior bodies. But instead of invalidating any such jurisdictional restrictions, the Court might simply exercise its residual grants of mandamus and habeas authority as needed to preserve the inferiority of lower courts. Both sources of supervisory power derive from grants that first appeared in the Judiciary Act of 1789 and both survive today under the All Writs Act, 28 U.S.C. § 1651. So long as one reads the All Writs Act as conferring power to issue all writs necessary for the exercise of the Court's appellate jurisdiction (as conferred by Article III), the supervisory power should survive any statutory restriction on the Court's appellate role (just as its authority to issue the "original" writ of habeas corpus survived the repeal of other sources of appellate jurisdiction in *Ex parte Yerger*). See Pfander (2000).

Critics have raised questions about the historical accuracy of the supervisory account of Article III. First, some scholars point to the fact that eighteenth century England had created multiple superior courts of coordinate jurisdiction, rather than vesting judicial power in one supreme and multiple inferior courts. England's failure to provide a model for a hierarchical judicial system, in turn, may appear to cast doubt on the claim that the framers of Article III chose to institute a hierarchical system on their own. See Endahl (1991); Ritz (1990). Other scholars question whether a well-defined model of supervisory authority existed at the time of the framing. Both these concerns may be allayed to some extent by evidence that the framers looked to Scotland, as well as England, in crafting a hierarchical judiciary.

Scotland had but a single supreme court of civil law, the Court of Session, which enjoyed supervisory power over all inferior courts in the country. What's more, the Court of Session was protected from Parliamentary remodeling by the Acts of Union (1707), which joined Scotland and England into Great Britain. Article 19 of the Acts of Union appear to anticipate the terms of Article III in securing the role of Scotland's one "supream" court "in all time coming," in declaring that other courts would remain subordinate to the Court of Session, and in forbidding Parliament to adopt any regulations of the Court's traditional authority and privileges other than regulations aimed at the better administration of justice. Under these provisions, the Court of Session engaged in supervisory review of inferior tribunals, even in circumstances in which Parliament had curtailed that court's appellate jurisdiction. Scotland, under the Acts of Union, thus provides an example of a hierarchical judicial system in which the power to supervise inferior tribunals was seen as defining the "supremacy" of the high court. Although they have been overlooked by modern scholars, Scottish precedents for a hierarchical judicial system were well-known to the framers of Article III, including its Scottish-born draftsman, James Wilson. See Pfander & Birk (2011).

10.5.1   Inferior Courts and Tribunals Subject to Supervision

If the Court's power to supervise inferior courts and tribunals survives restrictions on its appellate jurisdiction, and if its supremacy necessitates the preservation of such supervisory authority, then much depends on what bodies qualify as inferior tribunals. This section sketches the basis on which one might conclude that all three of the principal inferior judicial bodies in the Article III hierarchy—lower federal courts, Article I tribunals, and state courts—may be properly regarded as tribunals inferior to the Supreme Court. Such inferiority, in turn, brings into play the common law powers of supervision that have long been associated with a court's supremacy.

The case for treating lower federal courts as inferior courts flows directly from the language of Article III. Article III, section 2 vests the judicial power in one supreme court and in such "inferior" courts as the Congress may from time to time ordain and establish. This requirement of inferiority seemingly complements the requirement that there be but a single Supreme Court. The framers of the Constitution deliberately rejected a provision that would have authorized the creation of one or more supreme tribunals, thereby rejecting the English model of multiple supreme courts. (England had four courts of superior jurisdiction, King's Bench, Chancery, Exchequer, and Common Pleas, and a court of admiralty. These supreme tribunals lacked a common head and their jurisdictional disagreements led to much wasteful and duplicative litigation.) The best way to preserve a unitary supreme court was to require that all other courts remain inferior in relation to that court. Inferiority thus ensured supremacy by enabling the higher court to oversee and resolve jurisdictional disputes.

The argument for treating Article I tribunals as inferior also finds relatively clear support in constitutional text. As noted in section 10.3.2, Article I provides for Congress to "constitute tribunals inferior to the supreme Court." By using the term tribunals to describe Article I bodies, the framers may have meant to encompass both Article I tribunals and Article III courts. After all, Article III vests the judicial power in inferior courts, but does not vest such power in tribunals. Similarly, Article III guarantees life tenure for the judges of inferior courts but does not extend such requirements to the judges of Article I tribunals. One might conclude, therefore, that Article I empowers Congress to fashion some Article I tribunals outside of Article III. Yet the language of Article I specifically requires that all such tribunals remain inferior to the Supreme Court. Together, Article III and Article I provide some reason to conclude that all courts and tribunals that Congress erects must satisfy the inferiority requirement.

One can also read the same language in Article I as empowering Congress to constitute or appoint the state courts to serve as inferior tribunals. Just as it does now, the word "constitute" carried two meanings at the time of the framing: it referred both to newly created courts and to existing courts appointed to perform a new function. The power to constitute tribunals inferior to the Supreme Court might therefore include both the power to fashion Article I tribunals and the power to appoint state courts as federal tribunals. Such a reading of Article I solves an important problem in the scholarly literature by clarifying the way state courts might hear matters that were seen as inherently federal. Just as Congress had done under the Articles of Confederation, when it had appointed the state courts to serve as federal courts to hear crimes on the high seas and piracy, perhaps Article I authorizes Congress to constitute state courts as federal tribunals for certain purposes. State courts could serve as federal tribunals without employing life-tenured judges, and without implicating the requirement that federal judges act as civil officers of the United States within the meaning of the Appointments Clause of the Constitution.

Once one perceives the lower federal courts, Article I tribunals, and state courts as inferior bodies within the Article III hierarchy, the requirement of inferiority plays a common role in restricting the power of Congress to curtail all review in the Supreme Court. Congress can, to be sure, restrict the as-of-right appellate jurisdiction of the Court, as it has done. But Congress arguably cannot foreclose the sort of supervisory review necessary to preserve the inferiority of such courts. The Court might rely on its supremacy in insisting that all inferior courts and tribunals continue to adhere to the Court's precedents in the wake of jurisdiction-stripping legislation. Moreover, the Court would presumably retain power to invalidate the decisions of any court that Congress established outside the Article III hierarchy or attempted to immunize from supreme judicial oversight. Congress appears to have understood the nature of the Court's obligation in 1789 when it conferred mandamus power to oversee not only the federal district and circuit courts but also any court appointed under the authority of the United States. The broad language of the mandamus grant in section 13 seemingly contemplates the exercise of supervisory power with respect to a broader range of inferior tribunals than federal courts alone.

10.5.2　Supervisory Power and Military Detention of Terror Suspects

As noted in section 8.3.2, the Supreme Court's decision in *Boumediene v. Bush* (2008) provides a landmark discussion of the constitutional guarantee of habeas review of the legality of the government's detention of terrorism suspects at Guantanamo Bay. While the Court focused its analysis on the constitutionality of restrictions contained in the Military Commission Act of 2006 (MCA), the Court's approach can teach important lessons about the role of the supervisory power in debates over Congress's power to strip jurisdiction. Indeed, Justice Kennedy's opinion for the Court embraced a view of habeas much in keeping with the historic conception of the supervisory power. Thus, at one point the majority acknowledged that the requirement of habeas review expressed an obligation that Congress might discharge with other provisions for judicial review. At another point, the majority observed that the determinations of courts of record were entitled to greater deference when tested by way of habeas than were those of "inferior tribunals of limited jurisdiction." Kennedy thus invoked the traditional flexibility of supervisory review in defending a role for the federal courts in overseeing military detention. While the availability of habeas will depend on the situation and the availability of alternative forms of review, habeas will continue to play a conspicuous part in anchoring the Court's fundamental powers of supervision and in establishing a background rule of judicial review.

The Court also gave an important, albeit implicit, answer to the problem of inherent judicial power. Some critics have argued that the recognition of a superintending power would be tantamount to the recognition of inherent judicial power, something that runs counter to the tradition of written law and the suspicion of claims of inherent powers. On this view, what Congress gives by way of jurisdiction Congress can take away by way of repeal. Congress apparently chose to highlight its repeal authority in the way it structured the MCA. Thus, Congress chose to amend 28 U.S.C. § 2241 directly, rather than simply setting out a restriction on habeas power in a separate statute. By providing for the insertion of new language in the statute that confers habeas authority, Congress was signaling that it meant to impose a fundamental restriction on the habeas power of the federal courts. But the Court did not regard the repeal of habeas authority over Guantanamo Bay as presenting it with a choice between denying all relief and becoming complicit in the exercise of inherent power. Rather, the Court viewed the MCA as posing a question concerning how far Congress could go in cutting back on a form of judicial authority that the Constitution clearly meant to vest in the judiciary. Much the same sort of analysis would presumably apply to jurisdiction-stripping legislation that threatened to undercut the Court's ability to maintain its constitutional role in the oversight and control of inferior tribunals.

One final note deserves mention. Justice Kennedy's methodology in *Boumediene* bears some resemblance to the approach taken suggested in the supervisory account. Kennedy paid close attention to the history of habeas authority but did not focus only on the history. Arguments from structure and function played a role as well. Similarly, Kennedy viewed the common law as a source of important insights into the nature of the judicial task. Just as common law norms define the core of federal habeas, the historic function of the supervisory writs helps to define the Court's supremacy in relation to inferior tribunals. The Court's willingness to invalidate habeas restrictions as a de facto suspension of the writ provides a framework within which the Court should evaluate the constitutionality of restrictions on its supervisory powers. In the end, the Court's status as the "one supreme Court" identified in Article III provides a firm basis on which to question wholesale jurisdictional restrictions.

10.6 Conclusion

Much has changed since the framing of the Constitution and its early implementation in the Judiciary Act of 1789. The First Congress sought to provide for an effective federal judicial power, establishing lower federal courts and relying upon state courts to hear federal claims. But there was reason to doubt that the federal courts would achieve their role as an independent branch of the government. Courts had long been seen in England as part of the executive branch, and the experience in the early American states had been one of legislative dominance. Early expressions of judicial will called down the wrath of legislators; the refusal of the Justices to hear the claims of pensioners in *Hayburn's Case* (1792) led to calls for their impeachment. The nation's first Chief Justice, John Jay, left the Court and refused to accept re-nomination, citing the Eleventh Amendment as evidence that Congress and the states would never learn to accept an independent judiciary.

If in those early days the Article III judiciary acted as the least dangerous branch, its authority has expanded considerably in the ensuing centuries. Due in part to its control over its docket, to the expansion of federal law that has come with the growth of the federal government, and to the rights revolution in constitutional law, the Court now sits atop a complex and far-reaching body of federal law that permeates American life. The Court's role as the final exponent of the meaning of all elements of federal law makes it a natural target of controversy. It has achieved much of what the anti-Federalists feared when they described the Court as having been given greater power than any tribunal under heaven. The Court's power has been enhanced by the Constitution's scheme for amendments; rarely has the Court been overturned by the requisite concurrence of two-thirds of the members of both houses of Congress and three-fourths of the states.

With no real prospect of securing a constitutional amendment, Congress has limited options when faced with decisions it finds objectionable. The impeachment threat no longer seems viable, at least for federal judicial decisions that follow the forms of legal rhetoric, and Congress's ability to adopt new federal statutes will have little impact on constitutional doctrine. Constitutional change may come eventually through the appointment of new Justices, a fact that certainly explains the contentiousness of the modern judicial confirmation hearing but provides little comfort to a Congress that wants to change the law today. Jurisdiction-stripping legislation may reflect legislative frustration with the absence of alternative mechanisms with which to influence the shape of federal constitutional law.

The Court's supremacy in relation to inferior courts and tribunals provides a textual and structural response to jurisdiction stripping under the appellate exceptions and regulations clause. But the Court may prefer not to rely too heavily on constitutional arguments alone. It may lose a measure of legitimacy if compelled to acknowledge that its jurisdiction lies beyond congressional control. As Professor Charles Black has argued, the existence of congressional control over federal jurisdiction (however ideal) provides a democratic underpinning to the exercise of judicial review. See Black (1969). So long as the Court can point to federal statutes that authorize its exercise of oversight, it can claim an ongoing popular mandate to conduct judicial review. The desire to portray its role as constitutionally and legislatively approved may help to explain why the Court prefers to rely upon the doctrine of constitutional doubt. Such reliance allows the Court to portray itself as exercising jurisdiction that Congress has conferred rather than jurisdiction said to have been inherent in the Constitution itself.

Appendix

SELECTED CONSTITUTIONAL AND STATUTORY PROVISIONS

The Constitution of the United States

We the People of the United States, in Order to form a more perfect Union, establish Justice, insure domestic Tranquility, provide for the common defence, promote the general Welfare, and secure the Blessings of Liberty to ourselves and our Posterity, do ordain and establish this Constitution for the United States of America.

ARTICLE I

Section 1. All legislative Powers herein granted shall be vested in a Congress of the United States, which shall consist of a Senate and House of Representatives.

Section 2. The House of Representatives shall be composed of Members chosen every second Year by the People of the several States, and the Electors in each State shall have the Qualifications requisite for Electors of the most numerous Branch of the State Legislature.

No Person shall be a Representative who shall not have attained to the Age of twenty five Years, and been seven Years a Citizen of the United States, and who shall not, when elected, be an Inhabitant of that State in which he shall be chosen.   * * *

Section 3. The Senate of the United States shall be composed of two Senators from each State, chosen by the Legislature thereof, for six Years; and each Senator shall have one Vote.

* * *

No person shall be a Senator who shall not have attained to the Age of thirty Years, and been nine Years a Citizen of the United States, and who shall not, when elected, be an Inhabitant of that State for which he shall be chosen.

The Vice President of the United States shall be President of the Senate, but shall have no Vote, unless they be equally divided.

* * *

Section 6. The Senators and Representatives shall receive a Compensation for their Services, to be ascertained by Law, and paid out of the Treasury of the United States. They shall in all Cases, except Treason, Felony and Breach of the Peace, be privileged from Arrest during their Attendance at the Session of their respective Houses, and in going to and returning from the same; and for any Speech or Debate in either House, they shall not be questioned in any other Place.

No Senator or Representative shall, during the Time for which he was elected, be appointed to any civil Office under the Authority of the United States, which shall have been created, or the Emoluments whereof shall have been encreased during such time; and no Person holding any Office under the United States, shall be a Member of either House during his Continuance in Office.

Section 7. All Bills for raising Revenue shall originate in the House of Representatives; but the Senate may propose or concur with Amendments as on other Bills.

* * *

Section 8. The Congress shall have Power To lay and collect Taxes, Duties, Imposts and Excises, to pay the Debts and provide for the common Defence and general Welfare of the United States; but all Duties, Imposts and Excises shall be uniform throughout the United States;

To borrow Money on the credit of the United States;

To regulate Commerce with foreign Nations, and among the several States, and with the Indian Tribes;

To establish an uniform Rule of Naturalization, and uniform Laws on the subject of Bankruptcies throughout the United States;

To coin Money, regulate the Value thereof, and of foreign Coin, and fix the Standard of Weights and Measures;

To provide for Punishment of counterfeiting the Securities and current Coin of the United States;

To Establish Post Offices and Post Roads;

To promote the Progress of Science and useful Arts, by securing for limited Times to Authors and Inventors the exclusive Right to their respective Writings and Discoveries;

To constitute Tribunals inferior to the supreme Court;

To define and punish Piracies and Felonies committed on the high Seas, and Offences against the Law of Nations;

To declare War, grant Letters of Marque and Reprisal, and make Rules concerning Captures on Land and Water;

To raise and support Armies, but no Appropriation of Money to that Use shall be for a longer Term than two Years;

To provide and maintain a Navy;

To make Rules for the Government and Regulation of the land and naval Forces;

To provide for calling forth the Militia to execute the Laws of the Union, suppress Insurrections and repel Invasions;

To provide for organizing, arming, and disciplining, the Militia, and for governing such Part of them as may be employed in the Service of the United States, reserving to the States respectively, the Appointment of the Officers, and the Authority of training the Militia according to the discipline prescribed by Congress;

To exercise exclusive Legislation in all Cases whatsoever, over such District (not exceeding ten Miles square) as may, by Cession of Particular States, and the Acceptance of Congress, become the Seat of the Government of the United States, and to exercise like Authority over all Places purchased by the Consent of the Legislature of the State in which the Same shall be, for the Erection of Forts, Magazines, Arsenals, dock-Yards, and other needful Buildings;—And

To make all Laws which shall be necessary and proper for carrying into Execution the foregoing Powers, and all other Powers vested by this Constitution in the Government of the United States, or in any Department or Officer thereof.

Section 9. The Migration or Importation of Such Persons as any of the States now existing shall think proper to admit, shall not be prohibited by the Congress prior to the Year one thousand eight hundred and eight, but a Tax or Duty may be imposed on such Importation, not exceeding ten Dollars for each Person.

The Privilege of the Writ of Habeas Corpus shall not be suspended, unless when in Cases of Rebellion or Invasion the public Safety may require it.

No Bill of Attainder or ex post facto Law shall be passed.

No Capitation, or other direct, Tax shall be laid, unless in Proportion to the Census or Enumeration herein before directed to be taken.

No Tax or Duty shall be laid on Articles exported from any States.

No Preference shall be given by any Regulation of Commerce or Revenue to the Ports of one State over those of another: nor shall Vessels bound to, or from, one State be obliged to enter, clear, or pay Duties in another.

No Money shall be drawn from the Treasury, but in Consequence of Appropriations made by Law; and a regular Statement and Account of the Receipts and Expenditures of all public Money shall be published from Time to Time.

No Title of Nobility shall be granted by the United States; and no Person holding any Office of Profit or Trust under them, shall, without the Consent of the Congress, accept of any Present, Emolument, Office, or Title, of any Kind whatever, from any King, Prince, or foreign State.

Section 10. No State shall enter into any Treaty, Alliance, or Confederation; grant Letters of Marque and Reprisal; coin Money; emit Bills of Credit; make any Thing but gold and silver Coin a Tender in Payment of Debts; pass any Bill of Attainder, ex post facto Law, or Law impairing the Obligation of Contracts, or grant any Title of Nobility.

No State shall, without the Consent of the Congress, lay any Imposts or Duties on Imports or Exports, except what may be absolutely necessary for executing its inspection Laws: and the net Produce of all Duties and Imposts, laid by any State on Imports or Exports, shall be for the Use of the Treasury of the Unites States; and all such Laws shall be subject to the Revision and Control of the Congress.

No State shall, without the consent of Congress, lay any Duty of Tonnage, keep Troops, or Ships of War in Time of Peace, enter into any Agreement or Compact with another State, or with a foreign Power, or engage in War, unless actually invaded, or in such imminent Danger as will not admit of Delay.

ARTICLE II

Section 1. The executive Power shall be vested in a President of the United States of America. He shall hold his Office during the Term of four Years, and together with the Vice President, chosen for the same Term, be elected, as follows:

* * *

No person except a natural born Citizen, or a Citizen of the United States, at the time of the Adoption of this Constitution, shall be eligible to the Office of President; neither shall any Person be eligible to that Office who shall not have attained to the Age of thirty five Years, and been fourteen Years a Resident within the United States.

* * *

The President shall, at stated Times, receive for his Services, a Compensation, which shall neither be encreased nor diminished during the Period for which he shall have been elected, and he shall not receive within that Period any other Emolument from the United States, or any of them.

* * *

Section 2.   The President shall be Commander in Chief of the Army and Navy of the United States, and of the militia of the several States, when called into the actual Service of the United States; he may require the Opinion, in writing, of the principal Officer in each of the executive Departments, upon any Subject relating to the Duties of their respective Offices, and he shall have Power to grant Reprieves and Pardons for Offenses against the United States, except in Cases of Impeachment.

He shall have Power, by and with the Advice and Consent of the Senate, to make Treaties, provided two thirds of the Senators present concur; and he shall nominate, and by and with the Advice and Consent of the Senate, shall appoint Ambassadors, other public Ministers and Consuls, Judges of the supreme Court, and all other Officers of the United States, whose Appointments are not herein otherwise provided for, and which shall be established by Law: but the congress may by Law vest the Appointment of such inferior Officers, as they think proper, in the President alone, in the Courts of Law, or in the Heads of Departments.

The President shall have Power to fill up all Vacancies that may happen during the Recess of the Senate, by granting Commissions which shall expire at the End of their next Session.

Section 3.   He shall from Time to Time give to the Congress Information of the State of the Union, and recommend to their Consideration such Measures as he shall judge necessary and expedient; he may, on extraordinary Occasions, convene both Houses, or either of them, and in Case of Disagreement between them, with Respect to the Time of Adjournment, he may adjourn them to such Time as he shall think proper; he shall receive Ambassadors and other public Ministers; he shall take Care that the Laws be faithfully executed, and shall Commission all the Officers of the United States.

Section 4.   The President, Vice President and all civil Officers of the United States, shall be removed from Office on impeachment for, and Conviction of, Treason, Bribery, or other high Crimes and Misdemeanors.

ARTICLE III

Section 1.   The judicial Power of the United States, shall be vested in one supreme Court, and in such inferior Courts as the Congress may from time to time ordain and establish.   The Judges, both of the supreme and inferior Courts, shall hold their Offices during good Behaviour, and shall, at stated Times, receive for their Services, a Compensation, which shall not be diminished during their Continuance in Office.

Section 2. The judicial Power shall extend to all Cases, in Law and Equity, arising under this Constitution, the Laws of the United States, and Treaties made, or which shall be made, under their Authority;—to all Cases affecting Ambassadors, other public Ministers and Consuls;—to all Cases of admiralty and maritime Jurisdiction;—to Controversies to which the United States shall be a Party;—to Controversies between two or more States;—between a State and Citizens of another State;—between Citizens of different States;—between Citizens of the same State claiming Lands under the Grants of different States, and between a State, or the Citizens thereof, and foreign States, Citizens or Subjects.

In all Cases affecting Ambassadors, other public Ministers and Consuls, and those in which a State shall be a Party, the supreme Court shall have original Jurisdiction. In all the other Cases before mentioned, the supreme Court shall have appellate Jurisdiction, both as to Law and Fact, with such Exceptions, and under such Regulations as the Congress shall make.

The Trial of all Crimes, except in Cases of Impeachment, shall be by Jury; and such Trial shall be held in the State where the said Crimes shall have been committed; but when not committed within any State, the Trial shall be at such Place or Places as the Congress may by Law have directed.

Section 3. Treason against the United States, shall consist only in levying War against them, or, in adhering to their Enemies, giving them Aid and Comfort. No person shall be convicted of Treason unless on the Testimony of two Witnesses to the same overt Act, or on Confession in open Court.

The Congress shall have Power to declare the Punishment of Treason, but no Attainder of Treason shall work Corruption of Blood, or Forfeiture except during the Life of the Person attained.

ARTICLE IV

Section 1. Full Faith and Credit shall be given in each State to the public Acts, Records, and judicial Proceedings of every other State. And the Congress may by general Laws prescribe the Manner in which such Acts, Records and Proceedings shall be proved, and the Effect thereof.

Section 2. The Citizens of each State shall be entitled to all Privileges and Immunities of Citizens in the several States.

A Person charged in any State with Treason, Felony, or other Crime, who shall flee from Justice, and be found in another State, shall on demand of the executive Authority of the State from which he fled, be delivered up, to be removed to the State having Jurisdiction of the Crime.

No Person held to Service of Labour in one State, under the Laws thereof, escaping into another, shall, in Consequence of any Law or Regulation therein, be discharged from such Service or Labour, but shall be delivered up on Claim of the Party to whom such Service or Labour may be due.

Section 3. New States may be admitted by the Congress into this Union; buy no new State shall be formed or erected within the Jurisdiction of any other State; nor any State be formed by the Junction of two or more States, or Parts of States, without the Consent of the Legislatures of the States concerned as well as of the Congress.

The Congress shall have Power to dispose of and make all needful Rules and Regulations respecting the Territory or other Property belonging to the United States; and nothing in this Constitution shall be so construed as to Prejudice any Claims of the United States, or of any particular State.

Section 4. The United States shall guarantee to every State in this Union a Republican Form of Government, and shall protect each of them against Invasion; and on Application of the Legislature, or of the Executive (when the Legislature cannot be convened) against domestic Violence.

ARTICLE V

The Congress, whenever two thirds of both Houses shall deem it necessary, shall propose Amendments to this Constitution, or, on the Application of the Legislatures of two thirds of the several States, shall call a Convention for proposing Amendments, which, in either Case, shall be valid to all Intents and Purposes, as part of this Constitution, when ratified by the Legislatures of three fourths of the several States, or by Conventions in three fourths thereof, as the one or the other Mode of Ratification may be proposed by the Congress; Provided that no Amendment which may be made prior to the Year One thousand eight hundred and eight shall in any Manner affect the first and fourth Clauses in the Ninth Section of the first Article; and that no State, without its Consent, shall be deprived of its equal Suffrage in the Senate.

ARTICLE VI

All Debts contracted and Engagements entered into, before the Adoption of this Constitution, shall be as valid against the United States under this Constitution, as under the Confederation.

This Constitution, and the Laws of the United States which shall be made in Pursuance thereof; and all Treaties made, or which shall be made, under the Authority of the United States, shall be the supreme Law of the Land; and the Judges in every State shall be bound thereby, any Thing in the Constitution or Laws of any State to the Contrary notwithstanding.

The Senators and Representatives before mentioned, and the Members of the several State Legislatures, and all executive and judicial Officers, both of the United States and of the several States, shall be bound by Oath or Affirmation, to support this Constitution; but no religious Test shall ever be required as a Qualification to any Office or public Trust under the United States.

ARTICLE VII

The Ratification of the Conventions of nine States shall be sufficient for the Establishment of this Constitution between the States so ratifying the Same.

ARTICLES IN ADDITION TO, AND AMENDMENT OF, THE CONSTITUTION OF THE UNITED STATES OF AMERICA, PROPOSED BY CONGRESS, AND RATIFIED BY THE LEGISLA-TURES OF THE SEVERAL STATES PURSUANT TO THE FIFTH ARTICLE OF THE ORIGINAL CONSTITUTION.

AMENDMENT I [1791]

Congress shall make no law respecting an establishment of religion, or prohibiting the free exercise thereof; or abridging the freedom of speech, or of the press; or the right of the people peaceably to assemble, and to petition the Government for a redress of grievances.

AMENDMENT II [1791]

A well regulated Militia, being necessary to the security of a free State, the right of the people to keep and bear Arms, shall not be infringed.

AMENDMENT III [1791]

No Soldier shall, in time of peace be quartered in any house, without the consent of the Owner, nor in time of war, but in a manner to be prescribed by law.

AMENDMENT IV [1791]

The right of the people to be secure in their persons, houses, papers, and effects, against unreasonable searches and seizures, shall not be violated, and no Warrants shall issue, but upon probable cause, supported by Oath or affirmation, and particularly describing the place to be searched, and the persons or things to be seized.

Amendment V [1791]

No person shall be held to answer for a capital, or otherwise infamous crime, unless on a presentment or indictment of a Grand Jury, except in cases arising in the land or naval forces, or in the Militia, when in actual service in time of War or public danger; nor shall any person be subject for the same offence to be twice put in jeopardy of life or limb; nor shall be compelled in any criminal case to be a witness against himself, nor be deprived of life, liberty, or property, without due process of law; nor shall private property be taken for public use, without just compensation.

Amendment VI [1791]

In all criminal prosecutions, the accused shall enjoy the right to a speedy and public trial, by an impartial jury of the State and district wherein the crime shall have been committed, which district shall have been previously ascertained by law, and to be informed of the nature and cause of the accusation; to be confronted with the witnesses against him; to have compulsory process for obtaining witnesses in his favor, and to have the Assistance of Counsel for his defence.

Amendment VII [1791]

In Suits at common law, where the value in controversy shall exceed twenty dollars, the right of trial by jury shall be preserved, and no fact tried by jury, shall be otherwise reexamined in any Court of the United States, than according to the rules of the common law.

Amendment VIII [1791]

Excessive bail shall not be required, nor excessive fines imposed, nor cruel and unusual punishments inflicted.

Amendment IX [1791]

The enumeration in the Constitution, of certain rights, shall not be construed to deny or disparage others retained by the people.

Amendment X [1791]

The powers not delegated to the United States by the Constitution, nor prohibited by it to the States, are reserved to the States respectively, or to the people.

AMENDMENT XI [1798]

The Judicial power of the United States shall not be construed to extend to any suit in law or equity, commenced or prosecuted against one of the United States by Citizens of another State, or by Citizens or Subjects of any Foreign State.

AMENDMENT XIII [1865]

Section 1.   Neither slavery nor involuntary servitude, except as a punishment for crime whereof the party shall have been duly convicted, shall exist within the United States, or any place subject to their jurisdiction.

Section 2.   Congress hall have power to enforce this article by appropriate legislation.

AMENDMENT XIV [1868]

Section 1.   All persons born or naturalized in the United States, and subject to the jurisdiction thereof, are citizens of the United States and of the State wherein they reside.   No State shall make or enforce any law which shall abridge the privileges or immunities of citizens of the United States; nor shall any State deprive any person of life, liberty, or property, without due process of law; nor deny to any person within its jurisdiction the equal protection of the laws.

Section 2.   Representatives shall be apportioned among the several States according to their respective numbers, counting the whole number of persons in each State, excluding Indians not taxed.   But when the right to vote at any election for the choice of electors for President and Vice President of the United States, Representatives in Congress, the Executive and Judicial officers of a State, or the members of the Legislature thereof, is denied to any of the male inhabitants of such State, being twenty-one years of age, and citizens of the United States, or in any way abridged, except for participation in rebellion, or other crime, the basis of representation therein shall be reduced in the proportion which the number of such male citizens shall bear to the whole number of male citizens twenty-one years of age in such State.

Section 3.   No person shall be a Senator or Representative in Congress, or elector of President and Vice President, or hold any office, civil or military, under the United States, or under any State, who having previously taken an oath, as a member of Congress, or as an officer of the United States, or as a member of any State legislature, or as an executive or judicial officer of any State, to support the Constitution of the United States, shall have engaged in insurrection or rebellion against the same, or given aid or comfort to the enemies thereof. But Congress may by a vote of two-thirds of each House, remove such disability.

Section 4. The validity of the public debt of the United States, authorized by law, including debts incurred for payment of pensions and bounties for services in suppressing insurrection or rebellion, shall not be questioned. But neither the United States nor any State shall assume or pay any debt or obligation incurred in aid of insurrection or rebellion against the United States, or any claim for the loss or emancipation of any slave; but all such debts, obligations and claims shall be held illegal and void.

Section 5. The Congress shall have power to enforce, by appropriate legislation, the provisions of this article.

AMENDMENT XV [1870]

Section 1. The right of citizens of the United States to vote shall not be denied or abridged by the United States or by any State on account of race, color, or previous condition of servitude.

Section 2. The Congress shall have power to enforce this article by appropriate legislation.

AMENDMENT XIX [1920]

[1] The right of citizens of the United States to vote shall not be denied or abridged by the United States or by any State on account of sex.

[2] Congress shall have power to enforce this article by appropriate legislation.

AMENDMENT XXIV [1964]

Section 1. The right of citizens of the United States to vote in any primary or other election for President or Vice President, for electors for President or Vice President, or for Senator or Representative in Congress, shall not be denied or abridged by the United States or any State by reason of failure to pay any poll tax or other tax.

Section 2. The Congress shall have power to enforce this article by appropriate legislation.

AMENDMENT XXVI [1971]

Section 1. The right of citizens of the United States, who are eighteen years of age or older, to vote shall not be denied or abridged by the United States or by any State on account of age.

Section 2. The Congress shall have power to enforce this article by appropriate legislation.

AMENDMENT XXVII [1992]

No Law, varying the compensation for the services of the Senators and Representatives, shall take effect, until an election of Representatives shall have intervened.

28 U.S.C.

§ 1251. Original jurisdiction

(a) The Supreme Court shall have original and exclusive jurisdiction of all controversies between two or more States.

(b) The Supreme Court shall have original but not exclusive jurisdiction of:

(1) All actions or proceedings to which ambassadors, other public ministers, consuls, or vice consuls of foreign states are parties;

(2) All controversies between the United States and a State;

(3) All actions or proceedings by a State against the citizens of another State or against aliens.

§ 1254. Courts of appeals; certiorari; certified questions

Cases in the courts of appeals may be reviewed by the Supreme Court by the following methods:

(1) By writ of certiorari granted upon the petition of any party to any civil or criminal case, before or after rendition of judgment or decree;

(2) By certification at any time by a court of appeals of any question of law in any civil or criminal case as to which instructions are desired, and upon such certification the Supreme Court may give binding instructions or require the entire record to be sent up for decision of the entire matter in controversy.

§ 1257. State courts; certiorari

(a) Final judgments or decrees rendered by the highest court of a State in which a decision could be had, may be reviewed by the Supreme Court by writ of certiorari where the validity of a treaty or statute of the United States is drawn in question or where the validity of a state of any State is drawn in question on the ground of its being repugnant to the Constitution, treaties, or laws of the United States, or where any title, right, privilege, or immunity is specially set up or claimed under the Constitution or the treaties or statutes of, or any commission held or authority exercised under, the United States.

(b) For the purposes of this section, the term "highest court of a State" includes the District of Columbia Court of Appeals.

§ 1291. Final decisions of district courts

The courts of appeals (other than the United States Court of Appeals for the Federal Circuit) shall have jurisdiction of appeals from all final decisions of the district courts of the United States, the United States District Court for the District of the Canal Zone, the District Court of Guam, and the District Court of the Virgin Islands, except where a direct review may be had in the Supreme Court.   The jurisdiction of the United States Court of Appeals for the Federal Circuit shall be limited to the jurisdiction described in sections 1292(c) and (d) and 1295 of this title.

§ 1331. Federal question

The district courts shall have original jurisdiction of all civil actions arising under the Constitution, laws, or treaties of the United States.

§ 1332. Diversity of citizenship; amount in controversy; costs

(a) The district courts shall have original jurisdiction of all civil actions where the matter in controversy exceeds the sum or value of $75,000, exclusive of interest and costs, and is between—

(1) citizens of different States;

(2) citizens of a State and citizens or subjects of a foreign state;

(3) citizens of different States and in which citizens or subjects of a foreign state are additional parties; and

(4) a foreign state, defined in section 1603(a) of this title, as plaintiff and citizens of a State or of different States.

For the purposes of this section, section 1335, and section 1441, an alien admitted to the United States for permanent residence shall be deemed a citizen of the State in which such alien is domiciled.

* * *

§ 1345. United States as plaintiff

Except as otherwise provided by Act of Congress, the district courts shall have original jurisdiction of all civil actions, suits or proceedings commenced by the United States, or by any agency or officer thereof expressly authorized to sue by Act of Congress.

§ 1350. Alien's action for tort*

The district courts shall have original jurisdiction, of any civil action by an alien for a tort only, committed in violation of the law of nations or a treaty of the United States.

§ 1367. Supplemental jurisdiction

(a) Except as provided in subsections (b) and (c) or as expressly provided otherwise by Federal statute, in any civil action of which the district courts have original jurisdiction, the district courts shall have supplemental jurisdiction over all other claims that are so related to claims in the action within such original jurisdiction that they form part of the same case or controversy under Article III of the United States Constitution. Such supplemental jurisdiction shall include claims that involve the joinder or intervention of additional parties.

(b) In any civil action of which the district courts have original jurisdiction founded solely on section 1332 of this title, the district courts shall not have supplemental jurisdiction under subsection (a) over claims by plaintiffs against persons made parties under Rule 14, 19, 20, or 24 of the Federal Rules of Civil Procedure, or over claims by persons proposed to be joined as plaintiffs under Rule 19 of such rules, or seeking to intervene as plaintiffs under Rule 24 of such rules, when exercising supplemental jurisdiction over such claims would be inconsistent with the jurisdictional requirements of section 1332.

(c) The district courts may decline to exercise supplemental jurisdiction over a claim under subsection (a) if—

(1) the claim raises a novel or complex issue of State law,

(2) the claim substantially predominates over the claim or claims over which the district court has original jurisdiction,

(3) the district court has dismissed all claims over which it has original jurisdiction, or

* See the Federal Torture Victim Protection Act of 1991, Pub.L. 102–256, 106 Stat. 73 (1992), which appears as a note to this section in the United States Code.

(4) in exceptional circumstances, there are other compelling reasons for declining jurisdiction.

(d) The period of limitations for any claim asserted under subsection (a), and for any other claim in the same action that is voluntarily dismissed at the same time as or after the dismissal of the claim under subsection (a), shall be tolled while the claim is pending and for a period of 30 days after it is dismissed unless State law provides for a longer tolling period.

(e) As used in this section, the term "State" includes the District of Columbia, the Commonwealth of Puerto Rico, and any territory or possession of the United States.

§ 1441. Actions removable generally

(a) Except as otherwise expressly provided by Act of Congress, any civil action brought in a State court of which the district courts of the United States have original jurisdiction, may be removed by the defendant or the defendants, to the district court of the United States for the district and division embracing the place where such action is pending. For purposes of removal under this chapter, the citizenship of defendants sued under fictitious names shall be disregarded.

(b) Any civil action of which the district courts have original jurisdiction founded on a claim or right arising under the Constitution, treaties or laws of the United States shall be removable without regard to the citizenship or residence of the parties. Any other such action shall be removable only if none of the parties in interest properly joined and served as defendants is a citizen of the state in which such action is brought.

(c) Whenever a separate and independent claim or cause of action, within the jurisdiction conferred by section 1331 of this title is joined with one or more otherwise non-removable claims or causes of action, the entire case may be removed and the district court may determine all issues therein, or, in its discretion, may remand all matters in which State law predominates.

(d) Any civil action brought in a State court against a foreign state as defined in section 1603(a) of this title may be removed by the foreign state to the district court of the United States for the district and division embracing the place where such action is pending. Upon removal the action shall be tried by the court without jury. Where removal is based upon this subsection, the time limitations of section 1446(b) of this chapter may be enlarged at any time for cause shown.

§ 1442.   Federal officers or agencies sued or prosecuted

(a) A civil action or criminal prosecution commenced in a State court against any of the following may be removed by them to the district court of the United States for the district and division embracing the place wherein it is pending:

(1) The United States or any agency thereof or any officer (or any person acting under that officer) of the United States or of any agency thereof, sued in an official or individual capacity for any act under color of such office or on account of any right, title or authority claimed under any Act of Congress for the apprehension or punishment of criminals or the collection of the revenue.

(2) A property holder whose title is derived from any such officer, where such action or prosecution affects the validity of any law of the United States.

(3) Any officer of the courts of the United States, for any act under color of office or in the performance of his duties;

(4) Any officer of either House of Congress, for any act in the discharge of his official duty under an order of such House.

(b) A personal action commenced in any State court by an alien against any citizen of a State who is, or at the time the alleged action accrued was, a civil officer of the United States and is a nonresident of such State, wherein jurisdiction is obtained by the State court by personal service of process, may be removed by the defendant to the district court of the United States for the district and division in which the defendant was served with process.

§ 1446.   Procedure for removal

(a) A defendant or defendants desiring to remove any civil action or criminal prosecution from a State court shall file in the district court of the United States for the district and division within which such action is pending a notice of removal signed pursuant to Rule 11 of the Federal Rules of Civil Procedure and containing a short and plain statement of the grounds for removal, together with a copy of all process, pleadings, and orders served upon such defendant or defendants in such action.

(b) The notice of removal of a civil action or proceeding shall be filed within thirty days after the receipt by the defendant, through service or otherwise, of a copy of the initial pleading setting forth the claim for relief upon which such action or proceeding is based, or within thirty days after the service of summons upon the defendant if such initial pleading has then been filed in court and is not required to be served on the defendant, whichever period is shorter.

If the case stated by the initial pleading is not removable, a notice of removal may be filed within thirty days after receipt by the defendant, through service or otherwise, of a copy of an amended pleading, motion, order or other paper from which it may first be ascertained that the case is one which is or has become removable except that a case may not be removed on the basis of jurisdiction conferred by section 1332 of this title more than 1 year after commencement of the action.

(c) (1) A notice of removal of a criminal prosecution shall be filed not later than thirty days after the arraignment in the State court, or at any time before trial, whichever is earlier, except that for good cause shown the United States district court may enter an order granting the defendant or defendants leave to file the notice at a later time.

(2) A notice of removal of a criminal prosecution shall include all grounds for such removal. A failure to state grounds which exist at the time of the filing of the notice shall constitute a waiver of such grounds, and a second notice may be filed only on grounds not existing at the time of the original notice. For good cause shown, the United States district court may grant relief from the limitations of this paragraph.

(3) The filing of a notice of removal of a criminal prosecution shall not prevent the State court in which such prosecution is pending from proceeding further, except that a judgment of conviction shall not be entered unless the prosecution is first remanded.

(4) The United States district court in which such notice is filed shall examine the notice promptly. If it clearly appears on the face of the notice and any exhibits annexed thereto that removal shall not be permitted, the court shall make an order for summary remand.

(5) If the United States district court does not order the summary remand of such prosecution, it shall order an evidentiary hearing to be held promptly and after such hearing shall make such disposition of the prosecution as justice shall require. If the United States district court determines that removal shall be permitted, it shall so notify the State court in which prosecution is pending, which shall proceed no further.

(c) Promptly after the filing of such notice of removal of a civil action the defendant or defendants shall give written notice thereof to all adverse parties and shall file a copy of the notice with the clerk of such State court, which shall effect the removal and the State court shall proceed no further unless and until the case is remanded.

(d) If the defendant or defendants are in actual custody on process issued by the State court, the district court shall issue its writ of habeas corpus, and the marshal shall thereupon take such defendant or defendants into his custody and deliver a copy of the writ to the clerk of such State court.

(e) With respect to any counterclaim removed to a district court pursuant to section 337(c) of the Tariff Act of 1930, the district court shall resolve such counterclaim in the same manner as an original complaint under the Federal Rules of Civil Procedure, except that the payment of a filing fee shall not be required in such cases and the counterclaim shall relate back to the date of the original complaint in the proceeding before the International Trade Commission under section 337 of that Act.

§ 1651. Writs

(a) The Supreme Court and all courts established by Act of Congress may issue all writs necessary or appropriate in aid of their respective jurisdictions and agreeable to the usages and principles of law.

(b) An alternative writ or rule nisi may be issued by a justice or judge of a court which has jurisdiction.

§ 1652. State laws as rules of decision

The laws of the several states, except where the Constitution or treaties of the United States or Acts of Congress otherwise require to provide, shall be regarded as rules of decision in civil actions in the courts of the United States, in cases where they apply.

§ 2201. Creation of remedy

(a) In a case of actual controversy within its jurisdiction, . . . upon the filing of an appropriate pleading, may declare the rights and other legal relations of any interested party seeking such declaration, whether or not further relief is or could be sought. Any such declaration shall have the force and effect of a final judgment or decree and shall be reviewable as such.

§ 2241. Power to grant writ

(a) Writs of habeas corpus may be granted by the Supreme Court, any justice thereof, the district courts and any circuit judge within their respective jurisdictions. The order of a circuit judge shall be entered in the records of the district court of the district wherein the restraint complained of is had.

(b) The Supreme Court, any justice thereof, and any circuit judge may decline to entertain an application for a writ of habeas corpus and may transfer the application for hearing and determination to the district court having jurisdiction to entertain it.

(c) The writ of habeas corpus shall not extend to a prisoner unless—

(1) He is in custody under or by color of the authority of the United States or is committed for trial before some court thereof; or

(2) He is in custody for an act done or omitted in pursuance of an Act of Congress, or an order, process, judgment or decree of a court or judge of the United States; or

(3) He is in custody in violation of the Constitution or laws or treaties of the United States; or

(4) He, being a citizen of a foreign state and domiciled therein is in custody for an act done or omitted under any alleged right, title, authority, privilege, protection, or exemption claimed under the commission, order or sanction of any foreign state, or under color thereof, the validity and effect of which depend upon the law of nations; or

(5) It is necessary to bring him into court to testify or for trial.

(d) Where an application for a writ of habeas corpus is made by a person in custody under the judgment and sentence of a State court of a State which contains two or more Federal judicial districts, the application may be filed in the district court for the district wherein such person is in custody or in the district court for the district within which the State court was held which convicted and sentenced him and each of such district court shall have concurrent jurisdiction to entertain the application. The district court for the district wherein such an application is filed in the exercise of its discretion and in furtherance of justice may transfer the application to the other district court for hearing and determination.

(e)(1) No court, justice, or judge shall have jurisdiction to hear or consider an application for a writ of habeas corpus filed by or on behalf of an alien detained by the United States who has been determined by the United States to have been properly detained as an enemy combatant or is awaiting such determination.

(2) Except as provided in paragraphs (2) and (3) of section 1005(e) of the Detainee Treatment Act of 2005 (10 U.S.C. 801 note), no court, justice, or judge shall have jurisdiction to hear or consider any other action against the United States or its agents relating to any aspect of the detention, transfer, treatment, trial, or conditions of confinement of an alien who is or was detained by the United States and has been determined by the United States to have been properly detained as an enemy combatant or is awaiting such determination.

42 U.S.C.

§ 1983. Civil action for deprivation of rights

Every person who, under color of any statute, ordinance, regulation, custom, or usage, of any State or Territory or the

District of Columbia, subjects, or causes to be subjected, any citizen of the United States or other person within the jurisdiction thereof to the deprivation of any rights, privileges, or immunities secured by the Constitution and laws, shall be liable to the party injured in an action at law, suit in equity, or other proper proceeding for redress, except that in any action brought against a judicial officer for an act or omission taken in such officer's judicial capacity, injunctive relief shall not be granted unless a declaratory decree was violated or declaratory relief was unavailable. For the purposes of this section, any Act of Congress applicable exclusively to the District of Columbia shall be considered to be a statute of the District of Columbia.

Table of Cases

A

C

2363, 162 L.Ed.2d 257 (2005)—§ **5.5;** § **6.7.**

Gravel v. United States, 408 U.S. 606, 92 S.Ct. 2614, 33 L.Ed.2d 583 (1972)—§ **7.6.2.**

Griffith v. Kentucky, 479 U.S. 314, 107 S.Ct. 708, 93 L.Ed.2d 649 (1987)— § **8.4.3.**

Groenvelt v. Burwell, 1699 WL 6 (KB 1699)—§ **10.5.**

Grutter v. Bollinger, 539 U.S. 306, 123 S.Ct. 2325, 156 L.Ed.2d 304 (2003)— § **2.5.**

Guaranty Trust Co. of N.Y. v. York, 326 U.S. 99, 65 S.Ct. 1464, 89 L.Ed. 2079 (1945)—§ **6.4;** § **6.5;** § **6.6.1.**

H

Hamdi v. Rumsfeld, 542 U.S. 507, 124 S.Ct. 2633, 159 L.Ed.2d 578 (2004)— § **8.3.1.**

Hanna v. Plumer, 380 U.S. 460, 85 S.Ct. 1136, 14 L.Ed.2d 8 (1965)—§ **6.4.**

Hans v. Louisiana, 134 U.S. 1, 10 S.Ct. 504, 33 L.Ed. 842 (1890)—§ **7.4.1;** § **7.4.2;** § **7.4.3;** § **7.4.4;** § **7.4.6;** § **7.5;** § **7.5.2.**

Harlow v. Fitzgerald, 457 U.S. 800, 102 S.Ct. 2727, 73 L.Ed.2d 396 (1982)— § **7.5.2;** § **7.6;** § **7.6.1.**

Hayburn, Case of, 2 U.S. 408, 2 Dall. 409, 1 L.Ed. 436 (1792)—§ **1.2;** § **1.5;** § **2.3;** § **7.3.1;** § **10.3.1;** § **10.6.**

Hayman, United States v., 342 U.S. 205, 72 S.Ct. 263, 96 L.Ed. 232 (1952)— § **8.3.**

Haywood v. Drown, ___ U.S. ___, 129 S.Ct. 2108, 173 L.Ed.2d 920 (2009)— § **10.2.2.**

Heck v. Humphrey, 512 U.S. 477, 114 S.Ct. 2364, 129 L.Ed.2d 383 (1994)— § **9.5;** § **9.5.7;** § **9.5.8.**

Hein v. Freedom From Religion Foundation, Inc., 551 U.S. 587, 127 S.Ct. 2553, 168 L.Ed.2d 424 (2007)— § **2.6.1.**

Hensley v. Municipal Court, San Jose Milpitas Judicial Dist., Santa Clara County, California, 411 U.S. 345, 93 S.Ct. 1571, 36 L.Ed.2d 294 (1973)— § **8.4.4.**

Hepburn & Dundas v. Ellzey, 6 U.S. 445, 2 L.Ed. 332 (1805)—§ **5.7.**

Herb v. Pitcairn, 324 U.S. 117, 65 S.Ct. 459, 89 L.Ed. 789 (1945)—§ **4.6.**

Herrera v. Collins, 506 U.S. 390, 113 S.Ct. 853, 122 L.Ed.2d 203 (1993)— § **8.4.5.**

Hertz Corp. v. Friend, ___ U.S. ___, 130 S.Ct. 1181 (2010)—§ **5.8.**

Hess v. Port Authority Trans–Hudson Corp., 513 U.S. 30, 115 S.Ct. 394, 130 L.Ed.2d 245 (1994)—§ **7.4.6.**

Hibbs v. Winn, 542 U.S. 88, 124 S.Ct. 2276, 159 L.Ed.2d 172 (2004)— § **7.4.5;** § **9.4.**

Hicks v. Miranda, 422 U.S. 332, 95 S.Ct. 2281, 45 L.Ed.2d 223 (1975)— § **9.5.4.**

Hilton v. South Carolina Public Railways Com'n, 502 U.S. 197, 112 S.Ct. 560, 116 L.Ed.2d 560 (1991)— § **7.4.4.**

Hinderlider v. La Plata River & Cherry Creek Ditch Co., 304 U.S. 92, 58 S.Ct. 803, 82 L.Ed. 1202 (1938)— § **6.6.3.**

Hodgson v. Bowerbank, 9 U.S. 303, 3 L.Ed. 108 (1809)—§ **5.8.**

Holland v. Florida, ___ U.S. ___, 130 S.Ct. 2549, 177 L.Ed.2d 130 (2010)— § **8.5.2.**

Hollingsworth v. Perry, ___ U.S. ___, 130 S.Ct. 705 (2010)—§ **4.8.**

Honig v. Doe, 484 U.S. 305, 108 S.Ct. 592, 98 L.Ed.2d 686 (1988)—§ **2.7.**

Hook v. Payne, 81 U.S. 252, 20 L.Ed. 887 (1871)—§ **9.5.5.**

Hope v. Pelzer, 536 U.S. 730, 122 S.Ct. 2508, 153 L.Ed.2d 666 (2002)— § **7.6.1.**

House v. Bell, 547 U.S. 518, 126 S.Ct. 2064, 165 L.Ed.2d 1 (2006)—§ **8.4.5.**

Houston v. Ormes, 252 U.S. 469, 40 S.Ct. 369, 64 L.Ed. 667 (1920)— § **7.3.2.**

Huffman v. Pursue, Ltd., 420 U.S. 592, 95 S.Ct. 1200, 43 L.Ed.2d 482 (1975)—§ **9.5.4.**

Hurley v. Shinmei Kisen K.K., 98 Or. App. 180, 779 P.2d 1041 (Or.App. 1989)—§ **6.5.**

Hutto v. Finney, 437 U.S. 678, 98 S.Ct. 2565, 57 L.Ed.2d 522 (1978)— § **7.4.3.**

I

Idaho v. Coeur d'Alene Tribe of Idaho, 521 U.S. 261, 117 S.Ct. 2028, 138 L.Ed.2d 438 (1997)—§ **7.4.3.**

Imbler v. Pachtman, 424 U.S. 409, 96 S.Ct. 984, 47 L.Ed.2d 128 (1976)— § **7.6.2.**

Indiana ex rel. Anderson, State of v. Brand, 303 U.S. 95, 58 S.Ct. 443, 82 L.Ed. 685 (1938)—§ **4.5.**

In re (see name of party)

I.N.S. v. St. Cyr, 533 U.S. 289, 121 S.Ct. 2271, 150 L.Ed.2d 347 (2001)—§ **8.3;** § **8.6;** § **10.4;** § **10.4.3.**

Intec USA v. Engle, 467 F.3d 1038 (7th Cir.2006)—§ **5.8.**

J

Jinks v. Richland County, S.C., 538 U.S. 456, 123 S.Ct. 1667, 155 L.Ed.2d 631 (2003)—§ **5.10.**

Johnson v. Eisentrager, 339 U.S. 763, 70 S.Ct. 936, 94 L.Ed. 1255 (1950)— § **8.3.1.**

Johnson v. New Jersey, 384 U.S. 719, 86 S.Ct. 1772, 16 L.Ed.2d 882 (1966)— § **8.4.3.**

Jones v. Cunningham, 371 U.S. 236, 83 S.Ct. 373, 9 L.Ed.2d 285 (1963)— § **8.4.4.**

Juidice v. Vail, 430 U.S. 327, 97 S.Ct. 1211, 51 L.Ed.2d 376 (1977)— § **9.5.4.**

K

Kamilewicz v. Bank of Boston Corp., 92 F.3d 506 (7th Cir.1996)—§ **9.2.1.**

Kendall v. United States ex rel. Stokes, 37 U.S. 524, 9 L.Ed. 1181 (1838)— § **7.3.2.**

Kilbourn v. Thompson, 103 U.S. 168, 26 L.Ed. 377 (1880)—§ **7.6.2.**

Kimbell Foods, Inc., United States v., 440 U.S. 715, 99 S.Ct. 1448, 59 L.Ed.2d 711 (1979)—§ **6.6.1.**

Kimel v. Florida Bd. of Regents, 528 U.S. 62, 120 S.Ct. 631, 145 L.Ed.2d 522 (2000)—§ **7.4.5.**

Klaxon Co. v. Stentor Electric Mfg. Co., 313 U.S. 487, 61 S.Ct. 1020, 85 L.Ed. 1477 (1941)—§ **6.3.**

Klein, United States v., 80 U.S. 128, 20 L.Ed. 519 (1871)—§ **10.4.5.**

Kline v. Burke Const. Co., 260 U.S. 226, 43 S.Ct. 79, 67 L.Ed. 226 (1922)— § **9.2;** § **9.2.1;** § **9.3;** § **9.5.4.**

Kramer v. Caribbean Mills, Inc., 394 U.S. 823, 89 S.Ct. 1487, 23 L.Ed.2d 9 (1969)—§ **5.9.**

L

Lane v. Hoglund, 244 U.S. 174, 37 S.Ct. 558, 61 L.Ed. 1066 (1917)—§ **7.3.2.**

Lane v. Pena, 518 U.S. 187, 116 S.Ct. 2092, 135 L.Ed.2d 486 (1996)— § **7.3.1.**

Larson v. Domestic & Foreign Commerce Corp., 337 U.S. 682, 69 S.Ct. 1457, 93 L.Ed. 1628 (1949)—§ **7.3.2;** § **7.3.3.**

Lee v. Kemna, 534 U.S. 362, 122 S.Ct. 877, 151 L.Ed.2d 820 (2002)—§ **4.6.**

Lee, United States v., 106 U.S. 196, 1 S.Ct. 240, 27 L.Ed. 171 (1882)— § **7.3.2.**

Lemonds v. St. Louis County, 222 F.3d 488 (8th Cir.2000)—§ **9.5.6.**

Lexecon Inc. v. Milberg Weiss Bershad Hynes & Lerach, 523 U.S. 26, 118 S.Ct. 956, 140 L.Ed.2d 62 (1998)— § **9.2.1.**

Lincoln County v. Luning, 133 U.S. 529, 10 S.Ct. 363, 33 L.Ed. 766 (1890)— § **7.4.6.**

Linda R.S. v. Richard D., 410 U.S. 614, 93 S.Ct. 1146, 35 L.Ed.2d 536 (1973)—§ **2.6.2.**

Lindh v. Murphy, 521 U.S. 320, 117 S.Ct. 2059, 138 L.Ed.2d 481 (1997)— § **8.5.**

Little v. Barreme, 6 U.S. 170, 2 L.Ed. 243 (1804)—§ **7.2.2;** § **7.6.**

Lochner v. New York, 198 U.S. 45, 25 S.Ct. 539, 49 L.Ed. 937 (1905)— § **9.5.2.**

Los Angeles, City of v. Lyons, 461 U.S. 95, 103 S.Ct. 1660, 75 L.Ed.2d 675 (1983)—§ **2.8.**

Louisville, C. & C.R. Co. v. Letson, 43 U.S. 497, 2 How. 497, 11 L.Ed. 353 (1844)—§ **5.8.**

Louisville & N.R. Co. v. Mottley, 211 U.S. 149, 29 S.Ct. 42, 53 L.Ed. 126 (1908)—§ **5.4;** § **5.5;** § **5.6.**

Loving v. Virginia, 388 U.S. 1, 87 S.Ct. 1817, 18 L.Ed.2d 1010 (1967)— § **2.10;** § **8.4.3.**

Lujan v. Defenders of Wildlife, 504 U.S. 555, 112 S.Ct. 2130, 119 L.Ed.2d 351 (1992)—§ **2.6.1;** § **2.6.3.**

Luther v. Borden, 48 U.S. 1, 7 How. 1, 12 L.Ed. 581 (1849)—§ **2.9.**

Lynce v. Mathis, 519 U.S. 433, 117 S.Ct. 891, 137 L.Ed.2d 63 (1997)—§ **8.4.4.**

M

Mackey v. United States, 401 U.S. 667, 91 S.Ct. 1160, 28 L.Ed.2d 404 (1971)—§ **8.4.3.**

Maine v. Thiboutot, 448 U.S. 1, 100 S.Ct. 2502, 65 L.Ed.2d 555 (1980)— § **7.5.3.**

Maleng v. Cook, 490 U.S. 488, 109 S.Ct. 1923, 104 L.Ed.2d 540 (1989)— § **8.4.4.**

Maley v. Shattuck, 7 U.S. 458, 2 L.Ed. 498 (1806)—§ **7.3.1.**

Marbury v. Madison, 5 U.S. 137, 2 L.Ed. 60 (1803)—§ **1.2;** § **1.7;** § **2.1;** § **2.2;** § **2.2.1;** § **2.2.2;** § **2.2.3;** § **2.2.4;**

N

Table of Statutes and Rules

Table of Authorities

dents?, 46 Stan. L. Rev. 817 (1994)—
§§ **1.3, 10.4.3.**

Erwin Chemerinsky, Parity Reconsidered: Defining a Role for the Federal Judiciary, 36 U.C.L.A.L.Rev. 233 (1988)—§ **9.5.**

Bradford R. Clark, The Eleventh Amendment and the Nature of the Union, 123 Harv. L. Rev. 1817 (2010)—§ **7.4.1.**

Robert N. Clinton, A Mandatory View of Federal Court Jurisdiction: Early Implementation of and Departures from the Constitutional Plan, 86 Colum.L.Rev. 1515 (1986)—§ **10.4.2.**

Robert N. Clinton, A Mandatory View of Federal Court Jurisdiction: A Guided Quest for the Original Understanding of Article III, 132 U.Pa.L.Rev. 741 (1986)—§ **10.4.2.**

Michael G. Collins, The Federal Courts, The First Congress, and the Non-Settlement of 1789, 91 Va. L.Rev. 1515 (2005)—§§ **10.2.1, 10.4.4.**

Michael G. Collins, Article III Cases, State Court Duties, and the Madisonian Compromise 1995 Wisc.L.Rev. 39 (1995)—§§ **1.4, 5.2, 10.2.1, 10.4.1, 10.4.4.**

Walter E. Dellinger, Of Rights and Remedies: The Constitution as a Sword, 85 Harv. L. Rev. 1532 (1972)— § **7.4.3.**

Christine Desan, The Constitutional Commitment to Legislative Adjudication in the Early American Tradition, 111 Harv. L. Rev. 1381 (1998)— § **7.2.1.**

William Duker, A Constitutional History of Habeas Corpus (1980)—§ **8.2.**

Theodore Eisenberg, Congressional Authority to Restrict Lower Federal Court Jurisdiction, 83 Yale L.J. 498 (1974)—§§ **5.2, 8.6, 10.4.4.**

David E. Engdahl, Intrinsic Limits of Congress' Power Regarding the Judicial Branch, 1999 B.Y.U. L. Rev. 75 (1999)—§ **10.4.3.**

David E. Engdahl, *What's in a Name? The Constitutionality of Multiple "Supreme" Courts*, 66 Ind. L.J. 457 (1991)—§§ **10.4.3, 10.5.**

Richard H. Fallon, Jr., Making Sense of Overbreadth, 100 Yale L.J. 853 (1991)—§§ **9.5.3, 9.5.4.**

Richard H. Fallon, Jr., Of Legislative Courts, Administrative Agencies, and Article III, 101 Harv. L. Rev. 915 (1988)—§ **10.3.1.**

Richard H. Fallon, Jr. & Daniel J. Meltzer, New Law, Non–Retroactivity, and Constitutional Remedies, 104 Harv. L. Rev. 1731 (1991)—§ **6.8.**

Richard H. Fallon, Jr., Jurisdiction Stripping Reconsidered, 26 Va. L. Rev. 1043 (2010)—§§ **8.3.1, 10.4.6.**

Richard H. Fallon, Jr., John F. Manning, Daniel J. Meltzer, & David L. Shapiro, Hart & Wechsler's The Federal Courts and The Federal System (H & W) (6th ed. Supp. 2009)— §§ **5.5, 8.4, 8.6, 9.3.2, 9.5.1, 10.2.1, 10.4.2.**

Paul F. Figley & Jay Tidmarsh, The Appropriations Power and Sovereign Immunity, 107 Mich. L. Rev. 1207 (2009)—§§ **2.3, 7.2.1.**

William A. Fletcher, Congressional Power Over the Jurisdiction of Federal Courts: The Meaning of the Word "All" in Article III, 59 Duke L.J. 929 (2010)—§ **10.4.2.**

William A. Fletcher, The General Common Law and Section 34 of the Judiciary Act of 1789: The Example of Marine Insurance, 97 Harv. L. Rev. 1513 (1984)—§ **6.2.**

William A. Fletcher, A Historical Interpretation of the Eleventh Amendment: A Narrow Construction of an Affirmative Grant of Jurisdiction Rather than a Prohibition Against Jurisdiction, 35 Stan. L. Rev. 1033 (1983)—§§ **7.4.1, 7.4.6.**

Barry Friedman, Under the Law of Federal Jurisdiction: Allocating Cases Between Federal and State Courts, 104 Colum. L. Rev. 1211 (2004)— § **9.5.4.**

Henry Friendly, Is Innocence Irrelevant? Collateral Attack on Criminal Judgments, 38 U. Chi. L. Rev. 142 (1070)—§ **8.4.2.**

Henry Friendly, In Praise of Erie—And of the New Federal Common Law, 39 N.Y.U. L. Rev. 383 (1964)—§§ **6.2, 6.6.1.**

John J. Gibbons, The Eleventh Amendment and State Sovereign Immunity: A Reinterpretation, 83 Colum. L. Rev. 1889 (1983)—§ **7.4.1.**

Samuel R. Gross, et al., Exonerations in the United States 1989 Through 2003, 95 J. Crim. L. & Criminology 523 (2005)—§ **8.4.**

Gerald Gunther, Congressional Power to Curtail Federal Court Jurisdiction: An Opinionated Guide to the Ongoing Debate, 36 Stan. L. Rev. 895 (1984)—§ **10.4.1.**

Philip Hamburger, Law and Judicial Duty (2008)—§ **2.2.2.**

John Harrison, The Power of Congress to Limit the Jurisdiction of Federal Courts and the Text of Article III, 64 U. Chi. L. Rev. 203 (1997)—§§ **1.6, 10.4.2.**

Henry Hart, The Power of Congress to Limit the Jurisdiction of Federal Courts: An Exercise in Dialectic, 66 Harv. L. Rev. 1362 (1953)—§§ **10.4.2, 10.4.3.**

Henry Hart & Herbert Wechsler, The Federal Courts and The Federal System (1953)—§ **6.3.**

Learned Hand, The Bill of Rights (1959)—§ **2.2.2.**

Louis Henkin, Is There a Political Question Doctrine?, 85 Yale L.J. 597 (1976)—§ **2.9.**

Alfred Hill, The Lawmaking Power of the Federal Courts: Constitutional Preemption, 67 Colum. L. Rev. 1024 (1967)—§ **6.6.**

Vicki C. Jackson, Suing the Federal Government: Sovereignty, Immunity, and Judicial Independence, 35 Geo. Wash. Int'l. L. Rev. 521 (2003)—§ **7.3.1.**

Vicki C. Jackson, Seminole Tribe, The Eleventh Amendment, and Potential Evisceration of Ex Parte Young, 72 N.Y.U. L. Rev. 495 (1997)—§ **7.4.4.**

Vicki C. Jackson, The Supreme Court, the Eleventh Amendment, and State Sovereign Immunity, 98 Yale L.J. 1 (1988)—§ **7.4.4.**

John C. Jeffries, Jr., Reversing the Order of Battle in Constitutional Torts, 2009 Sup. Ct. Rev. 115 (2010)—§ **7.6.1.**

John C. Jeffries, Jr., The Right–Remedy Gap in Constitutional Law, 109 Yale L.J. 87 (1999)—§ **7.7.**

John C. Jeffries, Jr., In Praise of the Eleventh Amendment and Section 1983, 84 Va. L. Rev. 47 (1998)—§§ **7.4.3, 7.7.**

Richard Kluger, Simple Justice: The History of *Brown v. Board of Education* and Black America's Struggle for Equality (1976)—§ **9.5.1.**

Harold J. Krent, Reconceptualizing Sovereign Immunity, 45 Vand. L. Rev. 1529 (1992)—§ **7.3.1.**

Douglas Laycock, The Death of the Irreparable Injury Rule, 103 Harv. L. Rev. 687 (1990)—§ **7.4.3.**

James S. Liebman & William F. Ryan, "Some Effectual Power": The Quantity and Quality of Decision-making Required of Article III Courts, 98 Colum. L. Rev. 696 (1998)—§§ **10.4.1, 10.4.2.**

William P. Marshall, The Diversity of the Eleventh Amendment: A Critical Evaluation, 102 Harv. L. Rev. 1372 (1989)—§ **7.4.1.**

Calvin R. Massey, State Sovereignty and the Tenth and Eleventh Amendments, 56 U. Chi. L. Rev. 61 (1989)—§ **7.4.1.**

Jane Mayer, The Dark Side (2008)—§ **2.9.**

Daniel J. Meltzer, Jurisdiction and Discretion Revisited, 79 Notre Dame L Rev. 1891 (2004)—§ **5.5.**

Daniel J. Meltzer, The Seminole Decision and State Sovereign Immunity, 1996 Sup. Ct. Rev. 1 (1996)—§ **7.4.4.**

Daniel J. Meltzer, The History and Structure of Article III, 138 U. Pa. L. Rev. 1569 (1990)—§ **10.4.2.**

Linda Meyer, "Nothing We Say Matters": *Teague* and New Rules, 61 U. Chi. L. Rev. 423 (1994)—§ **8.4.3.**

Paul J. Mishkin, The Variousness of "Federal Law": Competence and Discretion in the Choice of National and State Rules for Decision, 105 U. Pa. L. Rev. 797 (1957)—§ **6.6.1.**

Henry Monaghan, Overbreadth, 1981 Sup. Ct. Rev. 1 (1981)—§ **9.5.3.**

Henry Monaghan, Foreword: Constitutional Common Law, 89 Harv. L. Rev. 1 (1975)—§ **6.8.**

Burt Neuborne, The Myth of Parity, 90 Harv. L.Rev. 1105 (1977)—§ **9.5.**

Gerald L. Neuman, The Extraterritorial Constitution After Boumediene, 82 S. Cal. L. Rev. 259 (2009)—§ **8.3.1.**

Gerald L. Neuman, The Habeas Corpus Suspension Clause After Boumediene, 110 Colum. L. Rev. 537 (2010)—§ **8.3.1.**

John Nowak, The Scope of Congressional Power to Create Causes of Action Against State Governments and the History of the Eleventh and Fourteenth Amendments, 75 Colum. L. Rev. 1413 (1975)—§ **7.4.4.**

John V. Orth, History and the Eleventh Amendment, 75 Notre Dame L. Rev. 1147 (2000)—§ **7.4.2.**

Gary Peller, In Defense of Federal Habeas Corpus Relitigation, 16 Harv. C.R.-C.L. L. Rev. 579 (1982)—§ **8.4.**

James E. Pfander, *Public Wrongs and Private Bills: Indemnification and Government Accountability in the Early Republic*, 85 N.Y.U.L. Rev. 1862 (2010) (with Jonathan L. Hunt)—§§ **2.3, 6.8, 7.2.2, 7.3.1.**

James E. Pfander, *Collateral Review of Remand Orders: Reasserting the Supervisory Power of the Supreme Court*, 159 U. Pa. L. Rev. ___ (forthcoming 2010)—§ **5.11.**

James E. Pfander, *Reclaiming the Immigration Constitution of the Early Republic: Prospectivity, Uniformity, and Transparency*, 96 Va. L. Rev. 359 (2010) (with Theresa Wardon)—§ **2.3.**

James E. Pfander, One Supreme Court: Supremacy, Inferiority, and the Judicial Power of the United States (2009)—§§ **1.3, 10.5.**

James E. Pfander, *Rethinking* Bivens: *Legitimacy and Constitutional Adjudication*, 98 Geo. L.J. 117–151 (2009) (with David Baltmanis)—§ **6.8.**

James E. Pfander, *Removing Federal Judges*, 74 U. Chi. L. Rev. 1227 (2007)—§ **1.5.**

James E. Pfander, *Federal Supremacy, State Court Inferiority, and the Constitutionality of Jurisdiction Stripping*, 101 Nw. U.L. Rev. 191 (2007)—§§ **1.3, 1.4, 10.4.3.**

James E. Pfander, *Protective Jurisdiction, Aggregate Litigation, and the Limits of Article III*, 95 Cal. L. Rev. 1423 (2007)—§ **5.7.**

James E. Pfander, Brown II: Ordinary Remedies for Extraordinary Wrongs, 24 J.L. & Ineq. 47 (2006)—§§ **2.10, 9.5.1.**

James E. Pfander, The Limits of Habeas Jurisdiction and the Global War on Terror, 91 Cornell L. Rev. 497 (2006)—§ **8.3.1.**

James E. Pfander, Article I Tribunals, Article III courts, and the Judicial Power of the United States, 118 Harv.L.Rev. 643 (2004)—§ **10.3.1.**

James E. Pfander, The Tidewater Problem, 79 Notre Dame L. Rev. 1925 (2004)—§§ **1.3, 5.2, 5.7.**

James E. Pfander, Marbury, Original Jurisdiction, and the Supreme Court's Supervisory Powers, 101 Colum. L. Rev. 1515 (2001)—§ **2.2.1.**

James E. Pfander, Jurisdiction–Stripping and the Supreme Court's Power to Supervise Inferior Tribunals, 78 Tex. L. Rev. 1433 (2000)—§§ **4.8, 8.2.1, 10.4.5, 10.5.**

James E. Pfander, Supplemental Jurisdiction and Section 1367: The Case for a Sympathetic Textualism, 148 U. Pa. L. Rev. 109 (1999)—§ **5.10.**

James E. Pfander, History and State Suability: An "Explanatory" Account of the Eleventh Amendment, 83 Cornell L. Rev. 1269 (1998)—§§ **7.4.1, 7.4.4.**

James E. Pfander, Rethinking the Supreme Court's Original Jurisdiction, 82 Cal. L. Rev. 555 (1994)—§§ **1.6, 3.5.**

James E. Pfander, Judicial Purpose and the Scholarly Process: *The Lincoln Mills Case*, 69 Wash. U.L.Q. 243 (1991)—§ **5.3.**

James E. Pfander, Sovereign Immunity and the Right to Petition, 91 Nw. U.L. Rev. 899 (1997)—§ **7.2.1.**

James E. Pfander & Daniel D. Birk, *Article III and the Scottish Enlightenment*, 124 Harv. L. Rev. ___ (forthcoming 2011)—§ **10.5.**

Richard Posner, Foreword: A Political Court, 119 Harv. L. Rev. 31 (2005)—§ **2.2.2.**

Richard Posner, The Federal Courts: Challenge and Reform (2d Printing, 1999)—§ **5.4.**

Saikrishna Bangalore Prakash, Field Office Federalism, 79 Va. L. Rev. 1957 (1993)—§ **10.4.1.**

Saikrishna Prakash & Steve D. Smith, *How to Remove a Federal Judge*, 116 Yale L.J. 72 (2006)—§ **1.5.**

Edward A. Purcell, Jr., The Particularly Dubious Case of *Hans v. Louisiana*: An Essay on Law, Race, History, and "Federal Courts", 81 N.C. L. Rev. 1927 (2003)—§ **7.4.2.**

Edward A. Purcell, Jr., Brandeis and the Progressive Constitution: Erie, the Judicial Power, and the Politics of the Federal Courts in Twentieth-Century America (2000)—§ **6.2.**

Robert J. Pushaw, Jr., The Inherent Powers of Federal Courts and the Structural Constitution, 86 Iowa L. Rev. 735 (2001)—§ **4.8.**

Robert J. Pushaw, Jr., Congressional Power Over Federal Court Jurisdiction: A Defense of the Neo–Federalist Interpretation of Article III, 1997 B.Y.U. L. Rev. 847 (1997)—§ **10.4.2.**

Robert J. Pushaw, Jr., Article III's Case/Controversy Distinction, 69 Notre Dame L. Rev. 447 (1994)—§ **1.6.**

Leonard G. Ratner, Congressional Power Over the Appellate Jurisdiction of the Supreme Court, 109 U. Pa. L. Rev. 157 (1960)—§ **10.4.2.**

Martin H. Redish, The Federal Courts in the Political Order: Judicial Jurisdiction and American Political Theory (1991)—§ **9.5.**

Martin H. Redish, Federal Jurisdiction: Tensions in the Allocation of Judicial Power (2d ed. 1990)—§ **5.2.**

Martin H. Redish, Legislative Courts, Administrative Agencies, and the Northern Pipeline Decision, 1983 Duke L.J. 197 (1983)—§ **10.3.1.**

Martin H. Redish, Constitutional Limitations on Congressional Power to Control Federal Jurisdiction: A Reaction to Professor Sager, 77 Nw. U. L. Rev. 143 (1982)—§ **10.4.1.**

Martin H. Redish, Federal Jurisdiction: Tensions in the Allocation of Judicial Power (1980)—§ **5.5.**

Martin H. Redish & Curtis E. Woods, Congressoinal Power to Control the Jurisdiction of Lower Federal Courts: A Critical Review and New Synthesis, 124 U. Pa. L. Rev. 45 (1975)—§ **10.2.1.**

William Rehnquist, Year End Report on the Federal Judiciary (January 1, 2005)—§ **1.5.**

Judith Resnik, Uncle Sam Modernizes His Justice, Georgetown L. J (2002)—§ **1.8.**

Judith Resnik, Rereading "The Federal Courts": Revising the Domain of Federal Courts Jurisprudence at the End of the Twentieth Century, 47 Vand. L. Rev. 1021 (1994)—§ **9.5.1.**

Wilfred J. Ritz, Rewriting the History of the Judiciary Acts of 1789 (Wythe Holt & L.H. Larue eds., 1990)—§ **10.5.**

Theodore W. Ruger, Pauline T. Kim, Andrew D. Martin, & Kevin M. Quinn, The Supreme Court Forecasting Project: Legal and Political Science Approaches to Predicting Supreme Court Decisionmaking, 104 Colum. L. Rev. 1150 (2004)—§ **9.5.**

Richard B. Saphire & Michael E. Solimine, Shoring up Article III: Legislative Court Doctrine in the Post CFTC v. Shor Era, 68 B.U.L.Rev. 85 (1988)—§ **10.3.1.**

Steven L. Schooner, The Future: Scrutinizing the Empirical Case for the Court of Federal Claims, 71 Geo. Wash. L. Rev. 714 (2003)—§ **7.3.3.**

David Shapiro, Jurisdiction and Discretion, 60 N.Y.U. L. Rev. 543 (1985)—§§ **5.5, 9.5.**

R. J. Sharpe, The Law of Habeas Corpus (2d ed. 1989)—§ **8.2.**

Jonathan R. Siegel, Congress's Power to Authorize Suits Against States, 68 Geo. Wash. L. Rev. 44 (1999)—§ **7.4.4.**

Scott Silliman, Prosecuting Alleged Terrorists by Military Commission: A Prudent Option, 42 Case W. Res. J. Int'l L. 289 (2009)—§ **8.3.2.**

Michael E. Solimine & James L. Walker, Constitutional Litigation in Federal and State Courts: An Empirical Analysis of Judicial Parity, 10 Hastings Const. L.Q. 213 (1983)—§ **9.5.**

Jordan Steiker, Innocence and Federal Habeas, 41 U.C.L.A. L. Rev. 303 (1993)—§ **8.4.5.**

William Treanor, Judicial Review Before Marbury, 58 Stan L. Rev. 455 (2005)—§ **2.2.2.**

Laurence H. Tribe, Jurisdictional Gerrymandering: Zoning Disfavored Rights Out of the Federal Courts, 16 Harv. C.R.-C.L.L. Rev. 129 (1981)—§ **10.4.2.**

William Van Alstyne, A Critical Guide to *Ex Parte McCardle*, 15 Ariz. L. Rev. 229 (1973)—§ **10.4.1.**

William Van Alstyne, A Critical Guide to *Marbury v. Madison*, 1969 Duke L.J. 1 (1969)—§ **2.2.1.**

Carlos Manuel Vazquez, Treaties as the Law of the Land: The Supremacy Clause and Judicial Enforcement of Treaties, 122 Harv. L. Rev. 599 (2008)—§ **6.9.**

Carlos Vazquez, What is Eleventh Amendment Immunity?, 106 Yale L.J. 1683 (1997)—§§ **7.4.4, 10.2.2.**

Julian Velasco, Congressional Control Over Federal Court Jurisdiction: A Defense of the Traditional View, 46 Cath. U. L. Rev. 671 (1997)— § **10.4.2.**

Charles Warren, Federal and State Court Interference, 43 Harv. L.Rev. 345 (1930)—§ **10.2.1.**
Herbert Wechsler, The Courts and the Constitution, 65 Colum. L. Rev. 1001 (1965)—§§ **5.4, 10.4.1, 10.4.3.**

Louise Weinberg, Our Marbury, 89 Va. L. Rev. 1235 (2003)—§ **2.2.1.**
Ann Woolhandler & Caleb Nelson, Does History Defeat Standing Doctrine?, 102 Mich. L. Rev. 689 (2004)—§ **2.6.**

Ernest A. Young, Constitutional Avoidance, Resistance Norms, and the Preservation of Judicial Review, 78 Tex. L. Rev. 1549 (2000)—§ **10.4.3.**

Index